NICKY EPSTEIN

Knitting On Top of the World

THE GLOBAL GUIDE TO
TRADITIONS, TECHNIQUES AND DESIGN

NICKY EPSTEIN

Knitting On Top of the World

{ THE GLOBAL GUIDE TO
TRADITIONS, TECHNIQUES AND DESIGN

Nicky
Epstein
Books
An imprint of Sixth&Spring Books

■ to all knitters past, present and future

Nicky Epstein Books

An imprint of Sixth&Spring Books
233 Spring Street, New York, NY 10013

Managing Editor
WENDY WILLIAMS

Technical Editor
CARLA SCOTT

Senior Editor
MICHELLE BREDESON

Art Director
DIANE LAMPHRON

Associate Art Director
SHEENA T. PAUL

Research Editor
DARYL BROWER

Yarn Editor
TANIS GRAY

Instructions Editors
EVE NG
PEGGY GREIG
JEANNIE CHIN
WENDY PRESTON

Technical Illustrations
JEANNIE CHIN, JANE FAY

Instructions Proofreaders
JENN JARVIS
LISA BUCCELLATO
NANCY HENDERSON

Copy Editor
KRISTINA SIGLER

Bookings Manager
RACHAEL STEIN

Still Photography
MARCUS TULLIS

Fashion Stylist
JULIE HINES

Hair and Makeup
INGEBORG KAIJZER
ELENA LYAKIR

■ ■ ■

Vice President, Publisher
TRISHA MALCOLM

Creative Director
JOE VIOR

Production Manager
DAVID JOINNIDES

President
ART JOINNIDES

Library of Congress Control Number: 2008925038
ISBN 1-933027-67-3
ISBN-13: 978-1-933027-67-8
Manufactured in China

3 5 7 9 10 8 6 4 2
First Edition

Cover and principal photography by Rose Callahan

4

Londonderry Rose Coat
page 56

J'aime tricoter...Adoro tejer...Ich liebe zu stricken... Amo lavorare a maglia...Jeg elsker at strikke...

I Love to Knit. No matter in what language you say it, millions of people around the world feel the same about the timeless craft and art of knitting. I feel a kinship with these knitters, past and present, and that close-knit feeling (pun intended) was my inspiration to create this ambitious work about the traditions, techniques and designs of knitting cultures around the world. I then set out to create original pieces and new traditions based on those wonderful styles. It's the kind of knitting book that I've always wanted to own, and I hope you will feel the same.

In lands from ancient Egypt to the boulevards of Paris, to the Great Plains of the American West, knitting has been enriching lives since early civilization. It goes back centuries, some say to the eleventh century, but exactly where it began is a matter of many differing opinions. In Europe, it first appeared in the fourteenth century. That's a long history, and in the beginning, of course, there were no yarn shops or online knitting resources, just lots of innovative people who at first created the craft as a necessity for making clothing, and then, as the centuries went on, turned it into the joyous pastime and art form it is today.

Some of the first knitted pieces that we know about are socks from ancient Egypt. (Who knows...maybe Cleopatra knitted a pair of Argyles for Mark Antony? Wait a minute, Argyles weren't around until centuries later.) As knitting evolved, people added their own creativity, and that gave birth to distinctive cultural and geographic styles and techniques. The international potpourri that we now enjoy is the fruit of their labors.

This book *is not meant to be a scholarly approach to knitting*. (There are some wonderful books on the subject, and I think we've garnered some fascinating historical and technique information.) I created these fashions as an incentive for all knitters to explore new horizons and for you to add your own personal touches.

I loved bouncing (literally and figuratively) from Scotland to Iceland to Japan to Sweden to Russia to Latvia and around the globe, learning the history and then designing pieces inspired by some of the knitting marvels that these lands have produced.

I can't help thinking of a woman or a man in ancient times picking up a stick or piece of bone and perhaps a bit of animal hair and, through trial and error, creating a scoop-necked, raglan-sleeved, stockinette-stitch, bobble-embellished, cocktail sweater....uhhh...maybe not! But somewhere, someone started knitting, and we are all the better for it!

Perhaps, one day, future generations will look back on my new designs in this book and think of them as "heritage." The popularity of knitting has survived through the ages and is now enjoying a renaissance that goes beyond geographical, political, gender, demographic and social borders. That's what makes knitting so exciting. So get out your beautiful needles and those gorgeous balls of yarn, and in no time, you'll find yourself Knitting On Top of the World!

Nicky Epstein

Nicky's Design Tips

Many people have asked me how I go through the design process and what elements I use to create my fashions. This book, with its myriad of techniques and designs, presented the challenge—and the opportunity—to use so many of my favorites. Here is a list of 10 key design elements that I use, and you can, too.

page 20

1. Silhouette
■ Choose the style and shape of the garment. Will it be a coat, cardigan or dress? This capelet is made up of three large counterpane triangles and a rectangle that are sewn together.

page 218

2. Sizing
■ Fashions change. One year fitted is in, the next year oversized is all the rage. Consider the width and length of your project. I've oversized this Cowichan sweater but kept its traditional feeling.

page 214

3. Yarn
■ So many textures…so many weights…so choose wisely. For this skirt I've chosen a lightweight yarn that drapes beautifully over the body, and a fur yarn for an accent.

page 106

4. Color
■ Color is a personal choice. Take your inspiration from nature's hues, fashion forecasts or even paint chips. Green was the perfect choice to capture the essence of Ireland for this shawl.

page 194

5. Stitch
■ Your choice of stitches will determine the basic style of the garment. Mix and match stitches for dramatic results. This unusual lace stitch pattern creates its own waved side edging.

page 86

6. Edging
■ Like a frame on a painting, the right edging can beautifully enhance your work. Here I've used a subtle eyelet-lace rib edging that does not distract from the Shetland lace body.

page 156

7. Detail
■ Pockets, embroidery, zippers, fringes, belts, ruffles, hoods…use them! The cable-woven bib on this dress is a detail that became a major part of the overall design.

page 160

8. Appliqué
■ One of my favorite techniques, appliqué, is used in many of my designs. Dimensional flowers, leaves, bobbles, etc., are a real passion of mine. On this sweater I let the flowers grow wild.

page 222

9. Closures
■ Knit them…tie them…buy them. Choose a closure that will blend or contrast with your garment. I've used a zipper discreetly here, along with more traditional horn buttons at the sides.

page 56

10. Combining Design Elements
■ The more the merrier…within the bounds of good taste, of course. Combine any number of the elements on this list and let your inner creativity show the world who you are!

FAR NORTH

Scandinavia

Iceland

Latvia

Russia

Estonia

■ NORTHERN WINDS, ICE AND SNOW, AND WARM AND WONDERFUL KNITS

The landscape of the North is stark and stunning, and the knitting styles that developed in this part of the world echo that cool, collected beauty. Pattern, symmetry and skill can be found in all aspects of northern knits, along with a streak of practicality.

Snowflake Sweater Cape
page 38

An artful eye for pleasing pattern, consideration for the cold, and painstaking attention to detail brought us the striking colorwork of Scandinavia, the lovely Orenburg laces of Russia, the shawls and sweaters of the Faroe Islands, and the intricate geometric patterning of Latvia and Estonia.

Knitting may have begun in Northern Europe as early as the seventeenth century; mittens dating from the eleventh century have been found in Latvia and Estonia. The Royal Museum in Copenhagen has a silver knitting-needle holder in its collection that dates to the mid-sixteenth century; a mitten excavated in Iceland dates to around the same period.

Where the first stitches were actually picked up will probably never be resolved, but we can be fairly certain that knitting evolved in pretty much the same fashion throughout Northern Europe. As in England, silk stockings, gloves and jackets made their way in from Spain and Italy, followed by the more practical wool stockings and working garments. And, as was the case in Britain, the patterns we think of as so typical of the North—stranded colorwork sweaters in snowflake designs, Faroese shawls and delicate Orenburg lace—are relative newcomers to the knitting scene.

Collective Color:
Sweden and the Bohus Stickning

■ Swedes were exporting native wool as early as the 1500s, but they didn't start knitting with the wool themselves until a century or so later. Once established, however, knitting became a popular—and somewhat profitable—undertaking. With sheep in abundance, the supply of wool was plentiful and inexpensive, and the portable nature of the work itself fit in perfectly with farm life. All members of the family knit, efficiently filling trunks that were then sold to the traveling salesmen who passed through the villages. Knitting proficiency was expected in all women, no matter what their age, and girls were often sent off to larger farms where a bigger market could be found for their handiwork.

The early knits slipping off Swedish needles were not the patterned ski sweaters so commonplace today, but rather mittens, socks and hats. These were done in textural patterns, most of them adapted from the damask and jacquard fabrics that were being imported from Germany and Italy at the time. They were beautiful, but quite stiff—a result of being worked to a very tight gauge in thin yarns. (Swedes have never seemed like a particularly uptight bunch to me, but perhaps it's the cold weather that made them so rigid in their tension.) The precisely patterned, color-stranded styles most of us associate with the region probably drifted over from Norway around 1830. The familiar stylized stars, flowers and iconic snowflakes of Nordic knits were most likely adaptations of German or Dutch designs.

The Knitting Co-ops

■ By the time sweaters made their way north in the early 1800s, the industrial revolution and the introduction of the knitting machine had all but eliminated the traveling salesman and the demand for hand-knits. But in the twentieth century, hand-knitting showed some signs of revival, aided by two similarly minded, if differently directed, collective knitting experiments. Begun in 1907 by Berta Borgstrom as winter relief work for women struggling to feed their families, the Halland Knitting Cooperative, better known as Binge, began turning out rather uninspired "traditional" designs in red, white and blue wool.

Established for similar reasons, but executed in a much more innovative manner, was the Bohus Stickning. Founded in 1939 by Emma Jacobsson, the wife of the governor of the Swedish province of Bohuslan, this cooperative provided work for the wives of unemployed stonecutters and farmers. By 1947, some 870 knitters were employed by Bohus, busily turning out designs created by Emma Jacobsson herself. (In later years, she'd bring in professional designers.) The first products were plain socks and gloves in strong wools, but the energetic and enthusiastic Jacobsson soon had her knitters moving on to stylish sweaters in fine wool and angora blends. Knit back-and-forth in stranded colorwork patterns, and using a minimum of three to four colors in a single row (some designs contained as many as seven colors), the sweaters became showpieces for Swedish handicraft and were often presented to visiting dignitaries. (Nikita Khrushchev received one during a state visit.)

By the 1950s Bohus sweaters had become a coveted fashion item and were being exported on a huge scale. But as the economy improved and the level of skill needed to knit the patterns increased, it became harder and harder to find knitters willing or able to do the work. Emma Jacobsson retired from the cooperative in 1956, and when no replacement could be found for her, Bohus Stickning struggled, eventually closing shop in 1969. All is not lost, however. If, like me, you feel you just can't live without one of these amazing creations on your needles, the Bohuslan Museum has done some bang-up research on the designs and offers patterns for authentic Bohus sweaters. Or, you can knit my version on page 34, so beautiful it would make a Viking weep.

Techniques

■ Along with their famed colorwork, Bohus designs often brought purl stitches to the front of the garment, which looks complicated but is not.

Sweden also introduced the technique of tvåändsstickning, (say that three times fast), or two-end knitting. This circular technique, in which both ends of the same ball of yarn are used and the strands are twisted between each stitch, produces a firm, wind-resistant fabric well-suited to the northern climes. The technique is similar to color stranding, shown on page 237 (using two colors alternating over two stitches instead of one).

Sheep Into Gold: The Faroe Islands

■ Built up from layer upon layer of volcanic basalt, the Faroe Islands (eighteen of them in all) sit about 200 miles north of Shetland and halfway between Iceland and Norway. Gorgeously green, the island's shores slope to the sea, while on the western coast the land rises to soaring cliffs. Inland, sheltered fjords and sounds create a tranquil oasis. Irish monks found refuge here in the seventh century; Vikings came ashore about 100 years later. In this windy, wet climate, the islanders have been knee-deep in wool and knitted garments for centuries.

The inhabitants of Faroe clothed themselves in wool from head to toe, donning knit hats, sweaters, jackets, leggings, stockings and even undergarments. Men generally did the spinning of the wool, while the knitting was left to the women and children—and there was plenty of

■ A knitting smörgassbord of Northern Knits featuring Bohus sweaters with their seamless yokes and spectacular color patterning.

it to do. When the fishing boats made their treks to the deep waters off Greenland (a four-month trip), it became a matter of family pride and practicality to outfit the seafaring men of the house with at least seven changes of warm woolen hand-knits to endure the journey.

Techniques
FAROESE KNITTING

■ The earliest Faroe knits were felted to increase their durability and wind and rain resistance (and anyone who has spent time on the islands will tell you there is plenty of both to resist). The more colorful patterned sweater style now associated with the Faroe Islands emerged sometime in the mid-eighteenth century. The basic sweater shape resembles that of Icelandic and Scandinavian designs, but Faroe sweaters are decorated with small geometric shapes, usually worked in narrow bands of alternating ground and pattern colors. In later

Bohus Swing Coat
page 34

Wooly Wonders

Faroe literally means "sheep island," and the islands' flocks have had more than 1,000 years to develop a particularly hardy constitution and a wonderfully warm, weather-repellent wool that is spun into a marvelous combination of both coarse and fine fibers. The quality of the fleece is said to fluctuate with the weather. During rainy, windy spells the animals develop a hairier and more dense outer coat that produces a stronger wool; when the winter is mild and the grass good, the fibers are finer. The sheep are only clipped at the head and neck; the remainder of the fleece is pulled and gathered by hand. Faroese wool is left unwashed to retain the water-repellent qualities of the lanolin, so don't be surprised if you find find few strands of grass spun in with your Faroese fiber.

■ *For information on these ram buttons/pins, go to nickyepstein.com.*

years, the knitters began incorporating wider bands into the work. Wool fell out of favor when newer, cheaper textiles began streaming into the islands, but the patterns were well preserved, and the knitters of Faroe have kept a tight grip on their needles. Inspired, rather than bound, by tradition, today's Faroese designers draw on the old patterns to create fashion-forward designs that are exported throughout the world.

Faroe is also famed for another form of knitting: paneled shawls cleverly constructed so that they won't slip off the shoulders. These elegant wraps have a butterfly shape that provides both a flattering fit and an attractive appearance. Typically knit in garter stitch, they are made up of two triangles and a trapezoid with borders set off by yarn overs or faggoting. The triangles decrease to a single stitch while the trapezoid decreases to about three inches in width. Decreases in the triangles create the shoulder shaping that gives the shawls such fabulous fit and drape. There are many wonderful resources for learning the traditional method of constructing these beauties, but I've decided to use the traditional techniques as a jumping-off point for my own interpretation of the art.

Land of the Midnight Sun: On to Iceland

■ Declared by the United Nations in 2007 to be the world's best place to live, Iceland is also a great place to knit. An island about the size of Ohio, it holds a place in the Atlantic midway between North America and Europe. More than 100 fjords dot the coastline; beyond these are volcanoes (two of which have erupted in the last two centuries), green valleys, more than 10,000 waterfalls and countless hot springs. Much of the country is uninhabitable, covered in treeless mountains and outcroppings of rock left behind by ancient lava flows. Many Icelanders believe the rocks to be home to the "little people"—Icelandic elves. Over the years more than one road has been diverted so as not to disturb its unseen residents. The abundance of hot springs (there are 800 in all) makes the country seem like one big day spa.

In the nineteenth century, knitted goods became the country's principal export and a source of income for its poorest people. Most of what was produced was practical in nature—warm socks, mittens and hats. Felting was often employed (Icelandic wool is ideal for this purpose), and the resulting items were bartered or sold among villagers and to the foreign sailors who set ashore. As in the rural areas of Europe and the rest of Scandinavia, all hands were expected to stay busy. During the long evenings someone would read aloud from the Norse sagas

while the rest of the household knit, spun or embroidered—children included. An old nursery rhyme shows the regard in which knitting was held:

Now you have come to your fourth year
Your work you will begin
That is learning the three arts:
To read, to knit, to spin.

Knitting's importance can also be seen in a more romantic practice. A young man in love would present the girl of his dreams with an elaborately carved case for her knitting needles, called a prjønastokkur. So much more practical than flowers, don't you think?

As in many countries, the sweater that Iceland is so famed for is a relatively recent development. Iceland's "national" garment, the lopapeysa, a yoked sweater knit from soft roving, called lopi, came to fame sometime in the 1940s or 1950s. Lopi wasn't considered suitable for knitting until about 1920, when a woman named Elin Goumundsdottir Snaeholm (is it any wonder Icelanders always address each other by first names only?) decided she didn't feel like spinning, threw some lopi onto her knitting frame and successfully stitched a scarf. Her patterns were soon published in craft magazines, and before long knitters across the country were casting lopi onto their needles. Icelanders built upon the Norwegian "sunburst" sweaters and Swedish Bohus designs of the 1940s. By 1957, manufacturers were turning out lopi yarns on a large scale, and the lofty bulk of the yarn, which works up quickly and easily, soon made hand-knitting profitable. Rural Icelanders began knitting in the evenings once more, this time turning out sweaters, mittens and hats for the tourist trade. This knitting tradition continues today. Lopi hats, mittens and sweaters hand-knit by locals can be found everywhere from gift shops to gas stations—a friend of mind even recalls the attendants on an Icelandair flight offering mittens and hats along with snacks and drinks. (Coffee, tea or lopi?)

Techniques

■ Icelandic sweaters sport a round yoke stitched in a pattern of naturally colored lopi yarn. It looks complicated, but is actually fairly simple to work. The body and sleeves are worked separately to the underarm, then joined on a large circular needle. The yoke forms the sleeve cap, shoulders and armhole of the sweater. Colorwork pattern bands are separated by plain decrease rounds in the main color. As you decrease closer to the neck, you may need to switch to a shorter needle to avoid stretching the

stitches. The most important part of this type of design is the join between the body and sleeves. See how to accomplish it on page 246.

Beauty and the Baltic: Latvia and Estonia

■ Bordered by Russia and the Baltic Sea, Latvia and Estonia (along with Lithuania) make up what is known today as the Baltic States. While language and origins differ between the two countries, their knitting techniques share a common culture and tradition.

The ancestors of modern-day Estonians left the forests west of the Ural Mountains 11,000 years ago, settling in what is known as Estonia and establishing hunting and fishing communities along the coast. By the end of the Bronze Age they had established themselves as farmers and found themselves subject to raids both from neighboring Baltic tribes and the Vikings, lending the Estonians a starring role in several of the Scandinavian sagas. With the Middle Ages came the Crusades and the "Livonian Brothers of the Sword," German "warrior monks" who conquered southern Estonia as part of the Northern Crusades. Along with Christianity, these knights—or at least the servants and craftsmen they brought with them—most likely introduced knitting to the Estonian tribes. The Estonians were a smart bunch and no doubt recognized the practical application the craft could have in protecting them from the elements. In 1950 a mitten cuff dating from the late thirteenth or early fourteenth century was found in a woman's grave in northeastern Estonia, indicating that knitted items, if not the act of knitting itself, were known to the peoples of the region.

Wedded to Knitting

■ By the nineteenth century, knitting had stitched itself into the very center of Estonian and Latvian folk traditions. Mittens and stockings were used symbolically during all of life's major milestones: birth, marriage and death. Men were urged to wear mittens to bed on their wedding night in hopes of producing a boy (what the bride thought of being fondled by bulky wool gloves is not mentioned) and godparents were presented with mittens and stockings upon a child's birth. When a young man decided it was time to find a wife, he paid a visit to his intended's family, bringing with him a bottle of liquor (a welcome gift for any occasion). If the bottle was returned empty with a pair of mittens or socks tied around it, the lucky lad had found himself a match. His next step was to pay a visit to his future in-laws, who would send him home with a stack of gifts that included hand-knit mittens.

The bride-to-be had a lot of handwork to attend to, and set about filling her hope chest with the knitted necessities for her new life. She was expected to turn out at least fifty pairs of mittens for the occasion (one hopes the engagement was a long one), along with 100 or so belts and various stockings, socks and other small items. Quality counted as much as quantity, as her handiwork would be on display at the wedding celebration. The wool for this endeavor was often obtained through a custom known as "chasing the wolf's tail." Armed with a bottle of wine, the bride would visit neighbors and friends, who would in turn gave her wool, or sometimes (if she was lucky) completed mittens and stockings.

The wedding ceremony itself lasted several days, and the mittens the bride had worked so hard to complete were handed out to everyone involved. The groom kept his mittens on throughout the day (and, as we noted earlier, into the wedding night). Groomsmen were dispatched to recover the bride (who had been hidden away) from her parents' house, and as they left were given gifts of belts and mittens. Mittens were tied to the carriage harness—a gift for whomever attended to the horse. The bride was lifted from the carriage and set down on a patterned blanket or fur throw (to ensure luck and fertility for the new couple and their livestock) on which she placed mittens or stockings. She then made her way into the house, leaving mittens on the threshold as she passed through the door. The groom's mother led her new daughter-in-law through the rooms of the house, the barns and the outer buildings—the bride leaving mittens or stockings at each stop. This distribution of mittens continued throughout the wedding festivities with relatives, guests and the wedding party receiving carefully crafted pairs as gifts of thanks. (A much more practical party favor than tulle bag filled with Jordan almonds, if you ask me.)

Inspired by...
These Princess Bride mittens have a Baltic "smitten with the mitten" heritage.

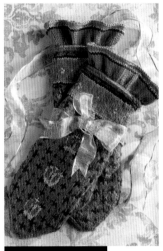

Princess Bride Mittens page 24

Northern Lights Cardigan page 16

Charting the Baltic

The geometric patterns of dots, squares, stars, crosses and triangles decorating Estonian designs were taken from traditional folk patterns; in Latvia they provide an illustrated reference to Baltic mythology. The zigzag design called "Mara," for example, protects cattle and water; "Jumis," a pair of crisscrossed upside-down check marks, personifies fertility and well-being. In western Estonia, animal and plant motifs derived from the original geometric patterns were often done in bolder colors than the more traditional designs. The patterns are very symmetrical in nature and leave little if any background space. Borders, centers and other design elements are elaborated and expanded as far as they can be—an aesthetic with which I can truly identify!

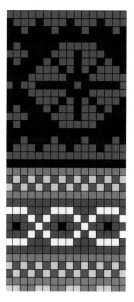

Baltic Cuffs and Cap
page 32

Superstitions and Death

■ Mittens were also believed to provide luck and protection. When it came time for the couple to choose a location for their home, three mittens filled with grain, dirt, and ashes respectively were placed on the intended building site. A child was then asked to choose a mitten. If it contained soil or grain, the land was good to go. If the mitten filled with ash was picked, a new location needed to be found, as there was a good chance that any house built there would burn to the ground. Farmers wore a mitten on their left hand when they planted crops, mittens were used to apply healing treatments, and those who became lost had only to turn their mittens inside out to find their way to the correct path (how this worked exactly is something I haven't been able to figure out). People literally took their mittens to the grave with them. They were buried wearing mittens, and the casket maker, gravediggers, and those who washed the body were given mittens in thanks for their work. These people were definitely smitten with the mitten!

Techniques

■ The mittens of Latvia and Estonia share a similar shape, a triangular point at the top of the mitten, straight sides, and a simple, gusset-less thumb worked from the palm. Traditionally, five double-pointed needles are used to stitch the mittens. Some end in a simple straight cuff, others sport decorative edges or a longer flared cuff. In later years, many of these gauntlet styles were decorated with a kind of entrelac diamond patterning; at other times, slanting patterns were used to create an entrelac-like effect. Braided or other decorative cast-ons were often used to create the cuffs, and lacy or zigzag patterns also found their way into the designs. Women's styles often added fringe to the cuffs—since I have a particular love

for edgings, I find these pieces particularly fascinating. The traditional technique is to work the decorative finish into the cast-on. I have expanded upon it by adding a separate ruffled edging to the mittens on page 24. The intricate colorwork patterns that decorate Latvian and Estonian mittens and socks provide more than decoration. Like the colorwork patterns of their neighbors in Scandinavia and Shetland, Baltic knitters used (and still use) stranding (see page 237) to create their two-color designs. The floats of yarn on the back of the work create an air pocket that traps body heat, providing a double layer of warmth essential in this cold region. Dyes made from plants, bark and moss created the wonderful colors used in the designs—at least until aniline dyes were introduced in the mid-nineteenth century. Latvia was partial to green, yellow red and blue; Estonia added red (from madder root) and brown (achieved with pinecones, alder bark and buckthorn) to the mix. Blue was the hardest shade to come by, as the indigo used to create it had to be imported from India or Africa, making it quite expensive. In Estonia, hanks of yarn were often wrapped with linen thread before being submerged in a dye bath. When the thread was removed (once the yarn was completely dry) the areas under the thread were lighter, resulting in a tie-dye like appearance when knit.

On Gossamer Wings:
The Orenburg Lace of Russia

■ The city of Orenburg, located on the steppes of Russia's Ural Mountains, is home to glassy lakes, rolling green hills and an exquisite form of shawl knitting known as Orenburg lace. Cobweb-like in appearance, knit from goat down and surprisingly warm, they've been worn as a layering piece since the seventeenth century in an attempt to combat the severe cold of the Russian winter. Folklore tells us that an old Cossack woman knit the first of these delicate pieces—a shawl so fine that the entire thing could be slipped through a wedding ring—and sent it to Catherine the Great. The empress was delighted with her gift, and knowing the value of such a well-crafted item, ordered that the woman be well provided for, for the rest of her life. There was, however, one caveat to Catherine's largesse: She also instructed that the knitter be blinded so that no other woman would be able to wear the same shawl. (You can't trust those empresses!) Sadly for Catherine, but thankfully for the rest of us, she neglected to take the old woman's daughter into account, who, as it turns out, possessed the same skill as her mother. So the techniques for knitting such exquisite lace endured, passed down through the generations.

The key to the softness and beauty of the Orenburg

St. Petersburg Camisole
page 28

Stash Envy

One Orenburg legend tells of Boguotchikha, a master knitter whose yarn, technique and shawls were the finest in the region. However, she had a bit of a problem sharing, and forbade anyone to enter her home for fear that he or she would see her work and somehow surpass her in skill. Hearing that a young knitter in a neighboring village was doing a much better job of things, Boguotchikha's paranoia increased. She fretted endlessly over whether or not the rival shawls were softer, more finely stitched, and more beautifully finished than her own. Her worries were well founded. When she finally saw the shawls in question, it's said she was so overcome with envy that she fell ill and died. Her own shawls, hidden away in her dreary house, fell prey to moths and were lost forever. Fortunately for the craft, most knitters of Orenburg lace are a little more open to sharing their techniques.

(You can't trust those goats!)

By the mid-nineteenth century, Orenburg shawls were being displayed and shown outside the boundaries of Russia (where, by the way, they were little valued), winning medals and gaining admiration from the world at large. In 1917, Lenin decreed folk crafts a state industry and the Orenburg knitters found themselves part of a grander plan. Working from home, they were supplied with materials and paid a monthly salary to create shawls for sale and exhibition. By 1938, a center known as the Orenburg Kombinat Knitted Lace Cooperative was established, supplying tools and materials to the knitters and setting production standards and marketing goals for the finished shawls. The kombinat closed its doors at the end of 1995, a casualty of the collapse of communism, leaving the knitters to fend for themselves. Shawl production since then has turned out many imitations, but recently the Orenburg Kombinat was resurrected, so there is a strong possibility that the city's lace traditions will continue.

Techniques

■ Orenburg shawls are knit as squares ranging from 47 to 70 inches across and feature a central geometric design of a five-diamond medallion or allover lace pattern. In the diamond designs, the central motif is surrounded by four smaller or equal-sized diamonds, with patterns of strawberries or cats' paws framing the central diamond. In the medallion styles, the central diamond is increased to fill the square, leaving four triangles at the corners. In the allover patterns, you'll find diamond grids or honeycomb or strawberry patterns. More lace patterning and borders of repeating snowflakes, trees, diamonds or other motifs frame the central design.

The shawls incorporate both knitted lace (patterning on every row) and lace knitting (patterning on every other row) and are knit in one piece. Most knitters work from memory rather than charts—the latter were only introduced in recent years—using short needles in very small sizes (no larger than a U.S. size 2). It takes more than 3,000 yards of goat down plied with silk to make a 60-inch shawl, meaning you'll need at least three ounces of fine lace yarn to copy the look. To complete them, one has to understand how to stitch the basic lace patterns, knit borders and turn corners. As each section is completed, it's tied up in a handkerchief to keep the knitting clean and out of the way. Extensive blocking is required to get the finished shawl into shape (the short needles cause them to bunch up). ❖❖

shawls lies in the fine goat down spun to create them. Similar in feel to cashmere, the fiber has wonderful softness, strength, heat retention and wrinkle resistance. Like the shawls, the goats come with their own legends. Long ago (just how long, no one really knows, but knitting did not catch on in Russia until the seventeenth century) their use was reserved for milk, meat and leather. The Cossacks, it's said, began offering to clean the "dirty" goats by combing them. Amused by what they considered the stupidity of the request, the peasants agreed. The Cossack carted off the hair from the combing, but it wasn't until the following spring, when the offer to clean up the goats was repeated, that the peasants finally got wise to the scheme. The Cossacks were selling and trading the down collected from the goats and making a nice profit doing so. (You can't trust those Cossacks!) The peasants quickly began combing their own animals and trading the fiber for tobacco and cloth, which they sold for profit. At the same time, the local women began copying and improving upon the knitted shawls worn by the Kashuk and Kalmyk nomads who roamed the area, perfecting the technique sometime in the early eighteenth century. In the mid-to-late 1700s a scientist named Peter Ritchlov began breeding goats for the quality of their down and organizing the local knitters, eventually registering Orenburg shawl knitting as an official peasant handicraft industry. Attempts were made to export first the down, then the goats, but both projects failed. The shawls crafted in Europe from the imported yarn were much too expensive to produce, and the goats—after a few years removed from brutal cold of the Urals—failed to produce down with the wonderful qualities for which the fiber was prized.

Copenhagen Royal Shawl
page 20

Northern Lights Cardigan

This Icelandic-style cardigan, yoked and cropped, with its sparkling beads and shimmering colors, reflects the spirit of the Aurora Borealis.

■ SKILLED KNITTER

WHAT YOU'LL NEED

- 9 (10, 12) 1¾oz/50g balls (ea. approx 92yds/85m) of Berroco Inc.'s *Pure Merino* (100% extrafine merino wool) in #8516 ensign blue (MC)
- 2 (3, 3) balls in #8534 black magic(D)
- 1 ball ea. in #8519 lavender (A), #8549 fuschia (B) and #8550 grape jelly (C)
- Sizes 7 (4.5mm) and 8 (5mm) 16" and 32" circular needles
- Sizes 7 (4.5mm) and 8 (5mm) double-pointed needles
- 70 (81, 90) 7mm faceted beads (purchase extra in case of breakage or loss)
- Tapestry needle
- Five 1"/2.5cm buttons
- Scrap yarn for stitch holders
- Fur collar optional

Sizes
Small (Medium, Large)

Finished Measurements
Bust (closed): 37 (41¼, 47)"/94 (106, 118)cm
Length: 18½ (20, 21¼)"/45.5 (51, 54)cm

Gauge
20 sts and 25 rows = 4"/10cm in Ridged rib on larger needles
TAKE TIME TO CHECK GAUGE.

Special stitches
■ Ridged rib
Row 1 (RS) Knit.
Row 2 Knit.
Row 3 P1, *k1, p1; rep from * to end.
Row 4 K1, *p1, k1; rep from * to end.
Rep rows 1-4.

Body
■ With MC and smaller needles, cast on 177 (201, 227) sts.
Work in St st for 7 rows beg with a p row.
Next row (RS) Purl for turning ridge.
Change to larger needle and beg with row 2, work in Ridged rib for 10 (11, 12)"/25.5 (28, 30.5)cm, ending with row 4.

Divide fronts and back
■ *Next row* (RS) K37 (43, 49) right front sts, bind off 14 sts, k75 (87, 101) back sts, bind off 14 sts, k37 (43, 49) left front sts. Place on scrap yarn or stitch holder.

Sleeves
■ With MC and smaller dpns, cast on 51 (55, 59) sts. Pm and join for knitting in the rnd. K 7 rnds, p 1 rnd.
Change to larger dpns and work in Ridged rib as foll:
Inc rnd K1, m1, work in Ridged rib to 1 st before marker, m1, k1.
Rep inc rnd every 8th rnd twice more—57 (61, 65) sts. Work even in pat until piece measures 14"/35.5cm from turning ridge, ending with row 4.
Set-up rnd K to last 7 sts, bind off 14 sts—43 (47, 51) sts.
Place on scrap yarn or stitch holder and work 2nd sleeve as for first.

Yoke
■ *Joining row* (WS) P37 (43, 49) sts of left front, p43 (47, 51) sts of sleeve, p75 (87, 101) sts of back, p43 (47, 51) sts of sleeve, p37 (43, 49) sts of right front—235 (267, 301) sts.
Working 4 (4, 6) rows in St st with MC, dec 4 (0, 4) sts evenly across first row—231 (267, 297) sts.

BEG CHART 1
■ NOTE: Beads appearing on chart appear for placement only and will be sewn on after knitting is complete.
Row 1 (RS) Cont in St st, work sts 1 and 2, work 6-st rep a total of 38 (44, 49) times, then work st 9.

CHART 1

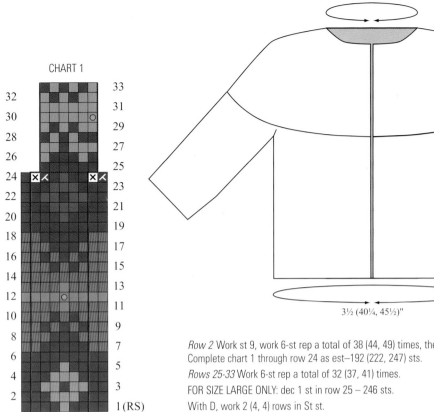

16¼ (20¼, 23¾)"

8½ (9, 9¼)"

14"

10 (11, 12)"

10¼ (11, 11½)"

3½ (40¼, 45½)"

CHART 2

KEY

☐	K on RS, P on WS
⊟	P on RS, K on WS
☒	K2tog on RS, p2tog on WS
⊙	Bead
☒	No Stitch
	Lt Blue (MC)
	Lt Purple (A)
	Hot Pink (B)
	Dk Purple (C)
	Black (D)

Row 2 Work st 9, work 6-st rep a total of 38 (44, 49) times, then work sts 2 and 1. Complete chart 1 through row 24 as est—192 (222, 247) sts.

Rows 25-33 Work 6-st rep a total of 32 (37, 41) times.

FOR SIZE LARGE ONLY: dec 1 st in row 25 – 246 sts.

With D, work 2 (4, 4) rows in St st.

Next row (WS) Purl, dec 59 (65, 71) sts evenly across – 133 (157, 175) sts.

RIDGED RIB

2-st rep

BEG CHART 2

■ *Row 1* (RS) Cont in St st, work st 1, then work 6-st rep a total of 22 (26, 29) times.

Row 2 Work 6-st rep a total of 22 (26, 29) times, then work st 1.

Complete chart 2 through row 11 as est. Change to smaller needles.

Next row (WS) With MC, knit, dec 52 (62, 68) sts evenly across – 81 (95, 107) sts.

Neckband

■ Work in p1, k1 rib for 3"/7.5cm, dec 0 (10, 18) sts evenly across first row—81 (85, 89) sts. Bind off in rib.

Hems

■ Fold lower edge and sleeve hems to inside of garment and sew in place.

Front bands

■ BUTTON BAND

With RS facing, beg at neck edge, pick up 107 (115, 123) sts evenly along left front opening, working through both layers of hem. Work in p1, k1 rib for 8 rows. Bind off in rib. Position 5 markers for buttons evenly spaced from beginning of Chart 1 to ½"/1.25cm from top of neckband.

■ BUTTONHOLE BAND

With RS facing, beg at lower right front, pick up 107 (115, 123) sts evenly along right front opening, working through both layers of hem. Work in p1, k1 rib for 4 rows.

Buttonhole row (WS) Rib 3 sts, *yo, p2tog, rib to next corresponding marker of buttonhole band; rep from * 4 times more, rib to end.

Cont in rib for 3 more rows as est. Bind off in rib.

Finishing

■ Sew underarm seams. Sew buttons in place. Sew beads to yoke as marked on chart 1.

Copenhagen Royal Shawl

If Ophelia had worn this shawl Hamlet might not have been such the melancholy Dane!

■ SKILLED KNITTER

WHAT YOU'LL NEED
- ■ 8 balls 1 ¾oz/50g balls (each approx 186yd/170m) of GGH/Muench *Merino Soft* (100% extrafine merino superwash) in #81 periwinkle
- ■ One set (5) size 7 (4.5mm) double-pointed needles
- ■ Stitch markers
- ■ Tapestry needle

Finished Measurements
Length at center back: 29½"/75cm

Gauge
18 sts and 24 rows = 4"/10cm in St st.
NOTE: Each Counterpane is worked in the round on double-pointed
needles from center out to edges. Chart is one-quarter of finished counterpane and
represents the repeat worked between markers.

Lace Counterpane (make 35)
■ Cast on 8 sts.
Join, taking care not to twist sts to work in the round. Divide sts evenly over 4 double-pointed needles, placing a marker to indicate beginning of round. (See page 239 for how-to on working a counterpane)
Rnd 1 Knit.
Rnd 2 Kfb around—16 sts.
Rnd 3 Knit.
Rnd 4 (Yo, p3, yo, k1) 4 times—24 sts.
Rnd 5 (K1, p3, k2) 4 times.
Rnd 6 (Yo, k5, yo, k1) 4 times—32 sts.
Rnd 7 Knit.
Rnd 8 (Yo, k7, yo, k1) 4 times – 40 sts.
Rnd 9 Knit.

Rnd 10 (Yo, p9, yo, k1) 4 times—48 sts.
Rnd 11 (K1, p9, k2) 4 times.
Rnd 12 (Yo, k11, yo, k1) 4 times—56 sts.
Rnd 13 Knit.
Rnd 14 (Yo, k13, yo, k1) 4 times—64 sts.
Rnd 15 Knit.
Rnd 16 (Yo, p15, yo, k1) 4 times—72 sts.
Rnd 17 (K1, p15, k2) 4 times.
Rnd 18 (Yo, k17, yo, k1) 4 times—80 sts.
Rnd 19 Knit.
Rnd 20 (Yo, k19, yo, k1) 4 times—88 sts.
Rnd 21 Knit.
Rnd 22 (Yo, p21, yo, k1) 4 times—96 sts.
Rnd 23 (K1, p21, k2) 4 times.
Rnd 24 *Yo, k5, (yo, k2tog tbl, k4) 3 times, yo, k1; rep from * 3 more times – 104 sts.
Rnd 25 Knit.
Rnd 26 *Yo, (k1, yo, k2tog tbl, k1, k2tog, yo) 4 times, k1, yo, k1; rep from * 3 more times—112 sts.
Rnd 27 Knit.
Rnd 28 *Yo, (k3, yo, k3tog tbl, yo) 4 times, k3, yo, k1; rep from * 3 more times—120 sts.
Rnd 29 Knit.
Bind off.

The drape of this shawl is flattering to all figures.

Finishing

- Sew 18 counterpanes together to make a rectangle, 3 counterpanes wide by 6 counterpanes long. Sew 9 counterpanes together to make a square, 3 counterpanes wide by 3 counterpanes long. Sew one edge of square to last 3 counterpanes along one long edge of rectangle to make an L-shape.

NECK TIE

- Sew remaining 8 counterpanes into a strip, 1 counterpane wide by 8 counterpanes long. Sew center 2 counterpanes of neck tie together with center 2 counterpanes in crook of L-shape.

- Weave in ends. ❖❖

Nicky's Notes
If you just knit the neck tie of this piece, it makes a lovely scarf!

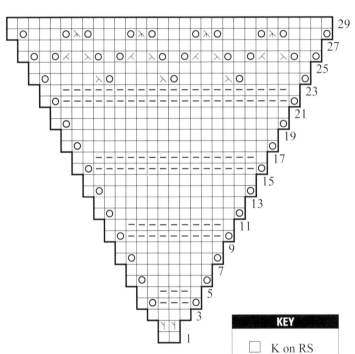

KEY	
□	K on RS
─	P on RS
⅄	Kfb
⊙	Yo
⧄	k2tog
⧅	k2tog tbl
⧆	k3tog tbl

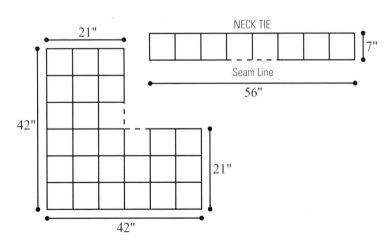

NECK TIE

Seam Line

56"

21"

42"

42"

21"

7"

Princess Bride Mittens

These traditional *durani* (Latvian for mittens) with a princess crown motif will keep your hands *silts* (warm) and *skaists* (beautiful).

■ SKILLED KNITTER

WHAT YOU'LL NEED
- ■ 1 1¾oz/50g ball (ea. approx 186yds/170m) of Filatura di Crosa *Maxime* (80% merino wool/20% soft polyamide) each in #10 grape (A), #8 royal blue (B) and #9 midnight blue (C)
- ■ 1 .88oz/25g ball (ea. approx 132yds/120m) of Filatura de Crosa/Tahki•Stacy Charles, Inc.'s *New Smoking* (65% viscose/35% polyester) in #1 gold (D)
- ■ Size 2 (2.75mm) double-pointed needles (set of 5) OR SIZE TO OBTAIN GAUGE
- ■ One pair size 2 (2.75mm) needles
- ■ Stitch markers
- ■ Waste yarn
- ■ Tapestry needle

Size

Length: 9¾"/25cm, excluding ruffle
Circumference: 7½"/19cm

Gauge

■ 34 sts and 32 rows = 4"/10cm in St st over Chart pat.
NOTE: Crowns are worked in duplicate stitch after mittens are complete.

Left Mitten

■ BRAIDED EDGING
With A and B held together, make a slip knot and place on needle. Slip knot does not count as stitch and can be dropped at end of row 1. Using the long tail cast-on with A over your index finger and B over your thumb, cast on 60 sts.

Inspired by...

In this traditional style, I incorporate bits of gold metallic yarn in a crown motif. I was inspired by this 18th-century crown pin.

Row 1 (RS) *P1 A, drop A and bring B under dropped strand, p1 B, drop B and bring A under dropped strand; rep from * to end. Pm and join.
Rnd 2 (RS) *Bring A over dropped strand and p1 A, drop A and bring B over dropped strand, p1 B, drop B; rep from * to end.
BEG CHART 1
■ Work rnds 1-21 of Chart 1, inc 4 sts evenly around on last rnd – 64 sts.

BEG CHART 2
■ Work rnds 1-19 of Chart 2
Rnd 20 Work 31 sts of Chart 2, place last 13 sts worked onto waste yarn, (yellow line on Chart 2) work Chart 2 to end.
Rnd 21 Work 18 sts of Chart 2, cast on 13 sts using backward loop cast-on (see page 234); work Chart 2 to end.
Cont with rnds 22-60 of Chart 2, working decs as charted–12 sts. Graft sts (see page 240).

Thumb

■ Place 13 sts from holder onto needle, pick up 3 sts between last st and cast-on, pick up 13 sts along cast-on edge, pick up 3 sts between cast-on and first st–32 sts. Work rnds 1-20 of Chart 3, working decs as charted–6 sts.
Graft sts.

Right Mitten

■ Work same as Left mitten through rnd 19 of Chart 2.
Rnd 20 Work 15 sts of Chart 2, place last 13 sts worked onto waste yarn (red line on Chart 2), work Chart 2 to end.
Rnd 21 Work 2 sts of Chart 2, cast on 13 sts using backward loop cast-on;

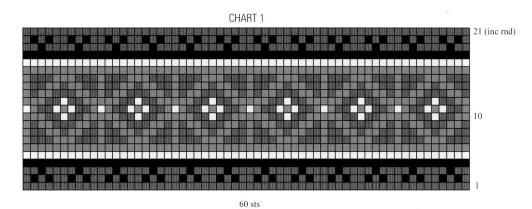

CHART 1

21 (inc rnd)

10

1

60 sts

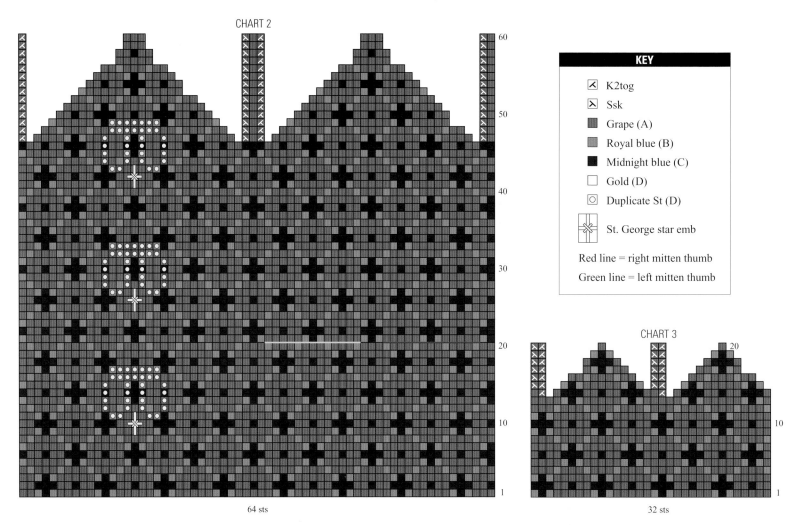

CHART 2

60

50

40

30

20

10

1

64 sts

KEY

⊼	K2tog
⊼	Ssk
■	Grape (A)
▨	Royal blue (B)
■	Midnight blue (C)
□	Gold (D)
⊙	Duplicate St (D)
✻	St. George star emb

Red line = right mitten thumb

Green line = left mitten thumb

CHART 3

20

10

1

32 sts

work Chart 2 to end.

Complete same as Left Mitten.

Finishing

RUFFLE

■ With straight needles and B, cast on 46 sts.

Next (inc) row (RS) Working back and forth, *kfb; rep from * to end – 92 sts.

Work in St st for 1"/2.5cm. Cont in St st, work 1 row C, 1 row D, then 1 row B. Bind off with B, leaving a long tail.

Sew side seam and attach to inside edge of mitten just above braid.

■ Using cast-on tail, sew seam at braided edge.

Embroidery

■ Using duplicate stitch (see page 238) and D, embroider crowns on each mitten as charted.

■ Embroider St. George's Star above each crown as foll:

Beg with D on WS, bring needle to RS at top of crown and insert needle into st 3 rows above. Bring needle to RS one st to the left of center of vertical st and insert needle into st 2 sts to the right to form a cross. Then work a cross-stitch (X) over the point where the sts cross. ❖

Nicky's Notes
A striped ruffle adds a softer touch to the cuff.

St. Petersburg Camisole

Poetically inspired by the Orenburg lace patterns, this camisole creation is made modern by the bold color contrasts and the lovely shape.

■ SKILLED KNITTER

WHAY YOU'LL NEED
- 9 (10, 13) 1¾oz/50g balls (each approx 109yd/100m) of RYC/Westminster Fibers, Inc. *Baby Alpaca* (100% baby alpaca) in #202 thistle
- Size 6 (4mm) needles
- Stitch holders
- Cable needle
- Tapestry needle
- 6yd/5.5m 1"/23mm wide pleated imported velvet ribbon in Wine
- Sewing needle and thread

Sizes
S (M, L)

Finished Measurements
Bust: 38 (46, 56)"/96.5 (117, 142)cm
Length: 27½ (27½, 28)"/70 (70, 71)cm

Gauge
21 sts and 28 rows = 4"/10cm in St st. TAKE TIME TO CHECK GAUGE.

Pattern Stitch
- Lace Pattern (multiple of 24 sts)
Row 1 (RS) *(P2tog) 4 times, (yo, k1) 8 times, (p2tog) 4 times; rep from * to end.
Row 2 (WS) Purl.
Row 3 Knit.
Row 4 Purl.
Repeat Rows 1-4 for Lace Pattern.
NOTE: Keep first and last st in St st for selvage St st.

Front and Back (make 2)
- Cast on 122 (146, 170) sts.
Row 1 (RS) K1 for selvedge st, work Row 1 of Lace Pattern across to last st, k1 for selvage st.
Repeat Rows 1-4 of Lace Pattern 4 times, working selvage sts in St st.

Change to St st and work until piece measures 11"/28cm from beginning, end with WS row.
Next (dec) Row (RS) K1, *k2 (2, 3), k2tog, k1 (2, 2); rep from * across to last st, k1—98 (122, 146) sts.
Leave sts aside on a spare needle.

Shape Ruffle
- Cast on 98 (122, 146) sts.
Repeat rows 1–4 of Lace Pattern 4 times, working selvage sts in St st.
Work in St st for ½"/.5cm.

- *Joining Row* (RS) With RS facing, position spare needle with body sts in back of left-hand needle. *Knit together 1 st from left-hand needle with next st on spare needle; rep from * across row to join pieces—98 (122, 146) sts.

- Work in St st until piece measures 9"/23cm from Joining Row, end with WS row.

Shape Armhole
- *Next (dec) Row* (RS) K1, k2tog, k to last 3 sts, ssk, k1.
Purl 1 row.
Repeat last 2 rows 12 (12, 15) more times—72 (96, 114) sts.

Shape Neck
- *Next Row* (RS) K12, join a second ball of yarn and k3tog and bind off at the same

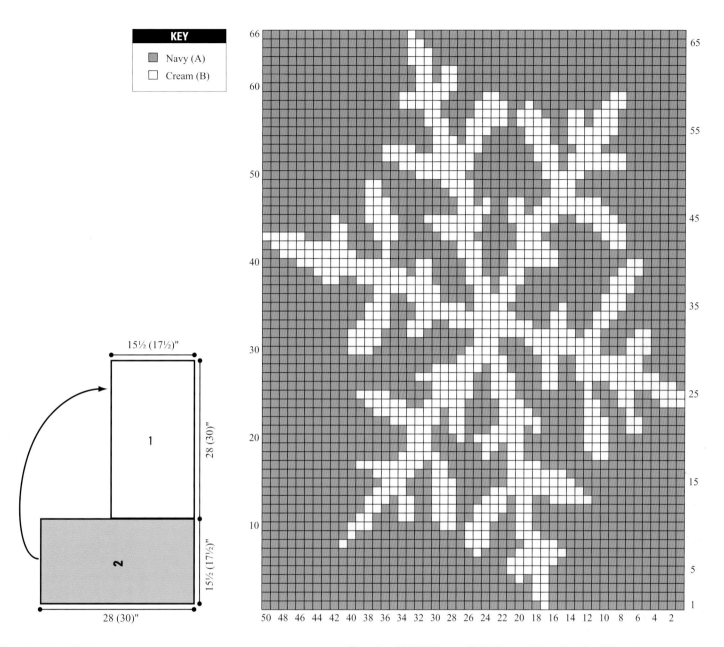

KEY

- ▨ Navy (A)
- ☐ Cream (B)

15½ (17½)"

1

28 (30)"

2

15½ (17½)"

28 (30)"

Rows 3, 5, 7 and 9 Knit.
Row 11 *K2tog; rep from * to end - 8 sts.
Row 12 *P2tog; rep from * to end - 4 sts.

■ CORD
Work I-cord (see page 240) over 4 sts for 4"/10cm. Place on spare dpn.
Make a second ball and work I-cord for 2½"/6.5cm. Place on spare dpn.
Make a third ball and work I-cord for 5"/12.5cm.

■ Place dpn with 4"/10cm cord behind current dpn and *k one st from front
dpn tog with one st from back dpn; rep from * to end. Work I-cord for 2"/5cm.

Place dpn with 2½"/6.5cm cord behind current dpn and rep from * to end.
Work I-cord for 24"/61cm. Bind off.

■ Thread cast-on tail through cast-on sts, gather and secure.
Stuff ball with fiberfill and sew side seam.

■ Fold turtleneck down. Thread each cord through eyelet row starting at
center front and fasten at center back. Tie in front.

■ Work snowflake in duplicate st, referring to photo for placement.
Block lightly. ❖

You'll love the oversized cowl collar and the draw-
string I-cord. The snowballs are a whimsical addition.

41

Liten Olaf Sweater

Your little Norseman will be stylishly warm
in this classically updated sweater and cap (even
if his name is Sheldon).

■ SKILLED KNITTER

WHAT YOU'LL NEED
- 1 1¾oz/50g skeins (ea. approx 110yd/100m) of Alpaca with a Twist *Baby Twist* (100% baby alpaca) in #100 natural (A), #1005 corn flower (B), #1006 nautical blue (C) and #3007 red wagon (D)
- Size 6 (4mm) needle, circular needle, 16"/40cm long
- Stitch markers
- Stitch holders
- Tapestry needle
- Transparent iridescent sequins (eliminate if knitting for an infant)
- Clear iridescent seed beads (eliminate if knitting for an infant)

One size
Finished circumference: 18"/45.5cm
Finished length: 9"/23cm

Gauge
27 sts and 28 rows = 4"/10cm in Chart 1. TAKE TIME TO CHECK GAUGE.
NOTES:
Carry colors loosely along wrong side of work. Pick up new color from underneath old color to twist yarns and prevent holes.

Body
■ With C, cast on 100 sts.
Change to B and purl 1 row on WS.
Join, taking care not to twist sts to work in the round. Place a marker for beginning of round.
Work in k2, p2 rib until piece measures 2"/5cm from beginning, ending with RS row.

■ *Inc Rnd* (RS) K2, M1, *k5, M1; repeat from * to last 3 sts, k3 – 120 sts.

BEGIN CHART 1
■ *Rnd 1* Work 12-st repeat of Chart 1 around.
Work Rnds 2-12 of Chart I once, then work Rnds 1-7 once more.

BEGIN CHART 2
■ *Rnd 1* Work 4-st repeat of Chart 2 around.
Work Rnds 2-4 of Chart 2 once.

Divide for Front and Back
FRONT
BEGIN CHART 3
■ *Row 1* (RS) With A, k1, M1, k59 (for Row 1 of chart 3) – 61 sts.

Leave remaining 60 sts unworked for Back. Turn. Cont to work back and forth as foll:
Row 2 P9, work Row 2 of Chart 3 across 43 sts, p9.

Shape Raglan
■ *Dec Row* (RS) Working as established, k1, k2tog, work across to last 3 sts, ssk, k1. Continue to work through Row 15 of Chart 3, working Dec Row every other row 6 times more—47 sts.

BEGIN CHART 2
■ *Row 1* (WS) Work 4-st repeat of Chart 2 across.
Work through Row 4 of Chart 2 once, working Dec Row at armhole edges twice more – 43 sts.
Next Row (WS) With A, p8, join second ball of yarn and p27 and slip sts to stitch holder for Front neck, p8.
Working both sides at same time with A, continue to work Dec Row at Raglan edge 4 more times and k2tog at each neck edge every other row twice. Bind off rem 2 sts each side.

BACK
■ BEGIN CHART 3
Slip 60 sts from holder to needle and work as foll: *Row 1* (RS) With A, k1, M1, k59 (Row 1 of Chart 3)–61 sts.
Row 2 P9, work Row 2 of Chart 3 across 43 sts, p9.

Shape Raglan
■ *Dec Row* (RS) Working as established, k1, k2tog, work across to last 3 sts, ssk, k1.Continue to work through Row 15 of Chart 3, working dec row every other row 6 times more—47 sts.

BEGIN CHART 2
■ *Row 1* (WS) Work 4-st repeat of Chart 2 across.

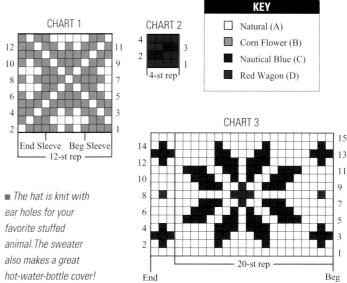

KEY
- ☐ Natural (A)
- ▨ Corn Flower (B)
- ■ Nautical Blue (C)
- ■ Red Wagon (D)

CHART 1

CHART 2

4-st rep

End Sleeve Beg Sleeve
12-st rep

CHART 3

20-st rep
End Beg

■ *The hat is knit with ear holes for your favorite stuffed animal. The sweater also makes a great hot-water-bottle cover!*

Continue to work through Row 15 of Chart 3, working dec row every other row 6 times more–27 sts.
BEGIN CHART 2
■ *Row 1* (WS) Work 4-st repeat of Chart 2 across.
Work through Row 4 of Chart 2 once, working Dec Row at armhole edges twice more – 23 sts.

■ *Next Row* (WS) With A only, continue to work dec row every other row 4 more times–15 sts. Slip sts to stitch holder for Sleeve.

Finishing
COLLAR
■ With RS facing and B, knit 35 sts from Back stitch holder, 15 sts from one Sleeve stitch holder, pick up and knit 2 sts from side front neck, 27 sts from Front stitch holder, pick up and knit 2 sts from side front neck, 15 sts from second Sleeve stitch holder–96 sts.
Join to work in the round, place marker for beginning of round.
Work in k2, p2 rib until Collar measures 4"/10cm from beginning.
Purl 1 round.
Change to C and bind off purlwise.

■ Sew raglan seams. Sew Sleeve seams. Weave in ends. Position a seed bead in the center of each sequin and sew one sequin/bead at each cross stitch of Chart 1.

Hat (make 2)
■ With C, cast on 36 sts.
Change to B and purl 1 row on WS.
Working back and forth in rows, work in k2, p2 rib for 4"/10cm from beg, ending with WS row.

■ *Dec Row* (RS) *K2tog, p2tog; rep from * to end – 18 sts.
Cut yarn leaving a long tail. Thread tail through sts and pull to close. Knot to secure.

Finishing
■ Sew top of Hat pieces together. Sew 1"/2.5cm from lower edge along sides closed, leaving a space for ears. With C, make a pompom (see page 241). Sew pompom to top of Hat. Weave in ends. ❖❖

Work through Row 4 of Chart 2 once, working Dec Row at armhole edges twice more–43 sts.
■ Continue to work with A only, working dec row every other row 4 times more–35 sts.
Slip sts to stitch holder for Back neck.

Sleeves
CUFF
■ With C, cast on 28 sts.
Change to B and purl 1 row.
Working back and forth in rows, work in k2, p2 rib until piece measures 2"/5cm from beginning, ending with RS row of Cuff. Sleeve cuff is meant to be folded up so RS of cuff is WS of Sleeve.

■ *Inc Row* (WS) P1, M1, *p2, M1; repeat from * to last st, p1–42 sts.

BEGIN CHART 1
■ *Row 1* (RS) Beginning and ending where indicated, work 12-st repeat of Chart 1 across.
Work through Row 12 of Chart 1 once, then work Row 1 once more.

BEGIN CHART 2
■ *Row 1* (WS) Work 4-st repeat of Chart 2 across.
Work through Row 4 of Chart 2 once.

BEGIN CHART 3
■ *Row 1* (RS) With A, k1, work Row 1 of Chart 3 across, dec 1 st – 41 sts.
Row 2 P9, work Row 2 of Chart 3 across 23 sts, p9.

Shape Raglan
■ *Dec Row* (RS) Working as established, k1, k2tog, work across to last 3 sts, ssk, k1.

WINDSWEPT ISLES

England

Scotland

Ireland

Isle of Aran

Guernsey

Shetland Isles

Fair Isle

■ TINY VILLAGES CREATED BIG KNITTING TRADITIONS

England, Scotland and Ireland, with their legendary damp, rolling hills and plentiful sheep, are well suited to the pursuit of sweaters. Whiling away the hours knitting seems as quintessentially British as tea and scones. But while tweedy wools, complex cables, and fishermen's sweaters figure prominently in our romantic notions of English knitting, these "traditional" British designs are actually rather recent developments in the region's needlework history.

Edwardian Lace Coat
page 86

Knitting probably arrived in England sometime around the fourteenth century, brought to the isles by sailors and merchants from Spain and Norway. Knitted caps framed the foundation of Britain's soon-to-be-booming knitting industry and were skillfully turned out by tradesmen licensed by the government. Becoming one of these knitting professionals was no easy task. Aspiring master knitters had to complete six years of training to become eligible for guild membership and were only accepted after turning out a felted cap, a pair of stockings or gloves (complete with embroidered decoration), a shirt or waistcoat and an elaborately knitted carpet—all within the space of thirteen weeks. (Think of that the next time you're feeling pressured to complete a project.)

The Shetland Story

■ Huddled between Norway and Scotland at the northernmost point of Britain, and often touted as the place where Scotland meets Scandinavia, the storm-battered Shetland Islands are home to unspoiled wilderness, abundant wildlife and a whole lot of knitting. It's a starkly beautiful place, barren of trees with striking landscapes of rock, peat and sea. Home to fishermen, crofters, long, dark winters and a sturdy breed of native sheep prized for their fine wool, Shetland was also the ideal breeding ground for knitting innovation.

Shetland knitters first picked up their needles sometime around 1500, presumably introduced to the craft by the English, though all parts of Northern Europe influenced the evolution of Shetland knits. The sheep native to the island produced a wonderfully soft and warm wool, and the human inhabitants of the Isles proved quite skillful at both spinning and stitching it into fine stockings, blankets and

shawls that they traded with visiting fishermen, particularly the crews of the Dutch herring boats. Remote, yet far from isolated, the Isles were a regular stop on the maritime merchant routes, and by the early eighteenth century, Shetland had established a flourishing trade in knitted goods.

The exquisite lace knitting for which the Isles are famed—gossamer shawls fine enough to slip through a wedding band—took hold in the 1840s; the legends of its origin were probably created at about the same time. The stories vary. In one, a fairy teaches a lame little girl to knit a spider web; in another a Shetland knitter prays for design inspiration that will bring riches and recognition to the Isles. In my favorite, a mermaid pining for the fisherman she loves weaves the foam of the sea into an intricate robe that so enchants the islanders, they decide to copy the design into their knitting.

These stories are delightful (and even more so when heard in the lilting accents of the storytellers), but the true origins of Shetland lace come from beyond the islands. By the late 1840s, the shawls produced on the island had become quite fashionable. Charitable upper-class Victorian ladies, both in Shetland and on the Scottish mainland, began patronizing the work of the knitters, encouraging those within their social circles to purchase the delicate concoctions. Examples of lace knitting were sent to Queen Victoria, who was so impressed that she ordered a pair of lace stockings, endorsing the quality of Shetland lace in doing so. With the social changes of the First World War came a demand for more practical clothing, and the market for lace knitting began to wane. By the 1920s Fair Isle had become the golden child of Shetland knitting (more on that later) and the majority of the islands' knitters turned their

■ *This Shetland lace shawl in the Victoria and Albert Museum is a prime example of the art of knitted lace.*

openwork pattern repeats with solid areas of stockinette or garter stitch. "Fern," "Cat's Paw" and "Cobweb" are among the more popular patterns.

The wedding band remains the litmus test of quality: The shawl should be so fine that the full length can be slipped through the ring with ease. In knitting the piece, every effort is made to eliminate firm edges. There are no discernable cast-ons or cast-offs, and any joining of pieces is accomplished by grafting, not seaming, to keep things as fluid and elastic as possible. Shawls begin with a single stitch as the knitter stitches the edge in its complete length. Stitches are then picked up continuously to knit each of four sections, one of which is continued to form a center panel. The whole shawl then forms a seamless square or triangle.

All lace, Shetland or otherwise, is composed of a series of yarn overs and compensating decreases that are combined to create stable "holes" in the knitted fabric. Combining rows of yarn overs with stretches of solid background stitches in stockinette or garter stitch creates the lace design. For yarn over technique, see page 245.

The Fairest of Fair Isle

■ By 1900, with orders for lace dwindling, Shetland knitters found themselves in need of a new knitted enterprise. They found it on Fair Isle. Once known as the Island of Sheep, Fair Isle, which sits at the southernmost point in the Shetland Isles, is sparse in population but rich in flora, fauna and inspired knitting. Surrounded by massive cliffs and awash in color and creativity, it is truly a jewel of the sea.

The seventy or so inhabitants of Fair Isle live in traditional crofts on the low-lying southern third of the island, leaving the rocky moorlands of the north to their rugged, wonderful wool-producing sheep. With that wool, Fair Isle's knitters devised the distinctive type of color knitting that bears the island's name. Today the term Fair Isle tends to be used to describe any type of banded colorwork, but in its pure form, stranding is used to create small geometric motifs that are repeated across the piece, with no more than two colors used in a single row. The first Fair Isle pieces were hats, stockings and scarves (sweaters didn't appear until about 1912).

Just how the inhabitants of Fair Isle came up with their unique brand of knitting is somewhat a mystery. The most

Fair Isle Tam Capelet
page 102

Faux Fair Isle Fairy Socks
page 82

attention to those patterns. Today, fine Shetland lace knitting is the work of a few dedicated, highly skilled women who carry on the lace tradition. Visit the Isle of Unst today and you'll still find them spinning beautiful yarns and knitting cobweb-thin shawls that both preserve and develop Shetland's rich textile history.

Techniques

■ The breathtaking beauty that is Shetland lace relies on three factors: sheep that produce a fine, soft wool, talented spinners able to draw that wool to a hairsbreadth thickness, and skillful knitters with an innate feel for combining stitch patterns. Unst, Shetland's northernmost isle, is home to all three.

Unst knitters work without instructions, relying on generations of skill and stitch knowledge to combine simple

A knitter may use as much as 6,000 yards of wool to create a six-foot-square Shetland shawl, but the finished product will weigh less than two ounces.

■ *Classic Fair Isle V-neck pullover*

Simply Smashing Cardigan
page 64

Inspired by...

The classic Fair Isle pattern is given a new spin in this striking cardigan and wee tea cozy.

Petite Fancy Fair Isle Tea Cozy, page 92

likely story, and one recounted by the islanders, is that a seaman from Fair Isle returned from the Baltics and presented his love with a beautifully patterned woven shawl. Ever practical and innovative, she and her fellow knitters adapted the designs for knitting and then began working out ever-more complex variations of the pattern. This legend seems to be close to the truth. Given Shetland's constant contact with the fishing and merchant fleets of the Far North, it's possible that patterns were picked up from the knits worn and traded by sailors from those countries.

However the Fair Isle designs developed, they would soon provide an economic lifeline for Shetland knitters. In 1927, the handsome young Prince of Wales was photographed on the golf green at St. Andrews clad in a Fair Isle sweater. The prince was popular and the photo widely circulated, resulting in a wild demand for similar knitwear. Fair Isle sweaters became the must-have fashion item for the bright young things of the Jazz Age, and Shetland knitters were soon working tirelessly to keep up with the

demand. The frenzy faded, but the sweaters never lost their hold on fashion. By the 1930s the brighter dyes had given way to beiges, fawns and grays, echoing the nation's nostalgia for simple country life. Waved, peaked and graded backgrounds began appearing around 1945; in the 1970s designers like Patricia Roberts began injecting new colors and silhouettes into the old patterns, something that continues in the design world to this day (Alice Starmore has beautiful books on the subject). On Fair Isle, a small cooperative still makes the sweaters in the traditional manner; they can be ordered made to measure and come labeled with the Fair Isle trademark.

Techniques

■ The colorful patterns that make up Fair Isle designs may look complicated, but in reality they're well within the skill range of the experienced beginner. The patterns are worked in simple stockinette, and no more than two colors are ever worked across a single row of knitting. Since the pattern repeats are short, the nonworking color is simply stranded loosely along the back, eliminating the need for bobbins or the twisting together of different-colored strands. You can strand using one or two hands (for the two-handed method, you'll need to know how to use both the English and Continental styles of knitting). The most important (and most difficult) aspect of Fair Isle technique is to maintain an even tension. If you pull too tightly, the work will pucker. You want the stranding to have the same elasticity as the knitted stitches. When you pick up a new color, try stretching the stitches on the needle farther than you intend to carry the yarn.

To simplify Fair Isle knitting even further, you can employ a method called Mock Fair Isle. (I love this technique.) To do this you simply alternate rows of a solid-color yarn (this forms the background) with a variegated yarn (this one creates the multicolor pattern motifs without the need to change colors on different rows). The yarns should coordinate but not match—there needs to be enough contrast in color between the two for the pattern to show up. An even easier option is to use one of the wonderful self-patterning yarns that are so plentiful these days. You'll get a gorgeous look without the need to follow a chart, and you'll have the added excitement of watching a pattern develop as if by magic. Turn to page 237 for a tutorial on Mock Fair Isle.

Construction

■ The traditional way of working Fair Isle is in the round. Not only does this method make the knitting go quicker (a must for the knitters whose income was based on the number of sweaters produced), it also results in a much

more durable garment. Since you are always working on the right side of the garment, it's easier to see how the stitch pattern is developing. There's no need to turn at the end of the row, and you'll always be working in stockinette. Knitting in the round is done on circular needles, which consist of two needles joined by a length of cord. Cord lengths vary; choose one that is short enough to keep the stitches from stretching when they are joined. See the techniques for casting on and knitting in the round on page 241.

A traditional Fair Isle sweater is worked circularly to the armhole, which is then cut in, or "steeked." This can be done in one of two ways. The traditional Scottish method involves casting on an extra eight to ten stitches at the beginning of the armhole, the first and last of which serve as edge stitches to be picked up later. On two-color rounds, you'll want to work the steek stitches in the same pattern as the sweater. When the knitting is complete, the armhole or sweater front is cut up the center of the steek, between the fourth and fifth stitches. The steek then creates a small facing that can be slip-stitched down. In the second method, you machine-baste down the length of the armhole, across the underarm and up the other side, then cut down the center of the basted stitch. See a tutorial for steeking on page 242.

Mad for Plaid (And Argyle)

■ From Shetland it's a relatively short journey to Scotland and another type of color knitting that, while relatively new to knitting history, takes inspiration from a centuries-old Scots' tradition. Like their neighbors in Shetland, the knitters of the Scottish mainland were farmers and fishermen, stitching stockings and other woolen garments out on the moors as they tended to their flocks or awaited the next seafaring trip.

Scotland, of course, is home to the kilt, that slightly silly yet oddly sexy tartan man-skirt that's been worn in the region for centuries. There's a running argument about what a Scotsman wears under his kilt. Last year in Edinburgh, a Scotsman told me, "In Edinburgh we wear an undergarment beneath our kilts, but in Glasgow the only thing under their kilts is what nature put there."

What's worn over the legs is obvious to all: long, knee-topping socks, better known as argyle stockings.

Argyle, a diamond colorwork design arranged in a

Inspired by...
The Highland Fling Plaid Jacket has a heritage dating back to the eighteenth-century Plaids.

diagonal checkerboard pattern is now a classic for men's socks and collegiate sweaters and the pattern gets its name from the Argyll region, home to Clan Campbell and the plaids from which the design supposedly derives.

Techniques

■ Traditional Scottish argyle stockings are worked flat and seamed up the back. Since the patterns usually cover wide areas of color, stranding is not practical. Instead, intarsia is the method of choice, with each color worked from a separate bobbin or butterfly. With this method, the yarns must be twisted at color changes. If it's not, you'll end up with holes in the work. Once a section is completed, the bobbin or butterfly is left behind and a new one picked up. See page 240 for techniques on intarsia.

Many modern-day patterns (my own included) use duplicate stitch to create the overlying pattern of diagonal lines. This makes for a much less complicated but equally attractive knitted piece. To create an argyle pattern this way, you'll first knit the diamond designs using the intarsia technique. When these are complete, take a contrasting yarn and create the thinner diagonal lines by covering the knit stitches with embroidered duplicate stitches. See page 238 for the duplicate stitch technique.

Modern knitters have adapted the ancient tartan

Highland Fling Plaid Jacket
page 74

Guernsey Cowl Collar Jumper
page 68

designs in the form of plaid knitting, a technique easily accomplished by employing the same intarsia and duplicate-stitch combinations described above.

Sanquhar, a little town in Dumfriesshire, Scotland, has a long tradition of tweed and hosiery manufacture. Among knitters, it's better known for a distinctive checked pattern which goes by the name of the town. Traditionally worked in two-color combinations of browns, grays, creams and whites, the patterns have wonderful names like "Duke," "Shepherd's Plaid," "Midge and Fly" and "Prince of Wales".

The Art of the Aran

■ Off the west coast of Ireland, tucked in the mouth of Galway Bay, lie Inishmore, Inishmaan and Inisheer, otherwise known as the Isles of Aran. Almost surreal in appearance, the landscape is one of endless expanses of silver-gray rock ending in massive limestone cliffs relentlessly pounded by the waves of the Atlantic. The land is literally scoured, the soil stripped away by the movement of glaciers during the Ice Age. Impossible as it seems, people have made their homes here for almost 4,000 years, subsiding on fishing and farming. Ever practical and tenacious, the inhabitants of Aran managed to support a handful of basic crops and a few hardy breeds of sheep and cattle. Fishing was done from caurraghs, lath crafts covered in tarred canvas. Flimsy and prone to crashing on the rocks if the waves were not caught at the right angle, these boats served as the only means of transportation between the three islands and the mainland. The rough waters of the Atlantic and rougher hours in the pubs made the caurraghs

Rewriting History

The connection between Aran knitting and ancient art is largely the work of Heinz Edgar Kiewe, a fashion journalist who in 1936 "discovered" a cream-colored Aran sweater in a Dublin shop. Inspired in part by the Robert Flaherty film *Man of Aran* (1934), Kiewe devoted the next thirty years to promoting and producing Aran sweaters. For his part, Flaherty stirred up interest in his film (and in the Isles of Aran) with a marketing campaign that would make any modern PR agency proud. Natives of Aran were brought to London for public appearances, theater ushers at screenings of the film were decked out in fishermen's sweaters, and tam-'o-shanters dubbed "Man of Aran Berets" were handed out to the fashionable. No marketing slouch himself, Kiewe romanticized the origins of Aran knitting, calling it a "thousands-year-old tradition" and assigning every bobble and cable symbolic meaning. In truth Aran traditions didn't develop before 1946, but the fashion industry knew as well then as now that a good background story can help move merchandise, and so the legends persist.

ROBERT FLAHERTY'S
MAN of ARAN

even more dangerous. As Alice Starmore so succinctly puts it in her book *Aran Knitting*, the men of Aran were "either expert in their use or drowned quite early in life."

As with the knits of Fair Isle, the origins of Aran designs are shrouded in myth and mystery. Some claim the traditions of Aran knitting and its distinctive cable patterning are rooted in Celtic symbolism and stretch back over the centuries. The patterns, which symbolize blessing and protections, were handed down through generations, with each family privy to its own patterns and stitch combinations. When it came time for the men to go to sea, the women of the family would knit these protective patterns into their sweaters. Should the knitted protections fail and a shipwreck or other unfortunate accident befall her loved one, the knitter would be able to identify her drowned husband, father or brother by the patterns stitched into his sweater.

The story of cable-stitch patterns being used to identify a drowned sailor most likely stems from a misinterpretation of J. M. Synge's play Riders to the Sea (first performed in 1904), in which a drowned man is identified not by the pattern of cables on his sweater but by dropped stitches in one of his stockings. Here's the pivotal scene:

NORA [who has taken up the stocking and counted the stitches]: It's Michael, Cathleen, it's Michael…

CATHLEEN [taking the stocking]: It's a plain knitted stocking.

NORA: It's the second of a third pair I knitted, and I put up three-score stitches, and I dropped four of them.

CATHLEEN [counts the stitches]: It's that number is in it. [Crying out] Ah, Nora, isn't it a bitter thing to think of him floating that way to the far north, and no one to keen him but the black hags that do be flying on the sea?

NORA [swinging herself round, and throwing out her arms on the clothes]: And isn't it a pitiful thing when there is nothing left of a man who was a great rower and fisher, but a bit of an old shirt and a plain stocking?

Not only is this a hauntingly sad and beautiful tale, but also one that's quite unlikely. Sweaters were not a part of traditional Aran dress. In 1907 the writer J. M. Synge noted that some of the younger men were beginning to adopt "the usual fisherman's jersey" common around British and Scottish coasts at the time. Any tradition surrounding the Aran sweater is a recent one, and the first Aran designs almost certainly did not appear on Aran or anywhere else prior to the 1930s.

What the women of Aran were knitting was a more practical, purpose-driven garment known as the gansey or guernsey. Knit from thick wool, usually dark in color (that wonderful creamy shade of white so many of us associate with the style was too impractical for a working garment), the gansey was knit in the round so that there would be no

Celtic Hooded Coat
page 78

seams to burst or tear (meaning, of course, less need for mending—remember, those islanders are a practical bunch). Gussets and shoulder straps added strength to the gansey and provided more freedom of movement and ease to the fit. Arans, by contrast, depart from features that made the gansey such an ideal working garment. For one thing, they are knit in flat pieces that are seamed together—far less suited for hard wear than the circular construction of the gansey. And while ganseys did often sport decorative patterns of knit and purl stitches or simple rope cables on the chest, the patterns did not require the copious amounts of yarn and time.

Aran Patterns

■ While they can't be traced back for centuries, Aran patterns have been passed down through generations, with knitters relying on memory rather than written instructions to create them. But where did the designs come from in the first place? One theory, proposed by the Churchill scholar Rohana Darlington, is that the Aran style actually emigrated from America by way of Austria. As it is told, two young women from the Aran Isles immigrate to America in 1906, settling in Boston where they learn intricately patterned Bavarian-style knitting from a German or Austrian immigrant. Unable to resist the call of the Isles, they eventually return home to Aran, where they incorporate their newfound stitch patterns into the traditional gansey structure used on the islands, and voilà— the Aran sweater is born.

While the American connection is certainly possible, the more plausible explanation (and the one accepted by most experts) is that the Aran developed from the traditional Scottish gansey, which was introduced by the "herring lassies," skilled Scottish girls brought to Aran to gut, filet and pack for the fishing industry. Young, unmarried and naturally gregarious, they spent the lulls between fishing boats knitting, and no doubt shared their techniques with the Aran women who worked alongside them. Riffing on the Scottish styles, a few creative Aran knitters probably began incorporating bobbles, ribs and braids in the Scottish gansey construction, using multiple stitches in a single sweater.

Vogue Knitting introduced American knitters to the Aran with the publication of a pattern for the style in 1956, and by 1957 the sweaters were popular in the U.S. Today most of the Arans sold to Ireland's tourist trade are machine-made of acrylic; wool and the time needed to produce the handmade versions are just too costly to be profitable.

Techniques

■ In modern knitting terms, Aran is used to describe a flat-constructed garment featuring a central panel, usually

Inspired by...
The curls, swirls and scrolls found on ancient Celtic carvings now find expression in yarn.

worked in an intricate cable design with a textured background, that is flanked by symmetrical side panels. The patterns, however complex, all begin with a basic cable construction. A predetermined number of stitches are slipped onto a cable needle and crossed to the front or back of the work. To see a cable stitch tutorial, turn to page 236.

And the Bead Goes On

■ Anyone who knows me knows that I can't just leave a piece of knitting alone. "Less is more" is certainly not my mantra. So when I looked at the sweater on page 52, I thought it needed just "a little extra" to give it some punch. In keeping with the refined tastes of the English, I thought pearls would be perfect. Now, bead knitting isn't a particularly English technique, but it was a popular pastime for Victorian ladies of the eighteenth and nineteenth centuries. They used a painstaking method in which beads were threaded onto the yarn then slipped between each stitch to completely cover the knitted fabric. The modern method of beaded knitting (bead knitting refers to the former technique) threads the beads onto the working yarn and then slips them between stitches in a random or planned pattern. The beads tend to fall over, rather than between, stitches, so your knitted fabric will be visible.

I sometimes make things even simpler by just sewing the beads to the finished piece. That way I can control when and where the beads appear. And if I decide I'd like to do something different, I can change the design without having to rip out stitches. If you try this, use an embroidery floss in a color that matches your yarn for a polished result. (For bead knitting how-to, see page 235.) ❖❖

Evening Aran Gala
page 52

Evening Gala Aran

Aran goes elegant! This chic and very feminine update of the classic sweater will definitely turn heads.

■ MASTER KNITTER

WHAT YOU'LL NEED

- ■ 9 (9, 11) 1¾oz/50g hanks (each approx 109yd/100m) of Cascade Yarns *Dolce* (55% *superfine* alpaca, 23% silk, 22% wool) in #909 ecru
- ■ Size 6 (4mm) needles
- ■ Size 6 (4mm) circular needles, 24"/60cm
- ■ Cable needle
- ■ Stitch holders
- ■ Stitch markers
- ■ Tapestry needle
- ■ Rainbow elastic, 1mm wide
- ■ 1yd/m ostrich feather fringe in ecru
- ■ 66 pearl beads, 6mm, in Ecru
- ■ 22 pearl beads, 9mm, in Ecru
- ■ 68 pearl beads, 12mm, in Ecru
- ■ 1 yd ½"-wide ecru velvet ribbon (optional)

Sizes
S (M, L)

Finished Measurements
Bust: 34 (37, 40)"/86.5 (94, 101.5)cm
Length: 17 (17, 17½)"/43 (43, 44.5)cm

Gauge
20 sts and 26 rows = 4"/10cm in k1, p1 rib unstretched. TAKE TIME TO CHECK GAUGE.

Pattern Stitches
2-st LPC Slip 1 st to cable needle and hold in front, p1, k1 from cable needle.
2-st RPC Slip 1 st to cable needle and hold in

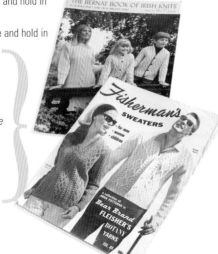

Inspired by...
Starting in 1940s, and going forward into the mid-'60s, traditional Aran sweaters were a staple in knitwear. V-neck pullovers, comfy cardis, artsy turtlenecks and vests graced the fashion pages.

back, k1, p1 from cable needle.
3-st LPC Slip 2 sts to cable needle and hold in front, p1, k2 from cable needle.
3-st RPC Slip 1 st to cable needle and hold in back, k2, p1 from cable needle.
4-st LC Slip 2 sts to a cable needle and hold in front, k2, k2 from cable needle.
4-st RC Slip 2 sts to a cable needle and hold in back, k2, k2 from cable needle.

CHART 1 (Worked over 13 sts)
Row 1 (RS) P5, (k1 tbl) 3 times, p5.
Row 2 K5, (p1 tbl) 3 times, k5.
Row 3 P4, 2-st RPC, k1 tbl, 2-st LPC, p4.
Row 4 K4, (p1 tbl, k1) 2 times, p1 tbl, k4.
Row 5 P3, 2-st RPC, p1, k1 tbl, p1, 2-st LPC, p3.
Row 6 K3, (p1 tbl, k2) 2 times, p1 tbl, k3.
Row 7 P2, 2-st RPC, p1, (k1 tbl) 3 times, p1, 2-st LPC, p2.
Row 8 K2, p1 tbl, k2, (p1 tbl) 3 times, k2, p1 tbl, k2.
Repeat Rows 1-8 for Chart I.

CHART 2 (Worked over 14 sts)
NOTE: Work all slipped sts with yarn in back of work.
Row 1 (RS) P1, slip 1 knitwise, p1, k8, p1, slip 1 knitwise, p1.
Row 2 K1, p1, k1, p8, k1, p1, k1.
Row 3 P1, slip 1 knitwise, p1, 4-st RC, 4-st LC, p1, slip 1 knitwise, p1.
Row 4 K1, p1, k1, p8, k1, p1, k1.
Row 5 P1, slip 1 knitwise, p1, k8, p1, slip 1 knitwise, p1.

Nicky's Notes
Under the ostrich feathers, you'll see this sweater has a 1½" x 1 x 1" rib. Leave the feathers and pearls off for a more casual look.

6 (6, 7)"

4"

SLEEVE

17"

3"

15 (15, 16)"

6 (6, 7)"

11 (12, 13)"

4"

FRONT AND
BACK

10"

17 (18, 20)"

17 (18½, 20)

CHART 1

13 sts

CHART 2

14 sts

CHART 3

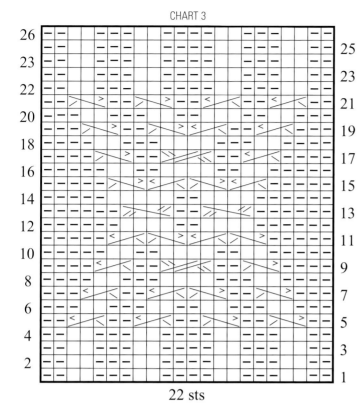

22 sts

Row 6 K1, p1, k1, p8, k1, p1, k1.
Row 7 P1, slip 1 knitwise, p1, 4-st LC, 4-st RC, p1, slip 1 knitwise, p1.
Row 8 Repeat Row 6.
Repeat Rows 1-8 for Chart 2.

CHART 3 (Worked over 22 sts)
Rows 1 and 3 (RS) P2, k2, p3, k2, p4, k2, p3, k2, p2.
Row 2 and All WS rows Knit the knit and purl the purl sts as they appear.
Row 5 P2, [3-st LPC, p2] twice, [3-st RPC, p2] twice.
Row 7 P3, 3-st LPC, p2, 3-st LPC, 3-st RPC, p2, 3-st RPC, p3.
Row 9 P4, 3-st LPC, p2, 4-st RC, p2, 3-st RPC, p4.
Row 11 P5, [3-st LPC, 3-st RPC] twice, p5.
Row 13 P6, 4-st LC, p2, 4-st LC, p6.
Row 15 P5, [3-st RPC, 3-st LPC] twice, p5.
Row 17 P4, 3-st RPC, p2, 4-st RC, p2, 3-st LPC, p4.
Row 19 P3, 3-st RPC, p2, 3-st RPC, 3-st LPC, p2, 3-st LPC, p3.
Row 21 P2, [3-st RPC, p2] twice, [3-st LPC, p2] twice.
Rows 23 and 25 P2, k2, p3, k2, p4, k2, p3, k2, p2.
Repeat Rows 1-26 for Chart III.

Back

■ Cast on 103 (111, 119) sts.
Work k1, p1 rib for 4 rows, dec 1 st on last row – 102 (110, 118) sts.

BEGIN CHARTS
Row 1 (RS) P1, work k1, p1 rib for 9 (13, 17) sts, p2, slip 1 knitwise wyib, work Row 1 of Chart 1over 13 sts, 14 sts of Chart 2, 22 stitches of Chart 3, 14 sts of Chart 2, 13 sts of Chart 1, slip 1 knitwise wyib, p2, work k1, p1 rib for 9 (13, 17) sts, p1.
Row 2 K1, work k1, p1 rib for 9 (13, 17) sts, k2, p1, working Row 2, work 13 sts of Chart 1, 14 sts of Chart 2, 22 stitches of Chart 3, 14 sts of Chart 2, 13 sts of Chart 1, p1, k2, work k1, p1 rib for 9 (13, 17) sts, p1.
■ Work in patterns as established until piece measures 10"/25.5cm, from beg, ending with WS row.

Shape Raglan Armhole
■ Bind off 5 sts at beginning of next 2 rows–92 (100, 108) sts.
Dec Row (RS) K1, ssk, work to last 3 sts, k2tog, k1.
Next Row P3, work to last 3 sts, p3.
Repeat last 2 rows 12 more times–66 (74, 82) sts.
Slip sts to a stitch holder.

Back
■ Work same as back.

Sleeves
CUFF
■ Cast on 47 (47, 53) sts.
Knit 2 rows.
Row 1 K21 (21, 24), ssk, place marker, k1, k2tog, k21 (21, 24)–45 (45, 51) sts.
Purl 1 row
Row 3 Work to first marker, ssk, k1, k2tog, work to end.
Purl 1 row.
Repeat last 2 rows 6 more times–31 (31, 37) sts.

WRIST
■ Work in k1, p1 rib for 2 rows, dec 1 st on last row–30 (30, 36) sts.

BEGIN CHART 3
Row 1 (RS) [K1, p1, k1] 0 [0, 1] time, p2, slip 1 knitwise wyib, p1, work Row 1 of Chart 3 over 22 sts, p1, slip 1 knitwise wyib, p2, [k1, p1, k1] 0 [0, 1] time.
Row 2 [P1, k1, p1] 0 [0, 1] time, k2, p1, k1, work Row 2 of Chart 3 over 22 sts, k1, p1, k2, [p1, k1, p1] 0 [0, 1] time.
Work in patterns as established, inc 1 st each edge every 4th row (working new sts in k1, p1 rib) 24 times–78 (78, 84) sts.
Work until piece measures 17"/43cm from k1, p1 wrist rib, ending with WS row.

Shape Raglan Cap
■ Bind off 5 sts at the beginning of the next 2 rows–68 (68, 74) sts.
Dec row (RS) K1, ssk, work to last 3 sts, k2tog, k1.
Next row P3, work to last 3 sts, p3.
Repeat last 2 rows 12 more times–42 (42, 48) sts.
Slip sts to a stitch holder.

Neckband
■ With RS facing and circular needle, work k1, p1 rib across 66 (74, 82) sts from Back stitch holder, 42 (42, 48) sts from Sleeve stitch holder, 66 (74, 82) sts from Front stitch holder, 42 (42, 48) sts from Sleeve stitch holder–216 (232, 260) sts.
Join, place marker for beginning of rnd.
Work in k1, p1 rib in rounds for 1½"/4cm. Bind off in rib.

Finishing
■ Sew raglan seams to raglan armholes. Sew side and sleeve seams.
Thread two lengths of elastic through sts on WS of neckband, gathering in neckline. Weave in ends.

■ Sew ostrich fringe around neckband.
Sew a line of 6mm beads along decreases of Cuff. Sew one 6mm bead at the tip of each knit stitch branch on Row 8 of Chart 1. Sew one 9mm in center on Row 5 of Chart 2. Sew three 12mm beads vertically between Rows 22–Row 4 in center of Chart 3. Sew one 12mm bead on either side of 4-st LC on Row 13 of Chart 3.
■ *Cut velvet ribbon, stitch to cuff and tie.*

Londonderry Rose Coat

What do you get when an Aran knit meets a British rose? A gorgeous coat that's equally at home on a trek through the moors or a stroll down Picadilly.

■ MASTER KNITTER

WHAT YOU'LL NEED
- 19 (24) 1 ¾oz/50g balls (ea. approx 124yds/113m) of Rowan/Westminster Fibers, Inc. *Scottish Tweed DK* in #19 peat (MC)
- 1 ball ea. in #18 thatch (A), #15 apple (B), #17 lobster (C) and #11 sunset (D)
- Size 10 (6mm) needles (circular needles)
- Size 9 (5.5mm) needles (circular needle)
- Three 1 ⅝"x ¾"/41mm x 19mm buttons
- Stitch markers
- Tapestry needle

Sizes
S/M (L/XL)

Final Measurements
Bust: 45 (59)"/114 (150)cm
Length: 37 (38)"/94 (96.5)cm

Gauge
17 sts and 19 rows = 4"/10cm in cable pat using larger needles.
TAKE TIME TO CHECK GAUGE.

Pattern Stitches
4-st LC (left cross) Sl 2 sts to cn and hold to front, k2, k2 from cn.
4-st RC (right cross) Sl 2 sts to cn and hold to back, k2, k2 from cn.
3-st LPC (left purl cross) Sl 2 sts to cn and hold to front, p1, k2 from cn.
3-st RPC (right purl cross) Sl 1 st to cn and hold to back, k2, p1 from cn.

Cable Pattern (multiple of 15 sts + 1)
Row 1 (RS) K1, p1 *4-st LC, p4, 4-st RC, p1, k1 tbl, p1; rep from * to last 14 sts, 4-st LC, p4, 4-st RC, p1, k1.
Row 2 P1, k1, p4, k4, p4, *k1, p1 tbl, k1, p4, k4, p4; rep from * to last 2 sts, k1, pl.
Row 3 K1, p1, *k2, 3-st LPC, p2, 3-st RPC, k2, p1, k1 tbl, p1;
rep from * to last 14 sts, k2, 3-st LPC, p2, 3-st RPC, k2, p1, k1.
Row 4 P1, k1, p2, k1, p2, k2, p2, k1, p2, *k1, p1 tbl, k1, p2, k1, p2, k2, p2, k1, p2;
rep from * to last 2 sts, k1, pl.
Row 5 K1, p1, *k2, p1, 3-st LPC, 3-st RPC, p1, k2, p1, k1 tbl, p1; rep from * to last 14 sts, k2, p1, 3-st LPC, 3-st RPC, p1, k2, p1, k1.
Row 6 P1, k1, p2, k2, p4, k2, p2, *k1, p1 tbl, k1, p2, k2, p4, k2, p2;

rep from * to last 2 sts, k1, p1.
Row 7 K1, p1, *k2, p2, 4-st RC, p2, k2, p1, k1 tbl, p1; rep from * to last 14 sts, k2, p2, 4-st RC, p2, k2, p1, k1.
Row 8 P1, k1, p2, k2, p4, k2, p2, *k1, p1 tbl, k1, p2, k2, p4, k2, p2;
rep from * to last 2 sts, k1, pl.
Row 9 K1, p1, *k2, p1, 3-st RPC, 3-st LPC, p1, k2, p1, k1 tbl, p1;
rep from * to last 14 sts, k2, p1, 3-st RPC, 3-st LPC, p1, k2, p1, k1.
Row 10 P1, k1, p2, k1, p2, k2, p2, k1, p2, *k1, p1 tbl, k1, p2, k1, p2, k2, p2, k1, p2;
rep from * to last 2 sts, k1, p1.
Row 11 K1, p1, *k2, 3-st RPC, p2, 3-st LPC, k2, p1, k1 tbl, p1;
rep from * to last 14 sts, k2, 3-st RPC, p2, 3-st LPC, k2, p1, k1.
Row 12 P1, k1, p4, k4, p4, *k1, p1 tbl, k1, p4, k4, p4; rep from * to last 2 sts, k1, p1.
Rep rows 1-12 for cable pat.

Back
■ With MC and smaller needles, cast on 91 (121) sts. K 4 rows.
Change to larger needles and work in cable pat until piece measures 28"/71cm from beg. Pm at each end of row to mark beg of armhole. Cont in cable pat until piece measures 37 (38)"/94 (96.5)cm from beg. Bind off.

Left front and sleeve
■ With MC and smaller needles, cast on 16 (31) sts. K 4 rows.
Change to larger needles.
Size S/M Work first 2 and last 14 sts of cable pat.
Size L/XL Work in cable pat.
Both sizes Cont in pat as established until piece measures approx 5¼"/14cm from beg, ending with row 9.
**Next row* (WS) Cast on 15 sts, k15, work in cable pat to end.

A

B

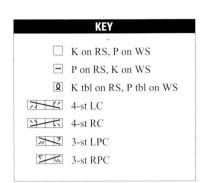

KEY
☐ K on RS, P on WS
⊟ P on RS, K on WS
⊠ K tbl on RS, P tbl on WS
⬚ 4-st LC
⬚ 4-st RC
⬚ 3-st LPC
⬚ 3-st RPC

■ Use the first 2 rows to make the twist to form a small stem, and the rose will shape itself.

■ Secure the first two rows using the cast-on tail and a tapestry needle.

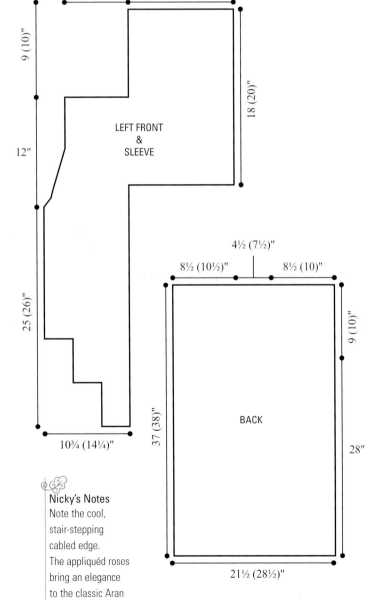

LEFT FRONT & SLEEVE

8½ (10½)"   14"

9 (10)"

18 (20)"

12"

25 (26)"

10¾ (14¼)"

4½ (7½)"

8½ (10½)"   8½ (10)"

BACK

9 (10)"

37 (38)"

28"

21½ (28½)"

Note the cool, stair-stepping cabled edge. The appliquéd roses bring an elegance to the classic Aran fisherman's cables.

Next row Work in cable pat to last 15 sts, k15.
Next row K15, work in cable pat to end.
Next row Work in cable pat across all sts.**
Cont in cable pat until piece measures approx 11½"/29cm from beg, ending with row 9.
Rep from ** to ** once more–46 (61) sts.
Cont in cable pat until piece measures 25 (26)"/63.5 (66)cm from beg.

Neck shaping

■ Dec 1 st at neck edge (end of RS rows) every other row 3 (9) times, then every 4th row 7 times, AT THE SAME TIME, when piece measures 28"/71cm from beg, ending with a WS row, beg sleeve.

Sleeve

■ *Next row* (RS) With larger needles, cast on 60 sts. K60, work in cable pat (including neck shaping) to end.
Next row Work in cable pat across all sts.
Cont in cable pat, completing neck shaping, then working even until front measures 37 (38)"/94 (96.5)cm from beg, ending with a RS row.
Bind off 36 (45) sts for shoulder. Cont in cable pat on rem 60 sts for sleeve until sleeve measures 17¾ (19¾)" from beg, ending with a RS row. K 1 row. Bind off.

Right front and sleeve

■ With MC and smaller needles, cast on 16 (31) sts. K 4 rows. Change to larger needles.
Size S/M Work first 2 and last 14 sts of cable pat.
Size L/XL Work in cable pat.
Both sizes Cont in pat as established until piece measures 5¾"/14.5cm from beg, ending with row 10.
**Next row* (RS) Cast on 15 sts. K15, work in cable pat to end.
Next row Work in cable pat to last 15 sts, k15.
Next row K15, work in cable pat to end.
Next row Work in cable pat over all sts.**
Cont in cable pat until piece measures 11½"/29cm from beg, ending with row 10. Rep from ** to **.
Cont in cable pat until piece measures 25 (26)"/63.5 (66)cm from beg.

CABLE CHART

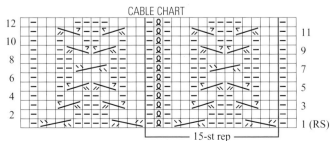

— 15-st rep —

Neck shaping

■ Dec 1 st at neck edge (beg of RS rows) every other row 3 (9) times, then every 4th row 7 times, AT THE SAME TIME, when piece measures 28"/71cm from beg, ending with a RS row, beg sleeve.

Sleeve

■ Cast on 60 sts. *Next row* (WS) P60, work in cable pat as est to end.
Next row Work in cable pat (including neck shaping) across all sts.
Cont in cable pat, completing neck shaping, then working even until front measures 37 (38)"/94 (96.5)cm from beg, ending with a WS row. Bind off 36 (45) sts for shoulder. Cont in cable pat on rem 60 sts for sleeve until sleeve measures 17¾ (19¾)" from beg, ending with a WS row. K 1 row. Bind off.

Finishing

■ Sew shoulder seams. Sew back half of sleeve to back armhole opening to marker.

Cuff

■ With RS facing and smaller needles, pick up 32 sts evenly across lower edge of sleeve. Work in k2, p2 rib for 2"/5cm. Bind off.

Collar

■ Pm on each front edge at beg of neck shaping. With RS facing and smaller needles, starting 6"/15cm before marker on right front, pick up 28 sts to marker, pick up 98 sts evenly around neck opening to next marker, pick up 28 sts from marker to 6"/15cm after – 154 sts.
Next row (WS) P2, *k2, p2; rep from * to end.
Cont in k2, p2 rib as established for 1¾"/4.5cm, ending with a WS row.
Buttonhole row (RS) Work 2 sts in rib, *bind off 2 sts, work 10 sts in rib; rep from * once more, bind off 2 sts, work to end.
Return row Work in rib, casting on 2 sts over each bound-off space.
Cont in rib, working short rows between markers as foll:
First 2 short rows Rib to 2 sts before marker, W&T.
Next 2 short rows Rib to 2 sts before wrapped st, W&T.
Rep last 2 short rows 8 times more—20 short rows total.
Next row Work in rib to end, picking up wraps and working them tog with st. Bind off in rib. Sew on buttons.

Roses (make 30 in assorted and/or mixed colors as desired)

■ With smaller needles, cast on 8 sts.
Rows 1, 3 and 5 Purl.
Row 2 *Kfb (k in front and back of st); rep from * to end – 16 sts.
Row 4 *Kfb; rep from * to end–32 sts.
Row 6 *Kfb; rep from * to end–64 sts.
Row 7 Purl.
Bind off with a different color if desired.
Roll strip to form flower and sew tog for center at cast on edge.

Garter leaves (make 18 with A and 18 with B)

■ With smaller needles, cast on 9 sts.
Rows 1, 3 and 5 (RS) K3, SK2P, k3–7 sts.
Rows 2 and 4 K1, M1, k2, p1, k2, M1, k1–9 sts.
Row 6 K3, p1, k3.
Row 7 K2, SK2P, k2–5 sts.
Row 8 K2, p1, k2.
Row 9 K1, SK2P, k1–3 sts.
Row 10 K1, p1, k1.
Row 11 SK2P–1 st. Fasten off.

■ Sew roses and leaves around collar as pictured.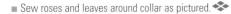

Sanquhar Bonny Socks

These footsie warmers, in patterns developed by knitters in the tiny town of Sanquhar, can be warn by lassies or laddies.

■ SKILLED KNITTER

WHAT YOU'LL NEED
- 2 1¾oz/50g skeins each (ea. approx 110yd/100m) of Alpaca with a Twist *Baby Twist* (100% baby alpaca) in #284 brindle (A) and #1006 nautical blue (B)
- 1 ball #3007 red wagon (C)
- One set (4) size 2 (2.25 mm) double-pointed needles
- One set (4) size 4 (3.5 mm) double-pointed needles
- Stitch markers
- Tapestry needle

One Size
Adult Woman's

Gauge
32 sts and 22 rows = 4"/10 cm over Sanquhar Chart using larger needles. TAKE TIME TO CHECK GAUGE.
NOTE: Carry colors loosely along wrong side of work. Pick up new color from underneath old color to twist yarns and prevent holes.

Sock
CUFF
■ With B and smaller needles, cast on 72 sts. Divide sts evenly over 3 needles.

Join, taking care not to twist sts to work in the round. Place a marker for beginning of round. Work in k1, p1 rib for 4 rnds.

BEGIN SANQUHAR CHART
■ Change to larger needles. Beginning with Rnd 1, repeat 18 sts of Sanquhar Chart around. Work 18 rnds of Sanquhar Chart.

■ Change to smaller needles and with A only, knit 1 round.
Next rnd (K4, k2tog) around – 60 sts.
Work in k1, p1 rib for 3"/7.5cm.
Turn work inside out to reverse fabric.

Inspired by...

The distinctive two-colored patterned knitting, widely known as "Sanquhar" takes its name from the small parish and ancient burgh of Sanquahar in Upper Nithsdale. There are about a dozen known, named traditional patterns with as many variations of cuff patterns. The most popular and most common: the "Duke."

BEGIN SANQUHAR SEED CHART

■ Change to larger needles. Beginning with Rnd 1, repeat 6 sts of Sanquhar Seed Chart around.
Continue to work in Sanquhar Seed Chart for 7"/18cm.

BEGIN HEEL

Row 1 Change to C. [Slip 1, k1] 15 times—30 sts. Turn.
Leave remaining 42 sts unworked.
Row 2 [Slip 1, p1] 15 times.
Repeat last 2 rows for 18 rows.

TURN HEEL

K17, ssk, k1, turn.
Slip 1, p5, p2tog, p1, turn.
Slip 1, k6, ssk, k1 turn.
Slip 1, p7, p2tog, p1, turn.
Continue in this manner, working 1 more st between decreases, until 18 sts remain.

Shape Foot

■ With C, k9, place marker for beginning of rnd, k9, pick up and knit 12 sts along edge of Heel, place second marker, working in Sanquhar Seed Chart on 30 sts, place third marker, with C, pick up and knit 12 st along edge of Heel, k9—72 sts.
Dec rnd Cut C. Keeping in Sanquhar Seed St as established on 30 instep sts, work to 3 sts before second marker, k2tog, k1, work across to third marker, k1, ssk, work to end of rnd.
Work 1 rnd in pattern.
Repeat last 2 rnds 5 more times—60 sts.
Work until 30 rnds from Heel have been worked.

Shape Toe

■ Change to C. K15 sts, place second marker, k30 sts, place third marker, k15.
Dec rnd Work to 3 sts before second marker, k2tog, k2, ssk, work to last 3 sts before third marker, k2tog, k2, ssk, work to end.
Repeat Dec Rnd 10 more times—16 sts.
Divide sts evenly between 2 needles. Graft sts together (see page 240) to close toe.

■ Weave in ends. ❖

SANQUHAR CHART

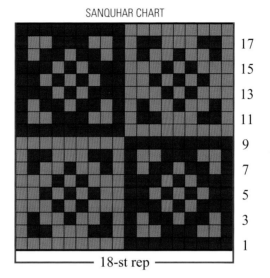

17
15
13
11
9
7
5
3
1

└─ 18-st rep ─┘

SANQUHAR SEED CHART

1

└─ 6-st rep ─┘

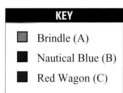

KEY
■ Brindle (A)
■ Nautical Blue (B)
■ Red Wagon (C)

I've used an authentic box pattern from the Sanquhar knitters to give these socks their unique look.

Simply Smashing Cardigan

It's no wonder that Fair Isle is one of the most popular techniques in the world. This cardigan is warm, wonderful and perfect for damp, chilly nights.

■ SKILLED KNITTER

WHAT YOU'LL NEED
- 9 (11) 1¾oz/50g skeins (ea. approx 109yds/100m) of Reynolds/JCA, Inc.'s *Lite Lopi* (100% Icelandic wool) in #426 gold heather (A)
- 3 skeins #867 dark brown heather (B)
- 1 skein ea. in #427 rust heather (C), #421 celery heather (D), #422 sage heather (E), #431 brick heather (F), #85 oatmeal (G) and #418 light blue heather (H)
- Size 7 (4.5mm) needles
- Size 6 (4mm) needles
- Stitch holders
- Cable needle
- Tapestry needle
- 3 wooden toggle buttons, 1"/2.5cm wide

Sizes
S/M (L)

Finished Measurements
Bust: 47 (58)"/119.5 (147.5)cm
Length: 29"/73.5cm

Gauge
17 sts and 24 rows = 4"/10cm in Embossed Diamond St using larger needles.
TAKE TIME TO CHECK GAUGE.
NOTES: Carry colors loosely along wrong side of work. Pick up new color from underneath old color to twist yarns and prevent holes.

Pattern Stitches
■ Embossed Diamond Stitch (multiple of 8 sts + 1 extra)
Row 1 (RS) *K4, p1, k3; rep from * to last st, k1.
Row 2 *P4, k1, p3; rep from * to last st, p1.
Row 3 *K3, p1, k1, p1, k2; rep from * to last st, k1.
Row 4 *P3, k1, p1, k1, p2; rep from * to last st, p1.
Row 5 *K2, p1, k3, p1, k1; rep from * to last st, k1.
Row 6 *P2, k1, p3, k1, p1; rep from * to last st, p1.
Row 7 *K1, p1, k5, p1; rep from * to last st, k1.

Row 8 *P1, k1, p5, k1; rep from * to last st, p1.
Row 9 *P1, k7; rep from * to last st, p1.
Row 10 *K1, p7; rep from * to last st, k1.
Row 11 Repeat Row 7.
Row 12 Repeat Row 8.
Row 13 Repeat Row 5.
Row 14 Repeat Row 6.
Row 15 Repeat Row 3.
Row 16 Repeat Row 4.
Repeat Rows 1-16 for Embossed Diamond St.

Back
HEM
■ With smaller needles and B, cast on 96 (120) sts.
Work in St st until piece measures 1½"/4cm from beginning, end with a RS row.
Knit 1 row on WS for turning row.
Work in St st for 1½"/4cm from turning row, end with a WS row.

BEGIN FAIR ISLE CHART
Row 1 (RS) Change to larger needles. Work Row 1 of Fair Isle Chart across.
Continue to work Rows 1-45 of Fair Isle Chart.
With A, purl 1 row on wrong side, inc 1 st—97 (121) sts.

BEGIN EMBOSSED DIAMOND STITCH

Row 1 (RS) With A, work Row 1 of Embossed Diamond St across.
Continue in Embossed Diamond St until piece measures 18"/45.5cm from turning row, end with WS row.

Shape Armholes

■ Bind off 5 sts at beginning of next 2 rows–87 (111) sts.
Work until armholes measure 10"/25.5cm.

Shape Shoulders

■ Bind off 9 (12) sts at beginning of next 6 rows–33 (39) sts.
Bind off rem sts for back neck.

Left Front

■ With smaller needles and B, cast on 48 (60) sts.
Work Hem as for Back.

BEGIN FAIR ISLE CHART

Row 1 (RS) Change to larger needles. Work Row 1 of Fair Isle Chart across, ending where indicated for Large.
Continue to work Rows 1-45 of Fair Isle Chart.
With A, purl 1 row on wrong side, inc 1 (5) sts–49 (65) sts.

BEGIN EMBOSSED DIAMOND STITCH

Row 1 (RS) With A, work Row 1 of Embossed Diamond St across.
Continue in Embossed Diamond St until piece measures 12"/30.5cm from turning row, end with WS row.

Shape Neck

■ *Dec row* (RS) Work across to last 3 sts, k2tog, k1.
Continue to work in Embossed Diamond St, working Dec Row every other row 1 (11) times more, then every 6th row 15 (12) times.

■ At Same Time, when piece measures 18"/45.5cm from turning row, end with WS row.

Shape Armhole

■ Bind off 5 sts at beginning of next RS row.
Work until armholes measure 10"/25.5cm–27 (36) sts.

Shape Shoulders

■ Bind off 9 (12) sts at side edge (beg of RS rows) 3 times.
Bind off.

Right Front

■ Mark placement for 3 toggle buttons evenly spaced in Fair Isle section on Left Front.

■ Work as for Left Front, reversing shaping and pattern placement, working buttonholes opposite markers as follows:
Buttonhole row (RS) Work 3 sts, bind off 3 sts, work to end of row.
Cast on 3 sts over bound-off sts of previous row.

Sleeves

HEM

■ With smaller needles and B, cast on 48 sts.
Work in St st until piece measures 1"/2.5cm from beginning, end with a RS row.
Knit 1 row on WS for turning row.
Work in St st for 1"/2.5cm from turning row, end with a WS row.

BEGIN FAIR ISLE CHART

Row 1 (RS) Change to larger needles. Work Row 1 of Fair Isle Chart across.
Continue to work Rows 1-19 of Fair Isle Chart.
With F, purl 1 row on RS for cuff turning row, inc 1 st–49 sts. Sleeve cuff is meant to be folded up so RS of cuff is WS of Sleeve.

BEGIN EMBOSSED DIAMOND STITCH

■ With A, purl 1 row on WS.
Row 1 (RS) With A, work Row 1 of Embossed Diamond St across.
Continue in Embossed Diamond St for 4"/10cm, ending with WS row.
Continue as established, inc 1 st each side (working sts into Embossed Diamond St) every 4th row 18 times–85 sts.
Work until piece measures 19"/48cm from turning row, end with WS row.
Bind off.

Finishing

■ Sew shoulder seams. Set in Sleeves. Sew Sleeve and side seams.
Fold Hems to WS at turning row and sew in place. Sew buttons opposite buttonholes.
Fold Sleeve Cuff to RS.

Left Collar

■ With larger needles and A, cast on 3 sts.
Knit 1 row, purl 1 row.

BEGIN FAIR ISLE CHART

■ Beginning with Row 1, work Fair Isle Chart, inc 1 st at end of every other RS row 17 times, then every 4th row 10 times, working new sts in Fair Isle Chart–30 sts.
Continue in Fair Isle Chart until piece measures 21" (21½)/53.5 (54.5)cm from beginning, or length to fit from beginning of neck shaping to center of Back neck.
Bind off.

Right Collar

■ Work as for Left Collar, beginning with last 3 sts of Row 1 of Fair Isle Chart, working incs at beg of RS rows.

■ Sew bound-off edges of Collar pieces together. Sew Collar pieces around neck edge, beginning at neck shaping of Left Front around to Right Front. Weave in ends.

Front Bands Hems

■ With RS facing, smaller needles and B, pick up and knit 52 sts along Right Front edge from lower edge to beginning of Collar.
Work in St st for 1"/2.5cm, ending with RS row.
Knit 1 row on WS for turning row.
Work in St st for 1"/2.5cm more. Bind off.
Repeat on opposite Left Front edge.

Collar Hems

■ With RS facing, smaller needles and B, pick up and knit 116 (120) sts along Right Collar from beginning of Right Collar to center of Back neck.
Work in St st for 1"/2.5cm, ending with RS row.
Knit 1 row on WS for turning row.
Work in St st for 1"/2.5cm more. Bind off.
Repeat on opposite Left Collar piece.

■ Fold Hems to WS at turning row and sew in place. Sew edges of Hems together. Weave in ends. ❖❖

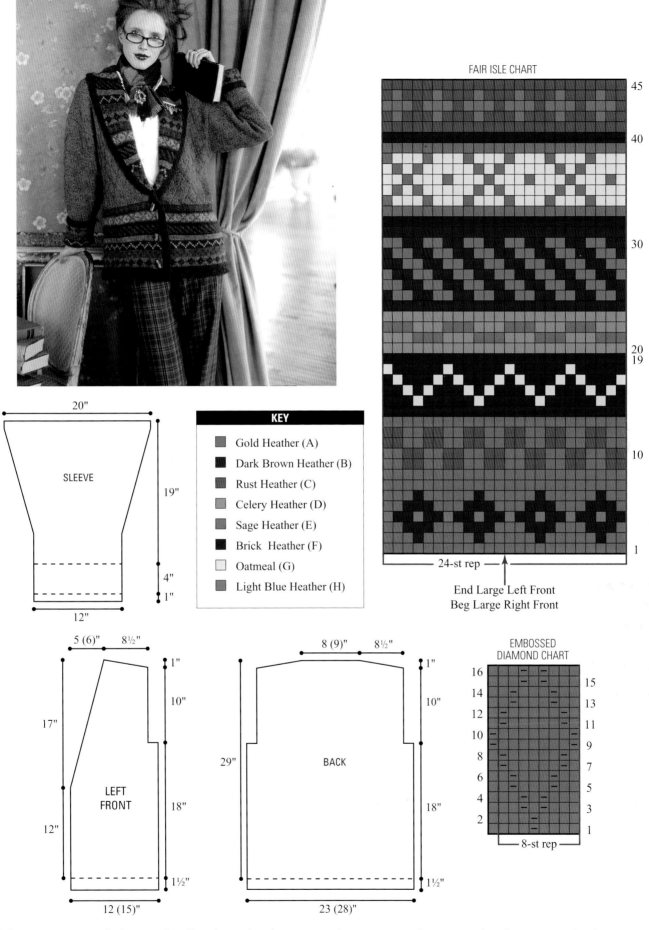

FAIR ISLE CHART

45

40

30

20
19

10

1

24-st rep

End Large Left Front
Beg Large Right Front

KEY

- Gold Heather (A)
- Dark Brown Heather (B)
- Rust Heather (C)
- Celery Heather (D)
- Sage Heather (E)
- Brick Heather (F)
- Oatmeal (G)
- Light Blue Heather (H)

20"

SLEEVE

19"

4"

1"

12"

EMBOSSED
DIAMOND CHART

16
14
12
10
8
6
4
2

15
13
11
9
7
5
3
1

8-st rep

5 (6)"   8½"

1"

10"

17"

18"

12"

LEFT
FRONT

12 (15)"

1½"

8 (9)"   8½"

1"

10"

29"

BACK

18"

23 (28)"

1½"

I've combined Fair Isle colorwork striping with a
subtle diamond texture stitch to create this update.

Cowl Collar Jumper

You say Guernsey and I say Gansey—original Guernsey fisherman sweaters had a waterproof, jersey-like texture. This update takes a much softer approach.

■ NOVICE KNITTER

WHAT YOU'LL NEED

- ■ 19 (26) 1¾oz/50g balls (ea. approx 65yd/60m) of Classic Elite Yarns *Bazic Wool* (100% superwash wool) in #2925 Sunflower
- ■ Size 8 (5mm) needles
- ■ Size 6 (4mm) needles
- ■ Size 6 (4mm) circular needle, 24"/60cm
- ■ Stitch holder
- ■ Stitch marker
- ■ Tapestry needle

Sizes
S/M (L)

Finished Measurements
Bust: 32 (42)"/81.5 (106.5)cm
Length: 36 (37)"/91.5 (94)cm

Gauge
18 sts and 26 rows = 4"/10cm in Box Stitch using larger needles.

Pattern Stitches
■ Box Stitch (worked over 10 sts)
Row 1 (RS) [K2, p2] twice, k2.
Rows 2 & 4 Knit the knit sts and purl the purl sts.
Row 3 K4, p2, k4.
Repeat Rows 1-4 rows for Box Stitch.

■ Diamond Panel (worked over 13 sts)
Row 1 P1, k11, p1.

Row 2 K1, p11, k1.
Row 3 P1, k5, p1, k5, p1.
Row 4 K1, p4, k1, p1, k1, p4, k1.
Row 5 P1, k3, [p1, k1] twice, p1, k3, p1.
Row 6 K1, p2, [k1, p1] 3 times, k1, p2, k1.
Row 7 P1, [k1, p1] 5 times, k1, p1.
Row 8 Repeat Row 6.
Row 9 Repeat Row 5.
Row 10 Repeat Row 4.
Row 11 Repeat Row 3.
Row 12 Repeat Row 2.
Repeat Rows 1-12 for Diamond Panel.

Back
■ With smaller needles, cast on 81 (104) sts.
Work in St st for 1"/2.5cm, ending with a RS row.
Knit 1 row on WS for turning ridge.
Change to larger needles.

I've made and
seen so many
Guernsey sweaters,
I thought it would
be fun to design a
dress! Hope you
think so, too!

BOX STITCH

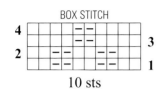

10 sts

DIAMOND PANEL

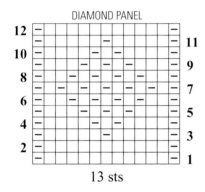

13 sts

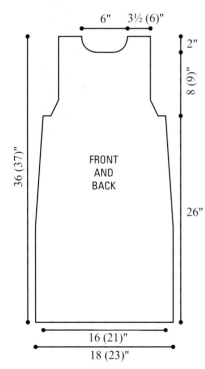

6"   3½ (6)"

2"

8 (9)"

36 (37)"

FRONT
AND
BACK

26"

16 (21)"

18 (23)"

KEY

☐	K on RS, p on WS
⊟	P on RS, k on WS

Traditional Knitting of The British Isles

**Fisher-Gansey Patterns
of Scotland and the Scottish Fleet**

Inspired by...

*As you can see styles change but
the basic feeling of a Gansey shines
through in the dress I've made.*

BEGIN PATTERNS

Row 1 (RS) P1, beginning with Row 1 *work Box St over 10 sts, Diamond Panel
over 13 sts; rep from * to last 11 sts, work Box St over 10 sts, p1.
Work as established until piece measures 13"/33cm from turning ridge.
Dec 1 st each edge every 10th row 4 times–73 (96) sts
Work until piece measures 26"/66cm from turning ridge.

Shape Armhole

■ Bind off 5 sts at beginning of next 2 rows–63 (86) sts.
Dec 1 st each edge every other row 3 times–57 (80) sts.
Work until armhole measures 8 (9)"/20.5 (23)cm, ending with WS row.

Shape Neck

■ *Next row* (RS) Work 20 (31) sts in pattern, slip next 17 (18) sts to
a stitch holder, join a second ball of yarn and work in pattern
across remaining 20 (31) sts.

■ Working both sides at same time with separate balls of yarn,
dec 2 sts at neck edge every other row twice–16 (27) sts.
Work until armhole measures 10 (11)"/25 (28)cm.
Bind off.

Front

■ Work same as back.

Finishing

■ Sew shoulder seams.

Cowl Collar

■ With RS facing and circular needle, join yarn at shoulder seam
and pick up and knit 126 evenly spaced around neck, working sts from stitch holders.
Join to work in the round. Place a marker for beginning of round.
Next rnd (knit) around, inc 78 sts evenly around – 204 sts.
Work in k2, p2 rib until Collar measures 8"/20.5cm.
Bind off in rib.

Armhole Bands

■ With RS facing and smaller needles, pick up and knit 58 (62) sts evenly
spaced along armhole edge.
Work in k2, p2 rib for 1"/2.5cm.
Bind off in rib.

■ Sew side seams, including armhole bands. Fold hem to WS along turning
ridge and sew in place. Weave in ends. ❖

Hunter's Argyle Socks

Even the Duke of Argyll would be reluctant to cover these resplendent socks with his boots.

■ SKILLED KNITTER

WHAT YOU'LL NEED
- 2 3½oz/100g hanks (ea. approx 450yd/410m) of Classic Elite Yarns *Alpaca Sox* (60% alpaca, 20% merino wool, 20% nylon) in #1838 toast (A)
- 1 hank ea. in #1881 granny smith (B), #1897 ivy (C) and #1855 russet (D)
- Size 2 (2.25 mm) needles
- Size 2 (2.25 mm) double-pointed needles
- Stitch markers
- Yarn bobbins
- Stitch holders
- Tapestry needle

One Size

Gauge
32 sts and 36 rows = 4"/10 cm in St st. TAKE TIME TO CHECK GAUGE.
NOTES:
- Use separate bobbins of yarn for each large block of color.
- Carry colors loosely along wrong side of work. Pick up new color from underneath old color to twist yarns and prevent holes.
- Cross lines of D on Argyle Chart may be embroidered in duplicate stitch after socks are finished.
- Legs of Socks are worked back and forth in rows. After foot is complete, stitches are then joined and Toe is worked in rounds.

Special Stitches
■ *Tuck Stitch* With right-hand needle pick up loop of next st 7 rows below, place on left-hand needle, then purl together picked-up loop and next st on left-hand needle.

Pleat Pattern (multiple of 8 sts + 6 extra)
Row 1 (WS) P5, *work Tuck st on 4 sts, p4; rep from * to last st, p1.
Rows 2-7 Work in St st.
Row 8 (WS) P1, work Tuck st on 4 sts, *p4, work Tuck st on 4 sts; repeat from * to last st, p1.
Rows 9-16 Work in St st.
Repeat Rows 1-16 for Pleat pattern.

Sock

CUFF
- With A, cast on 78 sts.
Beginning with RS row, work 9 rows in St st.
Beginning with Row 1, work Pleat pattern for 4"/10cm, ending with Row 1.
Knit 1 row, dec 11 stitches evenly across—67 sts.
Purl 1 row.

BEGIN ARGYLE CHART
- *Row 1* (RS) K1 for selvage st, work Argyle chart across 65 sts, k1 for selvage st.
Work 64 rows of Argyle Chart. Sock measures approx 11½"/29cm from beginning.

BEGIN INSTEP
- *Row 65* (RS) With A, k17 and slip to stitch holder for heel, continue in Argyle Chart on center 33 sts, slip last 17 sts to a second stitch holder for heel.
Work Rows 2-65 of Argyle Chart on 33 sts.
Cut yarn and slip sts to a third stitch holder.

BEGIN HEEL
- *Next Row* (WS) With WS facing, join A and p17 from second stitch holder then 17 sts from first stitch holder—34 sts.
Work 32 rows in St st slipping first st of each row, ending with RS row.
Turn Heel
Slip 1, p18, p2tog, p1, turn.
Slip 1, k5, ssk, k1, turn.
Slip 1, p6, p2tog, p1, turn.
Slip 1, k7, ssk, k1, turn.
Continue in this manner, working 1 more st between decreases, until 20 sts remain.
Cut yarn.

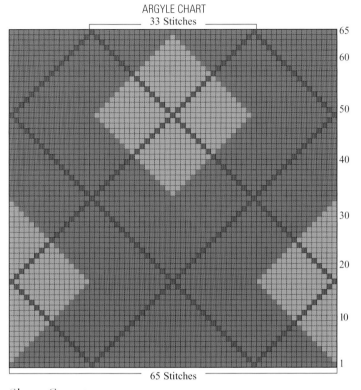

ARGYLE CHART
33 Stitches

65
60
50
40
30
20
10
1

65 Stitches

Shape Gusset

■ With RS facing and A, join yarn at edge of Heel and pick up and knit 17 sts along edge, k10 sts from Heel stitch holder, place marker, knit remaining 10 Heel sts, pick up and knit 17 sts along opposite edge of Heel—54 sts.

Working back and forth in rows with A, purl 1 row.

Dec row K1, ssk, knit to last 3 sts, k2tog, k1.

Repeat last 2 rows 8 more times—36 sts.

KEY	
■	Toast (A)
■	Granny Smith (B)
■	Ivy (C)
■	Russet (D)

Foot

■ Continue on 36 sts in St st with A until piece measures same length as Instep, dec 1 st on last row—35 sts.

Shape Toe

■ *Joining rnd* (RS) With double-pointed needles, work 17 sts of Foot on one needle, place marker for beginning of rnd, work 17 sts of Foot on second needle, place second marker, k1, work 33 sts from Instep stitch holder, place third marker—68 sts. Join and divide sts equally around needles.

■ *Dec rnd* Work to 3 sts before second marker, k2tog, k2, ssk, work to last 3 sts before third marker, k2tog, k2, ssk, work to end.

Knit 1 rnd.

Repeat last 2 rnds 11 more times—20 sts.

Divide sts evenly between 2 needles. Graft sts together (see page 240) to close toe.

Finishing

■ Embroider cross lines in duplicate stitch with D, following chart.
Sew back and instep seams. Weave in ends. ❖❖

Highland Fling Plaid Jacket

If you hear the lilting sounds of a bagpipe when you're knitting this modern plaid jacket, you'll know you're on the right track.

■ SKILLED KNITTER

WHAT YOU'LL NEED

- 7 1.48oz/42g balls (ea. approx 90yds/82m) of Classic Elite Yarns *La Gran* (76.5% mohair/17.5% wool/6% nylon) in #6516 natural (A)
- 4 balls #61538 mocha (B)
- 3 balls ea. of #6575 pebble (C) and #6555 infa red (F)
- 2 balls ea. #6545 barley (D) and #63520 winter sky (E)
- Size 9 (5.5mm) needles OR SIZE TO OBTAIN GAUGE
- Size 9 (5.5mm) double-pointed needles (2 dpns)
- Stitch holders (or waste yarn)
- Stitch markers
- Tapestry needle
- 2 Large hooks and eye in matching color

Sizes
S (M, L)

Finished Measurements
Bust (closed): 40 (48½, 57)"/101.5 (123, 145)cm
Length: 27½ (28, 28½)"/70 (71, 72.5)cm

Gauge
15 sts and 22 rows = 4"/10cm in St st. TAKE TIME TO CHECK GAUGE.
NOTE: vertical lines can be knit in or worked in duplicate st (see page 238) after the piece is knit.

Back
■ With B, cast on 75 (91, 107) sts. K 4 rows.
Change to St st and work 9 rows of Chart 1 for border, beg and end as noted on chart. Cont in St st, work rows 1-58 of Chart 2 once, rows 17-58 once, then rows 17-38 once more, AT THE SAME TIME, when back measures 18½"/47cm from beg, pm at each end of row for armholes. With A only, work even until back measures 27½ (28, 28½)"/70 (71, 72.5)cm from beg. Place sts on holder.

Right front
■ With B, cast on 39 (49, 59) sts. K 4 rows.
Change to St st and work same as back, dec 1 st at front edge every 10th (8th, 8th)

row 12 (14, 16) times as foll: Dec row (RS) K1, ssk, k to end, AT SAME TIME, pm at side edge when front measures 18½"/46cm from beg. Cont even on 27 (35, 43) sts until front is same length as back. Place sts on holder.

Left front
■ Work same as right front, working dec at front edge as foll:
Dec row (RS) K to last 3 sts, k2tog, k1.

Sleeves
■ With C, cast on 60 sts. K 3 rows.
Change to St st and work rows 39-58 of Chart 2 once, then rows 17-58 twice (or to desired length), AT THE SAME TIME, inc 1 st each side every 10th row 4 (6, 8) times–68 (72, 76) sts. Bind off.

Collar (make 2)
RIGHT SIDE
■ With A, cast on 29 sts. Work charts same as back, AT THE SAME TIME, dec 1 st at front edge every 10th row 10 times as foll:
Dec row (RS) K1, k2tog, k to end.
Cont even on 19 sts in stripe pat rep until collar measures 31 (31½, 32)"/78.5 (80, 81.5)cm from beg. Place sts on holder.

CHART 2

58

50

40

30

20

10

1

├── 16-st rep ──┤

LEFT SIDE
- Work same as right side, working dec at front edge as foll:
Dec row (RS) K to last 3 sts, ssk, k1.

Finishing
- Block all pieces.
- Join shoulder seams using 3-needle bind-off method (see page 244).
Set sleeves between markers and sew in place. Sew sleeve and side seams. Graft both sides of collar together. Sew decrease edge of collar to fronts and back neck.

Collar edging
- With dpns and B, cast on 5 sts. Work in I-cord (see page 240) until cord measures 62 (63, 64)"/157.5 (160, 162.5)cm. Do not bind off. Starting at cast-on end of cord, sew cord to edge of collar from one lower front edge to the other, adding or removing rows if necessary. Bind off and sew end in place. Fold collar back.

Vertical stripes
BACK
- Work duplicate st in color and column indicated on chart 2, starting at lower edge.

Fronts
- Work same as back, beg chart at side seams.

Collar
- Work each side of collar separately, centering a set of 3 vertical stripes on each side.

- Sew large hook and eye to center for closure. ❖

KEY
☐	Natural (A)
■	Mocha (B)
☐	Pebble (C)
▨	Barley (D)
▨	Winter sky (E)
■	Infa red (F)
•	Duplicate St (B)
✕	Duplicate St (F)

CHART 1

9

1

├─ 6-st rep ─┤
M
S
L

Nicky's Notes
The graduated collar folds back on this sweater, sporting a Fair Isle border.

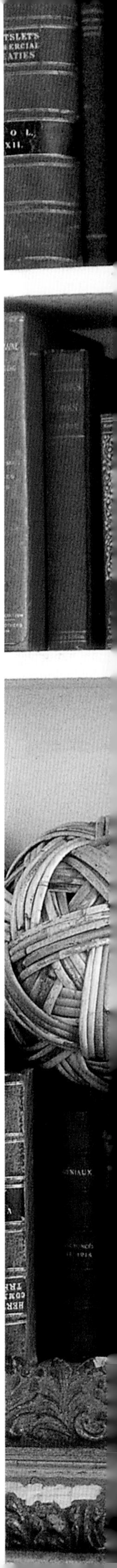

18 (19, 20)"

SLEEVE

12¼ (8½, 5)"

7¼ (11, 14½)"

16"

19½"

18½"

7¼ (9¼, 11½)"

RIGHT FRONT

9 (9½, 10)"

27½ (28, 28½)"

18½"

10½ (13, 15¾)"

5"

13 (13½, 14)"

RIGHT COLLAR

31 (31½, 32)"

18"

7¾"

7¼ (9¼, 11½)"   5½"   7¼ (9¼, 11¼)"

BACK

9 (9½, 10)"

27½ (28, 28½)"

18½"

20 (24¼, 28½)"

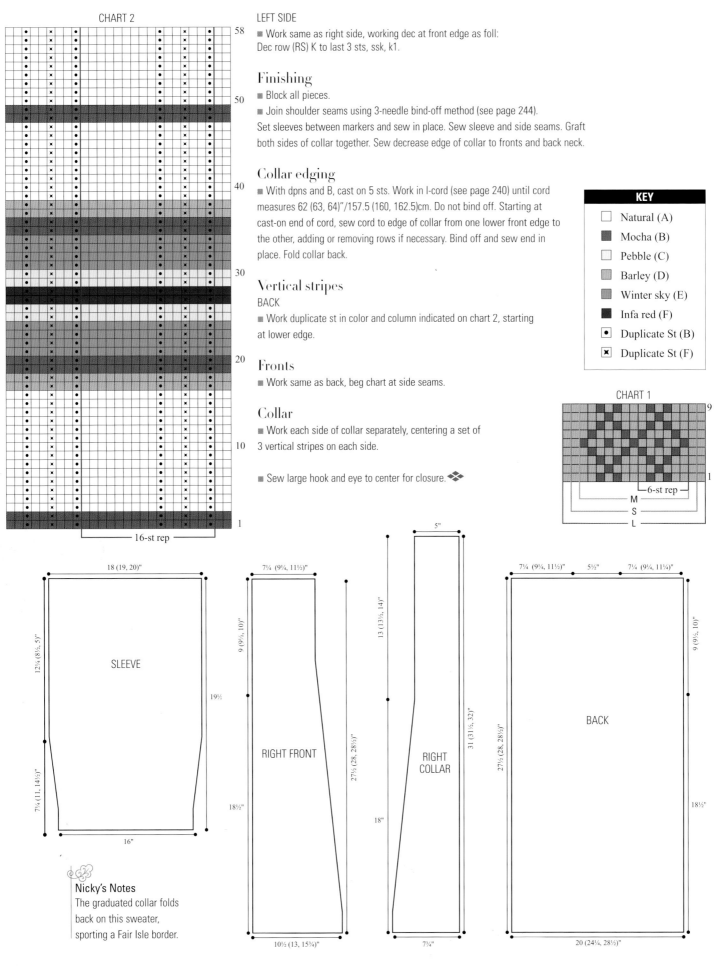

Celtic Hooded Coat

Classic Celtic cables combine to form this coat, as warm as an Irish welcome.

■ MASTER KNITTER

WHAT YOU'LL NEED
- 13 5oz/140g skeins (ea. approx 153yds/140m) of Lion Brand Yarn *Wool-Ease Chunky* (80% acrylic, 20% wool) in #99 fisherman
- Size 10 (6mm) needles or size to obtain gauge
- Size H-8 (5mm) crochet hook
- Cable needle
- Tapestry needle
- 2½ yds/2.3m 1½"/38mm plaid ribbon; ½ yd/.5m of 1"/2.5cm velvet ribbon (optional)
- Sewing needle and matching thread

Sizes
S/M (L/XL)

Finished Measurements
Bust: 54 (69)"/137 (175)cm
Length: 35"/89cm

Gauge
17 sts and 20 rows = 4"/10cm in cable pat. TAKE TIME TO CHECK GAUGE.

Special Stitches
3-st RPC SI 1 st to cn and hold in back, k2, p1 from cn.
3-st LPC SI 2 sts to cn and hold in front, p1, k2 from cn.
4-st RPC SI 1 st to cn and hold in back, k3, p1 from cn.
4-st LPC SI 3 sts to cn and hold in front, p1, k3 from cn.
5-st RC SI 3 sts to cn and hold in back, k2, sl the purl st to left needle and p1, k2 from cn.
5-st RPC SI 2 sts to cn and hold in back, k3, p2 from cn.
5-st LPC SI 3 sts to cn and hold in front, p2, k3 from cn.
6-st RC SI 3 sts to cn and hold in back, k3, k3 from cn.
6-st LC SI 3 sts to cn and hold in front, k3, k3 from cn.
7-st RC SI 4 sts to cn and hold in back, k3, sl the purl st to left needle and p1, k3 from cn.
5-to-1 Dec [SI 1 knitwise] 3 times,*pass 2nd st on RH needle over the last st, sl last st back to LH needle, sl 2nd st on LH needle over the first st, slip first st back to RH needle; rep from * once, then purl rem st.

Panel A (45 sts)
Row 1 (WS) K6, p3, k1, p3, k8, p6, k18.
Row 2 P18, 6-st RC, p8, 7-st RC, p6.
Row 3 and all WS rows Knit the k sts and purl the p sts, EXCEPT rows 15 and 35.

Row 4 P17, 4-st RPC, 5-st LPC, p4, 5-st RPC, p1, 5-st LPC, p4.
Row 6 P5, M1, k1, M1, p10, 4-st RPC, p3, 5-st LPC, 5-st RPC, p5, 5-st LPC, p2—47 sts.
Row 8 P5, [k1,M1] 3 times, p9, 4-st RPC, p6, 6-st RC, p9, k3, p2—50 sts.
Row 10 P3, 5-st RPC, 5-st LPC, p6, 4-st RPC, p6, 4-st RPC, 5-st LPC, p7, k3, p2.
Row 12 P2, 4-st RPC, p4, 5-st LPC, p3, 4-st RPC, p6, 4-st RPC, p3, 5-st LPC, p4, 4-st RPC, p2.
Row 14 P2, k3, p7, 5-st LPC, 4-st RPC, p6, 4-st RPC, p6, 5-st LPC, 5-st RPC, p3.
Row 15 K5, p2, p2tog, p2, k9, p3, k7, p6, k9, p3, k2—49 sts.
Row 16 P2, k3, p9, 6-st LC, p6, 4-st RPC, p9, 5-to-1 dec, p5—45 sts.
Row 18 P2, 5-st LPC, p5, 5-st RPC, 5-st LPC, p3, 4-st RPC, p16.
Row 20 P4, 5-st LPC, p1, 5-st RPC, p4, 5-st LPC, 4-st RPC, p17.
Row 22 P6, 7-st RC, p8, 6-st RC, p18.
Row 24 P4, 5-st RPC, p1, 5-st LPC, p4, 5-st RPC, 4-st LPC, p17.
Row 26 P2, 5-st RPC, p5, 5-st LPC, 5-st RPC, p3, 4-st LPC, p10, M1, k1, M1, p5—47 sts.
Row 28 P2, k3, p9, 6-st LC, p6, 4-st LPC, p9, [k1, M1] 3 times, p5—50 sts.
Row 30 P2, k3, p7, 5-st RPC, 4-st LPC, p6, 4-st LPC, p6, 5-st RPC, 5-st LPC, p3.
Row 32 P2, 4-st LPC, p4, 5-st RPC, p3, 4-st LPC, p6, 4-st LPC, p3, 5-st RPC, p4, 4-st LPC, p2.
Row 34 P3, 5-st LPC, 5-st RPC, p6, 4-st LPC, p6, 4-st LPC, 5-st RPC, p7, k3, p2.
Row 35 K2, p3, k9, p6, k7, p3, k9, p2, p2tog, p2, k5—49 sts.
Row 36 P5, 5-to-1 dec, p9, 4-st LPC, p6, 6-st LC, p9, k3, p2—45 sts.
Row 38 P16, 4-st LPC, p3, 5-st RPC, 5-st LPC, p5, 5-st RPC, p2.
Row 40 P17, 4-st LPC, 5-st RPC, p4, 5-st LPC, p1, 5-st RPC, p4.
Rep rows 1-40.

Panel B (11 sts)
Row 1 (WS) K3, p2, k1, p2, k3.
Row 2 P3, 5-st RC, p3.
Row 3 and all WS rows Knit the k sts and purl the p sts.
Row 4 P2, 3-st RPC, p1, 3-st LPC, p2.
Row 6 P1, 3-st RPC, p3, 3-st LPC, p1.

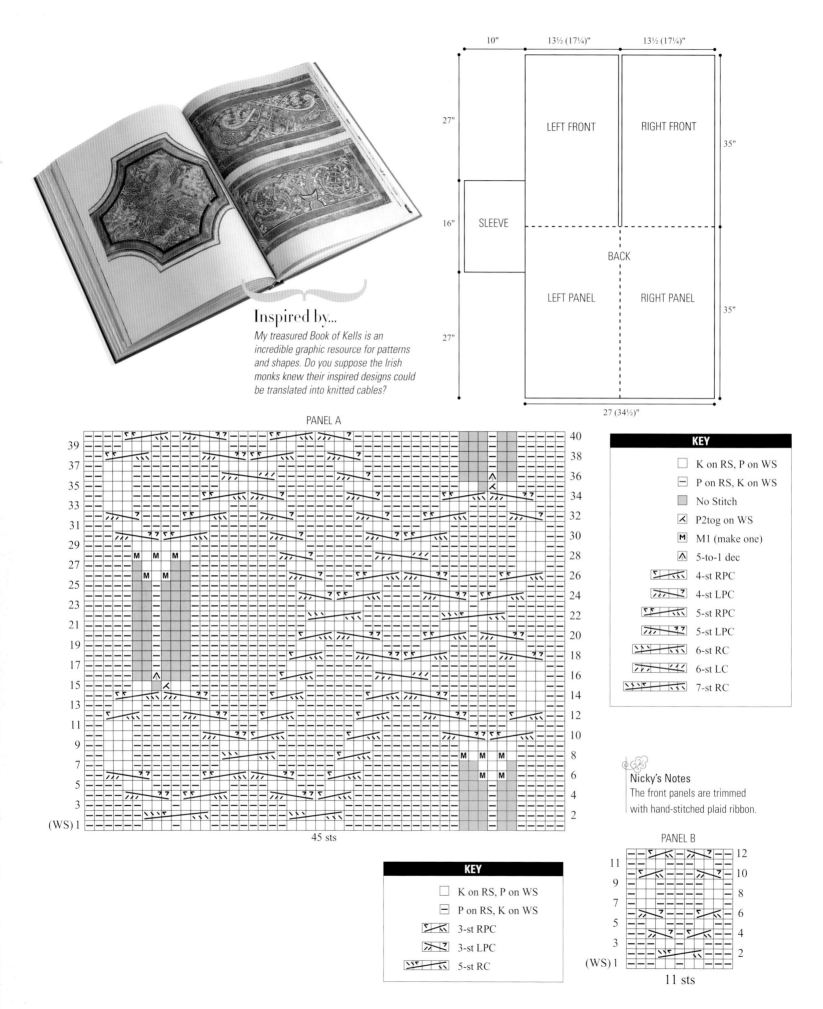

Inspired by...

My treasured Book of Kells is an incredible graphic resource for patterns and shapes. Do you suppose the Irish monks knew their inspired designs could be translated into knitted cables?

PANEL A

45 sts

KEY
☐ K on RS, P on WS
⊟ P on RS, K on WS
▨ No Stitch
P2tog on WS
M M1 (make one)
⋀ 5-to-1 dec
4-st RPC
4-st LPC
5-st RPC
5-st LPC
6-st RC
6-st LC
7-st RC

Nicky's Notes
The front panels are trimmed with hand-stitched plaid ribbon.

PANEL B

11 sts

KEY
☐ K on RS, P on WS
⊟ P on RS, K on WS
3-st RPC
3-st LPC
5-st RC

Row 8 P1, k2, p5, k2, p1.
Row 10 P1, 3-st LPC, p3, 3-st RPC, p1.
Row 12 P2, 3-st LPC, p1, 3-st RPC, p2.
Rep rows 1-12.

Body
LEFT PANEL
■ Cast on 58 (74) sts.
Row 1 (WS) Sl 1, p1, *k2, p2; rep from * to end.
Row 2 Sl 1, k1, *p2, k2; rep from * to end.
Rep rows 1 and 2 three times more, inc 4 (1) sts on last row–62 (75) sts.
Set-up row (WS) Sl 1, p1, work 0 (11) sts of Panel B, p0 (2), work 45 sts of
Panel A, p2, work 11 sts of Panel B, p2.
Cont in patterns as established, slipping the first stitch every row, until
piece measures 68"/172.5cm from beg, ending with a RS row.
Work rows 1 and 2 of rib for 8 rows, dec 4 (1) sts on first row.
Bind off in rib.

RIGHT PANEL
■ Work same as left panel EXCEPT for set-up row.
Set-up row (WS) P2, work 11 sts of Panel B, p2, work 45 sts of Panel A,
p 0 (2), work 0 (11) sts of Panel B, p2.
Complete same as right panel, being sure to end cable panels on the
same row.

Finishing
■ With RS facing, place both panels side by side, making sure B panels are
at center on smaller size. Place markers midpoint at inner edge of each
panel, 35"/89cm from bottom edge (shoulder line). Sew center back seam
from bottom edge to markers.

Sleeves
■ Place markers on outer edges, 8"/20cm down from shoulder line
on each piece.
With RS facing, pick up 46 sts evenly spaced between the 2 sleeve markers.
Row 1 (WS) P2, *k2, p2; rep from * to end.
Row 2 K2, *p2, k2; rep from * to end.
Rep rows 1 and 2 until sleeve measures 10"/25cm. Bind off in rib.
Rep on other side.
Sew sleeve and side seams.

Hood
■ Cast on 48 sts.
Set-up row (WS) Sl 1, p1, work 11 sts of Panel B 4 times, p2.
Cont in patterns as established, slipping first st every row, until piece
measures 28"/71cm from beg, ending with row 3 of Panel B. Bind off.
Fold in half lengthwise and sew back seam.

■ Place markers on inner edges of fronts, 12"/30.5cm from top of center
back seam. Sew hood between markers, easing in place if necessary.

Ribbon Facing
■ With sewing needle and thread, sew plaid ribbon along inside edge of
front opening, from hem to hem and around inner edge of hood.

Loop Closure (optional)
■ With crochet hook, attach 2 strands yarn to neck opening at base of hood
and ch 6. Form loop by sl st to base of ch. Fasten off. Rep on other side.
Slip velvet ribbon through loops and tie. ❖❖

Faux Fair Isle Fairy Socks

This innovative, mock-color variation of a Fair Isle pattern will make you want to go out without shoes.

■ SKILLED KNITTER

WHAT YOU'LL NEED

- 2 1¾oz/50g balls (ea. approx 208yds/187m) of Knit One, Crochet Too, Inc.'s *Soxx Appeal* (96% superwash Merino wool/3% nylon/1% elastic) in #9812 fawn (MC) 1 ball in #9851 chocolate cherry (CC)
- Size 2 (2.75mm) double-pointed needles (set of 4) OR SIZE TO OBTAIN GAUGE
- Stitch marker

Finished measurements

7¼"/18.5cm from cuff to heel
Approx 9"/23cm from heel to toe

Gauge

28 sts and 32 rnds = 4"/10cm in St st over chart patterns.
TAKE TIME TO CHECK GAUGE.

Sock

INNER CUFF (make 2)
■ With MC, cast on 60 sts onto one dpn.
Work in St st for 6 rows.
Twist row (RS) *K6, rotate LH needle counter-clockwise 360 degrees; rep from * to end.
Work in St st for 6 rows.
Bind off. With RS facing, sew side edges together to form a ring.

CUFF
■ Cast on 60 sts and work same as inner cuff for 7 rows. Divide sts over 3 needles as folls: 15 sts on needle 1, 30 sts on needle 2, 15 sts on needle 3. Pm and join.

BEG CHART
■ Work 40 rnds of Chart 1, then work rnds 1-20 once more.
With MC, k 1 rnd.

Heel

■ Cont with MC only, k15, turn.
Row 1 (WS) Sl 1, p29. Turn.
Row 2 [Sl 1, k1] 15 times. Turn.
Rep rows 1 and 2 until 28 rows have been worked.

Turn heel

Row 1 (WS) Sl 1, p16, p2tog, p1. Turn.
Row 2 Sl 1, k5, ssk, k1. Turn.
Row 3 Sl 1, p to 1 st before gap, p2tog, p1. Turn.
Row 4 Sl 1, k to 1 st before gap, ssk, k1. Turn.
Rep rows 3 and 4 until all heel sts have been worked — 18 sts.

Gusset

■ Using a spare needle (new needle 1), pick up and k15 sts along side of heel flap. With needle 2, k30 instep sts. With needle 3, pick up and k15 sts along other side of heel flap, k9. Slip rem 9 sts onto needle 1. Pm for new end of rnd between needles 3 and 1—78 sts.

■ Work Chart 2, making any chart adjustments at bottom of foot, as foll:
Rnd 1 Work to last 3 sts of needle 1, k2tog, k1; work even across needle 2; for needle 3, k1, ssk, work to end of rnd.
Rnd 2 Work even.

Inspired by...

The eternally dapper Prince of Wales. Always a trendsetter, the Prince donned this classic V-neck Fair Isle in 1922 and the rest is history.

Rep rnds 1 and 2 until 60 sts rem.

Foot

■ Work even in chart 2 until foot measures 7"/18cm or 2"/5cm less than desired foot length, ending with a MC row.

Toe

■ Work with MC only.

Rnd 1 Work to last 3 sts of needle 1, k2tog, k1; for needle 2, k1, ssk, k to last 3 sts, k2tog, k1; for needle 3, k1, ssk, work to end of rnd.

Rnd 2 Work even.

Rep rnds 1 and 2 until 32 sts rem.

Rep rnd 1 only until 16 sts rem.

With needle 3, k4 from needle 1.

Graft toe sts tog (see page 240).

Finishing

■ Sew back seam of sock cuff. Sew inner cuff in place, matching twists with outer cuff. ❖

CHART 1
(Leg)

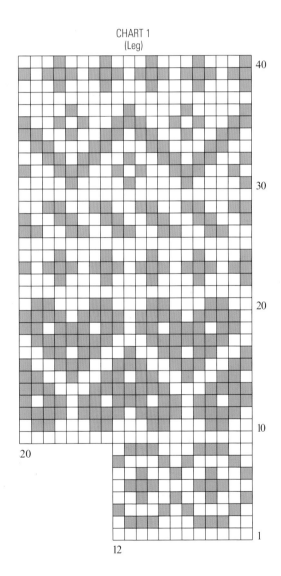

CHART 2
(Foot)

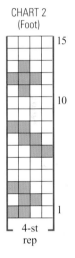

4-st rep

This faux-Fair-Isle look is achieved by using a multicolored yarn with a solid contrasting color. Once you try this technique, you'll be hooked!

Edwardian Lace Coat

Pure, 100-percent Shetland Islands lace patterns
led me to the creation of this elegant coat.

■ MASTER KNITTER

WHAT YOU'LL NEED

- 17 (24) 1¾oz/50g balls (each approx 110yd/100m) of Trendsetter Yarns *Kashmir* (65% cashmere/35% silk) in #1205 ecru
- Size 10 (6mm) needles
- Size 9 (5.5mm) needles
- Size 9 (5.5mm) 29"/74cm circular needle
- Stitch holders
- Cable needle
- Tapestry needle

Sizes
S/M (L/XL)

Finished Measurements
Bust: 42 (60)"/106.5 (152.5)cm
Length: 33"/84cm

Gauge
20 sts and 24 rows = 4"/10cm in Pattern I on smaller needles.
TAKE TIME TO CHECK GAUGE.

Shetland Pattern Stitches
PATTERN 1—Eyelet Rib (multiple of 7 sts + 2 extra)
Row 1 and 3 (WS) K2, *p5, k2; rep from * to end.
Row 2 (RS) P2, *k5, p2; rep from * to end.
Row 4 P2, *k2tog, yo, k1, yo, ssk, p2; rep from * to end.
Repeat Rows 1-4 for Pattern 1.

PATTERN 2—Old Shale Fan Stitch (multiple of 18 sts)
Row 1 (RS) Knit.
Row 2 (WS) Purl.
Row 3 *(K2tog) 3 times, (yo, k1) 6 times, (k2tog) 3 times; rep from * to end.
Row 4 Knit.
Repeat Rows 1-4 for Pattern 2.

PATTERN 3—Crest of Wave (multiple of 12 sts + 1 extra)
Rows 1-4 Knit.
Rows 5, 7, 9 and 11 (RS) K1, *(k2tog) twice, (yo, k1) 3 times, yo, (ssk) twice, k1;

rep from * to end.
Rows 6, 8, 10 and 12 (WS) Purl.
Repeat Rows 1-12 for Pattern 3.

PATTERN 4—Horseshoe (multiple of 10 sts + 1 extra)
Rows 1 and 3 (WS) Purl.
Row 2 (RS) K1, *yo, k3, sk2p, k3, yo, k1; rep from * to end.
Row 4 P1, *k1, yo, k2, sk2p, k2, yo, k1, p1; rep from * to end.
Rows 5 and 7 K1, *p9, k1; rep from * to end.
Row 6 P1, *k2, yo, k1, sk2p, k1, yo, k2, p1; rep from * to end.
Row 8 P1, *k3, yo, sk2p, yo, k3, p1; rep from * to end.
Repeat Rows 1-8 for Pattern 4.

PATTERN 5—Cable Feather (multiple of 18 sts)
Row 1 (WS) Purl.
Row 2 (RS) *(K2tog) 3 times, (yo, k1) 6 times, (k2tog) 3 times; rep from * to end.
Row 3 K15, *p6, k12; rep from * to last 3 sts, k3.
Row 4 K15, *slip 3 sts to cable needle and hold in back, k3,
k3 from cable needle — 6-st RC; k12; rep from * to last 3 sts, k3.
Rows 5-7 Repeat Rows 1-3.
Row 8 Knit.
Repeat Rows 1-8 for Pattern 5.

PATTERN 6—Fan Shell (multiple of 15 sts + 4 extra)
Row 1 (WS) P4, *k11, p4; rep from * to end.
Row 2 (RS) K4, *p11, k4; rep from *.
Row 3 P2, *p2tog, p11, p2tog tbl; rep from * to last 2 sts, p2.
Row 4 K2, *ssk, k9, k2tog; rep from * to last 2 sts, k2.

I love the scalloped edges of a Shetland lace pattern, so I designed this piece using my three-needle layering technique to showcase them.

Row 5 P2, *p2tog, p7, p2tog tbl; rep from * to last 2 sts, p2.
Row 6 K4, *(yo, k1) 5 times, yo, k4; rep from * to end.
Repeat Rows 1-6 for Pattern 6.

PATTERN 7–Lucina Shell (multiple of 9 sts + 3 extra)
Row 1 (RS) K2, *yo, k8, yo, k1; rep from * to last st, k1.
Row 2 (WS) K3, *p8, k3; rep from * to end.
Row 3 K3, *yo, k8, yo, k3; rep from * to end.
Row 4 K4, *p8, k5; rep from * to last 12 sts, p8, k4.
Row 5 K4, *yo, k8, yo, k5; rep from * to last 12 sts, yo, p8, yo, k4.
Row 6 K5, *p8, k7; rep from * to to last 13 sts, p8, k5.
Row 7 K5, *k4tog tbl, k4tog, k7; rep from * to last 13 sts, k4tog tbl, k4tog, k5.
Row 8 Knit.
Repeat Rows 1-8 for Pattern 7.

PATTERN 8–Vine Lace (multiple of 9 sts + 4 extra)
Row 1 and 3 (WS) Purl.
Row 2 (RS) K3, *yo, k2, ssk, k2tog, k2, yo, k1; rep from * to last st, k1.
Row 4 K2, *yo, k2, ssk, k2tog, k2, yo, k1; rep from * to last 2 sts, k2.
Repeat Rows 1-4 for Pattern 8.

Right Front
PATTERN 1
■ With smaller needles, cast on 51 (72) sts. Beginning with Row 1, repeat 4 rows of Pattern 1 for a total of 9 times, ending with Row 4. Work Row 1 once more, inc 3 (0) sts evenly spaced across–54 (72) sts. Leave sts aside on a spare needle.

PATTERN 2
■ With larger needles, cast on 54 (72) sts. Work 4 rows of Pattern 2.
Joining row (RS) With RS facing, position spare needle with Pattern 1 sts behind left-hand needle. *Working Row 1 of Pattern 2, knit together 1 st from left-hand needle with next st of Pattern 1 on spare needle; rep from * across row to join pieces–54 (72) sts.
Beg with Row 2, repeat 4 rows of Pattern 2 for 8 more times. Work Row 1 once more, dec 5 (inc 1) sts evenly spaced across–49 (73) sts. Leave sts aside on a spare needle.

PATTERN 3
■ With larger needles, cast on 49 (73) sts. Work Rows 1-5 of Pattern 3.
Joining row (WS) With WS facing, position spare needle with Pattern 2 sts in front of left-hand needle. *Working Row 6 of Pattern 3, purl together 1 st from left-hand needle with next st of Pattern 2 on spare needle; rep from * across row to join pieces–49 (73) sts.
Work through Row 12 of Pattern 3, then repeat Rows 1-12 for 3 more times. Knit 3 rows, dec 1 (inc 2) sts evenly spaced across last row–48 (75) sts. Leave sts aside on a spare needle.

PATTERN 7
■ With larger needles, cast on 68 (107) sts. Beginning with Row 4, work Rows 4-7 of Pattern 7–48 (75) sts.
Joining row (WS) With WS facing, position spare needle with Pattern 3 sts in front of left-hand needle. *Knit together 1 st from left-hand needle with next st of Pattern 3 on spare needle; rep from * across row to join pieces–48 (75) sts.
Beginning with Row 1, repeat 8 rows of Pattern 7 for 7 more times, ending with Row 8.

Shape Neck
■ *Next Row* (RS) Knit 11 (13) sts and slip to a stitch holder for right neck, work in Pattern 7 to end of row.
Continue to work as established, binding off 2 (3) sts at neck edge every other row twice. Work until Row 8 of Pattern 7, inc 3 (dec 2) sts evenly spaced on last row.
Slip 36 (54) sts to stitch holder for Right Shoulder.

Right Front Border
■ With RS facing and smaller circular needle, pick up and knit 149 sts evenly spaced along edge of Right Front from lower edge to beg of neck shaping.
Work rows 1-4 of Pattern 1 for 3 times, then work Row 1 once more.
Bind off.

Right Back
PATTERN 1
■ With smaller needles, cast on 51 (72) sts. Repeat 4 rows of Pattern 1 for a total of 9 times, ending with Row 4, dec 2 (inc 4) sts evenly spaced along last row–49 (76) sts. Leave sts aside on a spare needle.

PATTERN 8
■ With larger needles, cast on 49 (76) sts. Work 4 rows of Pattern 8.
Joining row (WS) With WS facing, position spare needle with Pattern 1 sts in front of left-hand needle. *Working Row 1 of Pattern 8, purl together 1 st from left-hand needle with next st of Pattern 1 on spare needle; rep from * across row to join pieces–49 (76) sts.
Repeat 4 rows of Pattern 8 for 16 more times, ending with Row 4, inc 2 (dec 5) sts evenly spaced along last row–51 (71) sts. Leave sts aside on a spare needle.

PATTERN 4
■ With larger needles, cast on 51 (71) sts. Work 6 rows of Pattern 4.
Joining row (WS) With WS facing, position spare needle with Pattern 8 sts in front of left-hand needle. *Working Row 7 of Pattern 4, purl together 1 st from left-hand needle with next st of Pattern 8 on spare needle; rep from * across row to join pieces–51 (71) sts. Work Row 8 of Pattern 4.
Repeat 8 rows of Pattern 4 for 4 more times, ending with Row 1, inc 3 (1) sts evenly spaced along last row–54 (72) sts. Leave sts aside on a spare needle.

PATTERN 5
■ With larger needles, cast on 54 (72) sts. Work Rows 1-4 of Pattern 5.
Joining row (WS) With WS facing, position spare needle with Pattern 4 sts in front of left-hand needle. *Working Row 5 of Pattern 5, purl together 1 st from left-hand needle with next st of Pattern 4 on spare needle; rep from * across row to join pieces–54 (72) sts.
Work Rows 6-8, then repeat 8 rows of Pattern 5 for 4 more times, then work Rows 1-5 once more.

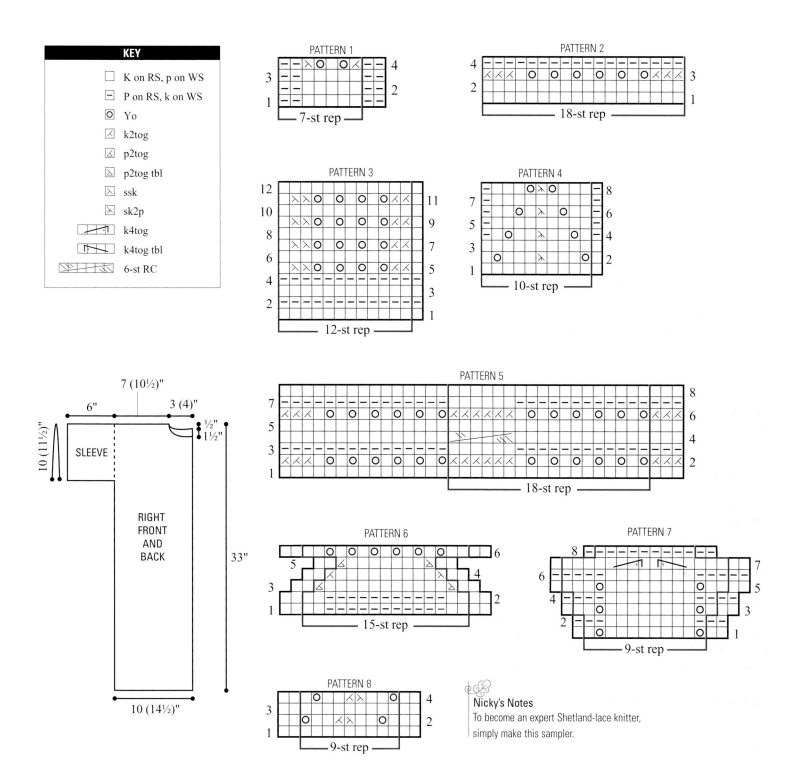

KEY

- ☐ K on RS, p on WS
- ⊟ P on RS, k on WS
- ⊡ Yo
- ⊠ k2tog
- ⊠ p2tog
- ⊠ p2tog tbl
- ⊠ ssk
- ⊠ sk2p
- ▱ k4tog
- ▱ k4tog tbl
- ▱ 6-st RC

Shape Neck

■ Next Row (RS) Work in Pattern Row 6 across 36 (54) sts, slip remaining 18 sts to stitch holder for right back neck.

Continue to work as established on 36 (54) sts until Row 8 of Pattern 5 has been worked. Leave sts aside on a spare needle.

Right Back Border

■ With RS facing and smaller circular needle, pick up and knit 163 sts evenly spaced along edge of Right Back from beg of neck shaping to lower edge.

Work rows 1-4 of Pattern 1 for 3 times, then work Row 1 once more.

Bind off.

Joining Right Shoulder

■ With RS of Right Front and Right Back together, use three-needle bind-off (see page 244), to join 36 (54) sts of shoulders together.

Right Sleeve

■ Measure and mark 10 (11½)"/25.5 (29)cm down from shoulder along side edge of Front and Back for Sleeve.

With RS facing and smaller circular needle, pick up and knit 100 (114) sts evenly spaced along side edge between markers. Beginning with Row 1, work 4 rows of Pattern I for 9 times, then work Row 1 once more.

Bind off.

Nicky's Notes
To become an expert Shetland-lace knitter, simply make this sampler.

■ The open back is my improvised addition.

Left Front

PATTERN 1
■ With smaller needles, cast on 51 (72) sts. Beginning with Row 1, repeat 4 rows of Pattern 1 for a total of 9 times, ending with Row 4, dec 2 (inc 7) sts evenly spaced along last row–49 (79) sts. Leave sts aside on a spare needle.

PATTERN 6
■ With larger needles, cast on 49 (79) sts. Work 6 rows of Pattern 6.
Joining row (WS) With WS facing, position spare needle with Pattern 1 sts in front of left-hand needle. *Working Row 1 of Pattern 6, work together 1 st from left-hand needle with next st of Pattern 1 on spare needle; rep from * across row to join pieces–49 (79) sts.
Repeat 6 rows of Pattern 6 for 12 more times, ending with Row 6, inc 2 (dec 8) sts evenly spaced along last row–51 (71) sts. Leave sts aside on a spare needle.

PATTERN 4
■ With larger needles, cast on 51 (71) sts. Work 6 rows of Pattern 4.
Joining row (WS) With WS facing, position spare needle with Pattern 6 sts in front of left-hand needle. *Working Row 7 of Pattern 4, purl together 1 st from left-hand needle with next st of Pattern 6 on spare needle; rep from * across row to join pieces–51 (71) sts. Work Row 8 of Pattern 4.
Repeat 8 rows of Pattern 4 for 5 more times, ending with Row 1, inc 3 (1) sts evenly spaced along last row–54 (72) sts. Leave sts aside on a spare needle.

PATTERN 5
■ With larger needles, cast on 54 (72) sts. Beginning with Row 1, work Rows 1-4 of Pattern 5.
Joining row (WS) With WS facing, position spare needle with Pattern 4 sts in front of left-hand needle. *Working Row 5 of Pattern 5, purl together 1 st from left-hand needle with next st of Pattern 4 on spare needle; rep from * across row to join pieces–54 (72) sts.
Work through Row 8, then repeat 8 rows of Pattern 5 for 2 more times.

Shape Neck
■ *Next Row* (WS) Purl 14 sts and slip to a stitch holder for left neck, work in Pattern 5 to end of row.
Continue to work as established, binding off 2 sts at neck edge every other row twice–36 (54) sts.
Work until Row 8 of Pattern 5. Slip 36 (54) sts to stitch holder for Left Shoulder.

Left Front Border
■ With RS facing and smaller circular needle, pick up and knit 149 sts evenly spaced along front of Left Front from beg of neck shaping to lower edge.
Work rows 1-4 of Pattern 1 for 3 times, then work Row 1 once more.
Bind off.

Left Back

PATTERN 1
■ With smaller needles, cast on 51 (72) sts. Repeat 4 rows of Pattern 1 for a total of 9 times, ending with Row 2, dec 2 (inc 1) sts evenly spaced across last row–49 (73) sts. Leave sts aside on a spare needle.

PATTERN 3
■ With larger needles, cast on 49 (73) sts. Work Rows 1-5 of Pattern 3.
Joining Row (WS) With WS facing, position spare needle with Pattern 1 sts in front of left-hand needle. *Working Row 6 of Pattern 3, purl together 1 st from left-hand needle with next st of Pattern 1 on spare needle; rep from * across row to join pieces – 49 (73) sts.
Work through Row 12 of Pattern 3, then repeat Rows 1-12 for 2 more times then work Rows 1-8, inc 5 (dec 1) sts evenly spaced across last row – 54 (72) sts.
Leave sts aside on a spare needle.

PATTERN 2
■ With larger needles, cast on 54 (72) sts. Work 4 rows of Pattern 2.
Joining row (RS) With RS facing, position spare needle with Pattern 3 sts behind left-hand needle. *Working Row 1 of Pattern 2, knit together 1 st from left-hand needle with next st of Pattern 3 on spare needle; rep from * across row to join pieces–54 (72) sts.
Repeat 4 rows of Pattern 2 for 11 more times, ending with Row 1, dec 6 (inc 3) sts evenly spaced along last row – 48 (75) sts. Leave sts aside on a spare needle.

PATTERN 7
■ With larger needles, cast on 68 (107) sts. Beginning with Row 4, work Rows 4-7 of Pattern 7 – 48 (75) sts.
Joining row (WS) With WS facing, position spare needle with Pattern 2 sts in front of left-hand needle. *Knit together 1 st from left-hand needle with next st of Pattern 2 on spare needle; rep from * across row to join pieces – 48 (75) sts.
Beginning with Row 1, repeat 8 rows of Pattern 7 for 7 more times, then work Rows 1-2–58 (91) sts.

Shape Neck
Row 3 (RS) K3, yo, ssk, k4, k2tog, yo, k3, yo, ssk, k3, slip these 19 sts to stitch holder for left back neck, k1, k2tog, *yo, k3, yo, ssk, k4, k2tog; rep from * across to last 3 sts yo, k3.
Row 4 K4, *p6, k5; rep from * to last 2 sts, p2.
Row 5 K2tog, *yo, k5, yo, ssk, k2, k2tog; rep from * to last 4 sts, yo, k4.
Row 6 K5, *p1, p2tog, p1, k7; rep from * to last st, p1–36 (66) sts.
Knit 1 row, dec 0 (12) sts evenly spaced across row. Leave 36 (54) sts aside on a spare needle.

Left Back Border
■ With RS facing and smaller circular needle, pick up and knit 163 sts evenly spaced along edge of Left Back from lower edge to beg of neck shaping.
Work rows 1-4 of Pattern 1 for 3 times, then work Row 1 once more.
Bind off.

Joining Left Shoulder
■ With RS of Left Front and Left Back together, use three-needle bind-off to join 36 (54) sts of shoulders together.

Left Sleeve
■ Work same as right sleeve.

Finishing
■ Sew sleeve and side seams, leaving side edges of scallops unsewn. Overlap Right Back border over Left Back border and sew together along neck edge.

Collar
■ With RS facing and smaller circular needle, join yarn at right front border and pick up and knit 114 (128) sts evenly spaced around neck edge, working neck sts from stitch holders.
Work rows 1-4 of Pattern 1 for 3 times, then work Row 1 once more.
Bind off.
■ Weave in ends. ❖

World Class Wee Sweaters

The little Aran, Argyle and Fair Isle classics will surprise and delight you with their versatile uses.

Mini Classic Aran

■ SKILLED KNITTER

WHAT YOU'LL NEED

■ 2 3oz/85g skeins (ea. approx 197yd/180m) of Lion Brand Yarn *Wool-Ease* (80% acrylic/20% wool) in #99 fisherman
■ Size 7 (4.5mm) needles
■ Stitch holders
■ Cable needle
■ Tapestry needle

Finished Measurements

Circumference: 20"/51cm
Length: 12"/30.5cm

Gauge

20 sts and 24 rows = 4"/10cm in Moss st. TAKE TIME TO CHECK GAUGE.

Pattern Stitches

■ *2-st LC* Skip 1 st but leave on left-hand needle, knit in the back loop of next st, leaving on left-hand needle, knit in the front loop of first st, slip both sts from left-handle needle.
■ *2-st RC* Skip 1 st but leave on left-hand needle, knit in the front loop of next st, leaving on left-hand needle, knit in the front loop of first st, slip both sts from left-handle needle.
■ *4-st LC* Slip 2 sts to a cable needle and hold in front, k2, k2 from cable needle.
■ *4-st RC* Slip 2 sts to a cable needle and hold in back, k2, k2 from cable needle.

Moss Stitch

Row 1 (RS) *K1, p1; rep from * to end.
Rows 2 and 4 Knit the knit sts and purl the purl sts.
Row 3 *P1, k1; rep from * to end.
Repeat Rows 1-4 for Moss st.

Front and Back (make 2)

■ Cast on 70 sts.
Work in k1, p1 rib for 4"/10cm, dec 4 sts evenly across last row — 66 sts.

BEGIN PATTERNS
Row 1 (RS) Beginning with Row 1, work 10 sts in Moss st, work 46 sts of Aran Chart over center 46 sts, work 10 sts in Moss st.
Continue as established until piece measures 8"/20.5cm from beginning, ending with WS row.

Shape Raglan

Next Row (RS) K1, sssk, work as established to last 4 sts, k3tog, k1–62 sts.
Next Row P2, work to last 2 sts, p2.
Repeat last 2 rows 8 times more.
Slip remaining 30 sts to stitch holder.

Sleeves

■ Cast on 26 sts.
Work in k1, p1 rib for 2"/5cm.
BEGIN PATTERNS
Row 1 (RS) Beginning with Row 1, work 2 sts in Moss st, work 7-st rep of Aran Chart 3 times, k1, work 2 sts in Moss st.

Mini Classic Aran

Foxy Little Argyle

Petite Fancy Fair Isle

Faux chapeau! Take this wee sweater and place it on your head. The arms can be tied in a simple knot.

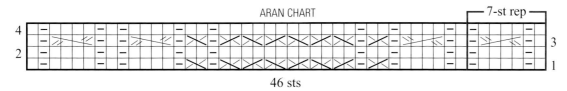

ARAN CHART

46 sts

KEY

☐	K on RS, p on WS
⊟	P on RS, k on WS
⊠	2-st RC
⊠	2-st LC
⊠⊠	4-st RC
⊠⊠	4-st LC

(continued from previous page)

Continue as established, inc 1 st each edge every 6th row 4 times, working inc sts into Moss st–34 sts.

Work even until piece measures 6"/15cm from beg, ending with WS row.

Shape Raglan

Next Row (RS) K1, ssk, work as established to last 3 sts, k2tog, k1–32 sts.
Next Row P2, work to last 2 sts, p2.
Repeat last 2 rows 8 times more.
Slip remaining 16 sts to stitch holder.

Finishing

■ Sew raglan seams, leaving one seam open.

Turtleneck

■ With RS facing, pick up and knit all sts from stitch holders – 92 sts.
Work in k1, p1 rib for 4"/10cm.
Bind off.

■ Sew remaining raglan seam and turtleneck closed.
Sew side seams and sleeve seams. Weave in ends. ❖

Little Foxy Argyle

■ SKILLED KNITTER

WHAT YOU'LL NEED

■ 2 1¾oz/50g balls (ea. approx 137yd/125m) of GGH/Muench *Wollywasch* (100% superwash wool) in #118 green (A)
■ 1 ball each of #81 yellow (B) and #130 burgundy (C)
■ Size 3 (3.25mm) needles
■ Size 4 (3.5mm) needles
■ Stitch bobbins
■ Tapestry needle

Finished Measurements

Circumference: 22"/56cm
Length: 11"/28cm

Gauge

23 sts and 28 rows = 4"/10cm in Argyle Chart using larger needles. TAKE TIME TO CHECK GAUGE.
NOTES: Use separate bobbins of yarn for each large block of color. Carry colors loosely along wrong side of work. Pick up new color from underneath old color to twist yarns and prevent holes. Cross lines of Argyle Chart may be embroidered in duplicate stitch after Chart is finished.

Back

LAYERED RIB–FIRST LAYER
■ With smaller needle and B, cast on 65 sts.
Work in k1, p1 rib for 2 rows.
Change to A and knit 1 row.
Work in k1, p1 rib with A until piece measures 2"/5cm from beginning,

end with WS row. Leave sts aside on a spare needle.

SECOND LAYER
■ With smaller needles and B, cast on 65 sts.
Work in k1, p1 rib for 2 rows.
Change to A and knit 1 row.
Work in k1, p1 rib with A until piece measures 1"/2.5cm from beginning, end with WS row.
Joining row (RS) With RS facing, position spare needle in back of left-hand needle.
*Knit together 1 st from left-hand needle with next st on spare needle; rep from * across row to join pieces – 65 sts.
Change to larger needles and work in St st with A until piece measures 7"/17.5cm from beginning, end with WS row.

Shape Armhole

■ Bind off 5 sts at beginning of next 2 rows – 55 sts.
Continue until piece measures 11"/28cm from beginning.
Bind off.

ARGYLE CHART

28-st rep

End   Beg

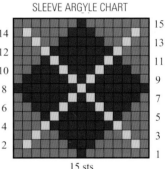

KEY

- ■ Green (A)
- □ Yellow (B)
- ■ Red (C)

SLEEVE ARGYLE CHART

15 sts

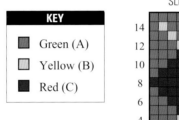

(continued from previous page)

Front

■ With smaller needles and B, cast on 65 sts.

LAYERED RIB

Work Layered Rib as for Back–65 sts.
Change to larger needles.
Purl 1 row.

BEGIN CHART

■ Beginning and ending where indicated, repeat 28 stitches of Argyle Chart across row.
Continue to repeat 32 rows of Argyle Chart until piece measures 7"/17.5cm from beginning, end with WS row.

Shape Armhole

■ Continuing to work in Argyle Chart, bind off 5 sts at beginning of next 2 rows–55 sts.
Continue until piece measures 9"/23cm from beginning, ending with WS row.

Shape Neck

■ Continuing to work in Argyle Chart, work 18 sts, join second balls of yarn and bind off center 19 sts, work remaining 18 sts to end.
Working both sides at same time, bind off 2 sts at neck edge every other row twice, then dec 1 st every other row twice–12 sts.
Work until same length as back to shoulders.
Bind off.

Sleeves

■ With smaller needle and B, cast on 29 sts.
Work in k1, p1 rib for 2 rows.
Change to A and knit 1 row.
Work in k1, p1 rib with A until piece measures 1"/2.5cm from beginning, end with WS row.
Change to larger needles and work in St st with A, inc 1 st every 4th row 4 times–37 sts.
At Same Time, when piece measures 4"/10cm from beginning, work 15 stitches of Sleeve Argyle Chart on center 15 sts.
Continue until piece measures 8"/20.5cm from beginning, end with WS row.

Shape Cap

■ Bind off 5 sts at beginning of next 2 rows.
Dec 1 st each side every other row 3 times–21 sts.
Work 1"/2.5cm more.
Dec 1 st each side every other row 5 more times–11 sts.
Bind off.

Finishing

■ Embroider cross lines in duplicate stitch (see page 238) following charts. Sew shoulders. Sew in Sleeves. Sew side and Sleeve seams. Weave in ends.

Neck Band

■ With smaller needles and A, cast on 15 sts.
Work in k1, p1 rib for 4"/10cm, ending with WS row.

Shape Braided Cable

■ *Next row* (RS) Continuing in k1, p1 rib, work 5 sts, join second strand of yarn, work 5 sts, join a third strand of yarn, work 5 sts.
Work each strip separately in st st with separate strands of yarn until strips measure 4"/10cm, ending with WS row.
Braid these 3 separate strips together.

JOINING ROW

■ With first strand of yarn, work in k1, p1 rib across all 15 sts.
Continue to work on 15 sts with one strand of yarn until piece measures 4"/10 from Joining Row.
Bind off.

■ Sew short ends of Neck Band together. Position seam at center of Back neck and sew Neck Band around neck. ❖

N o t   j u s t   f o r   s o c k s   a n d   g o l f e r s ,   m y   p e t i t e   A r g y l e
s u i t s   u p   y o u r   f a v o r i t e   s t u f f e d   a n i m a l   o r   d o l l .

Petite Fancy Fair Isle

■ MASTER KNITTER

WHAT YOU'LL NEED

- 1 .88oz/25g hank (ea. approx 115yd/105m) of Jamieson's/Simply Shetland *2-ply Spindrift* (100% shetland wool) in #104 natural white (A), #108 moorit (B), #1300 aubretia (C), #135 surf (D), #600 violet (E), and #764 cloud (F)
- Size 2 (2.75 mm) 16"/40cm circular needle
- Size 2 (2.75 mm) double-pointed needles
- Size 3 (3.25mm) 16"/40cm circular needle
- Size 3 (3.25mm) double-pointed needles
- Stitch markers
- Stitch holders
- Tapestry needle

Finished Measurements

Circumference: 21"/53.5cm
Length: 10"/25.5cm

Gauge

32 sts and 32 rows = 4"/10 cm over Fair Isle Chart using larger needles.
TAKE TIME TO CHECK GAUGE.
NOTE: Carry colors loosely along wrong side of work. Pick up new color from underneath old color to twist yarns and prevent holes.

Pattern Stitches

- *2-st LPC* Skip 1 st but leave on left-hand needle, purl in the back loop of next st, leaving on left-hand needle, knit in the front loop of first st, slip both sts from left-handle needle.
- *2-st RPC* Skip 1 st but leave on left-hand needle, knit in the front loop of next st, leaving on left-hand needle, purl in the front loop of first st, slip both sts from left-handle needle.

Body

EDGING RIB

- With E and smaller circular needle, cast on 160 sts. Join, taking care not to twist sts to work in the round. Place a marker for beginning of round.
Rnd 1 (RS) (K1, p1) around.
Rnd 2 *(K1, p1) 3 times, 2-st RPC, k1, 2-st LPC, (p1, k1) twice, p1; rep from * around.
Rnd 3 *(K1, p1) twice, k1, 2-st RPC, p1, k1, p1, 2-st LPC, (k1, p1) twice;
rep from * around.
Rnd 4 *(K1, p1) twice, (2-st RPC) twice, k1, (2-st LPC) twice, p1, k1, p1;
rep from * around.
Rnd 5 *K1, p1, k1, (2-st RPC) twice, p1, k1, p1, (2-st LPC) twice, k1, p1;
rep from * around.
Rnd 6 *K1, p1, (2-st RPC) 3 times, k1, (2-st LPC) 3 times, p1; rep from * around.
Rnd 7 Change to C. *K1, (2-st RPC) 3 times, p1, k1, p1, (2-st LPC) 3 times;
rep from * around.

Rnd 8 *K1, p1, (2-st RPC) 3 times, k1, (2-st LPC) 3 times, p1; rep from * around.
Rnd 9 *K1, (2-st RPC) 3 times, p1, k1, p1, (2-st LPC) 3 times; rep from * around.
Rnd 10 *K1, p1, (2-st RPC) 3 times, k1, (2-st LPC) 3 times, p1; rep from * around.
Rnd 11 Change to D. *K1, (2-st RPC) twice, (p1, k1) 3 times, p1, (2-st LPC) twice;
rep from * around.
Rnd 12 *K1, p1, 2-st RPC, (k1, p1) 4 times, k1, 2-st LPC, p1; rep from * around.
Rnds 13-16 Change to C. (K1, p1) around.
Change to larger circular needle and E, knit 1 round, inc 8 sts evenly spaced–168 sts.

BEGIN FAIR ISLE CHART

- Beginning with Rnd 1, work 12-st repeat of Fair Isle Chart around for 32 rnds.

Shape Gusset

- *Rnd 33* Work in Fair Isle Chart for 84 sts, place marker, M1 for Gusset, working new st following Gusset Chart, place marker, work 84 sts, place marker, M1 for Gusset, working new st following Gusset Chart–170 sts.
Rnds 34-40 Continue to work in Charts as established, work 84 sts until next marker, sl, marker, M1, work to next marker, M1 working new sts in Gusset Chart, sl, marker, work 84 sts to next marker, sl, marker, M1, work to next marker, M1 working new sts in Gusset Chart, sl, marker–198 sts.
Rnd 41 Work 84 sts for Front, slip next 15 sts of Gusset onto stitch holder, cast on 10 sts between Gusset markers for underarm steek (see page 242), work 84 sts for Back, slip next 15 sts gusset sts onto a stitch holder for Gusset, cast on 10 sts between Gusset markers for underarm steek.
Continue to work in Fair Isle Chart, alternating colors of working yarn across steek sts, ending with Rnd 57.

Shape Neck

- *Rnd 58* Work as established across 24 sts, slip next 36 sts onto stitch holder for front neck, place marker, cast on 10 sts for neck steek, place marker, continue as established around.
Dec 1 st on either side of neck steek sts every rnd 4 times.
Continue in Fair Isle Chart through Rnd 64.

Many tea cozies are hand-knit and resemble hats. They always bring a smile and are so much fun to make.

FAIR ISLE CHART

Rows numbered: 65, 63, 61, 59, 57, 55, 53, 51, 49, 47, 45, 43, 41, 39, 37, 35, 33, 31, 29, 27, 25, 23, 21, 19, 17, 15, 13, 11, 9, 7, 5, 3, 1

— 12-st rep —

KEY

☐	K on RS, p on WS
⊟	P on RS, k on WS
⧅	2-st LPC
⧄	2-st RPC
☐	Light Beige (A)
■	Taupe/Brown Mix (B)
■	Periwinkle (C)
▨	Light Blue Mix (D)
▨	Purple (E)
☐	Sky Blue (F)

GUSSET CHART

Rows numbered: 15, 13, 11, 9, 7, 5, 3, 1

EDGING CHART

Rows numbered: 11, 9, 7, 5, 3, 1

— 16-st rep —

Rnd 65 Work last rnd of chart, binding off 10 steek sts.

■ Using three-needle bind-off (see page 244), bind off across first and last 20 sts after and before underarm steek sts for shoulders. Slip center 44 sts of Back onto stitch holder for back neck.

Sleeve

■ Cut underarm steeks down the center.

With RS facing, C and larger double-pointed needles, begin at Front gusset and pick up and knit 24 sts to shoulder, pick up 1 st at center shoulder, pick up and knit 24 sts down Back, break yarn, place marker, slip Gusset sts onto needles, place marker for beginning of rnd—64 sts. Divide sts equally around needles.
Rnd 1 Beginning with Rnd 1, join A at beginning marker and repeat 12-st rep of Fair Isle Chart on 49 sts to second marker, working first st of chart once more, k2tog, work Gusset Chart across to 2 sts before beginning marker, k2tog, sl, marker. Continue to work in Fair Isle and Gusset Charts, dec 2 sts in Gusset every rnd 6 times more—50 sts.

Shape Sleeve

■ Dec 1 st after beginning marker and before second marker every 3rd row 4 times—42 sts. Continue as established, ending with Rnd 43.

Shape Cuff

■ *Next Rnd* With C, k1, (k2tog) to last st, k1 — 22 sts.
Change to smaller double-pointed needles and k1, p1 rib, work 2 rnds with C, 1 rnd with D, 2 rnds with C, 3 rnds with B. Bind off.

■ Repeat on opposite side for second Sleeve.

Neck

■ Cut neck steek down the center. With RS facing, smaller double-pointed needles and C, join yarn at left shoulder and pick up and knit 8 sts down left front neck, knit across 36 sts from front neck stitch holder, pick up and knit 8 sts up right front neck, knit across 44 sts from back neck holder—96 sts. Divide sts equally around needles.
Working in K1, p1 rib, work 2 rnds with C, 1 rnd each with D, C and B. Bind off.

Finishing

■ Trim sleeve and neck steeks and tack down trimmed stitches.
Weave in ends.

Flowers (make 9 in any 2-color combinations)

■ With larger needles, cast on 36 sts with any color.
Work 4 rows in St st.
Row 5 *K6, rotate left-hand needle counterclockwise 360-degrees; repeat from * across.
Purl 1 row.
Row 7 Change to contrasting color, (k2tog) across 18 sts.
Row 8 (P2tog) across 9 sts.
Row 9 (K2tog) 4 times, k1, slip sts one at a time over first st.
Fasten off. Sew seam closed.

Leaves

■ With B and larger needles, cast on 10 sts. Bind off 9 sts, slip remaining st to left-hand needle and cast on 12 sts. Bind off 12 sts.

■ Sew Flowers and Leaves evenly around neckline.

■ Weave in ends. ❖❖

Become a Master Knitter

This quartet of mini sweaters are examples of popular knitting styles: Aran, Fair Isle, Argyle and Jacquard Snowflake.
Each one incorporates a variety of special techniques and details. Even a novice can tackle these wee challenges, and knitting these sweaters is a great way to learn the techniques before investing hours on a larger project. When you complete these cuties, consider yourself an "International Master Knitter." I'd love to see your results; send photos to my website, nickyepstein.com.

Instructions for Liten Olaf sweater on page 42

Fair Isle Tam Capelet

Based on the classic tam design and one that I knit years ago, I've updated and expanded it to this capelet. The result: a piece that's both contemporary and a tribute to its Fair Isle heritage.

■ SKILLED KNITTER

WHAT YOU'LL NEED
- 2 3½oz/100g hanks (ea. approx 240yds/216m) of Harrisville Designs *Orchid* (25% mohair, 70% fine virgin wool, 5% cashmere) in #258 delphi teal (A)
- 1 hank ea. in #243 juniper (B), #249 golden curry (C), #262 sierra (D) and #246 wheat (E)
- 1 ball (approx .88oz/25g Filatura di Crosa/Tahki • Stacy Charles, Inc. *New Smoking* in #10 copper
- Size 7 (4.5mm) 24" circular needle OR SIZE TO OBTAIN GAUGE
- Size 7 (4.5mm) double-pointed needles (set of 5) OR SIZE TO OBTAIN GAUGE
- Stitch markers
- Tapestry needle

One Size

Finished Measurements
Each circle (tam) measures 17"/43cm in diameter

Gauge
22 sts and 26 rows = 4"/10cm in St st over chart pat.
TAKE TIME TO CHECK GAUGE.

Circles (make 3)
■ With circular needle and A, cast on 238 sts. Pm and join for working in the rnd.

Inspired by...
This St.Patrick's Day Blarney Tam appeared in my first book, Nicky Epstein's Knit Hat Book *in 1997. The snake is a real charmer!*

Rnds 1-3 Purl.
Rnd 4 (dec) [P15, p2tog] 14 times–224 sts.

BEG CHART 1
Work 11 rnds of Chart 1.
Rnd 12 With D, [k2tog, k30] 7 times–217 sts.
Rnd 13 With B, knit.
Rnd 14 With B, [k2tog, k29] 7 times–210 sts.
Rnd 15 With A, knit.
Rnd 16 With E, [k2tog, k28] 7 times–203 sts.
Rnd 17 With E, knit.
Rnd 18 With C, [k2tog, k27] 7 times–196 sts.
Rnd 19 With A, knit.
Rnd 20 With C, [k2tog, k10] 16 times, k4–180 sts.
Rnd 21 With C, knit.

BEG CHART 2
■ Work 4 rnds of Chart 2, inc 2 sts on rnd 4–182 sts.
Pm every 26 sts–7 sections.

BEG CHART 3
■ Work 25 rnds of Chart 3, changing to dpns as needed.

CHART 1

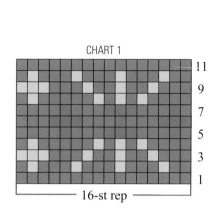

11
9
7
5
3
1

— 16-st rep —

CHART 3

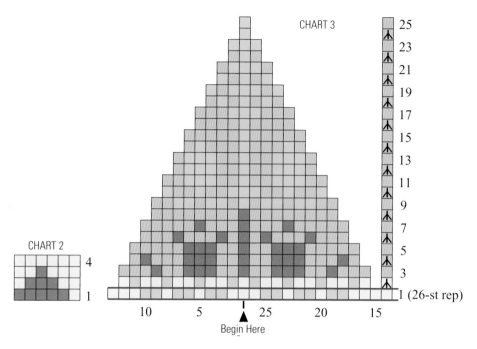

25
23
21
19
17
15
13
11
9
7
5
3
1 (26-st rep)

10   5   25   20   15

Begin Here

CHART 2

4
1

KEY
☐ Knit
🜋 S2KP
◼ Delphi Teal (A)
◻ Juniper (B)
▦ Golden Curry (C)
◼ Sierra (D)
☐ Wheat (E)

Rnd 26 With B, [k2tog] 7 times–7 sts.
Thread tail through rem sts, pull tight and fasten off.

Finishing
■ Block each circle with wet cloth and hot iron.
Arrange the 3 pieces in a row horizontally, with the top edge of the
center tam even with the center of each side tam.
Join the 3 tams with a 7"/18cm seam at the point where they touch,
leaving 9"/23cm at the top edge of the center tam.

Collar
■ With RS facing and A, starting and ending 2½"/6.5cm before
and after center tam, pick up 62 sts. Work in corrugated rib as foll,
reversing RS of work:
Row 1 (RS) K2 A, *p2 D, k2 A; rep from * to end.
Row 2 P2 A, *k2 D, p2 A; rep from * to end.
Rep rows 1 and 2 until collar measures 4"/10cm, ending with a WS row.
With A, k 2 rows. Bind off knitwise.

Embellishment (optional)
With 2 strands of F, work chevron st and lazy daisy stitch (see page 239)
on each tam as pictured. Fasten with your favorite shawl pin. ❖❖

Nicky's Notes
Circle size can be adjusted by removing outer
bands of colorwork if you want a snugger fit.

I used three repeats of a classic Fair Isle pattern to
create this (in all modesty) spectacular wrap.

Galway Bay Shrug Shawl

Isle of Aran cable patterns are an unmistakable and beautiful Irish icon. In this update, the original Aran fisherman cables are transformed into a shawl that goes from pub to palace.

■ SKILLED KNITTER

WHAT YOU'LL NEED
- 13 3½oz/100g hanks (ea. approx 45yd/41m) of Blue Sky *Alpacas Bulky* (50% alpaca/50% wool) in #1212 grasshopper
- Size 15 (10mm) needles OR SIZE TO OBTAIN GAUGES
- Cable needle
- Tapestry needle

One Size
Adult Woman's

Finished Measurements
Center back neck to sleeve edge: approx 21"/53.5cm
Length: 27"/68.5cm

Gauge
8 sts and 10 rows to 4"/10cm in St st.
10 sts and 10 rows to 4"/10cm in cable pat.
TAKE TIME TO CHECK GAUGES.

Special stitches
4-st RC Sl 2 sts to cn and hold to back, k2, k2 from cn.
4-st LC Sl 2 sts to cn and hold to front, k2, k2 from cn.
4-st RPC Sl 2 sts to cn and hold to back, k2, p2 from cn.
4-st LPC Sl 2 sts to cn and hold to front, p2, k2 from cn.

14-st Cable panel
Row 1 (RS) P1, k2, p2, k4, p2, k2, p1.
Rows 2, 4 and 6 K1, p2, k2, p4, k2, p2, k1.
Row 3 P1, k2, p2, 4-st RC, p2, k2, p1.
Row 5 Rep row 1.
Row 7 P1, 4-st LPC, 4-st RC, 4-st RPC, p1.
Row 8 and 18 K3, p8, k3.
Row 9 P3, 4-st RPC, 4-st LPC, p3.

Rows 10 and 16 K3, p2, k4, p2, k3.
Row 11 P1, 4-st RPC, p4, 4-st LPC, p1.
Rows 12 and 14 K1, p2, k8, p2, k1.
Row 13 P1, k2, p8, k2, p1.
Row 15 P1, 4-st LPC, p4, 4-st RPC, p1.
Row 17 P3, 4-st LC, 4-st RC, p3.
Row 19 P1, 4-st RPC, 4-st RC, 4-st LPC, p1.
Row 20 Rep row 2.
Rep rows 1-20 for 14-st cable panel.

Right side
■ Cast on 34 sts.
Row 1 (RS) K2, [p2, k2] twice, pm, work 14-st cable panel, pm, [k2, p2] twice, k2.
Row 2 P2, [k2, p2] twice, work 14-st cable panel, [p2, k2] twice, p2.
Cont in pats as established until piece measures 18"/45.5cm from beg, ending with a RS row.

Sleeve and shawl collar increases
■ *Row 1 (WS)* Cast on 14 sts for sleeve [K2, p2] 6 times, pm, work 14-st cable panel, [p2, k2] twice, pm, p1, M1, k1.
Row 2 K to marker, M1 (for collar), k1, work in rib as established over next 8 sts, work 14 sts of cable panel, work in rib to end.
Row 3 Cast on 1 st (for sleeve), work in rib to marker (incorporate each new sleeve st into rib), work 14 sts of cable panel, work in rib over next 8 sts, p1, m1 (for collar), k to end.
Rows 4-13 Rep rows 2 and 3 five times.

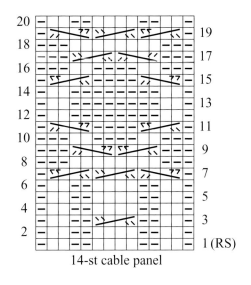

20 — — 19
18 — — 17
16 — — 15
14 — — 13
12 — — 11
10 — — 9
8 — — 7
6 — — 5
4 — — 3
2 — — 1 (RS)

14-st cable panel

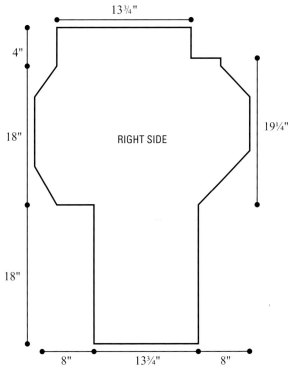

13¾"

4"

18"

18"

RIGHT SIDE

19¼"

8" 13¾" 8"

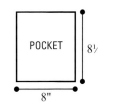

POCKET

8½

8"

KEY

☐	K on RS, P on WS
—	P on RS, K on WS
⧄	4-st RC
⧅	4-st LC
⧄	4-st RPC
⧅	4-st LPC

Row 14 Rep row 2.

Row 15 Work in rib to marker, work 14 sts of cable panel, work in rib over next 8 sts, p1, M1, k to end.

Rep last 2 rows 3 times more—74 sts.

Work even in pats as established until sleeve measures 14"/61cm, ending with a WS row.

Sleeve and shawl collar decreases

Row 1 (RS) K to 2 sts before marker, k2tog, work in rib over next 8 sts, work 14 sts of cable panel, work in rib to last 2 sts, k2tog.

Row 2 Work in rib to marker, work 14 sts of cable panel, work in rib to marker, p2tog, k to end.

Rows 3-10 Rep rows 1 and 2 four times.

Row 11 K to marker, work in rib over next 8 sts, work 14 sts of cable panel, work in rib to last 2 sts, k2tog.

Row 12 Bind off 14 sts of sleeve, work to end.

Row 13 Bind off 10 sts of collar, work to end—34 sts.

Work even in pats on rem 34 sts as established for 4"/10cm. Bind off.

LEFT SIDE

■ Work same as right side, reversing shaping for collar and sleeve.

Finishing

■ With RS facing, place right and left sides together. Sew 4"/10cm back seam and bound-off edges of collar for center back. Sew sleeve and 4"/10cm side seams.

Pockets (make 2)

■ Cast on 20 sts.

Row 1 (RS) P1, k2, work 14-st cable panel, k2, p1.

Row 2 K1, p2, work 14-st cable panel, p2, k1.

Rep rows 1 and 2 until 21 rows have been worked.

Bind off.

Sew a pocket to lower edge of each front panel.

Back closure

■ With RS facing, working from left side seam, skip 2 sts, pick up 8 sts.

Row 1 (WS) K1, p2, k2, p2, k1.

Row 2 P1, k2, p2, k2, p1.

Rep rows 1 and 2 for 9"/23cm. Bind off. Sew end to corresponding sts of right side. ❖❖

Original yarn used for this sweater, Duotones, is no longer available. A comparable substitution has been made and cited in the materials list.

Get out your big needles for this big cabled and ribbed showstopper! This easy knit's unusual structure has a flattering fit in one of my favorite colors.

OLD WORLD

Germany

Bavaria

France

Austria

Italy

■ THE OLD WORLD LIVES ON IN TIMELESS STITCHES

From the folkloric traditions of Austria and Germany to the fashion frenzy that is Paris and Milan, knitting on the European continent is ever evolving. Knitting here is and has always been a business and a passion, with methods and materials crossing all borders.

Tyrolean Leg Warmers
page 140

Behold Bavaria: The Knits of Austria and Germany

■ Like the region itself, the knits of Austria and Germany are a mix of different traditions and customs. The variation in pattern and design—from the folk-art feel of the felted and embroidered jackets of the Tyrol to the richly textured cables and bobbles of Bavaria to the delicate laces of Vienna—speak to widely varied senses of style, but a common passion for creating things of beauty. Given my love for adding texture and surface interest wherever and whenever I can, the knits of this region are among my favorites. They also inspire the occasional yodel as I knit them.

The knitters of Austria and Germany probably first picked up their needles early in the thirteenth century, using them to create simple stockings and hats. One hundred–plus years later, knitting was ingrained enough in everyday Germanic life to be included in one of the most famed of the "knitting Madonnas" (paintings and engravings showing the Virgin Mary busily at work with her needles), Master Bertram of Minden's "Buxtehude Madonna," painted circa 1390. In it, Mary sits in a lavishly appointed room knitting a crimson-colored shirt on a set of double-pointed needles. The Christ Child is at her feet, an open book before him, with his head turned to two angels standing at the left of the scene. The shirt Mary is knitting is thought to be the seamless robe stripped from Christ before the crucifixion—an item often represented in Passion paintings of the time period. It's unlikely that Mary really did any knitting herself (and if she did, the item in question would more likely have been a pair of stockings); the image of her knitting serves a more emotional than factual purpose.

■ Visit of the Angels to the Christ Child, *Master Bertram (1367–1414/5)*

By the 1700s, intricately ribbed and cabled stockings had become part of the Bavarian national costume. Though knit pieces were often felted and then cut and sewn into jackets and other garments, knit sweaters were not a big part of the German clothing tradition. Early in the twentieth century, however, some intrepid knitters made the creative leap, incorporating the textured patterns of the traditional stockings into cardigan-like jackets. These stitch patterns have much in common with the cabled "fishermen's knits" of Britain and Scotland, and were very likely the inspiration for the Aran technique.

Oktoberfest Glove Cuffs
page 136

Techniques

■ Unlike the Aran ganseys they inspired, Bavarian sweaters are knit flat in pieces and then seamed together, following the region's tailoring tradition. Jackets tend to be snugly shaped with cardigan-style openings and scooped necks. Panels of traveling stitches usually flank the center front opening and are repeated down the center back of the garment. The spaces between are filled with allover knit-and-purl combinations.

The sweaters of Tyrol followed a similar construction technique, substituting cables and bobbles for traveling stitches. But what I really love about them are the bits of embroidery that embellish the textural stitch designs. Meant to convey the beauty of the Alpine meadows where wildflowers grow in abundance, they use simple stitches (chains and daisy stitches are popular) to bring the piece into bloom. (See Embroidery Stitches on page 239.)

Knit into cables using the same color. I clustered the bobbles and changed colors, creating an unusual cuff on the fingerless gloves. To view a bobble tutorial, see page 235.

Bobbles are another big feature on Bavarian knits and one I love to use in my own designs. The knitters of Austria and Germany make their bobbles in the traditional way, but, as I possess little patience for all the intricate stitchwork (and am prone a high level of frustration when the placement doesn't work out the way I'd wanted), I devised a method of creating a separate bobble that can be attached anywhere you like. The big benefit here is that you can add or subtract bobbles without having to rip out rows and rows of stitching.

Along with traditional stitches, Germany is also home to an innovative method of construction known as Modular Knitting. Developed in the 1990s by Horst Schultz, a Berlin-based instructor and designer who learned to knit as a child in a Danish refugee camp after World War II, it involves building knitted squares and stripes upon one another to create a larger piece of knitting. Essentially you create a knitted shape, bind it off, cut the yarn, pick up new stitches and then continue knitting a new shape. The process repeats itself until you've completed a sleeve, sweater front or whatever else you've planned out. Also called Domino Knitting (a term coined by Danish knitter Vivian Høxbro) or Numbers Knitting, it is wildly addictive once you get the hang of it. (See chart for Oktoberfest Glove Cuffs, page 136.)

Ciao, Bella: Embracing Italian Knits

■ The Italians do everything with a little more flair than the rest of us, so why should knitting be an exception? Knitting came to Italy with visiting Spanish nobles, and once established, became much more sophisticated in both style and technique. (I'm half Italian and half Spanish, so I like to think I bring the best attributes of both cultures to my knitting.) Though knitting was very likely well-ensconced in Italy by the fourteenth century, there's little recorded history about what was being knit. Several Italian painters of the period, including the Lorenzetti brothers of Siena, Vitale da Bologna, and Tommaso da Modena painted images of the Virgin Mary with knitting needles and a work-in-progress in hand. While this tells us knitting was certainly known to Italians in the fourteenth century, it does not make clear who was doing the actual stitching (nuns? rural women? ladies of leisure?) or what exactly was being knit. All three pictures show Mary knitting in the round on double-pointed needles; in Vitale's version it's possible that she is making a small purse similar to several small bags discovered in Switzerland. Dating from the fourteenth century, the bags hold relics of the saints and are worked in colorwork patterns.

The so-called Florentine Jackets created in the seventeenth century and now in the collection of London's

Austrian Alps Zip Jacket
page 132

Black Forest Mitts
page 124

■ *Silk jacket, Italy, circa 1600.*

Florentine Shrug
page 142

Inspired by...

The elaborate jacquards of the spectacular knitted jackets of 1600s Venice fast forward to the winding grapevine and leaves on my Florentine Shrug.

113

Roman Holiday Shrug
page 116

Victoria and Albert Museum are perhaps the most famed examples of Italy's knitted past—though it's possible the jackets are not Italian at all. Knitted in two colors of silk, they feature wonderful jacquard patterns. The coats are sewn from blocks of knit fabric; the long floats on the backs of the pieces suggest that they may have been made by machine rather than by hand.

Some speculate these jackets were made by Spanish framework knitters in imitation of the woven brocades popular at the time and later replicated in England. We do know that knitting machines arrived in Venice around 1614, causing some consternation among the hand-knitters of that city. Commercial knitting was certainly taking place in Italy in the mid-1600s (both by hand and machine), but knitting historian Richard Rutt speculates that the jackets may actually have been made in London. After all, two Englishmen patented the technique in 1768.

Fast-forward several hundred years, and there's no doubt that Italy is the fashion center for both yarn and knitwear. Designers, editors and clothing manufacturers faithfully flock to Milan and Florence every year for Pitti Filati, the fiber-fueled exhibit that sets the trends in color, stitch and silhouette for the seasons to come. Italy produces some of the finest knitting fibers in the world, and all knitters swoon over the stunning yarns and fashion-forward patterns the country produces.

Mad for Missoni

Italy is home to the most recognized name in fashion knitwear: Missoni. The brand began as a small family-run shop in Milan owned by Rosita and Ottavio Missoni. The two met at the 1948 Olympic Games in London, where Ottavio was making track suits for the Italian team. They married and set up shop five years later, designing track suits and eventually moving on to knitwear. Their colorful patterns and stripes gained them worldwide fame when their knitwear line premiered in 1964. Two years later the Missonis were once again front-page fashion news. Rosita decided to send her models down the runway bra-less (so as not to ruin the line of her silk jersey dresses) causing quite the scandal. The bright lights rendered the dresses transparent—and the naughty bits clearly visible. Such a presentation would barely give today's fashion editors reason to look up from their BlackBerries, but it was considered absolutely shocking at the time.

Techniques

■ The Florentine Jackets may not have been made in Florence, but the hand-knit version of the jacquard technique used to create them was certainly in use at the time. I love the pretty patterns it creates and have learned to interpret it in my own way.

Yarn à la Mode: Knitting French Style

■ Ah, France. It should come as no surprise that the capital of fashion has made several outstanding contributions to the world's knitted legacy—after all, this is a country that prides itself on appreciation of quality and beauty, to say nothing of foie gras, duck confit and crème brûlée.

France picked up the knitting habit early in the game, following closely on the heels of the Spanish and Italians. By the sixteenth century, hand-knitting was a booming industry. French knitters made lace knitting their specialty, turning out elaborate stockings that were the envy of all Europe.

France's most famed knitter is of course the indomitable (albeit fictional) Madame Defarge in Dickens' *A Tale of Two Cities*. Madame counted the heads dropping from the guillotine with the click of her needles, all the while stitching into her work symbols representing condemned aristocrats. What she may have lacked in character she made up for in knitting skill. Dickens took inspiration for the madame from the real-life tricoteuses of the French Revolution, the women who knit their way through the debates of the National Convention in which the fates of the France's aristocrats were decided. The presence of knitting needles was likely more practical than political, (You need something to keep your hands busy during long stretches spent sitting, right?) but the tricoteuses' penchant for hurling insults at the condemned and nonchalantly turning sock heels as the heads rolled gave them a reputation for sadism. Dickens took full advantage of this sinister spin, using it as a metaphor for the stealthy, calculated vengefulness of the French revolutionaries.

Not surprisingly, it was the French who gave knitting a high-fashion spin, introducing knitwear to the cloistered world of couture. By the end of World War I, sweaters had become increasingly popular as outerwear for both

Chanel caused a sensation in 1914 by slipping a man's sweater over her head and cinching the waist with a handkerchief, summarily inventing the jersey knit dress.

men and women, but the French designers Elsa Schiaparelli (who was Italian-born) and Coco Chanel dominated the fashion scene of the 1920, turning knitwear into something fresh and exciting. Simple and striking, it became the height of chic. Chanel caused a sensation in the summer of 1914 by slipping a man's sweater over her head and cinching the waist with a handkerchief, summarily inventing the jersey knit dress. For the 1924 Diaghilev ballet Le Train Bleu, she created hand-knitted bathing suits, executing them in shocking colors like royal blue and cyclamen and mixing in bold stripes. The ballet and its designs, named for the train that shuttled fashionable Parisians from the city to the beach at Deauville, was considered the apotheosis of fashion. Schiaparelli created a fashion sensation of her own when she introduced her bow-knot sweater in 1927—a black V-neck with trompe l'oeil collar, floppy bow and cuffs stitched in white. The sweater was a must-have for the trendsetters, and Schiaparelli followed up her first success with designs featuring ties and handkerchiefs.

Techniques

■ One of my favorite textured stitch patterns is entrelac, that lovely interlacing of stitches. While the technique may not be French in origin, the term certainly is. It comes from the word entrelacer, which means to interlace or intertwine. It's also one of those wonderful techniques that looks incredibly complicated, but is actually quite simple once you get the hang of it. Entrelac is worked in one piece, beginning with a base of triangles, then working squares at right angles to one another.

I-cord (along with chocolate and cashmere) is one of my true loves, and I never tire of using it as an embellishment. I love the beautiful simplicity of both the technique and the end product. (I'm told the "I" stands for "idiot," a nod to how easy it is to make this versatile edging, but I like to think it stands for inventive.) My grandmother taught me ins and outs of I-cord when I was a young girl, though she called it "French cord," and I have created many unique I-cords and ways to use them. The I-cord is never given enough importance. (For more cord ideas, see my books *Knitted Embellishments* and *Knitting Over the Edge*.) The French connection probably lies in the spool knitters that were often used to create the cord. These

Inspired by...
The faux bow and cuff details of Schiaparelli's 1927 trompe l'oeil knitted sweater is restyled here with a large knitted rose and tiered sleeves.

little wooden tubes with pegs attached to the top are called by a variety of names, including the knitting spool, knitting noddy, knitting Nancy and French knitter. In France, the country of their origin, however, they're known as tricotins and have in production since World War I. Introduced by the big yarn factories of Roubaix as a way of unloading surplus yarn, the tricotins sold for about six francs and were distributed free of charge to schools in hopes that the fun and ease of using them would encourage the purchase of yarn. Made of wood or sometimes papier-mâché, tricotins came in the shape of country girls, housewives, soldiers, clowns, and, in the case of Pingouin Yarns, a penguin.

A few less politically correct, but popular, versions including an African figure modeled on the now-controversial Senegalese soldier featured on the packaging and ads for Banania, a chocolate drink mix, and the Chinese characters from the Tintin comics. The originals have become collector's items.

I prefer to do my French-cord knitting on double-pointed needles and have had great success (not to mention a lot of fun) experimenting by replacing standard stockinette with seed stitch, eyelet and cables, all the while sipping a glass of Sancerre. ❖

La Belle Cardigan
page 128

Parisian Entrelac Wrap
page 120

Roman Holiday Shrug

Fit for a princess, this embellished shrug is the perfect topper for your favorite dress—*bellissima!*

■ SKILLED KNITTER

WHAT YOU'LL NEED

- 5 (6) 3½oz/100g skeins (each approx 110yds/99m) of Reynolds/JCA *Andean Alpaca Regal* (90% alpaca/10% wool) in #6 off white
- Size 10 (6mm) needles OR SIZE TO OBTAIN GAUGE
- Cable needle
- Tapestry needle

Sizes

S/M (L/XL)

Finished back length: 9 (11¼)"/23 (28.5)cm

Cuff to cuff measurement: 30 (32)"/76 (81)cm

Gauge

16 sts and 22 rows = 4"/10cm in St st. TAKE TIME TO CHECK GAUGE.

Pattern Glossary

SMOCKING PATTERN (multiple of 16 sts + 12)

■ *Rows 1, 3, 5 and 7 (RS)* K3, p6, *[k2, p2] twice, k2, p6; rep from *, end k3.

Rows 2, 4, 6 and 8 P3, *k6, [p2, k2] twice, p2; rep from *, end k6, p3.

Row 9 K3, p2, k2, p2, *slip next 10 sts to cn and wind yarn 3 times around these sts, [k2, p6, k2] from cn, p2, k2, p2; rep from *, end k3.

Row 10 P3, *[k2, p2] twice, k6, p2; rep from *, end k2, p2, k2, p3.

Rows 11, 13, 15, and 17 K3, p2, k2, *p2, k2, p6, k2, p2, k2; rep from *, end p2, k3.

Rows 12, 14, 16 and 18 P3, k2, *p2, k2, p2, k6, p2, k2; rep from *, end p2, k2, p3.

Row 19 K1, *slip next 10 sts to cn and wind yarn 3 times around these sts, [k2, p6, k2] from cn, p2, k2, p2; rep from *, end slip next 10 sts to cn and wind yarn 3 times around these sts, [k2, p6, k2] from cn, k1.

Row 20 P3, k6, p2, *[k2, p2] twice, k6, p2; rep from *, end p1.

Rep rows 1–20.

HOLSTER PATTERN (multiple of 4 sts + 4)

Row 1 (RS) Purl.

Row 2 Knit.

Row 3 (RS) P4, turn, *cast on 8 sts using knitted on cast-on, p4 turn; rep from * to end.

Rows 4, 6, 8 and 10 K4, *p8, k4; rep from * to end.

Rows 5, 7, 9 and 11 P4, *k8, p4; rep from * to end.

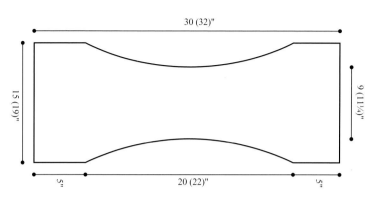

Row 12 K4, *bind off 8 sts purlwise, k4; rep from * to end.
Row 13 Purl.
Row 14 Knit.

Shrug

■ Cast on 60 (76) sts.
Work 14 rows in St st.
Work 14 rows of Holster pat.
Work in Smocked pat for 20 (22)"/51 (56)cm, ending with row 8.
Work 14 rows of Holster pat.
Work 14 rows in St st.
Bind off.

Bobbles (make 65)

■ **MB** (make bobble) ([K1, yo] twice, k1) in same st—5 sts, turn; k5, turn; p5, pass 2nd, 3rd, 4th and 5th sts over the first st.

■ Make a slip knot and place on needle. MB and fasten off.

Flowers (make 5)

■ Cast on 27 sts, leaving a long tail
Row 1 (RS) K1, *p1, k1; rep from * to end.
Row 2 P1, *k1, p1; rep from * to end.
Row 3 K1, *p1, M1p, k1; rep from * to end—40 sts.
Row 4 P1, *k2, p1; rep from * to end.
Row 5 K1, *p2, M1p, k1; rep from * to end—53 sts.
Row 6 *P1, k3; rep from *, end p1.
Row 7 K1, *p3, MB; rep from *, to end.
Bind off knitwise. With long tail, thread through cast-on sts, pull tightly to cinch and sew side seam to make a circle.

Bobble Flowers

■ Use 6 bobbles for each flower (one for center and 5 "petals") and place 5 flowers evenly spaced across each St st section at ends of shrug.

■ Flowers

With RS facing, attach 5 flowers evenly across neck edge of shrug.
Sew a bobble to center of each flower.

Finishing

■ Sew 7"/18cm sleeve seams at each end of shrug. ❖

Parisian Entrelac Wrap

From the Champs-Elysées to Pigalle to Montmartre, you'll be the belle of "Paree" in this lovely wrap.

■ SKILLED KNITTER

WHAT YOU'LL NEED
- ■ 8 1¾oz/50g balls (each approx 81yd/75m) of Tahki Yarns/Tahki•Stacy Charles, Inc. *Bunny Paint* (50% merino wool/25% alpaca/25% acrylic) in #76 grey/jewel tone multi (A)
- ■ 3 1¾oz/50g balls (each approx 81yd/75m) of Tahki Yarns/Tahki•Stacy Charles, Inc. *Bunny* (50% merino wool/25% alpaca/25% acrylic) each in #49 raspberry (B), #43 light olive (C) and #8 wine (D)
- ■ Size 9 (5.5mm) needles
- ■ 2 1¼" diameter (30mm) metal sew-on snaps
- ■ Tapestry needle

Finished Measurements:
Bust: 43"/109cm, closed
Length (back): 19¼"/49cm

Gauge
15 sts and 22 rows = 4"/10cm in St st. TAKE TIME TO CHECK GAUGE.

Entrelac
BASE TRIANGLES
■ Beg with a RS row *K2, turn, p2, turn. K3, turn, p3, turn. K4, turn, p4, turn.
Cont in this way until you have worked K9, turn, p9, turn. K10. Do not turn.
Rep from * to end. Change to next color.

FIRST ROW
■ Beg triangle
Beg with a WS row P2, turn, k1, m1, k1, turn. P2, p2tog, turn, k2, m1, k1, turn. P3, p2tog, turn, k3, m1, k1, turn. P4, p2tog, turn, k4, m1, k1, turn. Cont in this way until you have worked P8, p2tog, turn, k8, m1, k1, turn. P9, p2tog. Do not turn.

RECTANGLES
■ *Pick up and p 10 sts along side of triangle.
Beg with a RS row [K10, turn, p9, p2tog, turn] 9 times. K10, turn, p9, p2tog. Do not turn. Rep from * to last triangle.

END TRIANGLE
■ Pick up and p 10 sts along side of triangle.
Beg with a RS row K1, k2tog, k7, turn, p9, turn. K1, k2tog, k6, turn, p8, turn. K1, k2tog, k5, turn, p7, turn. Cont in this way until you have worked K1, k2tog, turn, p2, turn. K2tog. Do not turn. Change to next color.

SECOND ROW, FIRST RECTANGLE
■ *Pick up and k 9 sts along side of triangle.
Beg with a WS row [P10, turn, k9, ssk, turn] 9 times. P10, turn, k9, ssk. Do not turn.

NEXT AND SUBSEQUENT RECTANGLES
■ *Pick up and k 10 sts along side of rectangle.
Beg with a WS row [P10, turn, k9, ssk, turn] 9 times. P10, turn, k9, ssk. Do not turn.
Rep from * to end. Change to next color.
Rep first and second rows, ending with first row.

END TRIANGLES
■ Beg triangle
Beg with a WS row, P2, turn, k1, m1, k1, turn. P2, p2tog, turn, slip 1 st from RH needle to LH needle, k2tog, k1, m1, k1, turn. P3, p2tog, turn, slip 1 st from RH needle to LH needle, k2tog, k2, m1, k1, turn. P4, p2tog, turn, slip 1 st from RH needle to LH needle, k2tog, k3, m1, k1, turn. P5, p2tog, turn, k6, turn.
Bind off 6 sts purlwise—1 st on needle.

NEXT AND SUBSEQUENT TRIANGLES
■ *Pick up and p 9 sts along side of rectangle.
Beg with a RS row K8, k2tog, turn, p8, p2tog, turn. K7, k2tog, turn, p7, p2tog, turn. K6, k2tog, turn, p6, p2tog, turn. Cont in this way until you have worked K1, k2tog, turn, p1, p2tog, turn. K2tog, turn, p2tog, turn, k1, turn, p2tog. Do not turn.
Rep from * to last triangle.

END TRIANGLE
■ Pick up and p 9 sts along side of rectangle.
Beg with a RS row K1, k2tog, k7, turn, p2tog, p7, turn.
K1, k2tog, k5, turn, p2tog, p5, turn.
K1, k2tog, k3, turn, p2tog, p3, turn.
K1, k2tog, k1, turn, p2tog, p1, turn.
K2tog. Fasten off.

Right front
■ With A, cast on 30 sts. Work base triangles row.
Alternate first and second row of rectangles in stripe pattern as foll: *1 row B, 1 row A, 1 row C, 1 row A, 1 row D, 1 row A. Rep from * once more, then work 1 row B, 1 row A, 1 row C, 1 row A. Work end triangles row with D. Bind off.

Left front

■ With A, cast on 40 sts. Work base triangles row. Alternate first and second row of rectangles in strip pattern as foll: *1 row C, 1 row A, 1 row D, 1 row A, 1 row B, 1 row A, 1 row C, 1 row A. Work end triangles row with D. Bind off.

Back

■ With A, cast on 50 sts. Work same as right front through one stripe pattern rep, then 1 row B and 1 row A. Work end triangles row with C. Bind off.

Sleeves (make 2)

■ With A, cast on 40 sts. Work same as right front through one stripe pattern rep. Work end triangles row with B. Bind off.

Finishing

■ Sew pieces together and snaps to fronts following diagram.

FLOWERS (make 4)

■ With B, make a slip knot. *Cast on 4 sts, bind off 4 sts, slip rem st to left-hand needle; rep from * 5 times more. Thread cast-on tail through sts along base of petals and draw tight to form flower. Fasten end securely.

LEAVES (make 4)

■ With C, cast on 5 sts.
Row 1 (RS) K2, yo, k1, yo, k2—7 sts.
Row 2 and WS rows Purl.
Row 3 K3, yo, k1, yo, k3—9 sts.
Row 5 K4, yo, k1, yo, k4—11 sts.
Rows 7, 9, 11 and 13 Ssk, k to last 2 sts, k2tog—3 sts after row 13.
Row 15 Sk2p—1 st.
Fasten off.
Sew 4 leaves across short lower edge of right front. Sew a flower to the top of each leaf. With D, make a 3-wrap French knot in the center of each flower. ❖

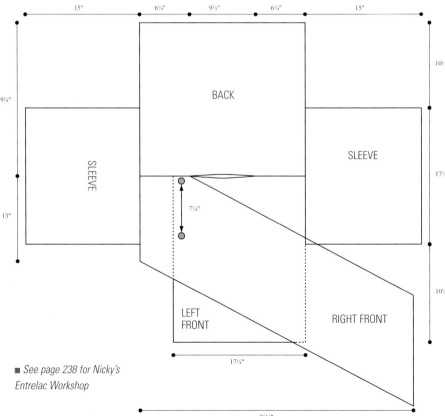

■ *See page 238 for Nicky's Entrelac Workshop*

Black Forest Mitts

With rich colors, textures and delicate embroidered flowers, the forest never looked lovelier.

■ SKILLED KNITTER

WHAT YOU'LL NEED
■ 2 1¾oz/50g skeins each (ea. approx 137yd/125m) of Knit One, Crochet Too Inc. *Ambrosia* (70% baby alpaca, 20% silk, 10% cashmere) in #249 garnet (A)
■ 1 skein each #688 french blue (B), #567 celery (C), #887 chocolate (D) and #900 jet (E)
■ Size 3 (3.25mm) needles
■ Stitch markers
■ Cable needle
■ Tapestry needle

One Size
Adult Woman's

Gauge
24 sts and 30 rows = 4"/10 cm in St st and A. TAKE TIME TO CHECK GAUGE.

Pattern Stitches
■ *MB* (Knit into front & back of st) twice, knit into front of st again—5 sts. Turn.
Purl 1 row, turn, knit 1 row, turn, purl 1 row, turn.
K2tog, k1, k2tog, turn.
Slip 1, p2tog, psso.

■ *2-st LPC* Skip 1 st but leave on left-hand needle, purl in the back loop of next st, leaving on left-hand needle, knit in the front loop of first st, slip both sts from left-hand needle.
2-st RPC Skip 1 st but leave on left-hand needle, knit in the front loop of next st, leaving on left-hand needle, purl in the front loop of first st, slip both sts from left-hand needle.

Inspired by...
My inspiration was actually the Black Forest itself, but I love this Bavarian oompah-band pin so much I wanted to share it with you.

3-st RC Slip 1 st to cable needle and hold in back, k1, p1, k1 from cable needle.
4-st RC Slip 2 sts to a cable needle and hold in back, k2, k2 from cable needle.

Bobble Pattern (multiple of 5 sts +2 extra)
Rows 1 and 3 (RS) P2, *k3, p2; rep from * to end.
Rows 2, 4 and 6 K2, *p3, k2; rep from * to end.
Row 5 P2, *k1, MB with desired color, k1, p2; rep from * to end.
Rep Rows 1–6 for Bobble Pattern.

Diamond Cable Panel (worked over 25 sts)
Row 1 (RS) P2, 4-st RC, p5, 3-st RC, p5, 4-st RC, p2.
Rows 2 and 4 Knit the knit sts and purl the purl sts as they appear.
Row 3 P2, k4, p4, 2-st RPC, p1, 2-st LPC, p4, k4, p2.
Row 5 P2, 4-st RC, p3, 2-st RPC, p3, 2-st LPC, p3, 4-st RC, p2.
Row 6 K2, p4, k3, p1, k2, p1, k2, p1, k3, p4, k2.
Row 7 P2, k4, p2, 2-st RPC, p2, k1, p2, 2-st LPC, p2, k4, p2.
Row 8 K2, p4, k2, p1, k2, p3, k2, p1, k2, p4, k2.
Row 9 P2, 4-st RC, p2, k1, p2, k3, p2, k1, p2, 4-st RC, p2.
Row 10 Repeat Row 8.
Row 11 P2, k4, p2, k1, p2, k3, p2, k1, p2, k4, p2.
Row 12 K2, p4, k2, p1, k3, p1, k3, p1, k2, p4, k2.
Row 13 P2, 4-st RC, p2, 2-st LPC, p2, k1, p2, 2-st RPC, p2, 4-st RC, p2.
Rows 14, 16, 18 and 20 Knit the knit sts and purl the purl sts as they appear.
Row 15 P2, k4, p3, 2-st LPC, p3, 2-st RPC, p3, k4, p2.
Row 17 P2, 4-st RC, p4, 2-st LPC, p1, 2-st RPC, p4, 4-st RC, p2.
Row 19 P2, k4, p5, 3-st RC, p5, k4, p2.
Repeat Rows 1–20 for Diamond Cable Panel.

Right Glove
■ With A, cast on 27 sts.

Work in Bobble Pattern, working bobbles in colors as desired and remaining sts with A, for 11 rows.

With A, cast on 45 sts at beg of next WS row—72 sts.

Continue in Bobble Pattern for 6 more rows, then work Rows 1–5 once more.

Next (dec) row (WS) K2tog, *p3, k2tog; rep from * to end—57 sts.

BEGIN DIAMOND CABLE PANEL

■ *Next Row* (RS) Work 9 sts in St st, 25 sts in Diamond Cable Panel, 23 sts in St st. Continue in patterns as established, dec 1 st each side every 14th row 5 times—47 sts. Work even until piece measures 11"/28cm from beg of Diamond Cable Panel, dec 1 st at end of last WS row—46 sts.

Thumb Gusset

■ *Next Row* K22, place marker, inc 1 st in next st, k2, inc 1 st in next st, place marker, k20.

Work 3 rows even—48 sts.

■ *Next (inc) Row* Knit to 1 st before marker, inc 1 st in next st, k to 1 st after second marker, inc 1 st in next st, k to end—50 sts.

Work 3 rows.

Repeat from * 3 times more.

Repeat Inc Row once more—58 sts.

Purl 1 row.

Thumb

■ *Next Row (RS)* Work 38 sts, turn. Leave remaining sts unworked.

Next Row P18, turn. Leave remaining sts unworked.

Next Row Cast on 3 sts for inside edge of Thumb, k18—21 sts.

Purl 1 row.

Knit 1 row.

Purl 1 row.

Bind off loosely knitwise.

Hand

■ Join yarn at base of 3 cast-on sts of Thumb and pick up and knit 3 sts in these sts, knit all stitches—43 sts.

Continue in St st for 1½"/4cm more, dec 1 st at center of last row—42 sts.

Index finger

■ *Next Row* K27, turn. Leave remaining sts unworked.

Next Row P12 turn. Leave remaining sts unworked.

Next Row Cast on 2 sts for inside edge of Finger, k12—14 sts.

Purl 1 row.

Knit 1 row.

Purl 1 row.

Bind off loosely knitwise.

Middle Finger

■ Join yarn at base of cast-on sts and pick up and knit 2 sts in these sts, k5, turn. Leave remaining sts unworked.

Next Row P12, turn. Leave remaining sts unworked.

Next Row Cast on 2 sts for inside edge of Finger, k12 – 14 sts.

Purl 1 row.

Knit 1 row.

Purl 1 row.

Bind off loosely knitwise.

Ring Finger

■ Work as for Middle Finger.

Little Finger

■ Join yarn at base of cast-on sts and pick up and knit 2 sts in these sts, k5, turn.

Next Row P12.

Next Row K12.

Purl 1 row.

Knit 1 row.

Purl 1 row.

Bind off loosely knitwise.

Left Glove

■ Work as for Right Glove, reversing the patterns and finger placement.

Finishing

■ Work 2 embroidered flowers randomly on back of hand. Work embroidered flowers on Row 1 of Diamond Cable Panel, reversing placement for mirror images. Work a circle of French knots with B. Work 3 lazy daisy stitches with C for flower petals. (See page 239 for embroidery stitches). Sew side seam. Weave in ends. ❖

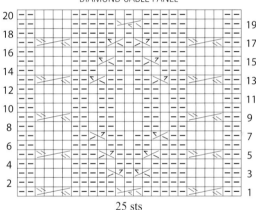

DIAMOND CABLE PANEL

25 sts

KEY
☐ K on RS, p on WS
⊟ P on RS, k on WS
⧅ 2-st LPC
⧄ 2-st RPC
⧅ 3-st RC
⧅ 4-st RC

La Belle Cardigan

Ooh la la! This very feminine cardigan is *très chic*.

■ SKILLED KNITTER

WHAT YOU'LL NEED

- ■ 4 (4, 5) 1¾oz/50g balls (ea. approx 137yds/125m) of Rowan/Westminster Fibers Inc. *Pure Wool DK* (100% superwash wool) in #24 petal (A)
- ■ 9 (11, 12) .88oz/25g balls (ea. approx 83yds/75m) of Rowan/Westminster Fibers Inc. *Kidsilk Aura* (75% kid mohair/25% silk) in #753 powder (B)
- ■ Size 7 (4.5mm) and 9 (5.5mm) needles OR SIZE TO OBTAIN GAUGE
- ■ Three 1⅛"/28.6mm buttons
- ■ 1 pkg Rainbow Elastic Thread (3mm bulky; 25yds/22m) in #83 pale rose
- ■ 3½ yds/3.2m ⅞"/21mm ribbon
- ■ Stitch holders
- ■ Tapestry needle

Sizes

S (M, L)

Finished Measurements

Bust: 34½ (39¾, 44½)"/87.5 (101, 113)cm
Length: 19½ (20, 20½)"/49.5, 51, 52)cm
Sleeve length: 31¼ (32, 32¼)"/79 (81, 82)cm

Gauge

18 sts and 25 rows = 4"/10cm in St st with A and B held together on larger needles. TAKE TIME TO CHECK GAUGE.
NOTE: Sleeves are worked with single strand of B. Body is worked with 1 strand each of A and B held together.

Fan Lace (multiple of 11 sts)

Row 1 (WS) Purl.
Row 2 *Ssk, k3 tbl, yo, k1, yo, k3 tbl, k2tog; rep from * to end.
Rows 3, 5 and 7 Purl.
Row 4 *Ssk, k2 tbl, yo, k1, yo, ssk, yo, k2 tbl, k2tog; rep from * to end.
Row 6 *Ssk, k1 tbl, yo, k1, [yo, ssk] twice, yo, k1 tbl, k2tog; rep from * to end.
Row 8 *Ssk, yo, k1, [yo, ssk] 3 times, yo, k2tog; rep from * to end.
Repeat rows 1–8.

Back

■ With larger needles and B, cast on 154 (176, 198) sts. Work in Fan lace pat for 32 rows–6"/15cm. Change to smaller needles and pick up A to work with A and B held together.
Dec row (WS) P0 (1, 0), *p2tog; rep from *, end p0 (1, 0)–77 (89, 99) sts.
Next row (RS) K1, *p1, k1; rep from * to end.
Work in k1, p1 rib as established for 1"/2.5cm.
Change to larger needles and work in St st for 4"/10cm, ending with a WS row.

ARMHOLE SHAPING

■ Bind off 5 (7, 9) sts at beg of next 2 rows.
Dec row (RS) K1, ssk, k to last 3 sts, k2tog, k1.
Rep dec row every RS row 2 (4, 5) times more–61 (65, 69) sts.
Work even in St st until armhole measures 8½ (9, 9½)"/21.5 (23, 24)cm.
Next row Work 14 (16, 18) sts and place these sts on holder, bind off next 33 sts, work to end of row and place rem 14 (16, 18) sts on holder.

Left Front

■ With larger needles and B, cast on 77 (88, 99) sts. Work in Fan lace pat same as back. Change to smaller needles and pick up A to work with A and B held together.
Dec row (WS) P1 (1, 1), *p2tog; rep from *, end p0 (1, 2)–39 (45, 51) sts.
Next row (RS) K1, *p1, k1; rep from * to end.
Work in k1, p1 rib as est for 1"/2.5cm, ending with a WS row.
Next row (RS) Knit, then cast on 6 sts for front facing–45 (51, 57) sts.
Cont in St st for 4"/10cm, ending with a WS row.

ARMHOLE SHAPING

■ Bind off 5 (7, 9) sts at beg of next RS row. P 1 row.
Dec row (RS) K1, ssk, k to end.
Rep dec row every RS row 2 (4, 5) times more–37 (39, 42) sts.
Work even in St st until armhole measures 7 (7½, 8)"/17.5 (19, 20)cm, ending with a RS row.

NECK SHAPING

■ Bind off 20 sts at beg of next WS row.
Dec row (RS) K to last 3 sts, k2tog, k1.
Rep dec row every RS row twice more–14 (16, 19) sts.
Work even in St st until armhole measures 8½ (9, 9½)"/21.5 (22.5, 24)cm.
Place sts on holder.
Place markers evenly along front edge for 3 buttons, beg ½"/1.5cm above ribbing and ending ½"/1.5cm below beg of neck shaping.

Blouson sleeves tied with ribbons and a lace peplum, collar and cuffs—all romantic touches.

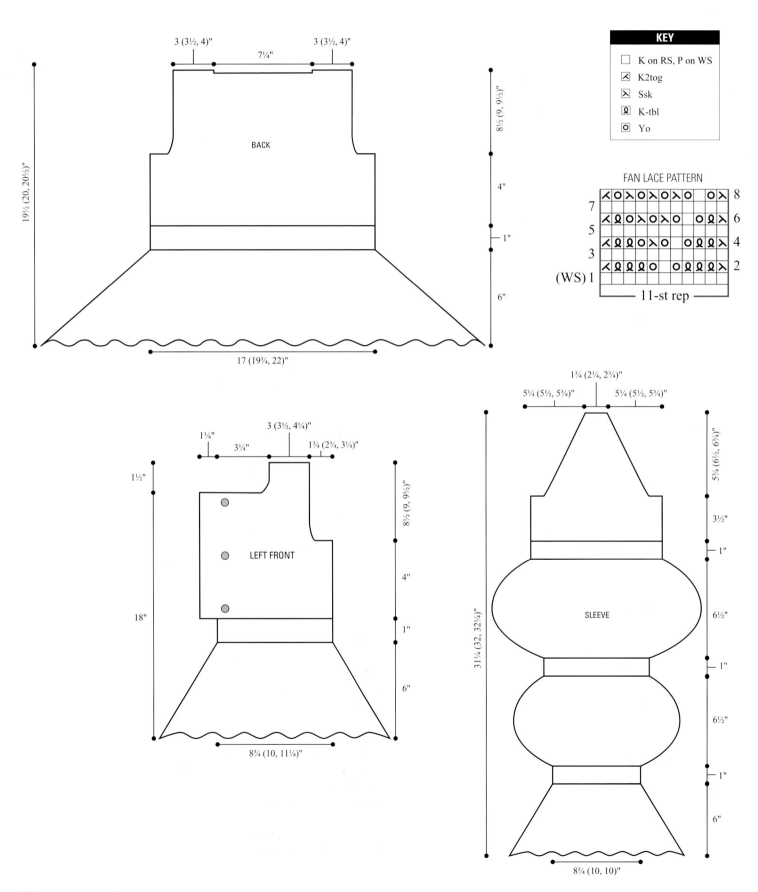

KEY

☐ K on RS, P on WS
☒ K2tog
☒ Ssk
☒ K-tbl
☒ Yo

FAN LACE PATTERN

11-st rep

BACK

3 (3½, 4)"   7¼"   3 (3½, 4)"

8½ (9, 9½)"

4"

1"

6"

19½ (20, 20½)"

17 (19¾, 22)"

LEFT FRONT

1¼"   3¼"   3 (3½, 4¼)"   1¾ (2¾, 3¼)"

1½"

18"

8½ (9, 9½)"

4"

1"

6"

8¾ (10, 11¼)"

SLEEVE

1¾ (2¼, 2¾)"

5¼ (5½, 5¾)"   5¼ (5½, 5¾)"

5¾ (6½, 6¾)"

3½"

1"

6½"

1"

6½"

1"

6"

31¼ (32, 32¼)"

8¾ (10, 10)"

Right front

■ With larger needles and B, cast on 77 (88, 99) sts. Work in Fan lace pat same as back.
Change to smaller needles and pick up A to work with A and B held together.
Dec row (WS) P1 (1, 1), *p2tog; rep from *, end p0 (1, 2)–39 (45, 51) sts.
Next row (RS) K1, *p1, k1; rep from * to end.
Work in k1, p1 rib as est for 1"/2.5cm, ending with a WS row. On last row,
cast on 6 sts for front facing–45 (51, 57 sts).
Next row (RS) Knit.
Cont in St st for 4"/10cm, ending with a RS row, AT THE SAME TIME,
work buttonholes to correspond with markers on left front as foll:
Buttonhole row 1 (RS) K2, bind off 2 sts, k4, bind off 2 sts, k to end.
Buttonhole row 2 P to bound-off sts, cast on 2 sts, p4, cast on 2 sts, p to end.

Armhole shaping

■ Bind off 5 (7, 9) sts at beg of next WS row.
Dec row (RS) K to last 3 sts, k2tog, k1.
Rep dec row every RS row 2 (4, 5) times more–37 (39, 42) sts.
Work even in St st until armhole measures 7 (7½, 8)"/17.5 (19, 20)cm,
ending with a WS row.

Neck shaping

■ Bind off 20 sts at beg of next RS row. P 1 row.
Dec row (RS) K1, ssk, k to end.
Rep dec row every RS row twice more–14 (16, 19) sts.
Work even in St st until armhole measures 8½ (9, 9½)"/18 (19, 20.5)cm.
Place sts on holder.

Sleeves

■ With larger needles and B, cast on 77 (88, 88) sts.
Work in Fan lace pat same as back. Change to smaller needles and pick up A
to work with A and B held together.
Dec row (WS) P1 (1, 1), *p2tog; rep from *, end p0 (1, 1)–39 (45, 45) sts.
Next row (RS) K1, *p1, k1; rep from * to end.
Work in k1, p1 rib as est for 1"/2.5cm, ending with a WS row.
Change to larger needles and B.
Inc row (RS) *Kfb; rep from * to end–78 (90, 90) sts.
Work in St st for 6½"/16.5cm, ending with a RS row.
Change to smaller needles and pick up A to work with A and B held together.
Dec row (WS) *P1, p2tog; rep from * to end–52 (60, 60) sts.
Work in k1, p1 rib for 1"/2.5cm, ending with a WS row.
Change to larger needles and B.
Inc row (RS) *Kfb; rep from * to end–104 (120, 120) sts.
Work in St st for 6½"/16.5cm, ending with a RS row.
Change to smaller needles and pick up A to work with A and B held together.
Dec row (WS) *[P2tog] 6 (6, 7) times, p1 (0, 1); rep from * to end–56 (60, 64) sts.
Work in k1, p1 rib for 1"/2.5cm, then work even in St st for 3½"/9cm.

Shape sleeve cap

■ Bind off 5 (7, 9) sts at beg of next 2 rows.
Dec row (RS) K1, ssk, k to last 3 sts, k2tog, k1.
Rep dec row every RS row 16 (12, 9) times more–12 (20, 26) sts.
Rep dec row every 4th row 0 (3, 5) times more–12 (14, 16) sts
Bind off 2 sts at beg of next 2 rows
Bind off rem 8 (10, 12) sts.

Finishing

■ Join shoulder seams using 3-needle bind-off (see page 244).
Set sleeves into armholes and sew in place.
Sew sleeve and side seams.
Fold facings to WS, matching buttonholes, and sew in place.
With B, sew around both layers of buttonholes.
Sew on buttons.
Sew a strand of elastic thread around the inside of each ribbing section
on each sleeve.
Sew ribbon around sleeves as pictured.

Collar

■ With RS facing, larger needles and B, cast on 275 sts.
Work in Fan lace pat for 16 rows–3"/7.5cm.
Next row (WS) K1, *k2tog; rep from * to end–138 sts.
Bind off. Ease bound-off edge of collar around neck opening
and sew in place.

Flower

■ With larger needles and B, cast on 176. Work in Fan lace pat
for 16 rows–3"/7.5cm.
Next row (WS) *K2tog; rep from * to end–88 sts.
Bind off leaving a long tail.
Thread tail through bound-off sts, pull firmly to gather and shape into a spiral.
Sew in place.

Flower center

■ With smaller needles and A and B held together, cast on 10 sts.
Rows 1 and 3 (RS) Kfb in each st to end–40 sts after row 3.
Rows 2 and 4 Purl.
Row 5 Kfb in each st to end–80 sts.
Bind off.
Shape into a spiral and sew to center of flower.
Attach flower to left front as pictured. ❖❖

Austrian Alps Zip Jacket

This lovely coat is perfect for hiking in the Alps or just strolling to the market. Note the unusual, undulating cable pattern, certain to turn heads.

■ MASTER KNITTER

WHAT YOU'LL NEED
- 18 (20, 28) 1¾oz/50g balls (ea. approx 137yd/125m) of Filatura Di Crosa/Tahki●Stacy Charles, Inc. *Zara* (100% merino wool) in #1451 oatmeal
- Size 6 (4mm) needles
- Size 6 (4mm) circular needle, 29"/74cm
- Stitch holders
- Stitch markers
- Tapestry needle
- 2yd/2m of ½"/13mm wide embroidered ribbon
- 22"/56cm long heavy separating zipper

Sizes
S (M, L)
Finished chest: 37 (41, 51)"/94 (104, 129.5)cm
Finished length: 27 (28, 31)"/68.5 (71, 78.5)cm

Gauge
30 sts and 32 rows = 4"/10cm in Cable Pattern unstretched.

Pattern Stitches
- Moss Stitch Rib (multiple of 7 + 3)
Row 1 (RS) P3, *k1, p1, k2, p3; repeat from * to end.
Row 2 K3, *p2, k1, p1, k3; repeat from * to end.
Row 3 P3, *k2, p1, k1, p3; repeat from * to end.
Row 4 K3, *p1, k1, p2, k3; repeat from * to end.

- *4-st LPC* Slip 2 sts to a cable needle and hold in front, p2, k2 from cable needle.
4-st RPC Slip 2 sts to a cable needle and hold in back, k2, p2 from cable needle.

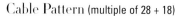

Inspired by...
The linear stitch pattern and color of these Old World gloves. Note the vintage knitting pins. A set like them probably created the gloves.

Cable Pattern (multiple of 28 + 18)
Row 1 (RS) P6, k6, *p4, [k2, p4] 3 times, k6; rep from * to last 6 sts, p6.
Row 2 K6, p6, *k4, p14, k4, p6; rep from * to last 6 sts, k6.
Row 3 P4, 4-st RPC, k2, *[4-st LPC, p2] twice, k2, [p2, 4-st RPC] twice, k2; rep from * to last 8 sts, 4-st LPC, p4.
Row 4 K4, * p10, k4; rep from * to end.
Row 5 P2, 4-st RPC, p2, k2 * [p2, 4-st LPC] twice, k2, [4-st RPC, p2] twice, k2; rep from * to last 8 sts, p2, 4-st LPC, p2.
Row 6 K2, p14, *k4, p6, k4, p14; rep from * to last 2 sts, k2.
Row 7 P2, *[k2, p4] 3 times, k6, p4; rep from * to last 16 sts—k2, [p4, k2] twice, p2.
Row 8 Repeat Row 6.
Row 9 P2, 4-st LPC, p2, k2, *[p2, 4-st RPC] twice, k2, [4-st LPC, p2] twice, k2; rep from * to last 8 sts p2, 4-st RPC, p2.
Row 10 Repeat Row 4.
Row 11 P4, 4-st LPC, k2, *[4-st RPC, p2] twice, k2, [p2, 4-st LPC] twice, k2; rep from * to last 8 sts, 4-st RPC, p4.
Row 12 Repeat Row 2.
Repeat Rows 1–12 for Cable Pattern.

Back
- Cast on 143 (171, 199) sts.
Beginning with Row 1, work in Moss St Rib for 8"/20.5cm, ending with a WS row and dec 19 (23, 27) sts evenly spaced on last row—124 (148, 172) sts.
Work in k1, p1 ribbing for ½"/1.5cm, ending with WS row.

- *Eyelet row* (RS) *[K1, p1] twice, yo, k2tog; rep from * to last 4 sts, [k1, p1] twice.
Work in k1, p1 rib for ½"/1.5cm more, ending with WS row, inc 6 (10, 14) sts evenly

spaced across last row—130 (158, 186) sts.

CABLE PATTERN
■ Beginning with Row 1, work 12 rows of Cable Pattern until piece measures 17"/43cm from beg, ending with WS row.

Shape Armhole
■ Bind off 6 sts at beginning of next 2 rows—118 (146, 174) sts.
Slip sts to a stitch holder for Back.

RIGHT FRONT
■ Cast on 87 (87, 115) sts.
Beginning with Row 1, work in Moss St Rib for 8"/20.5cm, ending with a WS row and dec 13 (13, 17) sts evenly spaced on last row—74 (74, 98) sts.
Work in k1, p1 ribbing for ½"/1.5cm, ending with WS row.

■ *Eyelet row* (RS) [K1, p1] twice, k1, yo, k2tog, *[p1, k1] 3 times, yo, k2tog; rep from * to last 3 sts, p1 k1, p1.
Work in k1, p1 rib for ½"/1.5cm more, ending with WS row, inc 0 (0, 4) sts evenly spaced across last row—74 (74, 102) sts.

CABLE PATTERN
■ Beginning with Row 1, work 12 rows of Cable Pattern until piece measures 17"/43cm from beg, ending with WS row.

SHAPE ARMHOLE
■ Bind off 6 sts at beginning of next row—68 (68, 96) sts.
Slip sts to a stitch holder for Right Front.

Left Front
■ Work same as Right Front, reversing shaping.

Sleeves
■ Cast on 50 (50, 78) sts.
Work in k1, p1 ribbing, inc 1 st each edge every 6th row 11 times—72 (72, 100) sts.
Work until piece measures 10"/25.5cm from beg, ending with WS row.
Leave sts aside on a spare needle.

SHAPE CUFF
■ Cast on 73 (73, 101) sts.
Beginning with Row 1, work in Moss St Rib for 4"/10cm, ending with WS row, dec 1 st on last row—72 (72, 100) sts.

■ *Joining Row (RS)* With RS facing, position spare needle with k1, p1 rib sts in back of left-hand needle. *knit together 1 st from left-hand needle with next st on spare needle; rep from * across row to join pieces.
Purl 1 row, inc 2 sts—74 (74, 102) sts.

CABLE PATTERN
■ Beginning with Row 1, work 12 rows of Cable Pattern, inc 1 st each edge every 6th row twice, then every 4th row 10 times, working new sts in rev St st—98 (98, 126) sts. Work as established until piece measures 17"/43cm from of k1, p1 rib, ending with WS row.

SHAPE ARMHOLE
■ Bind off 6 sts at beginning of next row—86 (86, 114) sts.
Slip sts to a stitch holder for Sleeve. Make a second Sleeve.

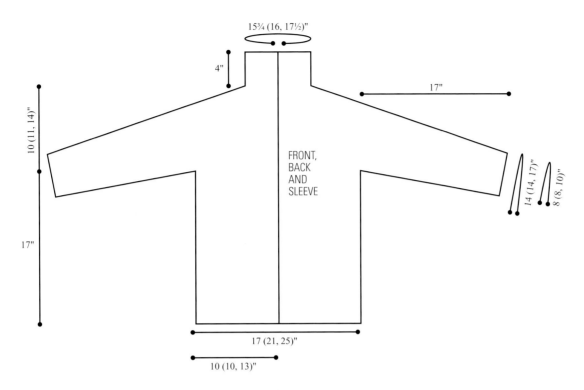

15¾ (16, 17½)"

4"

17"

10 (11, 14)"

17"

FRONT,
BACK
AND
SLEEVE

14 (14, 17)"

8 (8, 10)"

17 (21, 25)"

10 (10, 13)"

CABLE PATTERN

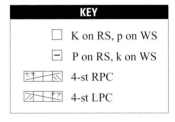

28-st rep

KEY

☐ K on RS, p on WS

— P on RS, k on WS

⟋⟍ ⟍⟋ 4-st RPC

⟍⟋ ⟋⟍ 4-st LPC

SHAPE RAGLAN

■ With RS facing and beginning with Row 1 of Moss St Rib as established, work 66 (66, 94) sts from Right Front stitch holder, place marker, k last 2 sts from stitch holder, k2 from Sleeve stitch holder, work 82 (82, 110) sts from Sleeve stitch holder, place marker, k last 2 sts from stitch holder, k2 from Back stitch holder, work 114 (142, 170) sts from Back stitch holder, place marker, k last 2 sts from stitch holder, k2 from Sleeve stitch holder, work 82 (82, 110) sts from Sleeve stitch holder, place marker, k last 2 sts from stitch holder, k2 from Left Front stitch holder, work 66 (66, 94) sts from Right Front stitch holder—426 (454, 594) sts. Work 1 row as established.

■ Next (dec) row (RS) *Work in pattern to 1 st before marker, k2tog, k2, ssk; rep from * 3 more times—418 (446, 586) sts. Work 1 row as established. Continue to work Dec Row every other row 25 (27, 35) more times—218 (230, 306) sts.

Next Row (RS) P3, work in Moss St Rib around, dec 28 (29, 40) by working (p2tog, p1) in each p section and continuing to work raglan dec as established—182 (193, 258) sts. Work 1 row as established. Continue to repeat dec row every other row 8 (9, 16) more times—118 (121, 130) sts, ending with a WS row.

Collar

■ Change to k1, p1 rib, dec 1 (0, 1) sts—117 (121, 129) sts. Continue to work in rib for 4"/10cm. Bind off.

Finishing

■ Sew side and Sleeve seams. Weave in ends. Sew zipper along front edges. Thread ribbon through eyelets made in Eyelet row. ❖

This raglan-sleeved zip jacket with a stylish rib-and-cable combo has a variety of special details.

Oktoberfest Glove Cuffs

Add these fashionable cuffs to your favorite pair of leather gloves and you won't want to take them off.

■ SKILLED KNITTER

WHAT YOU'LL NEED
- 1 3½oz/100g hank (ea. approx 225yds/200m) of Claudia Hand Painted Yarns *Sport* (100% merino wool) each in black (A) and bronze (B)
- Size 4 (3.5mm) needles OR SIZE TO OBTAIN GAUGE
- One pair black leather gloves
- Eight ½"/13mm black velvet buttons
- Tapestry needle

One size

Finished Measurement
approx 8½"/21.5cm wide and 7"/18cm high

Gauge
1 square = 1¾"/4.5cm. TAKE TIME TO CHECK GAUGE.

NOTES
- Use knitted-on cast-on throughout.
- When changing colors, bring new color under old color.
- Pick up and knit through both strands of edge stitches.

First Column
SQUARE A
- With A, cast on 19 sts using knitted-on cast-on.
Row 1 (WS) With A, k19.
Row 2 With B, k8, S2KP, k8—17 sts.
Row 3 With B, k8, p1, k8.
Row 4 With A, k7, S2KP, k7—15 sts.
Row 5 With A, k7, p1, k7.
Row 6 With B, k6, S2KP, k6—13 sts.

Row 7 With B, k6, p1, k6.
Cont in this way, dec 2 sts at center every RS row and p center st on WS row, and alternate 2 rows A with 2 rows B, until 3 sts rem.
Next row (WS) S2PP (insert right needle from back to front through 2nd st, then 1st st, and slip tog to right needle, p1, p2sso)—1 st (counts as 1st st for next square).

SQUARE B
- Turn square to work with RS facing and with A, pick up and k8 sts along side edge, pick up and k 1 in corner, cast on 9 sts—19 sts.
Beg with row 1, work same as Square A.

SQUARE C
- Work same as Square B.

SQUARE D
- Work same as Square B. Fasten off last st.

Second Column
SQUARE E
- With A, cast on 9 sts, pick up and k 10 sts along side of Square A—19 sts (see placement diagram).
Beg with row 1, work same as Square A (st 10 is the last st worked on Square A).

PLACEMENT DIAGRAM

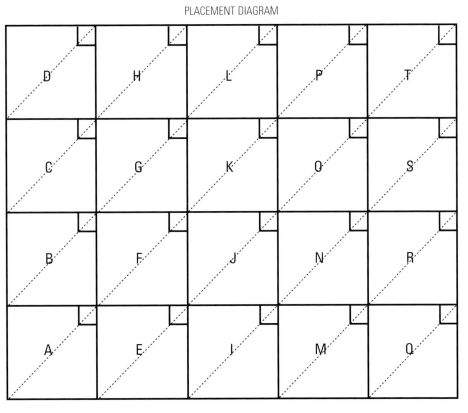

Nicky's Notes

Velvet buttons and a ruffled top
are delicious details, but feel
free to get creative here, adding
your own favorite buttons and
even mixing them up.

Square F

■ Pick up and k 8 sts along side of Square E, pick up and k 10 sts along side of
Square B—19 sts.

Beg with row 1, work same as square A (st 10 is the last st worked on Square B).

■ Cont to add squares in this way (foll placement diagram) until piece is
4 squares high and 5 squares wide. Fasten off last st.

Finishing

RUFFLE

■ With RS facing and A,
pick up 49 sts along width of piece.

Row 1 (WS) P1, *k1, p1; rep from * to end.

Row 2 K1, *p1, yo, k1; rep from *to end—73 sts.

Row 3 P1, *k2, p1; rep from * to end.

Row 4 K1, *p2, yo, k1; rep from * to end—97 sts.

Row 5 P1, *k3, p1; rep from * to end.

Row 6 K1, *p3, yo, k1; rep from * to end—121 sts.

Row 7 P1, *k4, p1; rep from * to end.

Row 8 K1, *p4, k1; rep from * to end.

Bind off purlwise.

■ Sew side seams, leaving last square above ruffle unsewn. Sew bottom into glove
lining. Sew buttons along side seam at base of each square, using button at
ruffle to connect both sides of slit. ❖❖

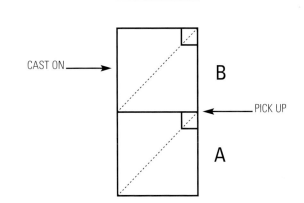

The mitered knitting was inspired by the designs of
Horst Schultz. It's a very addictive technique.

Tyrolean Leg Warmers

Heidi grows up! Warm your legs and your heart with these charming chill-chasers.

■ SKILLED KNITTER

WHAT YOU'LL NEED

- 5 1¾oz/50g balls (ea. approx 109yds/100m) of RYC/Westminster Fibers, Inc. *Silk Wool DK* in #308 brownstone (A)
- 1 ball each in #302 porcelain (B), #309 black (C), #301 limewash (D) and #304 cord (E)
- Size 6 (4mm) 16" circular needle
- Stitch marker
- Tapestry needle
- Fourteen ¾"/20mm buttons

One size

Finished Measurements

Length: 21"/53.5cm cuffed
Circumference: 14"/35.5cm at widest point

Gauge

21 sts and 28 rows = 4"/10cm over Chart 2.TAKE TIME TO CHECK GAUGE.

Left Legging

■ UPPER CUFF

With A, cast on 75 sts. Work 32 rows of Chart 1.
Next row (WS) Knit.
Pm and join.

Leg

NOTE: Patterns will not transition smoothly at the end of rnds.
The faux buttonband will cover the inconsistency.

■ Work in St st (k every rnd) for 3¾"/9.5cm.
Work 20 rnds of Chart 2 five times, dec 1 st at beg and end of every 10th rnd 9 times—57 sts.
Work 15 rnds of Chart 3—56 sts.

Lower Cuff

■ Work in k2, p2 rib for 1½"/4cm. Bind off in pattern.

Buttonband

■ With RS facing and A, starting at beginning of lower cuff and working below the line of decreases, pick up 102 sts evenly up to 1"/2.5cm past first repeat of Chart 2. Work in k2, p2 rib for 1½"/4cm. Bind off in pattern.

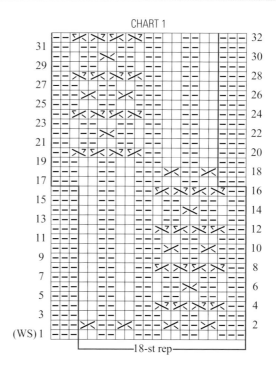

CHART 1

18-st rep

■ Using tails, sew ends of buttonband in place. Sew 7 buttons evenly spaced over buttonband, tacking down band in the process. Sew upper cuff seam with seam to WS of cuff to prevent it showing when folded.

Right Legging

■ Work same as left legging, except for buttonband. Start 1"/2.5cm before first repeat of Chart 2 and end at beginning of lower cuff. Complete as for left legging. ❖

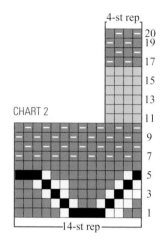

4-st rep

CHART 2

20
19
17
15
13
11
9
7
5
3
1

14-st rep

KEY

☐ K on RS, p on WS

− P on RS, k on WS

⊠ K2tog on RS, p2tog on WS

⊠ 2-st RC

⊠ 2-st LC

⊠ 2-st RPC

⊠ 2-st LPC

▦ Brownstone (A)

▦ Porcelain (B)

■ Black (C)

☐ Lime Wash (D)

▦ Cord (E)

CHART 3

15
13
11
9
7
5
3
1

14-st rep

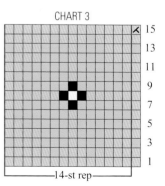

Florentine Shrug

Tuscany's wines are world famous, and this salute to its vineyards is utterly intoxicating.

■ MASTER KNITTER

WHAT YOU'LL NEED
■ 6 balls 1.75oz/50g balls (ea. approx 142 yds/130m) of RYC/Westminster Fibers, Inc. *Cashsoft DK* (57% extrafine merino/33% microfibre/10% cashmere) in #525 kingfisher (MC)
■ 1 ball ea. in #522 cashew (B), #521 opulence (C), #526 parma (D), #513 poison (E), #509 lime (F), #523 lichen (G) and #524 evergreen (H)
■ 2 .88oz/25g balls (each approx 132yds/120m) of Filatura Di Crosa/Tahki ● Stacy Charles, Inc. *New Smoking* (65% viscose/35% polyester) in #1 gold (A)
■ One pair ea. in size 4 (3.5mm) (for *New Smoking*) and 6 (4mm) needles OR SIZE TO OBTAIN GAUGE
■ 1 pkg (25 yds) of Rainbow Elastic, size 3mm bulky in #GMET Gold Metallic
■ Tapestry needle

One Size

Finished Measurements
Cuff to Cuff: 61"/155cm

Gauge
20 sts and 26 rows to 4"/10cm over st st using larger needles.
TAKE TIME TO CHECK GAUGE.
NOTE
■ Lame (A) sections are worked with 2 strands of yarn.
■ Motifs are worked in duplicate st after the piece is knitted.

Shrug
■ Beg at cuff, with 2 strands of A and smaller needles, cast on 43 sts.

GOLD BAND
■ Work in seed st for 1 inch as foll: K1, *p1, k1; rep from * to end. Cut A.

MAIN SECTION
Row 1 (WS) With MC and larger needles, purl.
Row 2 (RS) K1, KFB in each st across—85 sts.
Cont in st st until for an additional 185 rows.
Row 188 K2tog across, end k1—43 sts.
Row 189 Purl. Fasten off MC. Change to A and smaller needles.
Rep Gold Band and Main sections once more, then work the Gold Band section once more.

Embroidery
■ Using duplicate st (see page 238) and starting at cuff, follow chart for colors and motif(s) placement on left side. Repeat for right side.

Finishing
■ Fold piece lengthwise and sew sleeve seam beg at cuff for 18"/45.5cm. Rep for opposite side.
With 2 strands of elastic held tog, weave 2 rows, spaced evenly, around cuffs. Weave in ends.

Nicky's Notes
You may prefer using intarsia method rather than working all in duplicate stitch.

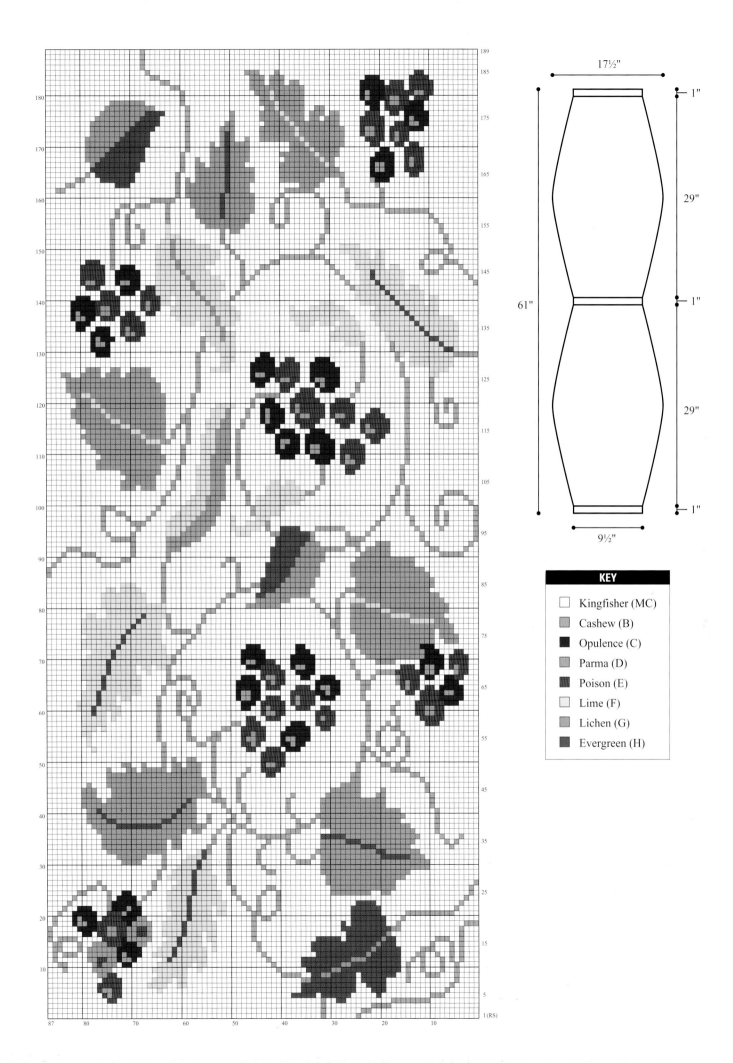

KEY	
☐	Kingfisher (MC)
▨	Cashew (B)
■	Opulence (C)
▤	Parma (D)
▦	Poison (E)
☐	Lime (F)
▨	Lichen (G)
▨	Evergreen (H)

17½"

1"

29"

61"

1"

29"

1"

9½"

AROUND THE MEDITERRANEAN

Spain

Portugal

Greece

Turkey

Syria

Egypt

■ THE MIDDLE EAST MAY HAVE GIVEN BIRTH TO KNITTING

Exactly when and where knitting began is a bit of a mystery, but most experts believe the Middle East to be the birthplace of the craft. Arabic nomads were probably the first to execute true knitting (as opposed to netting or nålebinding), carrying the craft into Egypt, where some of the oldest knitted pieces on record have been found. The Moors took the craft from the Middle East into Spain, and the Spanish in turn spread the craft throughout Europe.

Damascus Dream Dress
page 156

The Islamic Origins of Knitting

■ Egypt holds many treasures, among them some of the oldest examples of knitted, or least knit-like, textiles. Pick up any book on the history of knitting and you'll no doubt find a photo of the so-called Coptic socks, two ankle-high foot coverings with a split toe to accommodate the sandal-clad feet of the time. Excavated in the late nineteenth century from the burial grounds of Oxyrhynchus, an ancient Greek colony on the Nile, they're a beautiful example of nålebinding, a method of creating fabric by making multiple knots or loops with a single needle and thread that preceded two-needle knitting. The oldest examples of "true" knitting (or at least the oldest discovered so far) were made sometime in the eleventh to the thirteenth centuries and show quite a bit of sophisticated stitching.

Until evidence is unearthed to suggest otherwise, it's fairly certain that knitting evolved in the Middle East, either in Egypt or in the surrounding area. (King Tut's knits?) The skill presented in the socks and other fragments found so far suggests that the craft had been developing for some time—few novice knitters are likely to tackle such complicated patterning (and make such a good show of it) without some time to work out the kinks of the technique. The fact that knitting is done right to left, rather than left to right, also suggests Middle Eastern origins, since Arabic (and Hebrew) is written in this fashion.

From Egypt, knitting spread along the Silk Road and other trade routes, eventually finding its way to Spain via the Moors. A little conflict called the Crusades was going

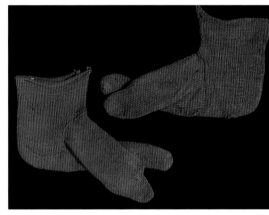

■ Knotless, knitted socks are some of the earliest knitted artifacts discovered. Egyptian, 300–499 AD.

on at the time, bringing an invading army of Europeans to the East. While it's unlikely that the knights were swapping knitting tips on the battlefield, it is possible that their servants may have picked up a few techniques and brought them home to Europe.

Techniques

■ The socks found at Oxyrhynchus (and others like them) were worked in the round using two-color stranding. See this technique on page 237. We can't be sure exactly how they were executed, but several knitters have worked out methods for copying the designs. Nancy Bush charted out patterns for the designs (and created instructions for the socks) in her book Folk Socks; charts for some of the designs also appear in Richard Rutt's History of Hand Knitting. The designs, like those of certain rare elaborate cushions found in Spain bring to mind the beautiful mosaics of the Moorish world. The originals were done in stockinette, but the patterns and motifs lend themselves

Greco Mosaic Bags
page 182

El Matador Sweater
page 170

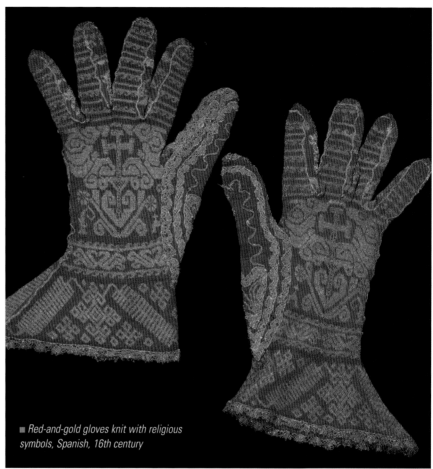

■ Red-and-gold gloves knit with religious symbols, Spanish, 16th century

beautifully to mosaic knitting—slip-stitched designs worked in two colors using two different strands, one at a time. Mosaic knitting requires no bobbin, no stranding, and no changing of colors mid-row (I highly recommend this technique to those of you who fear colorwork knitting). You can work it in stockinette, reverse stockinette or garter stitch. (Isn't it nice to have choices?) Only two colors are used in a motif, and each color is used alone for two rows. The first stitch shown in the chart tells you which color will be worked in that row. The second color is slipped purlwise over the same two rows. On the next two rows you reverse the process, working the second color and slipping the first. The first and last stitch of every row are always worked, never slipped.

Most mosaic charts show only the right-side rows, not the wrong-side rows. This is because colors are either slipped or worked exactly as they were on the right side of the work.

Spreading the Word: Spain and Portugal
■ The first pieces of knitting to be dated with real certainty are those found in tombs in the abbey of Santa Maria of Las Huelgas, in northern Spain. Founded by King Alfonso VIII and his queen, Leonora Plantagenet, in 1187, Las Huelgas was used as the royal mausoleum of Castile.

Inspired by...
The elaborate embellishment found on these early, bishop's gloves highlight the important relationship between religion, art, and design of the day.

When conservationists began cataloguing the contents of the tombs in 1944, they discovered several knitted cushions. The oldest of these was discovered in the tomb of Fernando de la Cerada, the heir of Alfonso X. Fernando died in 1275, so the cushion (on which it is believed his head was laid to rest) must date from that year or earlier. The cushion is the work of a master knitter, knit to about twenty stitches to the inch in elaborate patterns of fleurs-de-lis, castles, flowers and birds—all motifs I adore using in my designs. The Arabic word baraka, or blessing, is repeated around the border of Fernando's cushion, more evidence of the craft's ties to the Islamic world.

Spain's other claim to historical knitting fame is a pair of liturgical gloves made for a bishop in the sixteenth century. Now in the collection of the Victoria and Albert

Spanish Rose Trellis Scarf
page 152

Lisbon Lace Jacket
page 174

patterning soon worked its way into knits. Lace knitting reached its peak in the nineteenth century, when everything from gloves and shawls to table linens and bed covers were rendered in airy series of yarn overs.

In Portugal, knitters to this day still work with the yarn wound around their necks for tensioning. It's a technique probably picked up from the Turks and Moors who brought knitting to the region, and one that traveled to South America with the conquistadors. I learned to knit from a Spanish neighbor, and while she didn't teach me this method, she did like to use very long needles, tucking them under her armpits as she stitched. To this day I'm a pit knitter—and proud of it!

On the islands of the Azores (a Portuguese territory), a delicate form of knitting was developed known as pita lace, a nod to the Portuguese name for the aloe fiber from which it was knit. Incredibly light and detailed, the designs are created with single-thread construction, using traditional lace-knitting stitches. Most have a knitted border strip sewn to the edge of a medallion.

Techniques

■ Portugal's tradition of cutwork isn't based on knitting, but I'm a big fan of the beautiful table linens that are done in this fashion, and have always wanted to interpret this cut-and-sew technique in knitted stitches. My cutwork cardigan on page 174 is the result. To create it, I stitched up flowers and leaves in two different sizes, then pieced them together to make the fabric of the sweater. The neckline is done in one piece, with elastic thread woven in behind the stitches so you can adjust for a perfect fit. What I love about this method is that you can use it to create everything from pillows, throws and bags to skirts, shawls and sweaters. Just stitch up the number of flowers and leaves you think you'll need (remembering that you can always make more later), then lay them out on a flat surface a play around with the placement until you get the shape you want. Use a threaded tapestry needle to slip-stitch the pieces together, and you have a one-of-a-kind work of art.

With their passion for love, life and drama, the Spanish excel in the art of excess. My own Spanish heritage (by way of my father) may be the reason for my tendency to layer on lots of extras—be it the embellishments I use on my knits or all the icings I adore on my desserts. The wonderful flounces, flowers and ruffles of the flamenco dancer inspired the flowers and corkscrews I used in the sweaters and scarves on pages 152 and 160. Adding

Señorita's Floral Pullover
page 160

Museum in London, they're knit in the round in red silk and silver gilt thread and are adorned with religious symbols. Geometric designs decorate the cuffs, and a Greek wave motif appears on the fingers and wrists. Pieces such as these and the cushions found in the tombs of Las Huelgas show that knitting was more than likely reserved for luxury items.

Stockinette remained the only stitch in the knitters' repertoire until the mid-sixteenth century, when purling was introduced. A pair of stockings found in a tomb in Toledo and dated to 1562 is the first known example of this innovation, and for some time, purling was used only as a decorative element. At some point the Spanish began knitting silk stockings (we're not sure exactly when), the design and quality of which became much in demand across Europe. Spain was one of the few regions outside the Orient where silkworms would thrive, and as such silk became the fiber of choice. Spain was also famed for its meticulously made bobbin lace, and this type of

Greek Chic

Like Scotland, Greece has a long history of men in skirts. The Greek version, better-known as the *fustanella,* is considerably shorter than the Scottish kilt, leaving no mystery as to what is worn beneath it—thick white leggings that end in points at the ankle. The costume is worn by the *evezones,* the ceremonial guards of the royal court. These days the stockings are made by machine, but not so long ago they were the handiwork of rural knitters. In some areas of Thrace and Macedonia these stockings are decorated with patterned bands of gold or other colors.

On the island of Kimolos, the Greek women of centuries ago also wore short, lined white dresses over white knitted stockings. Subscribing to the notion that the thicker their legs appeared, the more beautiful they were, they tended to layer on several pairs at once, topping them off with lavishly decorated socks.

■ *Drawing of a Mykonos woman knitting a sock circa 1820*

these accents to any piece is actually quite easy, and I love the way they look—lush and lovely and marvelously exotic.

Bold Steps: Talking Turkey

■ It's not yet known when the Turks began knitting the beautifully patterned socks that make up the core of their country's knitting tradition. A pair of felt stockings bearing the ubiquitous çengal, or hook design, excavated from a burial mound in Pairik can be dated back to 600 bc, but it is unlikely the piece was knitted. Kenan Özbel, a Turkish professor of art and craft, believes the Turkish stocking traditions date back to the 17th century or thereabouts.

Whenever it began, there's no denying the beauty of the work. Turkish stockings are lavishly patterned with geometric motifs that represent everything from food (baklava and apple slices, walnuts and chestnuts) and nature (butterflies, birds' eyes) to protections and religious symbolism. Many patterns are worked in multiples of six—the "perfect" number according to the Koran. Five-pointed stars are incorporated to represent the five daily calls to prayer; other designs ward off the evil eye or offer blessings. (There are also plenty of designs that promote malice or bad luck, so research the symbols you incorporate in your designs carefully—unless, of course, sending a little ill will someone's way is your intent.)

As in the neighboring Balkans, the knitted patterns in Turkey can be used to identify the region or village from which the wearer hails or to indicate social rank and marital status. Socks are often given as gifts or used to relay a message or story; the acceptance of a pair of

socks can indicate the acceptance of a marriage proposal or a political alliance. In some cases, the patterns on the sock commemorate a natural disaster such as an earthquake or flood. Socks are still one of the most popular knitted gifts to give—all over the world. Interesting to think it all started so near the birthplace of civilization as we know it!

Techniques

■ Turkish socks are worked toe-up, with a pouchlike heel. Though they now knit in the Continental style, Turkish knitters traditionally tensioned their yarn much like their counterparts in Portugal and the Andes, draping it around their necks and working circularly on the inside of the work, purling all the stitches. As many as eight colors may be used in a single round. With diagonal lines predominating, many of the patterns have been created so that two repeats create one round on a sock, forming tall, vertical panels that flank the legs. Since it's customary in this country to remove one's shoes before entering a home and to pray with the soles of the feet exposed, it's not surprising that the soles of socks are as gorgeously patterned as the rest of the piece.

Interlocking patterns make up many of the geometric designs found in the socks, and the foreground and background are seemingly interchangeable in many designs. (Take a look at the sleeve chart on the Ottoman Empire Jacket on page 164.) This makes it quite easy to put a personal stamp on the design—one can simply change the background color or work various parts of a symbol in multiple colors to create a completely different effect. ❖

Ottoman Empire Jacket
page 164

Spanish Rose Trellis Scarf

This Moorish-inspired scarf gets the roses to the trellis without the gardener.

■ SKILLED KNITTER

WHAT YOU'LL NEED
- 4 1¾oz/50g skeins (ea. approx 93yds/85m) of Nashua Handknits/Westminster Fibers, Inc.'s *Julia* (50% wool/25% mohair/25% alpaca) in #50 forged iron (A)
- 2 skeins in #5185 spring green (B)
- 1 skein each in #2083 magenta (C), #3158 purple basil (D) and #3961 lady's mantle (E)
- Size 10 (6mm) needles
- Tapestry needle

Sizes
Instructions are written for one size.

Finished Measurements
Approx 10" x 50"/25.5 x 127cm, before felting.
Approx 6½" x 40"/16.5 x 101.5cm, after felting.

Gauge
Approx 19 sts and 24 rows = 4"/10cm over trellis pat, before felting.
Approx 30 sts and 30 rows = 4"/10cm over trellis pat, after felting.

Stitch Glossary
■ P1 wrapping yarn twice Insert needle into st as if to purl, wrap yarn twice around tip of needle, then complete as purl st.
Wrap sts [Wyib, sl last 3 sts worked back to LH needle, pass yarn to front, sl same 3 sts back again to RH needle, pass yarn to back] twice.

Trellis pattern (multiple of 8 sts + 1)
■ *Preparation row* (WS) With A, p1, *p1 wrapping yarn twice, p5, p1 wrapping yarn twice, p1; rep from * to end.

Row 1 (RS) With B, k1, *sl 1 wyib dropping extra wrap, k5, sl 1 wyib dropping extra wrap, k1; rep from * to end.
Row 2 With B, p1, *sl 1 wyif, p5, sl 1 wyif, p1; rep from * to end.
Row 3 With B, k1 *sl 1 wyib, k5, sl 1 wyib, k1; rep from * to end.
Row 4 With B, *p1, drop elongated sl st (color A) off LH needle to back (RS) of work, p5, drop elongated sl st (color A) off LH needle to back (RS) of work; rep from *, end p1.
Row 5 With A, k1, sl 1 wyib, k1, *pick up and knit dropped sl st, k1, pick up and knit dropped sl st, wrap sts, k1, sl 3 wyib, k1; rep from *, ending last rep with sl 1 wyib, k1.
Row 6 With A, p1, sl 1 wyif, *[p1, p1 wrapping yarn twice] twice, p1, sl 3 wyif; rep from *, ending last rep with sl 1 wyif, p1.
Row 7 With B, k3, *sl 1 wyib dropping extra wrap, k1, sl 1 wyib dropping extra wrap, k5; rep from * ending last rep with k3.
Row 8 With B, p3, *sl 1 wyif, p1, sl 1 wyif, p5; rep from *, ending last rep with p3.
Row 9 With B, k3, *sl 1 wyib, k1, sl 1 wyib, k5; rep from *, ending last rep with k3.
Row 10 With B, p3, *drop elongated sl st (color A) off LH needle to back (RS) of work, p1, drop elongated sl st (color A) off LH needle to back (RS) of work. p5; rep from *, ending last rep with p3.
Row 11 With A, k1, pick up and knit dropped sl st, *k1, sl 3 wyib, k1, pick up and knit dropped sl st, k1**, pick up and knit dropped sl st, wrap sts;

Inspired by...

A rose is a rose is a rose? Every rose is unique and there are more than 6000 varieties. What's more, every color has its own meaning: pink roses symbolize happiness; purple roses, unconscious beauty; and the red rose: true love.

rep from *, ending last rep at **.

Row 12 With A, p1, *p1 wrapping yarn twice, p1, sl 3 wyif, p1, p1 wrapping yarn twice, p1; rep from * to end.

Rep rows 1–12.

Scarf

■ With A, cast on 49 sts loosely. K 12 rows.

Work 12 rows of Trellis pat 23 times–276 pat rows.

With A, k 12 rows. Bind off loosely.

Rose (make 7 in C and 7 in D)

■ Cast on 37 sts, leaving a long tail for seaming.

Row 1 K1, *p1, k1; rep from * to end.

Rows 2, 4, 6 and 8 K the knit sts and p the purl sts.

Row 3 K1, *p1, m1 p, k1; rep from * to end–55 sts.

Row 5 K1, *p2, m1 p, k1; rep from * to end–73 sts.

Row 7 K1, *p3, m1 p, k1; rep from * to end–91 sts.

Row 9 K1, *p4, m1 p, k1; rep from * to end–109 sts. Bind off.

Roll ruffle edge from the outside and sew along cast-on edge to form rose.

Leaf (make 8 with 1 strand B, and 10 with B and E held tog)

■ Cast on 15 sts.

Row 1 (RS) K6, S2KP, k6–13 sts.

Row 2 K6, p1, k6.

Row 3 K5, S2KP, k5–11 sts.

Row 4 K5, p1, k5.

Row 5 K4, S2KP, k4–9 sts.

Row 6 K4, p1, k4.

Row 7 K3, S2KP, k3–7 sts.

Row 8 K3, p1, k3.

Row 9 K2, S2KP, k2–5 sts.

Row 10 K2, p1, k2.

Row 11 K1, S2KP, k1–3 sts.

Row 12 K1, p1, k2.

Row 13 S2KP–1 st. Fasten off.

Nicky's Notes
You can leave the scarf unfelted (as shown here) if you prefer.

Felting

■ Place all pieces into a pillowcase or net bag and felt (see Felting instructions on page 234), checking size of scarf occasionally to prevent over-felting.

Let dry completely.

Finishing

■ Sew roses and leaves to each end of scarf as pictured. ❖

The two-color drop-stitch textural pattern make up the trellis background. The roses and leaves are made separately and attached after the felting is done.

Damascus Dream Dress

Arabic tile patterns and desert colors will appeal to the sheik and the chic alike.

■ SKILLED KNITTER

WHAT YOU'LL NEED

- 6 (7, 8) 1¾oz/50g hanks (ea. approx 108yd/100m) of Tahki Yarns/Tahki•Stacy Charles, Inc.'s *Cotton Classic* (100% mercerized cotton) in #3226 oatmeal (A)
- 3 (3, 4) hanks in #3214 coffee (D)
- 1 hank ea. in #3559 butterscotch (B), #3358 tobacco brown (C), and #3774 pine green (E)
- Size 6 (4mm) needles
- Stitch holders
- Tapestry needle

Sizes

S (M, L)

Finished Measurements

Finished bust: 36 (40, 44)"/91.5 (101.5, 112)cm
Length: 35½"/90cm

Gauge

20 sts and 28 rows = 4"/10cm in St st.

Pattern Stitches

MOCK CABLE PATTERN

Row 1 (RS) P2, *k2, p2; rep from * to end.
Rows 2 and 4 K2, *p2, k2; rep from * to end.
Row 3 *P2, skip next st and knit the 2nd st, then knit the skipped st and slip both sts off needle; rep from * to last 2 sts, p2.

Yoke Piece (make 4)

FIRST STRIP

■ With A, cast on 14 sts.
Work in Mock Cable Pattern for 4"/10cm, ending with Row 4. Leave on needle.
Make 2 more strips – 3 strips on needle.
Joining row (RS) Working across all strips with same yarn to join, work in pattern across first strip to last 2 sts, p2tog, p2tog of second strip, work to last 2 sts, p2tog, p2tog of third strip, work to end–38 sts.

Continue in Mock Cable Pattern until piece measures 6"/15cm from
Joining row, ending with row 4.
Dividing row (RS) Work 13 sts in pattern, inc in last st, drop yarn, join second ball of yarn, inc in the first st of second strip, work pattern to last st, inc in last st, drop yarn, join third ball of yarn, inc in the first st of third strip, work pattern to end–14 sts each strip.
Work in pattern on three separate strips until pieces measure 4"/10cm from Dividing Row.
Bind off each strip separately.

Assembling Yoke

■ Arrange four Yoke Pieces into a square with the unattached strips overlapping in each corner. Weave the unattached strips over and under each other. Secure the strips in place by sewing corners of Yoke Pieces together along edges of the Strips. The open center of Yoke is neck.
Fold in half for Yoke.

Tunic Front and Back (make 2)

■ With E and using provisional method (see page 241), cast on 91 (101, 111) sts.

STRIPE SEQUENCE

■ Working in St st, work 8 rows with E, 6 rows with C, 6 rows with B, 6 rows with D.
Change to A and work for a total of 12"/30.5cm more.
Repeat Stripe Sequence.
Continue with D only for 6"/15cm.

The striking woven knit cable-bib is the perfect topper to this desert dazzler.

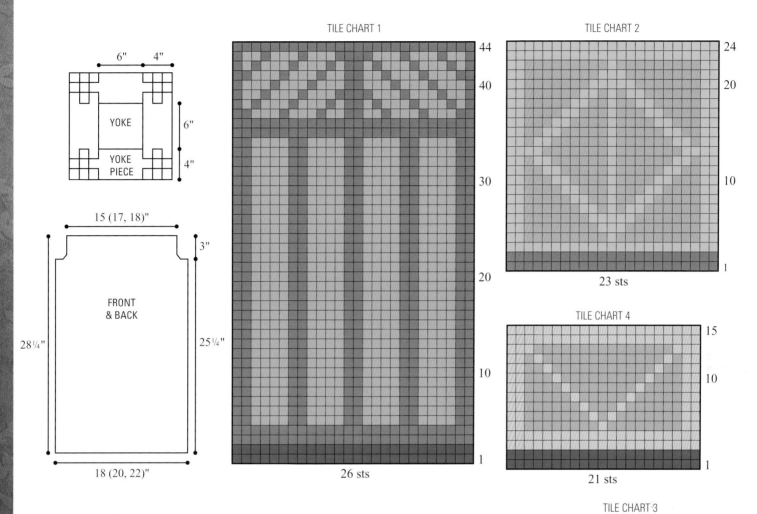

TILE CHART 1

26 sts

TILE CHART 2

23 sts

TILE CHART 4

21 sts

6"   4"

YOKE

YOKE PIECE

6"

4"

15 (17, 18)"

3"

28¼"

FRONT & BACK

25¼"

18 (20, 22)"

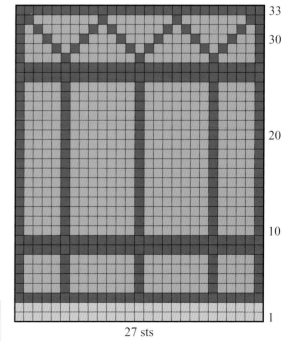

TILE CHART 3

27 sts

Shape Armhole

■ Bind off 5 sts at the beginning of next 2 rows–81 (91, 101) sts.
Dec 1 st each side every other row 3 (3, 6) times–75 (85, 89) sts.
Work until armhole measures 3"/7.5cm, ending with WS row.
Next Row (RS) Bind off 16 sts, (k2tog while continuing to bind off) 2 (5, 7) times, bind off to the last 20 (26, 30) sts, (k2tog while continuing to bind off) 2 (5, 7) times, bind off remaining 16 sts.

Finishing

■ Following Charts, duplicate stitch Tile patterns on Front piece in large section of A. Sew bound-off edge of Front and Back pieces to lower edge of Yoke.

Picot Edge

■ With RS facing and E, pick up 91 (101, 111) sts from provisional cast-on from Front.
Picot Row (RS) Bind off 2 sts, *slip remaining st back to left needle, using cable cast on (see page 236), cast on 3 sts, bind off 5 sts, repeat from * to last st, fasten off.

■ In same manner, work Picot Row across sts of Back.
Sew Front and Back together along sides.
Weave in ends. ❖

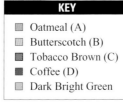

KEY

■ Oatmeal (A)
■ Butterscotch (B)
■ Tobacco Brown (C)
■ Coffee (D)
■ Dark Bright Green (E)

Señorita's Floral Pullover

The flowers from the gardens of Seville were the inspiration for this classic, and bloom anew in the dramatic, cascading ruffled collar.

■ SKILLED KNITTER

WHAT YOU'LL NEED
■ 8 1¾oz/50g balls (ea. approx 175yds/160m) of Rowan/Westminster Fibers, Inc. *Calmer* (75% cotton/25% acrylic/microfiber) in #465 onyx (A)
■ 2 balls in #492 garnet (B)
■ 1 1¾oz/50g ball (ea. approx 153yds/140m) of Rowan/Westminster Fibers, Inc. *Kid Classic* (70% lambswool/26% kid mohair/4% nylon) ea. in #847 cherry red (C) and #825 crushed velvet (D)
■ Size 8 (5mm) needles OR SIZE TO OBTAIN GAUGE
■ Size 8 (5mm) 16"/40cm circular needle
■ Stitch holders or waste yarn
■ Stitch marker
■ Tapestry needle
■ Decorative beads or buttons for flower centers (optional)

Sizes
S (M, L)

Finished Measurements
Bust: 33½ (40½, 48)"/85 (103, 122)cm
Length: 20¾ (22½, 24¼)"/52.5 (57, 61.5)cm
Lower edge circumference: 59 (66½, 73½)"/150 (169, 186.5)cm

Gauge
22 sts and 34 rows = 4"/10cm in St st with A using size 8 needles.
TAKE TIME TO CHECK GAUGE.

Back
■ With A, cast on 120 (140, 160) sts. Work in k2, p2 rib for 1"/2.5cm. Cont in St st, dec 1 st each side every 8th row 14 times—92 (112, 132) sts. Work even until piece measures 16½"/42cm from beg.

Raglan shaping
■ Bind off 5 (7, 9) sts at beg of next 2 rows—82 (98, 114) sts.
Next (dec) row (RS) K1, ssk, k to last 3 sts, k2tog, k1.
Rep dec row every other row until 48 sts rem. Place sts on holder.

Front
■ Work same as back.

Sleeves
■ With A, cast on 42 (46, 52) sts.
Row 1 (WS) P2, *k2, p2; rep from * to end.
Work in k2, p2 rib as est for 1"/2.5cm, then work in St st for 6"/15cm.
Next (inc) row (RS) K1, m1, k to last st, m1, k1—44 (48, 54) sts.
Rep inc row every 6th row 14 (15, 15) times more—72 (78, 84) sts.
Cont even in St st until sleeve measures 20"/51cm from beg.

Raglan shaping
■ Bind off 5 (7, 9) sts at beg of next 2 rows—62 (64, 66) sts.
Dec row (RS) K1, ssk, k to last 3 sts, k2tog, k1.
Work dec row every 4th row 0 (6, 11) times more, then every other row 16 (11, 7) times—28 sts rem. Work 1 (1, 5) rows st st. Place sts on holder.

Side inserts (make 2)
■ With B, cast on 42 sts.
Row 1 (WS) P2, *k2, p2; rep from * to end.
Work in k2, p2 rib as est for 1"/2.5cm, then work in St st for 1"/2.5cm. Cont in St st, dec 1 st each side every 6th row 19 times—4 sts. Work 5 rows St st.
Next (dec) row (RS) K2tog twice—2 sts.
Next (dec) row P2tog.
Fasten off.

Finishing

■ Sew raglan and sleeve seams. Sew side inserts to front and back and sew side seams.

Ribbed collar

■ With RS facing and starting with back, then sleeve, front and second sleeve, slip all sts from holders onto circular needle—152 sts. Pm at back left shoulder for end of rnd and attach A. Join to work in rnds.
Rnd 1 K1, *p2, k2; rep from *, end p2, k1.
Cont in k2, p2 rib as est for 3"/7.5cm, ending one st before end of rnd. Break off A and join C. Pm for new end of rnd.

Ruffled edging

Rnd 1 *K4, yo; rep from * to end.
Rnd 2 *K2, p3; rep from * to end.
Rnd 3 *K2, p3, yo; rep from * to end.
Rnd 4 *K2, p4; rep from * to end.
Rnd 5 *K2, p4, yo; rep from * to end.
Rnd 6 *K2, p5; rep from * to end.
Rnd 7 *K2, p5, yo; rep from * to end.
Rnd 8 *K2, p6; rep from * to end.
Bind off in pat.

Roses (make 5 with c and 8 with D)

■ With circular needles, cast on 6 sts.
Row 1 (RS) K3, yo, k3–7 sts.
Rows 2, 4, 6, 8, and 10 Knit.
Row 3 K3, yo, k4–8 sts.
Row 5 K3, yo, k5–9 sts.
Row 7 K3, yo, k6–10 sts.
Row 9 K3, yo, k7–11 sts.
Row 11 K3, yo, k8–12 sts.
Row 12 Bind off 6 sts, k to end - 6 sts.
Rep rows 1–12 four times more. Bind off leaving a long tail.
Sew cast on edge to bound-off edge. Weave tail in and out of eyelets, pull tightly to gather and secure. Using tails, tie flowers to sweater as pictured.

Scallop trim (make 2)

■ With B, cast on 156 sts (multiple of 11 sts + 2).
Row 1 (WS) Purl.
Row 2 K2, *k1 and sl back to LH needle; with RH needle, lift next 8 sts (one at a time) over this st and off needle, [yo] twice, k the slipped st again, k2; rep from * to end.
Row 3 K1, *p2tog, [k1, p1, k1, p1] in double yo, p1; rep from *, end k1 (multiple of 6 sts + 2).
Rows 4 and 5 Knit. Bind off.
Sew a strip to each side, along the front/side panel seam. ❖

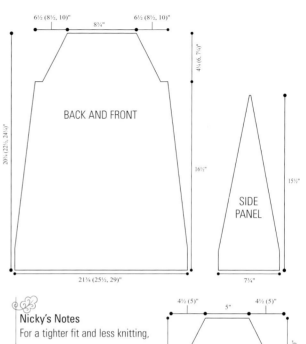

Nicky's Notes

For a tighter fit and less knitting, you can omit the side panel.

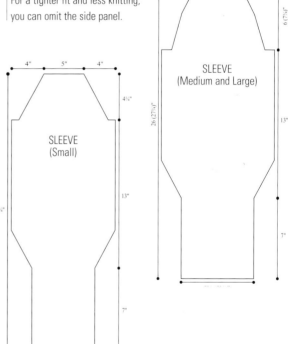

A ruffled collar, scalloped side trim, and lovely flowers combine to make any señorita spectacular!

Ottoman Empire Jacket

This jacket, with its stunning, traditional colorwork pattern, will be a sensation from Istanbul to Indianapolis.

■ MASTER KNITTER

WHAT YOU'LL NEED
- 7 (8, 8) 1¾oz/50g skeins (ea. approx 93yd/85m) of Nashua Handknits/Westminster Fibers, Inc. *Julia* (50% wool/25% mohair/25% alpaca) in #6396 deep blue sea (A) 1 skein ea. in #1220 tarnished brass (B), #1590 marine seas (C), #178 harvest spice (D), #4345 coleus (E), #2230 rock henna (F) #5185 spring green (G), #6086 velvet moss (H) and 3983 delphinium (J)
- Size 7 (4.5mm) needles
- Size 7 (4.5mm) double-pointed needles
- Size 6 (4mm) needles
- Stitch holders
- Cable needle
- Tapestry needle

Sizes
S (M, L)

Finished Measurements
Bust: 40 (44, 47)"/101.5 (111.5, 119.5)cm
Length: 18 (19, 20)"/45 (48 51)cm

Gauge
28 sts and 24 rows = 4"/10cm in Chart 1 on larger needles.
20 sts and 24 rows = 4"/10cm in Rev St st on larger needles.
22 sts and 24 rows = 4"/10cm in Chart 2 on larger needles.
TAKE TIME TO CHECK GAUGE.

Pattern Stitches
- *3-st LPC* Slip 2 sts to cable needle and hold in front, p1, k2 from cable needle.
- *3-st RPC* Slip 1 st to cable needle and hold in back, k2, p1 from cable needle.

Back
■ With smaller needles and A, cast on 93 (103, 115) sts. Work in k1, p1 rib for 1"/2.5cm, ending with RS row.
Next row (WS) Change to larger needles. Purl across, inc 22 sts evenly spaced–115 (125, 137) sts.

BEGIN CHART 1
NOTE: Chart 1 is begun on different rows at center of back to give a mirror image of chart.
■ *Row 1* (RS) P1 (6, 1) sts, beginning with Row 1, repeat 11 sts of Chart 1 for 5 (5, 6) times, beginning with Row 9, repeat 11 sts of Chart 1 for 5 (5, 6) times, k3, p1 (6, 1).
Continue to work in Chart as established keeping first and last 1 (6, 1) sts in Rev St st, inc 1 st each edge every 4th row once, then every 6th row 5 times, then every

4th row 3 times, working new sts in Rev St st–133 (143, 155) sts.
Work in Chart 1 as established until piece measures 10"/25.5cm from beg, ending with WS row.

Shape Armhole
■ Bind off 5 sts at beg of next 2 rows–123 (133, 145) sts.
Dec 1 st each edge every row 1 (4, 1) times, then every other row 2 (4, 2) times, then every 4th row twice–113 (113, 135) sts.
Continue to work in Chart 1 as established until piece measures 7 (8, 9)"/18 (20.5, 23)cm from beg of armhole shaping, ending with WS row.

Shape Neck and Shoulders
■ Bind off 11 (11, 14) sts at beg of next 6 rows–47 (47, 51) sts.
Bind off, dec 8 sts evenly spaced across.

Left Front
■ With smaller needles and A, cast on 59 (64, 70) sts. Work in k1, p1 rib for 1"/2.5cm, ending with RS row.
Next row (WS) Work in k1, p1 rib on first 6 sts and slip to stitch holder for Front Band, purl across remaining sts, inc 6 sts evenly spaced–59 (64, 70) sts.

BEGIN CHART 1
Row 1 (RS) Change to larger needles. P1 (6, 1) sts, beginning with Row 1, repeat 11 sts of Chart 1 for 5 (5, 6) times, k3.
Continue to work in Chart as established keeping first 1 (6, 1) sts in Rev St st, inc 1 st at beg of RS row every 4th row once, then every 6th row 5 times, then every 4th row 3 times, working new sts in Rev St st–68 (73, 79) sts.
Work in Chart 1 as established until piece measures 10"/25.5cm from beg, ending with WS row.

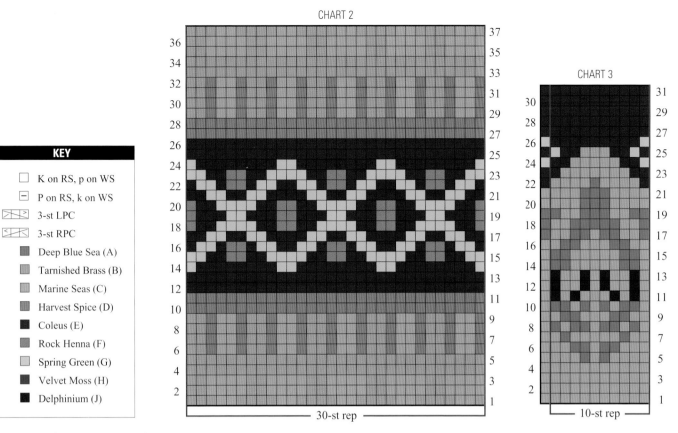

CHART 2

CHART 3

KEY

- □ K on RS, p on WS
- − P on RS, k on WS
- ⊠ 3-st LPC
- ⊠ 3-st RPC
- Deep Blue Sea (A)
- Tarnished Brass (B)
- Marine Seas (C)
- Harvest Spice (D)
- Coleus (E)
- Rock Henna (F)
- Spring Green (G)
- Velvet Moss (H)
- Delphinium (J)

30-st rep

10-st rep

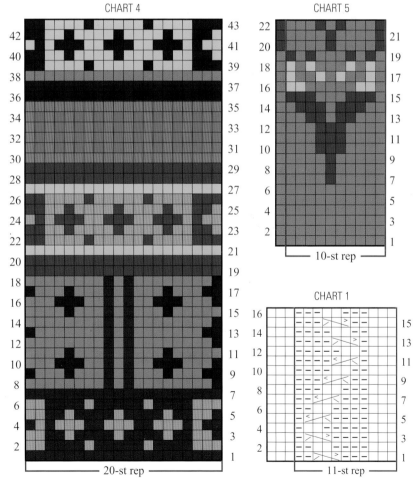

CHART 4

CHART 5

CHART 1

20-st rep

10-st rep

11-st rep

Shape Armhole and V-Neck

■ Bind off 5 sts, then dec 1 st at beg of RS rows every row 1 (4, 1) times, then every other row 2 (4, 2) times, then every 4th row twice.

At Same Time, dec 1 st at neck edge every row 10 (6, 4) times, then every other row 15 (19, 23) times—33 (33, 42) sts.

Continue to work in Chart 1 as established until piece measures 7 (8, 9)"/18 (20.5, 23)cm from beg of armhole shaping, ending with WS row.

Shape Shoulder

■ Bind off 11 (11, 14) sts at beg of next 3 rows.

RIGHT FRONT

■ With smaller needles and A, cast on 59 (64, 70) sts. Work in k1, p1 rib for 1"/2.5cm, ending with RS row.

Next row (WS) Work k1, p1 rib over next 53 (58, 64) sts, and inc 6 sts evenly spaced, then slip last 6 sts to st holder for Front Band—59 (64, 70) sts.

BEGIN CHART 1

Row 1 (RS) Change to larger needles. Beginning with Row 9, repeat 11 sts of Chart 1 for 5 (5, 6) times, k3, p1 (6, 1) sts.

Work as for Left Front reversing side and neck shaping.

Sleeves

BAND

■ With larger needles, cast on 12 sts.

BEGIN CHART 1

Row 1 (RS) Beginning with Row 1, work 11 sts of Chart 1, p1.

Continue to work Chart 1 as established until Band measures 8 (8, 10)"/20.5 (20.5, 25.5)cm from beg.

Bind off.

Sleeve

■ With RS facing, pick up and knit 50 (50, 60) sts along k3 edge.

Purl 1 row.
Knit 1 row, inc 20 (20, 30) sts evenly spaced across row–70 (70, 90) sts.
Purl 1 row.
Knit 1 row, inc 20 (20, 30) sts evenly spaced across row–90 (90, 120) sts.
Purl 1 row.

CHART 2
■ *Row 1* (RS) Beginning with Row 1, repeat 30 sts of Chart 2 across row.
Continue to work Chart 2 for 37 rows.

CHART 3
■ *Row 1* (WS) Beginning with Row 1, repeat 10 sts of Chart 3 across row.
Continue to work Chart 3 for 31 rows, dec 10 (10, 20) sts evenly spaced across
last row–80 (80, 100) sts.

CHART 4
■ *Row 1* (RS) Beginning with Row 1, repeat 20 sts of Chart 4 across row.
Continue to work Chart 4 for 19 rows.
Row 20 Work Row 20, dec 20 sts evenly space across row–60 (60, 80) sts.
Work Chart 4 through Row 28.

Shape Armhole
■ Bind off 5 sts at beg of next 2 rows–50 (50, 70) sts.
Dec 1 st each edge every other row 5 times–40 (40, 60) sts.
Continue to work Chart 4 until Row 43.

CHART V
■ Row 1 (WS) Beginning with Row 1, repeat 10 sts of Chart V across row.
Continue to work Chart V until piece measures 5 (6, 7)"/12.5 (15, 17.5)cm from
beg of armhole shaping, working with F only when Chart V is complete.

SHAPE CAP
■ Bind off 1 (1, 3) sts at beg of next 4 rows, then 2 (2, 4) sts at beg of next 6 rows,
then 4 sts at beg of next 6 rows. Fasten off.

Finishing
■ Sew shoulder seams.

Left Front Band and Collar
■ With RS facing and smaller needles, slip 6 sts from stitch holder and work in k1,
p1 rib until band, slightly stretched, fits to beg of neck shaping, ending with WS row.
Sew in place while knitting.

Shape Collar
■ *Next row* (RS) Inc 1 st, cont in k1 p1 rib to end of row-7 sts.
Cont to inc at neck edge every row 47 times more–54 sts.
Continue to work in k1, p1 rib until Collar fits to center of Back neck.
Bind off.
Place markers for 5 buttons evenly spaced on Band, from lower edge to
beg of neck shaping.

Right Front Band and Collar
■ Work as for Left Front Band and Collar, reversing Collar shaping and working
buttonholes opposite button markers as follows:
■ *Buttonhole row* (RS) Work 2 sts in k1, p1 rib, yo, k2tog , work 2 sts in k1, p1 rib.

■ Sew Collar pieces together at center of Back neck. Fit and sew Collar around neck.
Sew in Sleeves. Sew side and Sleeve seams. Weave in ends. Sew on buttons. ❖

Turkish Delight Buttons
(make 1 each with B, C, D, G and J)
■ With double-pointed needles, cast on 5
sts. Work in I-Cord (see page 240) for 18
rows. K2tog, k1, k2tog. P3tog. Fasten off.

■ Tie I-Cord into a square knot.
Pull cast-on tail to back, then bound-off tail
to back, one row below.

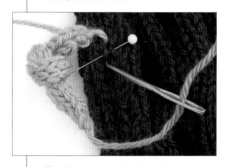

■ Tie tails together at back, pull to
front through center of button and cut as
shown to hide tails.

■ Snip off the excess yarn and you're done!

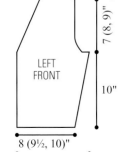

7"   4½ (4½, 6)"
18 (19, 20)"
BACK
1"
7 (8, 9)"
10"
16 (18, 19)"
20 (22, 23)"

7½ (8½, 9½)"
SLEEVE
17"
2"
11 (11, 14½)"
16 (16, 22)"
8 (8, 10)"

4½ (4½, 6)"
3½"
LEFT FRONT
1"
7 (8, 9)"
10"
8 (9½, 10)"
10 (11, 12)"

El Matador Jacket

Ole! The crowds will cheer you and throw roses at your feet in this stunning jacket.

■ SKILLED KNITTER

WHAT YOU'LL NEED
■ 12 (14, 15) 1¾oz/50g balls (ea. approx 109yd/100m) of Knit One, Crochet Too, Inc.'s *Camelino* (90% merino wool/10% camel) in #256 lipstick
■ Size 7 (4.5mm) needles, 1 pair plus 1 spare needle.
■ Size 7 (4.5mm) double-pointed needles
■ Tapestry needle
■ One large hook-and-eye closure

Sizes
S (M, L)

Finished Measurements
Bust: 31 (35, 37)"/78.5 (89, 94.5)cm
Length: 21 (21½, 22)"/53.5 (54.5, 56)cm

Gauge
24 sts and 24 rows = 4"/10cm in Pat St. TAKE TIME TO CHECK GAUGE.

Pattern Stitches
Slip Stitch Scallop (multiple of 6 sts + 5 extra)
Row 1 (RS) *(K1, p1) twice, k1, slip 1; rep from * to last 5 sts, (k1, p1) twice, k1.
Row 2 *(P1, k1) twice, p1, slip 1; rep from * to last 5 sts, (p1, k1) twice, p1.
Rows 3–6 Repeat Rows 1-2.
Work Rows 1-6 for Slip Stitch Scallop.

Vertical Bar Pattern Stitch (multiple of 4 sts + 1 extra)
Rows 1, 3 and 5 (RS) K1, *p3, k1; rep from * to end.
Rows 2, 4 and 6 P1, *k3, p1; rep from * to end.
Rows 7, 9 and 11 P2, k1, *p3, k1; rep from * to last 2 sts, p2.
Rows 8, 10 and 12 K2, p1, *k3, p1; rep from * to last 2 sts, k2.
Repeat Rows 1–12 for Vertical Bar Pat st.

Back
FIRST SCALLOP
■ Cast on 95 (101, 107) sts.
Work 6 rows in Slip St Scallop. Change to k1, p1 rib and work until piece measures 4"/10cm from beginning, ending with WS row. Leave sts aside on a spare needle.

SECOND SCALLOP
■ Cast on 95 (101, 107) sts. Work as for First Scallop until piece measures 2"/5cm from beginning, ending with WS row.

■ *Joining row* (RS) With RS facing, position needle with Second Scallop sts in front of sts on spare needle. *Working in rib as established, work together 1 st from left-hand needle with next st on spare needle; rep from * across row to join pieces – 95 (101, 107) sts.
Continue in k1, p1 rib until piece measures 6"/15cm from beginning of first scallop, dec 2 (0, 2) sts across last WS row – 93 (101, 105) sts.

■ Work in Vertical Bar Pattern St until piece measures 13"/33cm from beginning, ending with WS row.

Shape Armhole
■ Bind off 5 sts at beginning of next 2 rows – 83 (91, 95) sts.
Dec 1 st each edge every other row 7 times – 69 (77, 81) sts.
Continue until armhole measures 7 (7½, 8)"/18 (19, 20.5)cm from beginning, ending with WS row.

Shape Shoulders
■ Bind off 7 (8, 9) at beginning of next 4 rows, then 7 (9, 9) sts at beginning of next 2 rows – 27 sts.
Bind off.

Left Front
■ Cast on 47 (53, 59) sts.
Work 6 rows in Slip St Scallop. Change to k1, p1 rib and work until piece measures 4"/10cm from beginning, ending with WS row. Leave sts aside on a spare needle.

SECOND SCALLOP
■ Cast on 47 (53, 59) sts. Work as for First Scallop until piece measures 2"/5cm from beginning, ending with a WS row.

■ *Joining row* (RS) With RS facing, position needle with Second Scallop sts in front of sts on spare needle. *Working in rib as established, work together 1 st from left-hand needle with next st on spare needle; rep from * across row to join pieces – 47 (53, 59) sts.
Continue in k1, p1 rib until piece measures 6"/15cm from beginning of first

Inspired by...

Like the Matador's suit of lights, I wanted an impressive shoulder detail. I spiraled I-cord and attached one of my favorites of embellishments: clustered corkscrews.

pin available at nickyepstein.com

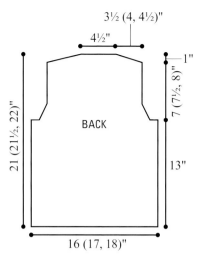

3½ (4, 4½)"

4½"

1"

7 (7½, 8)"

BACK

21 (21½, 22)"

13"

16 (17, 18)"

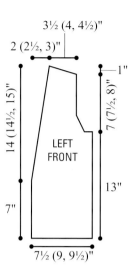

3½ (4, 4½)"

2 (2½, 3)"

1"

7 (7½, 8)"

14 (14½, 15)"

LEFT FRONT

13"

7"

7½ (9, 9½)"

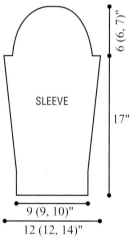

6 (6, 7)"

SLEEVE

17"

9 (9, 10)"

12 (12, 14)"

scallop, dec 2 (0, 2) sts across last WS row — 45 (53, 57) sts.

■ Work in Vertical Bar Pattern St for 1"/2.5cm, ending with a WS row.

V-NECK SHAPING

■ Continue to work in Pattern St, dec 1 st at the end of RS rows every 4th row 0 (8, 10) times then every 6th row 12 (8, 8) times.

At Same Time, work until piece measures 13"/33cm from beginning, ending with RS row to begin armhole shaping.

ARMHOLE SHAPING

■ Bind off 5 sts, then dec 1 st at side edge every other row 7 times.

When all shaping is finished, continue to work on 21 (25, 27) sts until armhole measures 7 (7-1/2, 8)"/18 (19, 20.5)cm from beginning, ending with WS row.

SHOULDER SHAPING

■ Bind off 7 (8, 9) at beginning of RS row twice, then 7 (9, 9) sts once.

RIGHT FRONT

■ Work as for Left Front reversing shaping.

Sleeves

■ Cast on 53 (53, 59) sts.

Work 6 rows of Slip Stitch Scallop. Continue in k1, p1 rib until piece measures 3"/7.5cm from beginning, dec 0 (0, 2) sts across last WS row — 53 (53, 57) sts.

■ Work in Vertical Bar Pattern St, inc 1 st each edge (working inc sts into pat) every 6th row 11 (11, 14) times — 75 (75, 85) sts. Continue to work until piece measures 17"/43cm from beginning, ending with a WS row.

CAP SHAPING

■ Bind off 5 sts at beginning of next 2 rows—65 (65, 75) sts.

Dec 1 st each edge every other row 12 times every row 5 (5, 10) times—31 sts.

Bind of 4 sts at beginning of next 4 rows.

Bind off 15 sts.

Finishing

■ Sew shoulder seams. Sew in Sleeves.

Sew side and sleeve seams.

Neck Trim

■ With double-pointed needles and holding

2 strands of yarn together, cast on 5 sts.

■ Work I-cord (see page 240) over 5 sts for 33 (34, 35)"/84 (86.5, 89)cm.

Bind off.

Arrange and sew I-cord around neckline beginning and ending at beginning of Pattern St.

■ Sew Hook and Eye closure to Front at beginning of Neck Trim. Weave in ends.

Epaulets (make 2)

■ With double-pointed needles and holding 2 strands of yarn together, cast on 5 sts.

Work I-cord over 5 sts for 28"/71cm. Bind off.

Arrange and sew I-cord into a spiral to make an oval, 5"/12.5cm long.

Corkscrew Trim (make 20)

■ With two needles held together, cast on 30 sts very loosely. Remove one needle.

Row 1 (K into front, back and front again) in each st across.

Bind off purlwise.

Use fingers to twist into corkscrew shape. (See page 243 for tutorial)

■ Sew one Epaulet to each shoulder. Arrange and sew 10 Corkscrew Trims to the end of each Epaulet, allowing Corkscrews to cascade over shoulder. ❖

Nicky's Notes
The unusual scallop 1 x 1 l rib is not original to this sweater. I created it from my *Knitting On the Edge* book.

Lisbon Lace Jacket

Inspired by the lovely, traditional Portuguese lace cutwork tablecloths, this jacket wants to be taken to dinner.

■ SKILLED KNITTER

WHAT YOU'LL NEED
- 13 1¾oz/50g skeins (ea. approx 112yds/102m) of Nashua Handknits/Westminster Fibers, Inc.'s *Desert Flower* (50% cotton/43% linen/7% nylon) in #3568 dove
- Size 7 (4.5mm) needles
- Tapestry needle
- large hook and eye
- 1 pkg (ea. approx 25yds/22m) of 3mm Rainbow Elastic in #122 mushroom

One Size
Adult Woman's

Finished Measurements
Bust: 43"/109cm
Length: 22"/56cm

Gauge
18 sts and 26 rows = 4"/10cm in St st. TAKE TIME TO CHECK GAUGE.

Cable Rib Pattern (Multiple of 4 sts + 2)
Row 1 (RS) P2, *k2, p2; rep from * to end.
Row 2 K2, *p2, k2; rep from * to end.
Row 3 *P2, skip the first st and k the 2nd st, then knit the first st, slipping both sts off needle, p2; rep from * to end.
Row 4 Rep row 2.
Rep rows 1-4.

Neckband
■ Cast on 106 sts. Work 12 rows in Cable rib, dec 2 sts on last row–104 sts. Do not fasten off. Turn.

Yoke Leaves
Row 1 (RS) *K6, yo, k1, yo, k6. Turn, leaving rem sts to be worked later–15 sts.
Row 2 and all WS rows Purl.
Row 3 K7, yo, k1, yo, k7–17 sts.

Row 5 K8, yo, k1, yo, k8–19 sts.
Rows 7, 9, 11, 13 Knit.
Rows 15, 17, 19, 21, 23, 25 and 27 K1, ssk, k to last 3 sts, k2tog, k1–5 sts after row 27.
Row 29 Ssk, k1, k2tog–3 sts.
Row 30 Sl 1, p2tog, psso. Fasten off.
Attach yarn to next st in neckband and rep from * 7 times more–8 leaves.

5-Scallop Flower (make 67; 3"/7.5cm diameter)
■ Cast on 57 sts, leaving an 8"/20cm tail.
Row 1 (WS) Purl.
Row 2 K2, *k1 and sl back to LH needle; with RH needle, lift next 8 sts (one at a time) over this st and off needle, [yo] twice, k the slipped st again, k2; rep from * to end.
Row 3 K1, *p2tog, [k1, p1, k1, p1] in double yo, p1; rep from *, end k1.
Row 4 Knit.
Row 5 *K2tog; rep from * to end.
Row 6 *K2tog; rep from * to end.
Thread tail through rem 8 sts, draw up tight to gather and fasten securely. Sew seam and weave in ends.

Lady's Lace Flower (make 26; 4"/10cm diameter)
■ Cast on 49 sts.
Row 1 (WS) Purl.
Row 2 K1, *yo, k1, sk2p, k1, yo, k1; rep from * to end.
Rows 3-8 Rep rows 1 and 2.
Row 9 Purl.

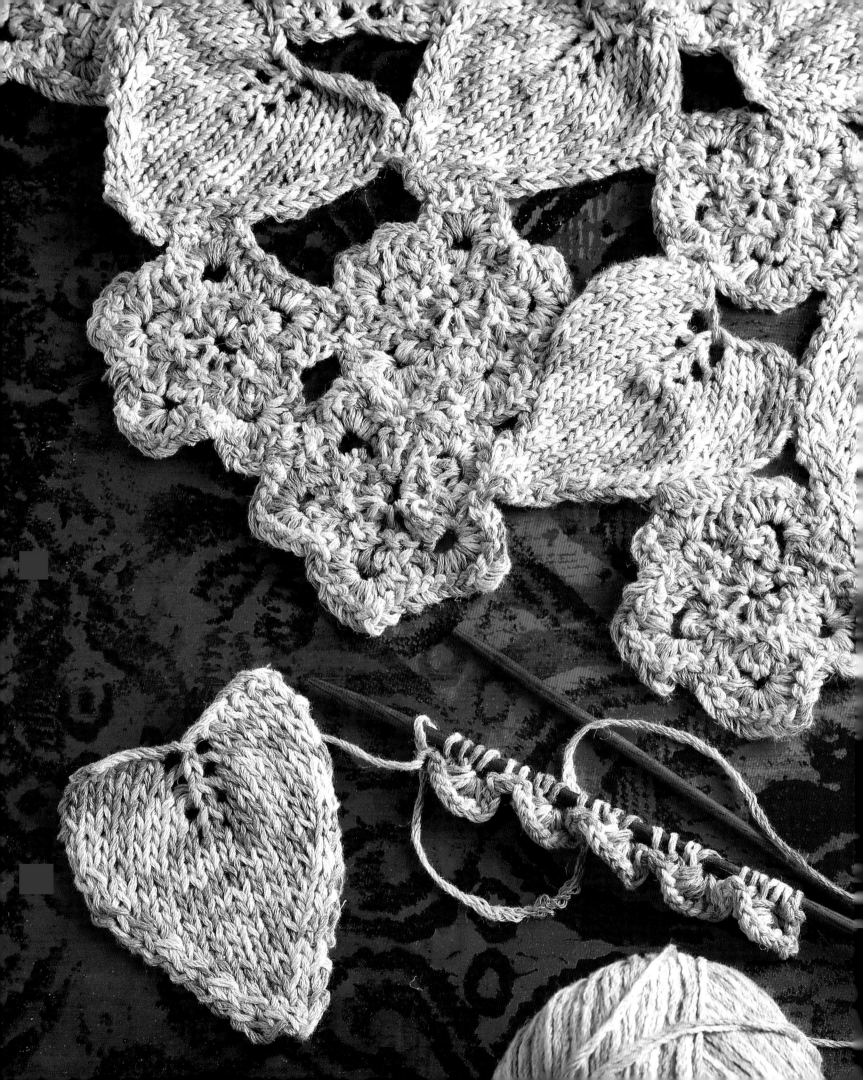

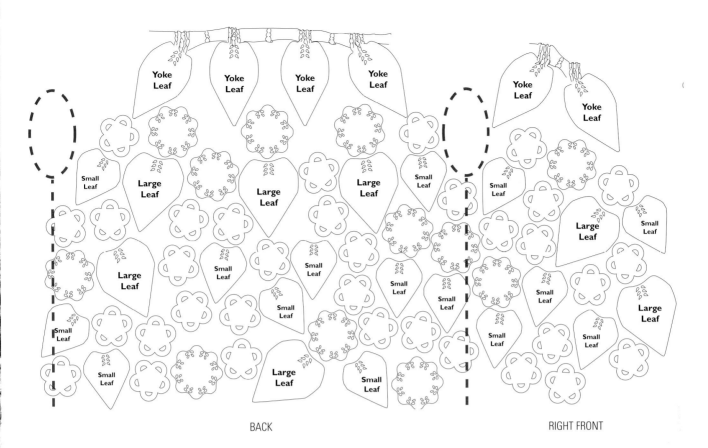

BACK

RIGHT FRONT

Row 10 *P2tog; rep from *, end p1—25 sts.
Row 11 *K2tog; rep from *, end k1—13 sts.
Thread tail through rem sts, draw up tight to gather and fasten securely.
Sew seam and weave in ends. (from *Nicky Epstein's Knitted Flowers,* pg 52)

Large Leaves (make 11; 4"L x 3½"W/10cm x 9cm)
■ Cast on 13 sts. Work rows 1-12 of yoke leaves, then rows 15-30.

Small Leaves (make 32; 3"L x 3¼"/7.5cm x 9.5cm)
■ Cast on 11 sts.
Row 1 (RS) K5, yo, k1, yo, k 5—13 sts.
Row 2 and all WS rows Purl.
Row 3 K6, yo, k1, yo, k6—15 sts.
Row 5 K7, yo, k1, yo, k7—17 sts.
Rows 7, 9, 11, 13, 15 and 17 K1, ssk, k to last 3 sts, k2tog, k1—5 sts.
Row 19 Ssk, k1, k2tog—3 sts.
Row 20 Sl l, p2tog, psso. Fasten off.

Finishing
■ Press all pieces. Position flowers and leaves referring to diagrams
(reversing placement of motifs on right front for left front and on left sleeve
for right sleeve) and sew in place at each point where motifs touch.
Fold sleeve in half over a piece of cardboard (for easier seaming) and sew
flowers together to close sleeves.

■ With 2 strands of elastic held together, thread across WS of top and bottom
of neckband to desired neck size. Sew hook and eye to center of cable rib,
or use your favorite pin as a closure. ❖❖

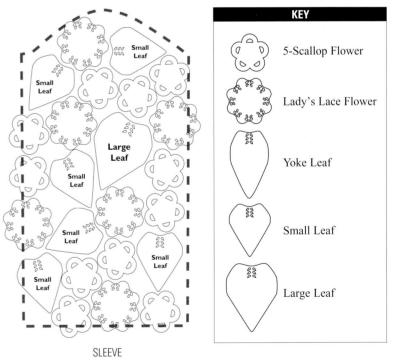

SLEEVE

KEY	
	5-Scallop Flower
	Lady's Lace Flower
	Yoke Leaf
	Small Leaf
	Large Leaf

This jacket is worked freeform by sewing knit flowers
and leaves together following the diagram.

Isis Tunic

This lovely creation would make the Sphinx blink and King Tut rise from his sarcophagus.

■ NOVICE KNITTER

WHAT YOU'LL NEED
- 6 1¾oz/50g hanks (ea. approx 77yds/71m) of Berroco Inc.'s *Bonsai* (97% bamboo/3% nylon) in #4143 kin gold (A)
- 1 hank ea. in #4121 raku brown (B), #4141 japanese maple (C) and #4148 sora blue (D)
- One pair size 7 (4.5mm) needles OR SIZE TO OBTAIN GAUGE
- Two size 7 dpn needles (for I-cord)
- Tapestry needle
- Stitch markers
- Sewing needle and matching thread

Sizes
S (M, L)

Finished Measurements
Bust: 35 (40, 44)"/99 (101.5, 111.5)cm
Length: 27 (27½, 28)"/68.5 (70, 71)cm

Gauge
22 sts and 30 rows = 4"/10cm in St st.
TAKE TIME TO CHECK GAUGE.

NOTES
- Garment is worked in one piece from lower edge of front to lower edge of back.
- Use the knitted on cast-on when casting on for back.

Front
■ With A, cast on 68 (82, 94) sts. Work in St st until front measures 12½"/32cm from beg, ending with a WS row. Work 14 rows B, 14 rows D, 14 rows C and 10 rows A. Mark center 32 (34, 36) sts.
Next row (RS) Bind off 0 (6, 11) sts, k to first marker and place these 18 sts on a holder, bind off center 32 (34, 36) sts, knit until there are 18 sts after bind-off and place these sts on a holder, bind off rem 0 (6, 11) sts. Place marker each end of last row.

Shoulder straps
■ *Place 6 sts from holder onto needle (12 sts remain on holder). Join yarn and work in St st for 20 (21, 22)"/51 (53.5, 56)cm. Rep 2 more times. Place marker each end of last row. Work second shoulder strap the same. Braid each side, keeping strips as flat as possible with RS of each strip facing at all times. Place each 18-st braid onto needle.

Back
■ Cast on 0 (6, 11) sts, with RS facing, k18 sts of first braid, cast on 32 (34, 36) sts, k18 sts of 2nd braid, cast on 0 (6, 11) sts–68 (82, 94) sts. Cont in St st same as front, working color pat in reverse. When back measures same as front, ending with a WS row. Bind off.

Side panels (make 2)
■ With A, cast on 37 sts.
Rows 1 and 3 (WS) K2, *p3, k2; rep from * to end.
Row 2 P2, *3-st RT (sl 2 sts to cn and hold to back, k1, k2 from cn), p2; rep from * to end.
Row 4 P2, *k3, p2; rep from * to end.
Rep rows 1-4 until panel measures 7 (7¾, 8½)"/17.5 (19.5, 21.5)cm from beg. Bind off.

Embroidery
■ Using duplicate stitch (see page 238), embroider hieroglyphics motifs following charts in striped section of front as pictured.

Finishing

■ Sew sides of cable panel to sides of front and back, matching the top edge of panel to markers, and sew along cable panel length. With RS facing, curve shoulder strap braid in half at top shoulder and sew 2½"/6.5cm center seam.

Edging (make 2)

■ With A, cast on 5 sts and work 8 rows I-cord (see page 240). Cont in I-cord, work 8 rows of each color until cord measures approx 39 (41, 43)"/99 (104, 109)cm. Place sts on holder. Using sewing needle and thread, beg at cast-on end, sew cord along edges of front from bottom of cable panel on one side to the other. Add or remove rows on cord as needed to fit. Bind off and sew ends to cable panels. Repeat for back. ❖❖

KEY	
☐	Background
▨	A
■	B
▨	C
▨	D

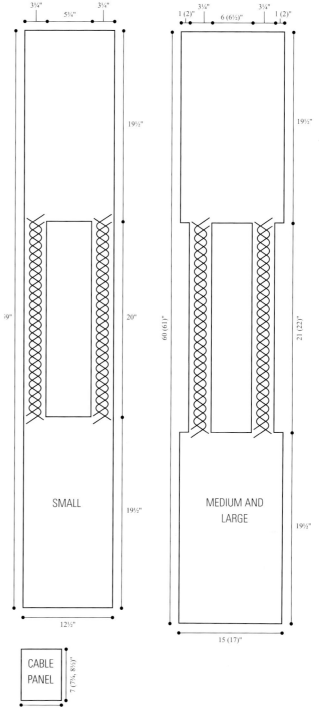

SMALL

MEDIUM AND LARGE

CABLE PANEL

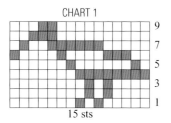
CHART 1
15 sts

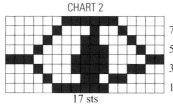
CHART 2
17 sts

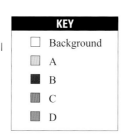
CHART 3
17 sts

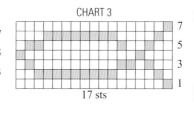

Inspired by...

The pictorial symbols used in the hieroglyphics of ancient Egypt were the genesis for this trio of simple yet evocative, duplicate-stitch motifs.

Braided cord straps and Egyptian-inspired I-cord color striping are a dramatic backdrop for the hieroglyphs.

Greco Mosaic Bags

From the land of Olympus, these bags would provoke the envy of the gods (or at least your office mates).

■ NOVICE KNITTER

Size
Approx 9"W x 7½"H/23cm x 19cm

Gauge
17 sts and 30 rows = 4"/10cm in Lucky Diamonds pattern. TAKE TIME TO CHECK GAUGE.

Mosaic stitch patterns
NOTE: Sl sts wyib on RS rows, and sl sts wyif on WS rows.

Version A
Lucky Diamonds
COLORS A (light) and B (dark)
(Multiple of 16 sts plus 3)
■ *Preparation row* (WS) With A, knit.
Row 1 With B, [k1, sl 1] 3 times, k7, *sl 1, [k1, sl 1] 4 times, k7; rep from *, end [sl 1, k1] 3 times.
Row 2 and all WS rows With same color as previous row, k all sts worked and sl all sl-sts.
Row 3 With A, k6, sl 1, [k1, sl 1] 3 times, *k9, sl 1, [k1, sl 1] 3 times; rep from * , end k6.
Row 5 With B, [k1, sl 1] twice, k5, sl 1, k5, *sl 1, [k1, sl 1] twice, k5, sl 1, k5; rep from *, end [sl 1, k1] twice.
Row 7 With A, k4, sl 1, k1, sl 1, *k5, sl 1, k1, sl 1; rep from *, end k4.
Row 9 With B, k1, sl 1, *k5, sl 1, [k1, sl 1] twice, k5, sl 1; rep from *, end k1.
Row 11 With A, k2, sl 1, k1, sl 1, k9, *sl 1, [k1, sl 1] 3 times, k9; rep from *, end sl 1, k1, sl 1, k2.
Row 13 With B, k5, sl 1, [k1, sl 1] 4 times, *k7, sl 1, [k1, sl 1] 4 times; rep from *, end k5.
Row 15 With A, k2, sl 1, k13, *sl 1, k1, sl 1, k13; rep from *, end sl 1, k2.
Row 17 Rep row 13.
Row 19 Rep row 11.
Row 21 Rep row 9.
Row 23 Rep row 7.
Row 25 Rep row 5.
Row 27 Rep row 3.
Row 28 See row 2.
Rep rows 1-28.

Chevron Chic
COLORS A (light) and B (dark) (Multiple of 24 sts plus 2)
■ *Preparation row* (WS) With A, purl.
Row 1 With B, k1, *sl 1, k2; rep from *, end k1.
Row 2 and all WS rows With same color as previous row, k1, p all sts worked and sl all sl-sts to last st, k1.
Row 3 With A, k1, *k1, sl 1, [k2, sl 1] 3 times, k3, [sl 1, k2] 3 times, sl 1; rep from *, end k1.
Row 5 With B, k1, *k2, [sl 1, k2] 3 times, sl 1, k1, sl 1, [k2, sl 1] 3 times, k1; rep from *, end k1.
Row 7 With A, rep row 1.
Row 9 With B, rep row 3.
Row 11 With A, rep row 5.
Row 12 See row 2.
Rep rows 1-12.

BACK AND FLAP
■ With A, cast on 35 sts. Work rows 1-28 of Lucky diamonds pat 3 times. Bind off with A.

FRONT
■ With A, cast on 26 sts. Work rows 1-12 of Chevron chic pat 4 times. Bind off with A.

Finishing
ASSEMBLY

Rows 15, 17, 19, 21, 23 and 25 Rep rows 11, 9, 7, 5, 3 and 1.
Rows 27 and 28 With B, knit.
Row 29 With A, k1, *sl 1, k1; rep from * to end.
Row 31 With B, k8, *sl 1, k15; rep from *, end last rep k8.
Row 33 With A, k2, *[sl 1, k1] twice, sl 1, k3; rep from *, end last rep k2.
Row 35 With B, k7, *sl 3, k13; rep from *, end last rep k7.
Row 37 With A, k4, *sl 1, k7; rep from *, end last rep k4.
Row 39 With B, k5, *sl 1, k1, sl 3, k1, sl 1, k9; rep from *, end last rep k5.
Rows 41-51 Rep rows 37, 35, 33, 31, 29 and 27.
Row 52 With B, knit.
Rep rows 1-52.

Magic Diamond
■ COLORS A (light) and B (dark) (Multiple of 4 sts plus 3)
Rows 1 and 2 With A, knit.
Row 3 (RS) With B, k3, *sl 1, k3; rep from * to end.
Row 4 and all WS rows With same color as previous row, k all sts worked and sl all sl-sts.
Row 5 With A, k1, *sl 1, k3; rep from *, end last rep sl 1, k1.
Row 7 With B, k2, *sl 1, k1; rep from *, end k1.
Row 9 With A, rep row 3.
Row 11 With B, rep row 5.
Rows 13 and 14 With A, knit.
Row 15 With B, rep row 5.
Row 17 With A, rep row 3.
Row 19 With B, rep row 7.
Row 21 With A, rep row 5.
Row 23 With B, rep row 3.
Row 24 See row 4.
Rep rows 1-24.

{ **Inspired by...**
The colors and patterns here remind me of the classic blue and white of the Agean Sea and the whitewashed, cliff-side buildings on the coast.

Back and flap
■ With A, cast on 33 sts. Work rows 1-52 of Assyrian Stripe pat, then work rows 1-26 once more. Bind off with A.

Front
■ With A, cast on 27 sts. Work rows 1-24 of Magic Diamond pat twice, then work rows 1-14 once more. Bind off with A.

Finishing
ASSEMBLY
■ With WS tog, place front piece sideways on top of back piece. Join B to top edge of front at right corner. Using crochet hook, single crochet evenly around through both layers to join, working 3 sc at each lower corner.

FLAP EMBELLISHMENT
■ With dpns and B, cast on 5 sts. Work I-cord for 6"/15cm. Bind off.
Starting with bound-off end, roll cord into a spiral leaving 1½"/4cm free. Sew to secure and sew to center edge of flap.

SHOULDER STRAP
■ With dpns and B, cast on 5 sts. Work I-cord for 48 (60)"/122 (152.5)cm. Bind off.
■ Sew one end of cord to top edge of side seam. Make 13 knots evenly spaced along length of cord. Sew end to other side seam.

LINING
■ Press ½"/1.5cm of each short end of fabric to WS. Fold fabric in half with RS together and sew ¼"/.5cm side seams. Insert lining into bag with WS together.

■ With WS tog, place front piece sideways on top of back piece. Join B to top edge of front at right corner. Using crochet hook, single crochet evenly around through both layers to join, working 3 sc at each lower corner.

FLAP EMBELLISHMENT
■ With dpns and B, cast on 5 sts. Work I-cord for 3½"/9cm. Bind off. Make a knot at center of cord and sew to center edge of flap.

SHOULDER STRAP
■ With dpns and B, cast on 5 sts. Work I-cord (see page 240) for 48 (60)"/122 (152.5)cm. Bind off.
■ Match halfway point of cord with center bottom edge of bag. Sew cord around lower edges of bag. Make 7 knots evenly spaced along each end of cord. Make a double-knot with ends to join.

LINING
■ Press ½"/1.5cm of each short end of fabric to WS. Fold fabric in half with RS together and sew ¼"/.5cm side seams. Insert lining into bag with WS together. Using whipstitch, sew top edge of lining in place.

Version B
Assyrian Stripe
■ COLORS A (light) and B (dark) (Multiple of 16 sts plus 1)
Rows 1 and 2 With A, knit.
Row 3 (RS) With B, k1, *sl 1, k1; rep from * to end.
Row 4 and all WS rows With same color as previous row, k all sts worked and sl all sl-sts.
Row 5 With A, k8, *sl 1, k15; rep from *, end last rep k8.
Row 7 With B, k2, *[sl 1, k1] twice, sl 1, k3; rep from *, end last rep k2.
Row 9 With A, k7, *sl 3, k13; rep from *, end last rep k7.
Row 11 With B, k4, *sl 1, k7; rep from *, end last rep k4.
Row 13 With A, k5, *sl 1, k1, sl 3, k1, sl 1, k9; rep from *, end last rep k5.

FAR EAST

Japan

China

Korea

■ EASTERN ART FUSES WITH WESTERN KNITTING

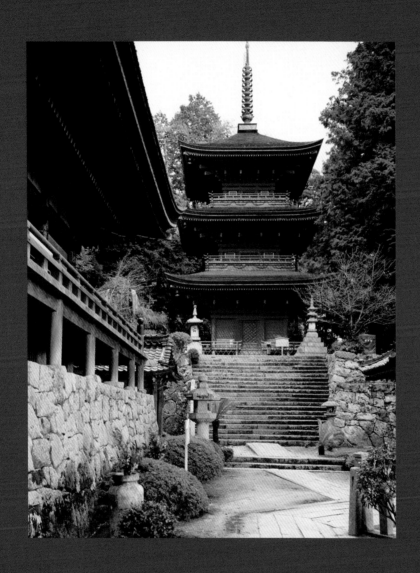

Though there was plenty of snow and cold to be had, China, Japan and Korea were slow to warm to knitting. In fact, when it comes to the history of the craft, the Far East is the new kid on the block.

Mongolian Warrior Pullover
page 196

Inspired by...

Mongol warriors wore strips of hardened laquered leather as armor...strong but lightweight. I've criss-crossed my strips.

Knitted items did appear in Japan, China and Korea long before knitting became common in the region, but it wasn't until the nineteenth and twentieth centuries that yarn and needles were picked up in earnest. However, once these crafts were in their grip, they never let them go.

All three countries derive their terms for knitting from words that describe netting and weaving, indicating no native tradition of the craft. *Meriyasu*, the term used in Japan and Korea since the sixteenth century to describe stockinette knit pieces, derives from the Spanish word for stocking (medias), suggesting that the Europeans introduced both the finished product and the technique to the Far East.

Warrior Knitters: Japan and the Samurai

■ Dutch and Portuguese traders probably brought knitted items to Japan sometime in the 1500s, but the Japanese did not begin knitting until a century or so later. Japan was a regular stop on the European trade routes during the 1600s, but there's no evidence that the knit stockings worn by the European merchants and sailors ended up on the feet of their Japanese hosts—or that the Japanese took to knitting their own stockings. During the Edo Period (1603–1867), Japan began to deliberately isolate itself from the rest of the world, which kept the adaptation of outside influences (including knitting) to a minimum. There was, however, some restricted trade between the Dutch and Chinese during this time, and hand-knit stockings and gloves were among the items bartered and sold in Nagasaki. In 1960, seven knitted stockings dating from about 1688 were discovered in a Japanese temple; they are believed to have belonged to Mito Komon Mitsukuni Tokugawa, grandson of the first Shogun of Japan. It's a fitting match, as the Shogun played an important, if peripheral, role in the in the development of knitting in Japan.

By 1853, as the Edo Period was nearing its end, social and political changes were taking place. Japan was interacting with the outside world, and the shoguns, along with the samurai who enforced their rule, were beginning to lose power and influence. The Japanese army began to reorganize its structure to resemble Western armies. With that reorganization came a need for uniforms, including knitted gloves and socks. To supplement their rapidly diminishing incomes, the samurai put down their swords and picked up knitting needles to make tabi, a traditional split-toe sock that they sold to the army. Gloves, covers for sword hilts and blades (tuka-bukuru and tuba-bukuru), and purses (kinchaku) were also knit by these former warriors. The year 1868 ushered in the Meiji Period and the total overthrow of the shoguns, establishing an emperor as head of state and leaving the samurai unemployed. Knitting became the sole occupation of many of these warriors, creating Japan's first cottage knitting industry. (Could this someday inspire yet another adaptation of Kurosawa's *Seven Samurai: The Magnificent Seven Take Up Crochet*?) Sadly for the samurai, knitting for income proved to be a short-lived prospect. The Meiji government fully embraced the industrial revolution, bringing in European knitting machines, looms and other textile equipment and rendering the samurai knitters obsolete.

Hand-knitting managed to hang on, reinventing itself (as it had in Europe) as a builder of character and a pursuit of leisure. Missionary schools were established, and handcrafts, knitting included, were often part of the core curriculum. During these same years Japanese women began traveling abroad, often returning to establish schools and universities for girls and women, which, like the mission schools, made knitting a part of the lesson

■ *Japanese woman spinning cotton*

plan. Well-to-do Japanese women began adopting the clothing, manners and leisure activities of their Western counterparts, and knitting became quite fashionable.

Meanwhile, textiles were becoming an important part of the Japanese economy. The outbreak of World War I further expanded the industry, as countries unable to obtain their fiber and fabrics from France, Germany or the United Kingdom turned to Japan for supplies. Hand-knitting was also going strong. Like their sisters abroad, the women of Japan were busily knitting socks and underwear to send to the troops on the front lines of the war.

Techniques
■ Asian patterns rely on a knitter being well versed in the craft—written instructions are almost nonexistent. Instead, diagrams, photos and the occasional chart provide a kind of outline for the project. For those accustomed to worded patterns, the Japanese approach can be a bit intimidating at first, but once you get used to it, it's actually quite easy to follow. (For extra help, take a gander at www.tata-tatao.to, which provides a Japanese-English knitting dictionary, among other knitting gems.)

Amigurumi
■ Nowadays we can thank the Japanese not only for cutting-edge fashion but also for amigurumi, those utterly adorable knit and crocheted anthropomorphic bunnies, cats and robots that can be found on just about every knitter's desktop—both physical and virtual. The majority of amigurumi are crocheted, but there are a few knitted ones out there, and that's the approach I've decided to go with. To crochet them, you simply work in rounds, adjusting the size and shape as you see fit. Gauge is more or less irrelevant—you simply want the stitches to be tight enough to keep the stuffing from showing through. Cuteness is the key factor. The typical amigurumi has an oversized sphere of a head set atop a cylindrical body, with or without undersized arms and legs.

Knit amigurumi are worked in the round using a number of stitches that can be evenly divided (usually by six). Think of it as a ring of concentric circles. Start by casting on a predetermined number of stitches, then decrease to form the head. You can then increase again to form the body or work separate pieces and stitch them together. Use embroidery to add eyes and other features. If you want inspiration, ideas or help making amigurumi, you'll find a plethora of patterns on the Internet.

Shibori
■ Shibori is form of Japanese resist-dyeing that involves folding, stitching, wrapping or otherwise binding fabric to create a pattern. I've always loved the technique, and so I decided to experiment with it on knit fabrics. Instead of colored dyes I use felting to create a dimensional surface

on the knitted fabric. It's incredibly easy to do. You simply slip any unshrinkable object under the knitted fabric—I used hazelnuts for the Shibori bag on page 192, but marbles or large, round beads will work just as well—secure them with a rubber band and felt the piece. The stitches wrapped around the object won't felt, and when you remove the object, you'll be left with a fabulous pattern of bubbles. You can go absolutely crazy with this technique (shown on page 242) and get all sorts of different designs by varying the size and spacing of the objects. (My book *Knitting Never Felt Better* has lots of ideas and examples.)

Block Parties: Knitting in China
■ Yarn was scarce when the Chinese first began knitting, mostly in cotton and silk imported from Germany and using dull colors and equally uninspired designs. That changed with the rise of the Communist government and the beginnings of an industrialized society. Wool imported from Australia was spun into basic yarns, while a Shanghai publishing house issued a comprehensive knitting guide that became the "knitting bible" of its day (roughly the Chinese equivalent of America's *Vogue Knitting Ultimate Knitting Book*). Design and color choices improved with the economic growth of the 1960s, only to be cut short by the Cultural Revolution and its utilitarian aesthetic. When synthetic yarns appeared in the 1970s, they were more expensive than wool, a pricing equation that has since reversed itself. Government factories produced much of China's knitting yarn, and state-run stores supplied it (in very limited quantities and color options) to knitters.

These days the knitting atmosphere in China is a bit more relaxed and leaves more room for innovation. In Shanghai, knitters are everywhere. You'll find them stitching at bus stops, in the streets and in the market stalls. Yarn stores are not as easy to spot, but with a little digging, you'll find lots of lovely wool. Patterns are plentiful, and like those in Japan, rely more on photos and diagrams than on written instructions to explain garment construction. Today the manufacture of yarns in China is booming, challenging the European and Australian dynasties.

Techniques
■ Chinese knitters work intricate stitch and intarsia patterns on long double-pointed needles (bamboo is the wood of choice, though it's a bit rougher than what we're used to), wielding them as easily as Western knitters do circulars. Stitches are divided among three needles, and the fourth is used to knit the stitches (see page 237 for the how-to). Keep an even tension as you knit, and if you find the stitches are slipping, do as the Chinese do and wrap rubber bands around the nonworking ends to make them stay put. ❖❖

Shanghai Garden Scarf
page 188

Fuji Feather Lace Wrap
page 194

Shanghai Garden Scarf

The romance of old Shanghai comes to life with floral, beaded appliquéd flowers and exotic pointed edges in a classic jade color.

■ MASTER KNITTER

WHAT YOU'LL NEED
- 2 .88oz/25g hanks ea. (ea. approx 95yds/87m) of Berroco Inc's. *Lumina* (54% cotton, 36% acrylic, 10% metallic) in #1618 space ship
- 6 strands of Deanna's Vintage Styles #6 seed beads in #588 aurora borealis
- 12 dagger beads in #588 aurora borealis
- Size 5 (3.75mm) needles
- Stitch markers
- Tapestry needle
- Beading needle

One size
9"/23cm at widest edge x 38"/96.5cm

Gauge
17 sts and 28 rows = 4"/10cm in St st. TAKE TIME TO CHECK GAUGE.

Pattern Stitches
■ SHORT ROWS

W & T. Bring yarn to front, slip next st, turn, wrap yarn around slip st and slip same st back onto right hand needle. Work wrapped st by picking up wrap and working together with st on left hand needle.

■ SB Slip one bead in place from the working yarn.

Half Scarf (make 2)
■ Thread 4 strands of beads onto each ball of yarn.

Border
■ Cast on 80 sts.
Row 1 (RS) K1, *(SB, k1); rep from *.
Repeat Row 1 three more times.

Body
Row 1 (RS) Slip 1, (SB, k1) 3 times, yo, knit to end of row—81 sts.
Row 2 Purl to last 4 sts, (k1, SB) 3 times, k1.
Rows 3-8 Repeat Rows 1-2—84 sts.

FIRST EYELET ROW
■ Row 9 (RS) Bind off 4 sts, *yo, k2tog; rep from * to last 4 sts, k4—80 sts.
Row 10 P4, place first marker, purl to end.
Row 11 Slip 1, (SB, k1) 3 times, yo, knit to 1 st before marker, W & T.
Row 12 P2, place movable marker, purl to last 4 sts, (k1, SB) 3 times, k1.
Rows 13, 15 and 17 Slip 1, (SB, k1) 3 times, yo, knit to 1 st before moveable marker, W & T.
Row 14, 16 and 18 Repeat Row 12, moving movable marker 2 sts before previous wrapped st.

SECOND EYELET ROW
■ Row 19 (RS) Bind off 4 sts, *yo, k2tog; rep from * to 1 st before moveable marker, W & T.
Row 20 P2, place second marker, purl to end.
Row 21 Slip 1, (SB, k1) 3 times, yo, knit to 1 st before second marker, W & T.
Row 22 P2, place moveable marker, purl to last 4 sts, (k1, SB) 3 times, k1.

Rows 23, 25 and 27 Slip 1, (SB, k1) 3 times, yo, knit to 1 st before moveable marker, W & T.

Row 24, 26 and 28 Repeat Row 22, moving moveable marker 2 sts before previous wrapped st.

THIRD EYELET ROW

■ *Row 29* (RS) Bind off 4 sts, *yo, k2tog; rep from * to 1 st before second marker, W & T.

Row 30 P2, place moveable marker, purl to end.

Row 31 Slip 1, (SB, k1) 3 times, yo, knit to 1 st before marker, W & T.

Row 32 P2, place moveable marker, purl to last 4 sts, (k1, SB) 3 times, k1.

Rows 33, 35 and 37 Slip 1, (SB, k1) 3 times, yo, knit to 1 st before moveable marker, W & T.

Row 34, 36 and 38 P2, place movable marker, purl to last 4 sts, (k1, SB) 3 times, k1, moving moveable marker 2 sts before previous wrapped st.

FOURTH EYELET ROW

■ *Row 39* (RS) Bind off 4 sts, *yo, k2tog; rep from * to 1 st before second marker, W & T.

Row 40 Purl to end.

Row 41 Slip 1, (SB, k1) 3 times, yo, knit to 2 sts after marker, W & T.

Row 42 Place moveable marker, purl to last 4 sts, (k1, SB) 3 times, k1.

Rows 43, 45 and 47 Slip 1, (SB, k1) 3 times, yo, knit to 2 sts after moveable marker, W & T.

Row 44, 46 and 48 Place moveable marker, purl to last 4 sts, (k1, SB) 3 times, k1, moving moveable marker 2 sts after previous wrapped st.

FIFTH EYELET ROW

■ Bind off 4 sts, *yo, k2tog; rep from * to first marker, W & T.

Row 50 Purl to end.

Row 51 Slip 1, (SB, k1) 3 times, yo, knit to end.

Row 52 Purl to last 4 sts, (k1, SB) 3 times, k1.

Rows 53, 55 and 57 Slip 1, (SB, k1) 3 times, yo, knit to end.

Row 54, 56 and 58 Purl to last 4 sts, (k1, SB) 3 times, k1.

Row 59 (RS) K1, *(SB, k1); rep from *.

Repeat Row 59 for 3 more times.

Bind off.

Large Beaded Flowers (make 6)

■ Thread 45 beads onto yarn.

Cast on 51 sts.

Row 1 (RS) K2, *[SB, k1, pass 2nd st on RH needle over first st to bind off 1 st] 9 times, k1; rep from * to end (omitting last k1)—6 sts on needle.

Cut yarn, leaving a long tail. Thread tail through sts and pull to close. Knot to secure.

Small Beaded Flowers (make 6)

■Thread 35 beads onto yarn.

Cast on 41 sts.

Row 1 (RS) K2, *[SB, k1, pass 2nd st on RH needle over first st to bind off 1 st] 7 times, k1; rep from * to end (omitting last k1)—6 sts on needle.

Cut yarn, leaving a long tail. Thread tail through sts and pull to close. Knot to secure.

Finishing

■ Sew short edges of Scarf pieces together. Arrange 3 each of large and small beaded flowers randomly to RS at each wider edge of Scarf and sew in place. Sew one dagger bead to each beaded point at wider edge of Scarf. Weave in ends. ❖

Worked in short rows with eyelets, this scarf is sure to catch the eye of the emperor!

Shibori Blossom Bag

The ancient art of Shibori, coupled with a good, contemporary felting process, will give you a bag perfect for a night out with your favorite Samurai.

■ NOVICE KNITTER

WHAT YOU'LL NEED
- 1 2oz/57g hank (ea. approx 120yds/110m) of Lorna's Laces *Glory* (mohair blend) in #205 irving park (A)
- 1 4oz/113g hank (ea. approx 190yds/174m) of Lorna's Laces *Bullfrogs and Butterflies* (85% wool, 15% mohair) in #205 irving park (B)
- 2 4oz/113g skeins in #16ns charcoal (C)
- Size 11 (8mm) needles
- Size 8 (5mm) double-pointed needles
- Tapestry needle
- Approx 75 hazelnuts or other round object that can be washed
- Rubber bands
- 2 laundry bags
- 3 lacquer buttons, 1¼"/3cm wide

One size
16"/40.5cm wide x 17"/43cm tall, before felting
12"/30.5cm wide x 11"/28cm tall, after felting

Gauge
16 sts and 22 rows = 4"/10cm in St st using larger needles and B, before felting.
NOTE: Diamond pattern is worked in duplicate stitch after piece is knit.

Bag
■ With larger needles and C, cast on 63 sts.
Working in St st, for 5"/12.5cm. Change to B and work for 5 rows. Change to C and work 2 rows. Rep last 7 rows until piece measures 29"/73.5cm from beginning, end with WS row.

Flap
■ Change to A, inc 3/ sts evenly across row – 100 sts.
Working in St st, (work 10 rows with A, 4 rows with C) 4 times.
Work 10 rows with A.
Bind off.

Loop
■ With RS facing and A, pick up 1 st at center of bound-off row of Flap. Cast on 17 sts. Bind off. Secure last st in same spot on Flap as first st.

Strap
■ With double-pointed needles and C, cast on 5 sts. Work I-cord (see page 240) over 5 sts for 100"/254cm. Bind off.

Edging
■ With double-pointed needles and C, cast on 8 sts. Work in St st for 75"/190cm.
Bind off.

Finishing
■ Following Chart, duplicate-stitch C over striped section of Bag.
Fold body of bag in half lengthwise. Solid C section should be lined up with beginning of Flap section. Sew side seams.
Weave in ends.

With WS facing, arrange nuts or round objects randomly and close together in flap section on RS. Secure each nut with a rubber band on RS.

Felting
■ Place knit bag, edging and strap into laundry bag. Felt pieces (see page 234). Pull Bag into shape and allow to dry. Remove nuts and rubber bands.

■ Position and sew Edging along sides and bottom edge of Bag. Cut excess. Fold Strap in half. Sew ends together and sew to inside seam on one side of bag. Tie an overhand knot in doubled strap. Sew folded end of Strap to inside seam on opposite side of bag.

■ Fold Flap over to front of Bag and mark placement of 3 buttons, vertically placed and lined up with Loop, on front of bag. Sew buttons in place. ❖

DUPLICATE STITCH CHART

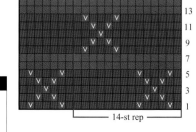

KEY	
■	Irving Park (B)
■	Charcoal (C)

Nicky's Notes
If you like a bag with a bolder look, choose a more high-contrasting color, such as black, to create a brighter duplicate stitch.

Nicky's Notes
The wave pattern works its way down to knitted, giant tassels wrapped with velvet ribbon that is also woven vertically into the lace eyelets.

Fuji Feather Lace Wrap

This rare lace pattern translates into an elegant wrap with a flowing natural wave at the sides.

■ SKILLED KNITTER

WHAT YOU'LL NEED

- 2 4oz/113g hanks (each approx 225yds/206m) of Lorna's Laces *Shepherd Worsted* (100% superwash wool) in #11ns bold red
- Size 10 (6mm) needles
- Tapestry needle
- Fiberfill
- 8yd/7.3m velvet ribbon, ⅝"/16mm wide, in Black

One size

12" x 80"/30.5cm x 203cm, excluding tassels

Gauge

15 sts and 16 rows = 4"/10cm in Feather Lace Stitch.

Pattern Stitches

■ Feather Lace Stitch (multiple of 11 sts + 1 extra)
Row 1 and all WS Rows K1, *p10, k1; rep from *.
Rows 2 and 4 P1, *k10, p1; rep from *.
Rows 6, 10 and 14 P1, *k1, (yo, k1) 3 times, (ssk) 3 times, p1; rep from *.
Rows 8 and 12 P1, *k1, (k1, yo) 3 times, (ssk) 3 times, p1; rep from *.
Rows 16 and 18 Repeat Row 2.
Rows 20, 24 and 28 P1, *(k2tog) 3 times, (k1, yo) 3 times, k1, p1; rep from *.
Rows 22 and 26 P1, *(k2tog) 3 times, (yo, k1) 3 times, k1, p1; rep from *.
Repeat Rows 1-28 for Feather Lace Stitch.

Shawl

■ Cast on 45 sts.
Work in garter st for 4 rows.
Beginning with Row 1, repeat 28 rows of Feather Lace St 11 times.
Work Rows 1–4.
Work in garter st for 4 rows.
Bind off.

Tassels (make 10)

■ Cast on 28 sts.
Rows 1, 2, 3, 5, 7, 9 and 11 Purl.
Rows 4, 6, 8 and 10 K1, *k2tog, k2, yo, k1, yo, k2, ssk; repeat from * to end.
Rows 12-19 Repeat Rows 4-11.
Rows 20-25 Repeat Rows 4-9.

Row 26 K1, (k2tog) across to last st, k1 – 15 sts.
Rows 27-32 Knit.
Row 33 K1, (k2tog) across – 8 sts.
Cut yarn, leaving a long tail. Pull tail through remaining sts on needle to close top.
Knot to secure. Sew side edge seam, stuffing Rows 26-33 with fiberfill to make a ball.
Cut a 3"/7.5cm strip of ribbon and wrap around Tassel under ball. Sew in place.

Finishing

■ Sew 5 Tassels evenly spaced along each short end of Shawl.
Thread ribbon length over and under purl stitches between Feather Lace Stitch repeats for the length of the Shawl.
Sew ends in place to secure.
Weave in ends. ❖

KEY	
☐	K on RS, p on WS
⊟	P on RS, k on WS
⊙	Yo
⊠	k2tog
⊠	Ssk

FEATHER LACE STITCH

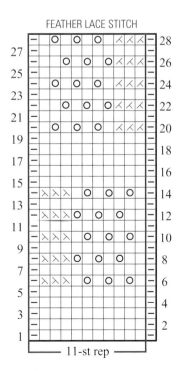

11-st rep

Silver Shawl Pins
designed by Nicky
available at
nickyepstein.com

Mongolian Warrior Pullover

The unique pattern has its roots in the armor used by the hordes of Genghis Khan.

■ NOVICE KNITTER

WHAT YOU'LL NEED
- 20 (22) 1 ¾oz/50g balls (each approx 66yds/60m) of Filatura di Crosa/Tahki•Stacy Charles, Inc. *North Pole* (70% merino wool, 30% soft polyamide) in #2 light olive
- Size 7 (4.5mm) needles, or size needed to obtain gauge
- Stitch holders or waste yarn
- Straight pins
- Tapestry needle

Sizes
S/M (L/XL)

Finished Measurements
Bust (unstretched): 32 (38)"/81 (96.5)cm
Bust (stretched): 36 (42)"/91.5 (106)cm
Upper arm (unstretched): 9¼ (10½)"/23.5 (26)cm
Upper arm (stretched): 11¼ (12½)"/28.5 (32)cm

Gauge
29 sts and 23 rows = 4"/10cm over k2, p2 rib (unstretched)

Right front
■ Cast on 56 (68) sts for lower edge.
Row 1 (RS) *[K2, p2] 4 (5) times, k2, p1; rep from * twice more, omitting p1 on last rep.
Row 2 *[P2, k2] 4 (5) times, p2, k1; rep from * twice more, omitting k1 on last rep.
Rep rows 1 and 2 until piece measures 6 (7)"/15 (18)cm from beg, end with a WS row.
DIVIDE FOR WEAVING STRIPS.

STRIP 1
■ *Next row* (RS) Work 18 (22) sts in rib for first strip, place rem sts on holder.

Work even in rib on these 18 (22) sts for 12 (13)"/30.5 (33)cm, end with a RS row.
Place sts on separate holder and cut yarn.

STRIP 2
■ Slip next 20 (24) sts from first holder onto needle.
Next row (RS) Ssk, k1, [p2, k2] 3 (4) times, p2, k1, k2tog.
Cont in k2, p2 rib on these 18 (22) sts for 13 (14)"/33 (35.5)cm, end with a RS row.
Place sts on separate holder and cut yarn.

STRIP 3
■ Slip rem 18 (22) sts from first holder onto needle and work even in rib
over these 18 (22) sts for 14 (15)"/35.5 (38)cm, end with a RS row.
Joining row (WS) Work 18 (22) sts of last strip in rib; place sts of center strip on
needle and pfb, work in rib to last st, pfb; place sts of first strip on needle
and work 18 (22) sts in rib—56 (68) sts.
Cont in rib as est for 5"/12.5cm. Bind off in rib for shoulder.

Left front
■ Work same as right front to joining row, reversing lengths of first
and last strips.
NOTE: Place sts of Strip 3 on a holder for easier weaving.

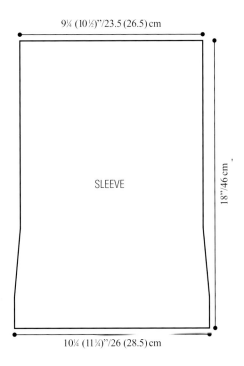

9¼ (10½)"/23.5 (26.5) cm

SLEEVE

18"/46 cm

10¼ (11¼)"/26 (28.5) cm

Weaving

■ With RS facing, and cast-on edges at bottom, lay left front across right front. Place all three sections of left front on separate holders. With RS facing, starting with the longest strip on the left front, weave over, under, and over the three strips on right front and pin in place. Weave the center strip on left front under, over and under the three strips on right front and pin in place. Weave the last strip same as the first strip. Adjust the position of the strips if necessary to create a tight basketweave as pictured. With WS facing, stitch strips in place.

■ Place sts from all three strips onto needle and join. Starting with a WS row, complete same as for right front.

Back

■ Work same as front.

Sleeves

■ Cast on 74 (82) sts. Next Row (k2, p2) across, end k2. Continue in k2, p2 rib, dec 1 st each side every 12th row 3 times–68 (76) sts. Work even until piece measures 18"/46cm from beg, or desired length. Bind off loosely in rib.

Finishing

■ Sew shoulder seams. Place markers 7 (8)"/18 (20.5)cm down from shoulder seams on front and back for armholes. Pin bound-off edge of sleeves between markers, stretching to fit, and sew in place. Sew sleeve seams. Tack front and back together at corner side seams at cast-on edge. ❖

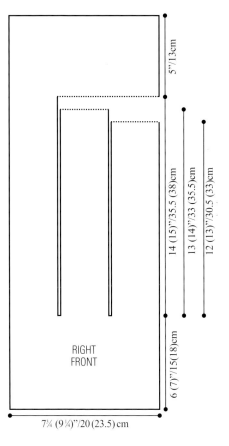

5"/13cm

14 (15)"/35.5 (38)cm

13 (14)"/33 (35.5)cm

12 (13)"/30.5 (33)cm

6 (7)"/15(18)cm

RIGHT FRONT

7¾ (9¼)"/20 (23.5) cm

The open-weave pattern is much easier than it appears. The entire piece is made with a 2×2 rib-stitch pattern that a beginner can make without too much trouble.

Inspired by...
...a fusion of Japanese
Amigurumi and a Chinese
New Year's celebration
dragon from my
Chinatown neighborhood.

Hai-Riyo

My fire-breathing, flying friend has more detail than the original Amigurumi animal patterns, and personality plus!

■ SKILLED KNITTER

WHAT YOU'LL NEED
- 1 3½oz/100g skein (ea. approx 210yds/193m) of Berroco Inc. *Comfort* (50% superfine nylon/50% superfine acrylic) in #9750 primary red (A)
- 1 .88oz/25g hank (ea. approx 95yds/87m) of Berroco Inc. *Lumina* (54% cotton/36% acrylic/10% metallic) in #1620 gold coast (B)
- Size 7 (4.5mm) needles or size to obtain gauge
- Stitch marker
- Tapestry needle
- Fiberfill
- Two 5mm beads for eyes
- Wire (optional)

Size
Approx 13½"H x 5¾"W x 8"D/34 x 14.5 x 20cm

Gauge
18 sts and 26 rows = 4"/10cm in St st. TAKE TIME TO CHECK GAUGE.
NOTE: Use 2 strands of B held together wherever B is used.

Tail
- With A, cast on 3 sts.
Rows 1-4 Work in St st.
Row 5 (RS) Kfb, k to last st, kfb—5 sts.
Row 6 Purl.
Rep rows 1-6 five times more—15 sts.
Cont even in St st until tail measures 6"/15cm from beg, end with a WS row.

Body
- *Next (inc) row* (RS) *Kfb; rep from * to end – 30 sts.
Next row Purl.
Rep inc row—60 sts.
Work even in St st for 2½"/6.5cm, end with a WS row.

Next row (RS) K20, ssk, k16, k2tog, pm, k20—58 sts.
Next row Purl.
Next row K20, ssk, k to 2 sts before next marker, k2tog, k20—56 sts.
Rep last 2 rows until 44 sts rem. P next WS row.
Next row K20, ssk, k2tog, k20—42 sts.

Neck
- *Next (dec) row* (RS) [K2, ssk] 5 times, [k2, k2tog] 5 times, k2—32 sts.
Next row Purl.
Next row [K1, ssk] 5 times, k2, [k2tog, k1] 5 times—22 sts.
Work even in St st for 1½"/4cm, end with a WS row.
Next (dec) row (RS) K1, k2tog, k to last 3 sts, ssk, k1—20 sts.
Cont in St st, working dec row every 10th row until 10 sts rem, then every 4th row twice—6 sts.
Work even in St st for 1½"/4cm, end with a WS row.

Head
- *Next (inc) row* (RS) *Kfb; rep from * to end—12 sts.
Next row Purl.
Next (inc) row [K1, kfb] 5 times, k2—17 sts.

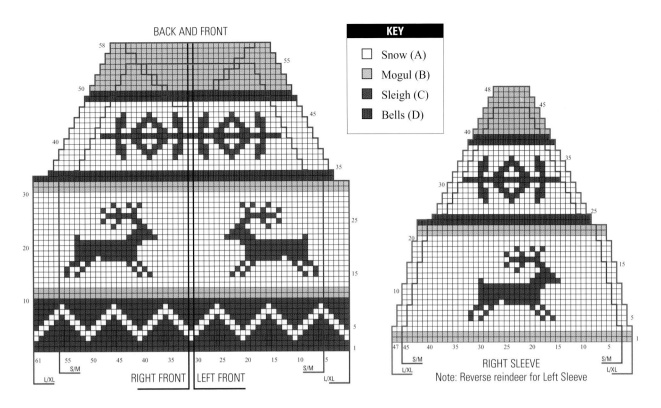

BACK AND FRONT

KEY

☐	Snow (A)
▨	Mogul (B)
▨	Sleigh (C)
■	Bells (D)

RIGHT FRONT   LEFT FRONT

RIGHT SLEEVE
Note: Reverse reindeer for Left Sleeve

NECK SHAPING

Next row (WS) Bind off 8 (9) sts, work chart to end.

Next row K1, k2tog, work chart to end.

Next row Bind off 2 sts, work chart to end.

Rep last 2 rows until 54 (58) rows of chart are complete—3 sts. Bind off.

Right sleeve

▪ With B, cast on 49 (53) sts and work in k1, p1 rib for 4½"/11.5cm.

Next row (RS) Knit, dec 6 sts evenly across—43 (47) sts.

Work 32 rows of right sleeve chart, dec 1 st each side every 4th row 5 times—33 (37) sts.

Foll chart, cont to work raglan shaping same as for back—7 sts. Bind off.

Left sleeve

▪ Work same as right sleeve, reversing direction of reindeer on sleeve chart.

Finishing

▪ Weave in ends. Sew raglan sleeve caps to raglan armholes. Sew sleeve and side seams.

COLLAR

▪ With RS facing, pick up 13 (16) sts along right front neck, 5 sts across top of right sleeve, place 25 (31) back neck sts from holder onto spare needle, and work across these sts as foll:

Size S/M: K4, [k2tog, k3] 4 times, k1—21 sts.

Size L/XL: K2, k2tog, [k3, k2tog] 5 times, k2—25 sts.

Pick up 5 sts across top of left sleeve, 13 (16) sts along left front neck—57 (67) sts.

Work in p1, k1 rib for 10 (11)"/25.5 (28)cm. Bind off in rib. ❖

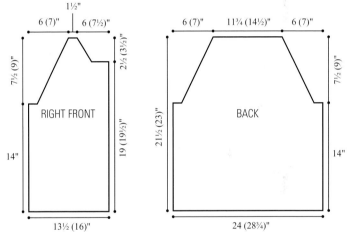

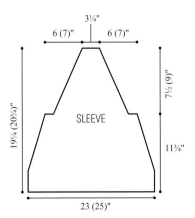

There are many wonderful resources online for knitting an original Cowichan collar. Check them out!

Great Bear Zip Tunic

This tunic, based on a beautiful Navajo blanket, takes a fresh look at a Southwestern classic.

■ SKILLED KNITTER

WHAT YOU'LL NEED

■ 5 3½oz/100g hanks (ea. approx 127yd/116m) of Classic Elite Yarns *Montera* (50% llama, 50% wool) in #3875 inca grey (A)
3 hanks in #3845 fieldstone heather (B)
■ 2 hanks ea. in #3862 kingfisher blue (C), #3831 turquoise (D), #3868 ancient orange (E) and #3833 honeybell (F)
■ Size 9 (5.5mm) needles
■ Stitch holder
■ Yarn bobbins
■ Tapestry needle
■ 35"/89cm long heavy separating zipper
■ Decorative zipper pull
■ 6 horn toggle buttons, 2½"/6.5cm long

Finished Measurements
Bust (closed): 50"/127cm
Length: 38"/96.5 (94)cm

Gauge
16 sts and 20 rows = 4"/10cm in St st.

Notes
Use separate bobbins of yarn for each large block of color.
Carry colors loosely along wrong side of work. Pick up new color from underneath old color to twist yarns and prevent holes.

Back
■ With A, cast on 100 sts.
Work 14 rows in garter st, ending with WS row.

BEGIN CHART 1
Row 1 (RS) K5 with A, work from st 1 to 45 of Chart 1, then work from st 45 to st 1, k5 with A.
Row 2 K5 with A, work Chart 1 in St st as established to last 5 sts, k5.
Keeping first and last 5 sts in garter st with A, work 12 rows of Chart 1.

BEGIN STRIPE
■*Keeping first and last 5 sts in garter st with A and center 90 sts in St st, work 10 rows with B, 2 rows with E, 10 rows with A and 2 rows with E.
Repeat these 24 rows from * once more, then work 10 rows with B, 2 rows with E.

BEGIN CHART 2
Row 1 (RS) K5 with A, work from st 1 to 45 of Chart 2, then work from st 45 to st 1, k5 with A.
Row 2 K5 with A, work Chart 2 in St st as established to last 5 sts, k5.
Keeping first and last 5 sts in garter st with A, work 40 rows of Chart II.

BEGIN STRIPE
■*Keeping first and last 5 sts in garter st with A and center 90 sts in St st, work 2 rows with E, 10 rows with B, 2 rows with E and 10 rows with A.
Repeat these 24 rows from * once more, then work 2 rows with E and 10 rows with B.

BEGIN REVERSE OF CHART 1
Row 1 (RS) K5 with A, beginning with Row 12, work from st 1 to 45 of Chart 1, then work from st 45 to st 1, k5 with A.
Row 2 K5 with A, work Row 11 of Chart 1 as established to last 5 sts, k5.
Keeping first and last 5 sts in garter st with A, work from Row 12 to Row 1 of Chart 1 in St st to reverse direction of chart.
Change to A.
Work 14 rows in garter st, ending with WS row.
Bind off.

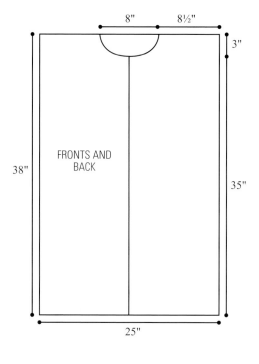

FRONTS AND BACK

8"   8½"   3"   38"   35"   25"

■ The casual fit of this sweater, with its zipper, side openings and patchwork bear-claw pockets transform the traditional pattern into a unique and modern style.

CHART 2

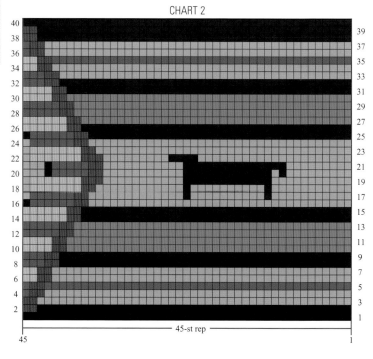

CHART 1

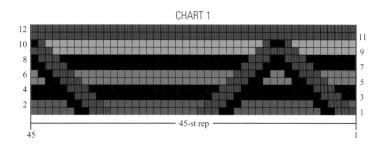

45-st rep

45-st rep

Left Front

■ With A, cast on 51 sts.
Work 14 rows in garter st, ending with WS row.

BEGIN CHART 1

■ *Row 1 (RS)* K5 with A, work from st 1 to 45 of Chart 1 k1 for selvage st.
Row 2 P1 for selvage st, work Chart 1 in St st as established to last 5 sts, k5 with A.
Keeping 5 sts in garter st with A for side border, work 12 rows of Chart 1.

BEGIN STRIPE

■ *Keeping 5 sts in garter st with A and remaining sts in St st, work 10 rows with B, 2 rows with E, 10 rows with A and 2 rows with E.
Repeat these 24 rows from * once more, then work 2 rows with E and 10 rows with B.

BEGIN CHART 2

Row 1 (RS) K5 with A, work from st 1 to 45 of Chart 2, k1 for selvage st.
Row 2 P1 for selvage st, work Chart 2 as established to last 5 sts, k5.
Keeping 5 sts in garter st with A, work 40 rows of Chart 2 in St st.

BEGIN STRIPE

■ *Keeping 5 sts in garter st with A and remaining sts in St st, work 2 rows with E, 10 rows with B, 2 rows with E and 10 rows with A.
Repeat these 24 rows from * once more, then work 2 rows with E and 10 rows with B.

BEGIN REVERSE OF CHART 1

Row 1 (RS) K5 with A, beginning with Row 12, work from st 1 to 45 of Chart 1, k1 for selvage st.
Row 2 P1 for selvage st, work Row 11 of Chart 1 as established to last 5 sts, k5.
Keeping 5 sts in garter st with A, work from Row 12 to Row 1 of Chart 1 in St st to reverse direction of chart. At Same Time, begin neck shaping on Row 9.

SHAPE NECK

■ Bind off 5 sts at neck edge twice. Dec 1 st at neck edge every row 3 times, then every other row 3 times—35 sts.
Continue to work Chart 1 as established through Row 1.
Change to A and work in garter st for 14 rows.
Bind off.

Right Front

■ Work as for Left Front, reversing shaping and Chart placements.

Finishing

■ Sew shoulder seams.

Frontbands

■ With RS facing and A, pick up and knit 140 sts along front edge. Bind off knitwise.
Repeat along opposite Front.

Collar

■ With RS facing and A, pick up and knit 72 sts evenly spaced around neck.
Work in garter st for 8 rows. Bind off.

Bear Claw Pockets (make 2)

SHAPE PALM

■ With A, cast on 11 sts.
Working in St st, inc 1 st each side every other row 7 times—25 sts.
Work for 2"/5cm more, ending with WS row.

FIRST CLAW

■ K5, turn, leaving remaining sts unworked.
Work on 5 sts for 1½"/4cm, ending with WS row.
Next Row (RS) Ssk, k1, k2tog.
Purl 1 row.
Slip 1, k1, pass slipped st over.
Fasten off.

SECOND CLAW

■ With RS facing, join yarn and work next 5 sts, turn, leaving remaining sts unworked.
Work on 5 sts for 2"/5cm, ending with WS row.
Next Row (RS) Ssk, k1, k2tog.
Purl 1 row.
Slip 1, k1, pass slipped st over.
Fasten off.

THIRD CLAW

■ With RS facing, join yarn and work next 5 sts, turn, leaving remaining sts unworked.
Work on 5 sts for 2½"/6.5cm, ending with WS row.
Next Row (RS) Ssk, k1, k2tog.
Purl 1 row.
Slip 1, k1, pass slipped st over.
Fasten off.

FOURTH CLAW

■ Work as for Second Claw.

FIFTH CLAW

■ Work as for First Claw.

■ Measure 10"/25.5cm down from shoulder along side edges and leave unsewn for armholes. Sew next 5"/12.5cm along side seams closed. Leave remaining side seams unsewn. Space 1 toggle button at the top of each sewn section of side seam and sew in place. Sew another button 5"/12.5cm down from sewn section on each side to join Front and Back. Sew zipper along front edge. Attach decorative zipper pull to zipper. Position one Pocket in striped section on each Front and sew along all edges, leaving a space along the straight side edge for inserting hand. Sew a toggle button on each Pocket. Weave in ends. ❖❖

The patchwork bear-claw pockets add a touch
of Native American authenticity.

La Paz Scarf & Cap

The bright colors and bold patterns hark back to ancient Bolivian and Peruvian textiles.

■ SKILLED KNITTER

WHAT YOU'LL NEED

SCARF
- ■ 2 4oz/113g skeins each (ea. approx 190yds/173m) of Brown Sheep Company *Lamb's Pride Worsted* (85% wool, 15% mohair) in #M113 oregano (B), #M97 rust (C) and #M174 wild mustard (F)
- ■ 1 skein ea. in #M151 chocolate souffle (A), #M145 spice (D) and #M175 bronze patina (E)

HAT
- ■ 1 4oz/113g skein each (each approx 190yds/173m) of Brown Sheep Company *Lamb's Pride Worsted* (85% wool, 15% mohair) in #M151 chocolate souffle (A), #M113 oregano (B), #M97 rust (C), #M145 spice (D), #M175 bronze patina (E) and #M174 wild mustard (F)

FOR BOTH
- ■ Size 8 (5mm) 16"/40cm circular needle
- ■ Size 8 (5mm) double-pointed needles
- ■ Stitch markers
- ■ Tapestry needle
- ■ Fiberfill

One size

Finished Measurements

SCARF
10½" x 74"/25.5cm x 188cm, omitting ball trim
HAT
Finished circumference 20"/51cm

Gauge

18 sts and 22 rows = 4"/10 cm over Chart pattern after blocking.
NOTE: Carry colors loosely along wrong side of work.
Pick up new color from underneath old color to twist yarns and prevent holes. TAKE TIME TO CHECK GAUGE. WHEN WORKING FROM CHART, READ ALL ROWS FROM RIGHT TO LEFT.

Scarf

■ With circular needle and C, cast on 24 sts.
Row 1 (RS) Knit into front and back of every st across—48 sts.
Purl 1 row.

Row 3 Knit into front and back of every st across—96 sts. Join, taking care not to twist sts to work in the round. Place a marker for beginning of round.

■ BEGIN CHART
Rnd 1 (RS) Beginning with Rnd 1, work 24-st repeat of Chart 4 times.
Work 94 rounds of Chart twice. Then work Rnds 1–28.
With D, purl 1 rnd, knit 1 rnd, purl 1 rnd.

Reversing Chart, work Rnds 13-1 once, then 94–1 twice.
Next row (K2tog) across—48 sts. Turn.
Purl 1 row.
Next row (K2tog) across—24 sts.
Bind off.

First Ball

■ With D, cast on 10 sts, leaving long tail for sewing.
Row 1 Knit into front and back of every st—20 sts.
Row 2 and all WS Rows Purl.
Row 3 Repeat Row 1—40 sts.
Row 5 Join F, *k3 with F, k3 with D; rep from * to last 4 sts, k4 with F.
Row 6 P4 with F, *p3 with D, p3 with F; rep from * to end.
Rows 7–10 Work in St st with F.
Rows 11–14 Change to A and work in St st.
Rows 15–16 Change to E and work in St st.
Rows 17–18 Change to B and work in St st.
Row 19 Join C, *k2 with C, k2 with B; rep from * end.
Row 20 *P2 with B, p2 with C; rep from * to end.
Rows 21–22 Work in St st with B.
Rows 23–24 Change to A and work in St st.
Rows 25–26 Change to F and work in St st.
Row 27 (K2tog) across row—20 sts.
Row 28 Purl.
Row 29 (K2tog) across row—10 sts.
Bind off.

Nicky's Notes
The balls on the scarf can also be used as unusual Christmas ornaments.

94

90

80

70

60

50

40

30

20

10

1

24-st rep

KEY

⊟ Purl on RS

■ Chocolate Souffle (A)

■ Oregano (B)

■ Rust (C)

■ Spice (D)

■ Bronze Patina (E)

■ Wild Mustard (F)

Second Ball

■ With E, cast on 10 sts, leaving long tail for sewing.

Row 1 Knit into front and back of every st—20 sts.

Row 2 and all WS Rows Purl.

Row 3 Repeat Row 2—40 sts.

Row 5–8 Work in St st with E.

Row 9 Join F, *k2 with E, k2 with F; rep from * to end.

Row 10 Purl with F.

Row 11 Knit with F.

Row 12 *P2 with F, p2 with E; rep from * to end.

Rows 13–14 Work in St st with E.

Rows 15–16 Change to C and work in St st.

Rows 17–18 Join D, and work in St st.

Rows 19–20 Change to A and work in St st.

Rows 21–26 Change to B and work in St st.

Row 27 (K2tog) across row—20 sts.

Row 28 Purl.

Row 29 (K2tog) across row—10 sts.

Bind off.

Third Ball

■ With A, cast on 10 sts, leaving long tail for sewing.

Row 1 Knit into front and back of every st—20 sts.

Row 2 and all WS Rows Purl.

Row 3 Repeat Row 1—40 sts.

Rows 5–10 Work in St st.

Rows 11–14 Change to F and work in St st.

Rows 15–16 Change to A and work in St st.

Rows 17–18 Change to C and work in St st.

Row 19 Join A, *k2 with C, k2 with A; rep from * to end.

Row 20 *P2 with A, p2 with C; rep from * to end.

Rows 21–22 Work in St st with A.

Rows 23–26 Change to B and work in St st.

Row 27 (K2tog) across row—20 sts.

Row 29 (K2tog) across row—10 sts.

Bind off.

Fourth Ball

■ With C, cast on 10 sts, leaving long tail for sewing.

Row 1 Knit into front and back of every st—20 sts.

Row 2 and all WS Rows Purl.

Row 3 Repeat Row 1—40 sts.

Rows 5–8 Work in St st.

Rows 9–10 Change to B and work in St st.

Row 11 Join F, *k3 with F, k2 with B; rep from * to end.

Rows 12–14 Work in St st with B.

Rows 15–22 Change to D and work in St st.

Rows 23 Join F, *k1 with F, k1 with D; rep from * to end.

Rows 24–26 Work in St st with F.

Row 27 (K2tog) across row—20 sts.

Row 28 Purl.

Row 29 (K2tog) across row—10 sts.

Bind off.

Finishing

■ Thread C through sts at cast-on edge of Scarf. Pull yarn to gather sts and knot to secure. Repeat on opposite short end of Scarf. Weave in ends.

■ Sew side seams of each ball. Thread yarn through sts at cast-on edge of Ball. Pull yarn to gather sts and knot to secure. Stuff firmly with fiberfill. Repeat on opposite end of Ball. Weave in ends.

■ Sew two Balls together at ends. Repeat with remaining two Balls. Sew one end of joined Balls at each end of scarf. ❖❖

Hat

■ With circular needle and C, cast on 84 sts. Join, taking care not to twist sts to work in the round. Place a marker for beginning of round. Change to double-pointed needles as necessary as stitches decrease.

BEGIN CHART

Rnd 1 (RS) Beginning with Rnd 1, work .

Work Rnds 1–50 of Chart.

Rnd 51 *K2tog, k5; rep from * to end—72 sts.

Work Chart through Rnd 58.

Rnd 59 *K2tog, k4; rep from * to end—60 sts.

Rnd 60 *K2tog, k3; rep from * to end—48 sts.

Continue to work Chart on 48 sts through Rnd 94, then work Rnds 1–32.

Rnd 33 *K2tog, k2; rep from * to end—36 sts.

Rnd 34 *K2tog, k1; rep from * to end—24 sts.

Work in Chart on 24 sts through Rnd 44.

Rnd 45 (K2tog) around—12 sts.

Knit 1 rnd.

Cut yarn leaving a long tail. Thread tail through sts and pull to close top of Hat. Knot to secure.

Ball

■ With D, cast on 10 sts, leaving long tail for sewing.

Row 1 Knit into front and back of every st—20 sts.

Row 2 and all WS Rows Purl.

Rows 3–6 Work in St st.

Row 7 Join F, *k1 with F, k1 with D; rep from * end.

Row 8 *P1 with D, p1 with F; rep from * to end.

Rows 9–12 Work in St st with F.

Rows 13–14 Change to B and work in St st.

Row 15 (K2tog) across row—10 sts.

Row 16 (P2tog) across row—5 sts.

Bind off.

Finishing

■ Sew side seams of Ball. Thread yarn through sts at cast-on edge of Ball. Pull yarn to gather sts and knot to secure. Stuff firmly with fiberfill. Repeat on opposite end of Ball.

■ Sew Ball to tip of Hat. Weave in ends.

Nicky's Notes

If any hat is too big, you can always run a few rows of elastic thread around the bottom edge and adjust it to fit. Or, make a pleated tuck at the center back and sew it in place.

The scarf is knit in the round...lots of knitting with spectacular results!

Great Plains Blanket Bag

The Native Americans of the West were wonderful artists; their designs inspired this beautiful bag.

■ SKILLED KNITTER

WHAT YOU'LL NEED

- 4 8oz/227g hanks (ea. approx 500yds/457m) of Lorna's Laces *Fisherman* (100% wool)
- 1 hank ea. of #38 mixed berries (MC), #6ns douglas fir (A), #0ns natural (B) #45ns cranberry (C), #41ns china blue (D), #2ns manzanita (E), #24ns navy (F), #8ns harvest (G), #20ns pine (H) and #23ns berry (I)
- One pair each in sizes 6 and 8 (4 and 5mm) needles OR SIZE TO OBTAIN GAUGE
- Bobbins
- 2 yds/1.85m fabric for lining
- Sewing needle and matching thread
- 16" wide x 3½" long/40.5 x 9cm cardboard (for base)
- Muench purse handles (these are "Urban Cowboy Handles" available at yarniverse.com)

Finished Measurements

- 23" wide x 25" long/58.5 x 63.5cm, before felting
- 20" wide x 19½" long/51 x 49.5cm, after felting

Gauge

18 sts and 23 rows to 4"/10cm in St st and colorwork using larger needles (before felting) TAKE TIME TO CHECK GAUGE.
NOTE: When working chart, use a separate bobbin of yarn for each large block of color.

} **Inspired by...**
This blanket bag originates from a wool sweater I designed for Vogue Knitting. I took it apart and felted it to make the bag.

Side (make 2)

■ Beg at top edge, with smaller needles and MC, cast on114 sts.
Work in k2, p2 rib for 3"/7.5cm, ending with a RS row. Change to larger needles and P 1 row, dec 11 sts evenly spaced across—103 sts.
BEG CHART
NOTE: When working rows 16 and 17 of chart, do not skip center st in order to keep in 4-st rep pat across row.
Row 1 (RS) Beg with first st, work to end of chart, skip center st and work from left to right, ending with first st.
Cont in chart pat through row 126—piece should measure approx 25"/63.5cm from beg. Bind off.

Finishing

■ Sew side seams beg from top edge, leaving approx 6"/15cm unsewn towards bottom. Sew bottom seam. Hold end of bottom seam and end of lower side seam tog and sew across to form gusset/base of bag. Rep for other side.
Felt bag (see felting instructions on page 234).

■ Check measurements of bag. If still larger than finished measurements, rep process with progressively shorter cycles, measuring every few minutes until measurement is achieved. Form bag into shape. Let air dry.

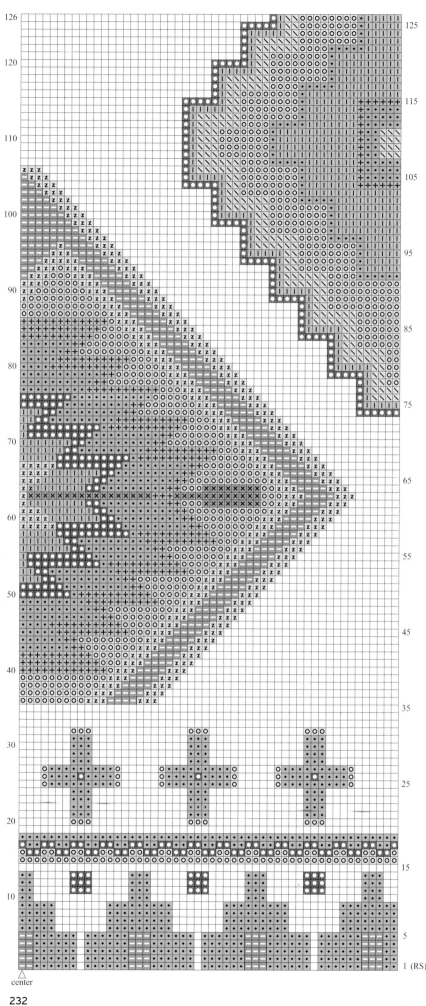

KEY

☐	Audubon ombre (MC)
⊡	Teal heather (A)
⊙	Oyster heather (B)
⊡	Cranberry (C)
⊟	Marine blue (D)
Ⅰ	Plum (E)
◨	Navy (F)
⚏	Chestnut heather (G)
⊞	Green heather (H)
⊠	Dark rose (I)

Lining

■ Cut the foll:

For lining: 19½"/50cm wide x 17"/43cm long (2 pieces)

For pocket: 11½"/29cm wide x 8"/20cm long (1 piece)

For base: 17"/43cm wide x 8½"/21.5cm long (1 piece)

POCKET

■ Fold over ½"/1.25cm seam towards WS around all 4 sides and press. Topstitch approx ⅜"/1cm along one side for top edge. With WS of pocket facing RS of lining, position and pin pocket in middle of lining. Sew approx ⅜"/1cm around rem 3 sides of pocket to lining.

LINING

■ With RS of linings tog, sew ½"/1.25cm seam around 3 sides, leaving 4th side for top opening. Turn felted bag inside out and insert into WS of lining (top edge opening should meet between ribbing and colorwork. Fold rib edge over lining and sew.

BASE

■ With RS tog, fold base fabric lengthwise and sew ½"/1.25cm seam, leaving opening at each end. Turn RS out and insert cardboard into one end positioning seam in middle of cardboard. Fold ends towards seam and sew edge and cardboard tog. Insert base into bag seamside down. Sew handles to top of bag. ◆

Abbreviations

approx approximate(ly)

beg begin(ning)(s)

CC contrast color

cn cable needle

cont continu(e)(ed)(es)(ing)

dec decrease

dpn(s) double-pointed needle(s)

est establish(ed)

foll follow(ing)(s)

inc increase

K knit

kfb k in front and back of st

LC left cable

LH left-hand

LPC left purl cable

M1 make 1—insert LH needle into horizontal strand between last st worked and next st on needle, k through back loop of this strand

M1p make 1 purlwise—same as M1, but p strand through back loop

MB make bobble

MC main color

P purl

pat pattern

pfb p in front and back of st

pm place marker

psso pass slipped stitch over

RC right cable

rm remain(ing)

rep repeat

RH right-hand

rnd(s) round(s)

RPC right purl cable

RS right side

S2KP sl 2 sts as if to k2tog, k1, pass slipped sts over k1

SK2P sl 1 st as if to k, k2tog, pass slipped st over k2tog

skp sl 1 knitwise, k1, pass slipped st over k1

sl slip stitch

ssk sl next 2 stitches knitwise, one at a time, to right-hand needle. Insert tip of left-hand needle into fronts of these stitches, from left to right. Knit them tog. Two stitches have been decreased.

St st stockinette st (k on RS, p on WS)

St(s) Stitch(es)

tbl through back loop

tog together

W&T wrap and turn (see glossary)

WS wrong side

wyib with yarn in back

wyif with yarn in front

yo yarn over

Glossary

BACKWARD LOOP CAST ON
■ Make a loop in the yarn and place it on the needle backward so that it doesn't unwind.
■ Repeat for desired number of stitches, adjusting as needed.

FELTING
■ Fill washing machine to low water setting at a hot temperature. Add ½ cup of gentle detergent.
■ Add all pieces (may be placed in a lingerie bag or pillowcase) and a pair of jeans to provide abrasion and balanced agitation.
■ Use 15–20 minute wash cycle, including cold rinse and spin. Repeat process until desired felting effect is achieved.
■ Lay flat to dry.

SHORT ROW WRAPPING
(wrap and turn—w&t)
KNIT SIDE
1 Wyib, sl next st purlwise.
2 Move yarn between the needles to the front.
3 Sl the same st back to LH needle. Turn work, bring yarn to the p side between needles. One st is wrapped. When short rows are completed, work to just before wrapped st, insert RH needle under the wrap and knitwise into the wrapped st, k them tog.

PURL SIDE
1 Wyif, sl next st purlwise.
2 Move yarn between the needles to the back of work.
3 Sl same st back to LH needle. Turn work, bring yarn back to the p side between the needles. One st is wrapped. When short rows are completed, work to just before wrapped st, insert RH needle from behind into the back lp of the wrap and place on LH needle; P wrap tog with st on needle.

Skill Levels

■ **NOVICE KNITTER**
Basic stitches, minimal shaping, simple finishing.

■ **SKILLED KNITTER**
For knitters with some experience.
More intricate stitches, shaping and finishing.

■ **MASTER KNITTER**
For knitters able to work patterns with complicated stitches, shaping and finishing.

Techniques A to Z

BEADED KNITTING

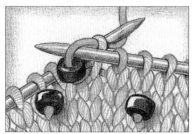

Adding beads with a slip stitch is done on stockinette stitch from the right side of the work. The bead falls directly in front of the slip stitch. Note: Make sure to use beads with holes large enough to thread yarn through.

Thread desired amount of yarn as follows: using a sturdy thread, loop it through a folded piece of yarn and then pull both ends of thread through the eye of the needle. Pass the bead over the needle and thread it onto the yarn.

From the right side
Work to the stitch to be beaded, then slip the bead up in back of the work. Insert needle as if to knit; wrap yarn around it. Push bead to front through the stitch on the left needle; complete the stitch.

BOBBLES

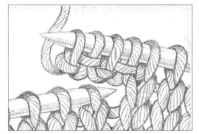

A bobble is a three-dimensional stitch made by working multiple increases in one stitch, sometimes working a few rows, and then decreasing back to one stitch. The following example is of a five-stitch bobble.

1 Make five stitches in one stitch as follows: [knit the stitch in the front loop and then knit in the back loop without slipping it from the left needle] twice, knit in the front loop once more. Slip the stitch from the left needle.

2 Turn the work and purl these five stitches as shown, turn the work and knit five. Do this twice.

3 With the left needle, pull the second, third, fourth, and fifth stitches, one at a time over the first stitch and off the needle. One stitch remains and one bobble has been made. For instructions on knitting a bobble separately and attaching it, see page 214.

CABLE

FRONT CABLE

Front (or left) cable

1 Slip the first three stitches of the cable purlwise to a cable needle and hold them to the front of the work. Be careful not to twist the stitches.

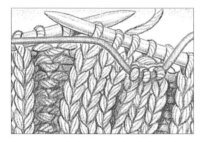

2 Leave the stitches suspended in front of the work, keeping them in the center of the cable needle where they won't slip off. Pull the yarn firmly and knit the next three stitches.

3 Knit the three stitches from the cable needle or return the stitches to the left needle and then knit them.

BACK CABLE

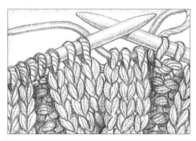

Back (or right) cable

1 Slip the first three stitches of the cable purlwise to a cable needle and hold them to the back of the work. Be careful not to twist the stitches.

2 Leave the stitches suspended in back of the work, keeping them in the center of the cable needle where they won't slip off. Pull the yarn firmly and knit the next three stitches.

3 Knit the three stitches from the cable needle or return the stitches to the left needle and then knit them.

CABLE CAST-ON

■ Begin with the Knitting on method using two needles and one length of yarn.

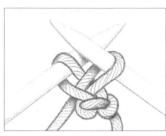

1 Make a slipknot on the left needle. Insert the right needle knitwise into the stitch on the left needle. Wrap the yarn around the right needle as if to knit.

2 Draw the yarn through the first stitch to make a new stitch, but do not drop the stitch from the left needle.

3 Slip the new stitch to the left needle as shown.

4 *Insert the right needle between the two stitches on the left needle.

5 Wrap the yarn around the right needle as if to knit and pull the yarn through to make a new stitch.

6 Place the new stitch on the left needle as shown. Repeat from * in step 4, always inserting the right needle in between the last two stitches on the left needle.

COLOR STRANDING/ FAIR ISLE

STRANDING: ONE-HANDED

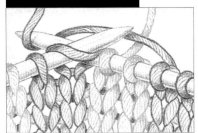

1 On the knit side, drop the working yarn. Bring the new color (now the working yarn) over the top of the dropped yarn and work to the next color change.

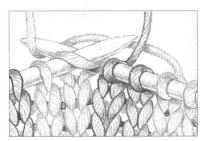

2 Drop the working yarn. Bring the new color under the dropped yarn and work to the next color change. Repeat steps 1 and 2.

1 On the purl side, drop the working yarn. Bring the new color (now the working yarn) over the top of the dropped yarn and work to the next color change.

2 Drop the working yarn. Bring the new color under the dropped yarn and work to the next color change. Repeat steps 1 and 2.

STRANDING: TWO-HANDED

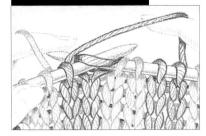

1 On the knit side, hold the working yarn in your right hand and the non-working yarn in your left hand. Bring the working yarn over the top of the yarn in your left hand and knit with the right hand to the next color change.

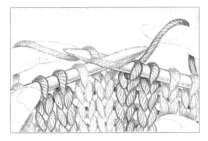

2 The yarn in your right hand is now the non-working yarn; the yarn in your left hand is the working yarn. Bring the working yarn under the non-working yarn and knit with the left hand to the next color change. Repeat steps 1 and 2.

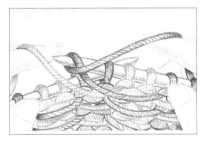

1 On the purl side, hold the working yarn in your right hand and the non-working yarn in your left hand. Bring the working yarn over the top of the yarn in your left hand and purl with the right hand to the next color change.

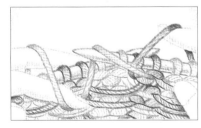

2 The yarn in your right hand is now the non-working yarn; the yarn in your left hand is the working yarn. Bring the working yarn under the non-working yarn and purl with the left hand to the next color change. Repeat steps 1 and 2.

CIRCULAR KNITTING ON DOUBLE-POINTED NEEDLES

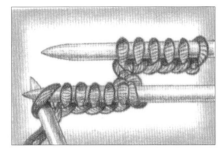

1 Cast on required number of stitches on the first needle, plus one extra. Slip extra stitch to next needle as shown. Continue in this way, casting on the required number of stitches on the needle (or, cast on all stitches onto one needle, then divide them evenly over the other needles).

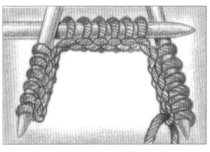

2 Arrange needles as shown, with cast-on edge facing center of triangle (or square), make sure not to twist the stitches.

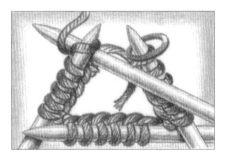

3 Place a stitch marker after the last cast-on stitch. With the free needle, knit the first cast-on stitch, pulling the yarn tightly. Continue knitting in rounds, slipping the marker before beginning each round.

DUPLICATE STITCH

Duplicate stitch covers a knit stitch. Bring the needle up below the stitch to be worked. Insert the needle under both loops one row above and pull it through. Insert it back into the stitch below and through the center of the next stitch in one motion, as shown.

  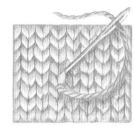

ENTRELAC

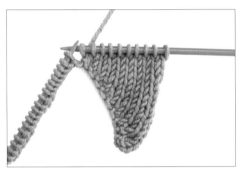 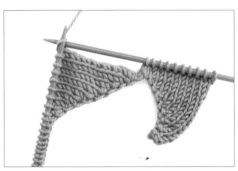 

1 Base Triangle Row: Cast on desired sts and work each triangle as foll: *K2, turn, p2, turn. K3, turn, p3, turn. K4, turn, p4, turn. Cont in this way until you have worked K9, turn, p9, turn. K10. Do not turn.

2 Leaving the first triangle on the right-hand needle, work the second triangle over the next 10 sts as in the previous step, that is, repeat from *.

3 Rep from * across row until all sts have been worked from the left-hand needle. Note how the triangles made after the first one curl up. Turn.

4 1st Row—Beg triangle: P2, turn, k1, M1, k1, turn. P2, p2tog, turn, k2, M1, k1, turn. P3, p2tog, turn, k3, M1, k1, turn. P4, p2tog, turn, k4, M1, k1, turn. Cont in this way until you have worked P8, p2tog, turn, k8, M1, k1, turn. P9, p2tog. Do not turn.

5 Rectangles: *Pick up and p 10 sts along side of triangle. Beg with a RS row [K10, turn, p9, p2tog, turn] 9 times. K10, turn, p9, p2tog. Do not turn. Rep from * to last triangle.

6 End triangle: Pick up and p 10 sts along side of last triangle. Turn. K1, k2tog, k7, turn, p9, turn. K1, k2tog, k6, turn, p8, turn. K1, k2tog, k5, turn, p7, turn. Cont in this way until you have worked K1, k2tog, turn, p2, turn. K2tog. Do not turn.

  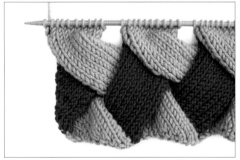

7 Second row—First rectangle: *Pick up and k 9 sts along side of triangle. Beg with a WS row [P10, turn, k9, ssk (shown here), turn] 9 times. P10, turn, k9, ssk. Do not turn.

8 Next and subsequent rectangles: *Pick up and k 10 sts along side of rectangle. [P10, turn, k9, ssk, turn] 9 times. P10, turn, k9, ssk. Do not turn.

9 Rep from * across the row. Cont to rep the 1st and 2nd rows to desired length, end with 1st row.

Bullion Stitch

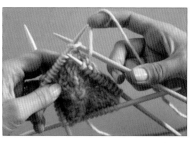

Chain Stitch

Chevron Stitch

French Knot

Jacobean Couching

Lazy Daisy Stitch

Leaf Stitch

Stem Stitch

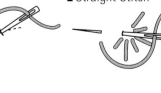

Straight Stitch

"FRENCH" MEDALLION COUNTERPANE

1 After casting on eight stitches or amount given, divide them evenly over four needles. Place a marker, as shown, to indicate the beginning of the round.

2 Work in the pattern stitch in rounds as stated in the instructions. To work a round that begins with a yarn over, simply wrap the yarn around the RH needle, as shown, then knit the next stitch.

3 When working from one needle to the next, work the first stitch on the next needle, then pull the yarn tight, as shown, before working the second stitch. This will keep the joins neat and even.

4 Joining medallions with slip stitch: Place the wrong sides of two medallions together on a flat surface. Insert a crochet hook under the bound-off edge on both pieces, as shown.

5 Draw the yarn through the knitting and through the loop on the hook to complete the slip stitch.

6 Continue until all counterpanes are sewn together to shape garment. For instructions on knitting a square counterpane made of triangles, see page 20.

GRAFTING

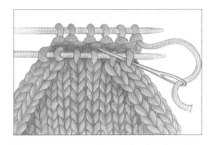

1 Insert tapestry needle purlwise (as shown) through first stitch on front needle. Pull yarn through, leaving that stitch on knitting needle.

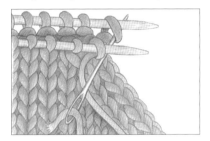

2 Insert tapestry needle knitwise (as shown) through first stitch on back needle. Pull yarn through, leaving stitch on knitting needle.

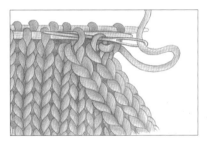

3 Insert tapestry needle knitwise through first stitch on front needle, slip stitch off needle and insert tapestry needle purlwise (as shown) through next stitch on front needle. Pull yarn through, leaving this stitch on needle.

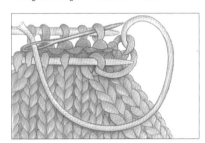

4 Insert tapestry needle purlwise through first stitch on back needle. Slip stitch off needle and insert tapestry needle knitwise (as shown) through next stitch on back needle. Pull yarn through, leaving this stitch on needle.
Repeat steps 3 and 4 until all stitches on both front and back needles have been grafted.
Fasten off and weave in end.

I-CORD OR KNIT CORD

■ Using 2 double-pointed needles, cast on three to five stitches.
*Knit one row on RS. Without turning the work, slip the stitches to right end of needle to work the next row on the RS. Repeat from * until desired length. Bind off.

INTARSIA

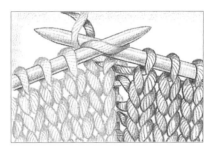

1 On the knit side, drop the old color. Pick up the new color from under the old color and knit to the next color change.

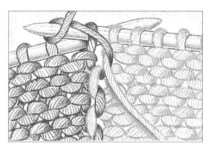

2 On the purl side, drop the old color. Pick up the new color from under the old color and purl to the next color change. Repeat steps 1 and 2.

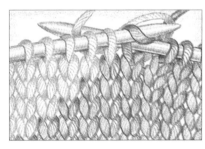

Changing colors in a diagonal line
1 When working a right diagonal on the knit side, bring the new color over the top of the old color and knit to the next color change.

2 On the purl side, pick up the new color from under the old color and purl to the next color change.

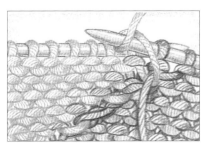

3 When working a left diagonal on the purl side, bring the new color over the top of the old color and purl to the next color change.

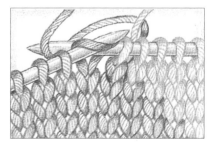

4 On the knit side, pick up the new color from under the old color and knit to the next color change.

KNITTING IN THE ROUND

■ Cast on as you would for straight knitting. Distribute the stitches evenly around the needle, being sure not to twist them. The last cast-on stitch is the last stitch of the round. Place a marker here to indicate the end of the round.

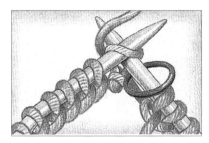

■ If the cast-on stitches are twisted, as shown, you will find that after you knit a few inches the fabric will be twisted. You will have to rip out your work to the cast-on row and straighten the stitches.

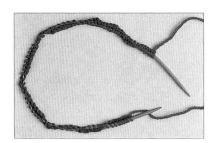

■ Hold the needle tip with the last cast-on stitch in your hand and the tip with the first cast-on stitch in your left hand. Knit the first cast-on stitch, pulling the yarn tight to avoid a gap.

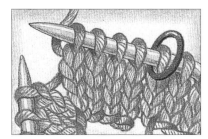

■ Work until you reached the marker. This completes the first round. Slip the marker to the right needle and work the next round.

POMPOM

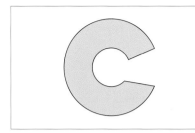

1 With two circular pieces of cardboard the width of the desired pompom, cut a center hole. Then cut a pie-shaded wedge out of the circle. Use the templates as guides.

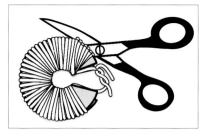

2 Hold the two circles together and wrap the yarn around the cardboard. Carefully cut around the cardboard.

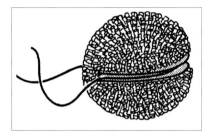

3 Tie a piece of yarn tightly between the two circles. Remove the cardboard.

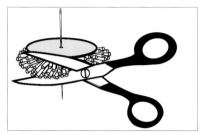

4 Sandwich pompom between two round pieces of cardboard held together with a long needle. Cut around circumference for a perfect pompom.

PROVISIONAL CAST-ON

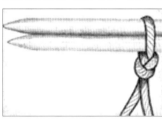

1 This is a cast-on method used when stitches are to be picked up and worked later, such as for hems or special edges. Using two needles held together, begin with a slipknot.

2 Hold a long strand of waste yarn beside the slipknot and take the working yarn under the waste yarn and then behind it again until all stitches are cast on.

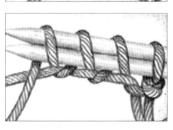

3 Before knitting, withdraw one needle, then knit into the front of the loops on the first row. Leave waste yarn in until you are ready to pick up stitches and add your edge later.

STEEKING Steeking is a traditional Scottish method of circular knitting where you add stitches to a section of the garment that will be cut for an opening, such as an armhole or front of a cardigan. After you cut down the center, the steek creates a small facing that folds back and is slip stitched down.

1 To work a steek, place eight stitches on a holder, then cast on eight stitches. When the body is complete, use the holder stitches plus picked-up stitches to work the band or the sleeve.

2 Pick up stitches through the inside loop of the first stitch before the steek by inserting the needle into the stitch and wrapping the yarn around the needle.

3 Once the steek is trimmed to a two-stitch width, fold it back and sew in place with a finer yarn. Overcast the steek in one direction and then in the other direction as shown.

KNITS WITH NUTS (SHIBORI)

Before

After

1 Insert hazelnuts randomly on back of piece, securing with rubber bands.
2 After felting, carefully remove rubber bands, cutting with a sharp scissors if necessary, and remove nuts. A variety of shrink-resistant objects can be used to achieve the Shibori technique. Experiment and have fun.

For more on felting see my book *Knitting Never Felt Better* (Sixth&Spring).

SHIBORI BLOSSOM BAG (see page 192)

Knit large! A bag like this can shrink more than a third of its size during the felting process.

Before

After

CORKSCREW TASSEL

Cast on over two needles or very loosely—over any number of sts.

The fringe is knitted separately and then attached.

The yarn weight and number of sts cast on will determine the length.

Loosely cast on any number of sts.

Row 1 K into the front, back and front again of each st across rows.

Row 2 Bind off purlwise.

Use fingers to twist each tassel into a corkscrew.

GARTER STITCH TASSEL

Note Tassel can be made with a single strand or multiple strands held together.

With A and B held tog, cast on 16 sts.

Work Garter Stitch for 2¾"/7cm, ending with a WS row.

Bind off 9 sts, fasten off 10th st.

Sl rem 6 sts off needle and unravel them on every row.

Weave yarn in and out of every other st along side edge and pull closed. Insert fiberfill into tassel and sew back seam.

Band

With A and B held tog, cast on 10 sts. K 1 row. Bind off. Sew band around neck of tassel. Trim evenly.

■ **Basic Tassel with Knitted Band**

■ **Basic Tassel**

BASIC WRAP TASSELS

Basic tassel

Wrap yarn around a piece of cardboard 4"/10cm wide by desired length of tassel plus 1"/2.5cm for tying and trimming. Wrap yarn 40 times (or to desired thickness) around length of cardboard. Insert a strand of yarn through cardboard and tie it at the top.

Cut the lower edge. Wrap a 12"/30.5cm piece of yarn 1½"/4cm below top knot to form tassel neck. Trim ends even.

Basic tassel with knitted band

Make Basic Tassel.

Band

With CC, cast on number of sts needed to fit around tassel neck.

K 2 rows. Bind off.

Wrap band around neck tie. Sew cast-on edge to bound-off edge.

ENRICHED FLOUR: This is actually flour that has been stripped of most of its natural nutritional benefits, which makes it necessary to add back nutrients. Go for whole-grain flour instead.

ARTIFICIAL COLORING: Avoid foods with the label "FD&C," which indicates a less-than-natural coloring in candies, cakes, and a variety of other foods.

MONOSODIUM GLUTAMATE: If you've got onion soup mix in your cabinet (and let's face it — who doesn't?) you've been using MSG. Since many people are allergic/sensitive to MSG, look out for this additive under its other names: hydrolized vegetable protein, autolyzed yeast, autolyzed plant protein, and vegetable protein extract.

NITRITES: Watch your hot dog intake! These preservatives, which are often found in hot dogs, cold cuts, and other preserved meats, could be toxic in large amounts. In some instances, they are thought to be carcinogenic when they undergo chemical reactions during cooking.

RESISTANT STARCH: Although it sounds like something you'd want to avoid, make room for resistant starch. What's the buzz about? Resistant starch is a fiber found in many carbohydrates like potatoes, barley, bananas, and beans that is formed when starch-containing foods are cooked and cooled, such as cooked-and-chilled potatoes. This nutrient literally "resists" digestion, and may play a significant role in promoting weight loss by keeping those hunger pangs at bay since it makes you feel full and satiated. Aside from helping you slim down, resistant starch improves blood sugar levels and may even protect against certain cancers.

Definitions

Here are simple, clear-cut definitions

to help you understand some popular terms used regularly in the media and referred to within this book.

ALLIUM: A chemical that boosts your immune system and fights infection. These compounds are naturally found in garlic.

ANTHOCYANIDIN: Substances that help to maintain healthy blood vessels and contribute to maintaining brain function and a healthy immune system. They are found in blueberries, blackberries, cranberries, cherries, red cabbage, and the skin of eggplant, just to name a few.

ANTIOXIDANTS: Substances or nutrients in our food that provide protection to the cells in the body by delaying or preventing damage caused by free radicals (see free radicals). Some of the most common antioxidants and the foods they appear in are lycopene (tomatoes), lutein (spinach), polyphenols (garlic), beta-carotene (sweet potatoes), and flavonoids (blueberries.)

BETA-CAROTENE: An antioxidant that the body converts to Vitamin A. Foods that are red, yellow, orange, and deep green are rich in beta-carotene, like sweet potatoes, cantaloupe, and carrots. These foods may be especially helpful in promoting heart and eye health.

BETA-CRYPTOXANTHIN: A potent carotenoid (see carotenoid) that helps maintain healthy eyes, skin, and bones and boost our immune system. Pumpkin and deep orange vegetables are rich in this nutrient.

BETA-SITOSTEROL: A substance (sterol) in certain plants that may reduce cholesterol levels and reduce the risks of heart disease. These sterols are found in cherries.

CAPSAICIN: A chemical in chile peppers that stimulates pain receptors which might help fight inflammation and arthritis pain. This active ingredient may also help your heart.

CARAVOL: A chemical in the spice oregano, which may help relieve respiratory problems.

CAROTENOIDS: Powerful antioxidants that provide the beautiful colors of orange and red vegetables. Vegetables like red and yellow peppers are carotenoids that may help reduce risks of heart disease, certain cancers, and age-related diseases of the eye.

CATECHIN: An antioxidant (flavonoid) found in cocoa and in white and green tea that may promote heart health.

CHOLESTEROL: A waxy-like substance found in foods of animal origin and found in every body cell. Foods high in dietary cholesterol (like butter, fatty meats, and whole-milk dairy products) can increase heart disease risks.

CURCUMIN: The active ingredient in the spice turmeric, used as an anti-inflammatory agent that helps to fight certain cancers, heart disease, and possibly Alzheimer's disease.

CRUCIFEROUS VEGETABLES: Vegetables in the cabbage family such as broccoli, cauliflower, and Brussels sprouts, which may protect against certain cancers.

ELLAGIC ACID: An antioxidant that boosts the immune system and helps ward off free radical production. Kiwi, grapes, and berries are high in ellagic acid.

FIBER: A form of complex carbohydrates that aids in digestion, promotes health, and may reduce the incidence of heart disease, stroke, and certain types of cancer. Fiber may also reduce the incidence of obesity by means of curbing the appetite by promoting a sense of fullness. (See soluble fiber and insoluble fiber)

FLAVANOLS: Substances that may contribute to heart health. Examples of flavanols are catechins, epicatechins, and procyanidins. They are found in apples, chocolate, cocoa, grapes, tea, and wine.

FLAVANONES: Substances that boost our immune systems by neutralizing damaging free radicals (see free radicals). The flavanones are hesperetin and naringenin and are found in citrus fruit, like oranges and grapefruit.

FLAVONOLS: Substances that bolster the antioxidant defenses in cells. The flavonol quercetin, found in onions, may reduce the risk of asthma, lung cancer, and heart disease.

FREE RADICALS: Atoms with unpaired electrons. Radicals damage cells, causing aging and cell destruction. Antioxidants may help eliminate or prevent damage by free radicals.

HDL (High-Density Lipoprotein) CHOLESTEROL: Also known as "good" cholesterol, HDLs carry cholesterol and other blood lipids away from body cells and are believed to be protective against heart disease.

INSOLUBLE FIBER: Aids in digestion because these fibers don't dissolve. Also known as "roughage," insoluble fibers help to move waste through the intestines, possibly decreasing the incidence of colon cancer. Wheat bran is high in insoluble fiber.

ISOFLAVONES: Phytochemicals believed to help strengthen bones, fight cancer, and protect your heart. Soy products are high in isoflavones.

LDL (Low-Density Lipoprotein) CHOLESTEROL: Often characterized as "bad" cholesterol, LDLs may form deposits on the walls of arteries and other blood vessels, increasing the risks of heart disease.

LUTEIN: An antioxidant known for its role in preventing age-related eye aliments like macular degeneration, as well as heart disease and certain types of cancer. Spinach is a rich source of lutein.

LYCOPENE: A powerful antioxidant found in red fruits such as tomatoes, watermelon, pink grapefruit, and guava, shown to ward off heart disease and certain types of cancer, particularly of the prostate, lung, breast, and digestive tract.

MONOUNSATURATED FATS: These fats may reduce LDL (bad) cholesterol levels and increase HDL (good) cholesterol levels. Canola, nut, and olive oils are high in monounsaturated fats.

OMEGA-3 FATTY ACIDS: Fatty acids (DHA and EPA) that are highly polyunsaturated and are known for thinning the blood and protecting us from heart disease and stroke. Although omega-3s are most commonly found in fatty fish like salmon and mackerel, they are also found in walnuts, canola, flaxseed, and soy oils.

OSTEOPOROSIS: A bone-thinning disease that can be treated with or prevented by an adequate intake of calcium and Vitamin D and regular exercise. Sometimes medications are needed as well. Regular consumption of fat-free or low-fat dairy products may prevent osteoporosis.

PHLORIDZIN: A flavonoid found only in apples that may increase bone strength to aid in the prevention of osteoporosis.

PHYTOCHEMICALS (Phytonutrients): Compounds found in plants that are responsible for the beautiful colors, flavors, textures, and aromas our foods provide for us. They are believed to reduce the risks of many diseases including heart disease, diabetes, and some cancers. There are hundreds of phytonutrients, such as carotenoids, flavonoids, and phenols.

PHYTOSTEROLS (Phytoestrogens): Substances found in plants that act like the hormone estrogen. Although they may reduce menopausal symptoms, contribute to bone health, and boost the immune system, it may be wise to not overdo your intake of phytoestrogens, mostly found in soy products.

POLYUNSATURATED FATS: Fats that are liquid at room temperature, which may help lower LDL (bad) cholesterol levels when they are substituted for trans and saturated fats. These fats are found in safflower, sunflower, sesame, corn, and soybean oils.

QUERCETIN: A flavonoid found in onions and garlic that may reduce the incidence of heart disease, asthma, and lung cancer.

RESVERATROL: A flavonoid that helps maintain urinary tract and heart health as well as boost the immune system. Red grapes, wine, cranberries, blueberries, and peanuts are rich in resveratrol.

SATURATED FATS: Fats that are solid at room temperature and may raise LDL (bad) cholesterol levels.

Foods high in saturated fats include fatty cuts of meat, butter, lard, cream, whole milk, and tropical oils (palm, coconut, and palm kernel).

SOLUBLE FIBER: Soluble fibers give foods their gummy texture and may help lower cholesterol and triglyceride levels and stabilize blood sugar levels, thereby reducing risks of heart disease and diabetes. Oatmeal, oatbran, beans, apples, and carrots are rich in soluble fiber.

SULFORAPHANE: A disease-fighting nutrient that may help reduce the incidence of cancer. This is present in vegetables of the cabbage family such as broccoli and cauliflower.

THYMOL: The active ingredient in the spice thyme, believed to have antibacterial and antifungal properties.

TRANS FATTY ACIDS (Trans Fats): A fat that is formed when fats are hydrogenated (made harder). Trans fats not only raise LDL (bad) cholesterol levels, but they also lower HDL (good) cholesterol. Trans fats are found in many stick margarines, pastries, cookies, and fried foods. Although the process of hydrogenation extends the shelf life of a food, trans fats should be avoided when possible.

TRIGLYCERIDES: The main form of fat in food. Levels of this fat should be kept in check to reduce your risk of heart disease. Treatment of high triglycerides may require weight loss, if needed, a reduction in fat and cholesterol intake, lowered alcohol consumption, and a decrease in the amount of sugar in the diet.

ZEAXANTHIN: An antioxidant found in green leafy vegetables, orange fruits and vegetables, and eggs, which may help promote eye health and possibly prevent macular degeneration.

Superfoods

Superfoods are creating a buzz!

These disease-fighting powerhouses pack a wallop when it comes to helping your body.

The bottom line, however, is that no one food will cure all your ailments, melt away your unwanted pounds, or give you superpowers. But by regularly including a variety of these nutrient-rich foods in proper portions, there's a much greater chance that you and your family can live longer, healthier lives.

This chart below only scratches the surface of the array of foods, herbs, and spices that are available to help empower you to take better care of yourself, but we hope that this gives you a head start.

FOOD	POTENT PROPERTIES	HEALTH BENEFIT
Salmon	Omega-3 Fatty Acids	Heart health; skin and hair; prevents Alzheimer's disease
Beans	Protein, Soluble Fiber	Prevents heart disease; rich in complex carbohydrates; lowers cholesterol and triglyceride levels; stabilizes blood sugar; prevents cancer
Blueberries	Antioxidants, Vitamin C	Brain function; heart health
Dark Chocolate	Flavenoids, Antioxidants	Reduces inflammation; releases endorfins; prevents heart disease; improves blood flow
Garlic/Onions	Vitamins C & E, Potassium, Polyphenols	Lowers blood pressure and cholesterol; heart health; antibacterial agent
Spinach & Leafy Greens	Folates, Fiber, Lutein, Beta-Carotene, Iron	Promotion of eye health; prevention of macular degeneration; cancer prevention; heart health
Red Foods: Tomatoes, Pink Grapefruit, Watermelon	Lycopene	Cancer prevention; eye health
Sweet Potatoes	Carotenoids, Vitamin C, Potassium, Fiber	Heart health; breast and colon cancer prevention
Tea	Flavonoids, Antioxidants	Cancer prevention; heart health; bone strength; digestive health

Tasty Tidbits

What does it all mean?

Sometimes it seems that you need a dictionary to eat healthily! I've broken down the basics so they're easy to understand.

ORGANIC: Foods bearing this special symbol adhere to specific standards of growing and processing.

ORGANIC FRUITS and VEGETABLES: No pesticides sprayed on crops; no chemicals used in growing.
The scoop: Generally believed to be healthier and better for the environment, especially when it comes to the "Dirty Dozen": apples, celery, cherries, grapes, nectarines, peaches, pears, peppers, potatoes, raspberries, spinach, and strawberries.

ORGANIC MEAT and POULTRY: No antibiotics or growth hormones used in raising the animals; no chemicals used in processing.
The scoop: Easier to get kosher organic poultry than red meat. Though many believe organic meat tastes better, there's no guarantee the animals have been treated more ethically than other livestock.

ORGANIC FISH: No chemical colorings, artificial feed, or growth hormones.
The scoop: Organic fish can be farmed and are not necessarily wild.

GMOS (Genetically Modified Organisms):
These are products (plants, fish, and animals) whose genetic makeup has been altered scientifically to incorporate characteristics that don't appear naturally (i.e., fusing peanut genes into rice genes to make heartier crops).
The scoop: Some worry that GMOs can make people sick because it's difficult to determine all the components in a scientifically altered crop. Others feel making stronger crops is a good idea.

FREE-RANGE:
Poultry and livestock are given space to roam on land, as opposed to being confined to a pen or cage.
The scoop: Many believe that free-range animals taste better, and that giving animals "room to breathe" is a more humane way of treating them.

FARMED FISH: Fish raised in ponds in a controlled environment. Some feel they are not as healthy as when the fish are free to swim and select their natural food choices.
The scoop: Farmed fish can be both organic and non-organic, and there is wide debate if it truly is less healthy than wild.

WILD FISH: Fish caught from a natural stream or body of water, not cultivated.
The scoop: Many feel that wild fish, though not necessarily organic, have firmer flesh and a gamier flavor; typically more expensive.

SEASONAL: Food (mostly produce) eaten in its natural growing months (i.e., asparagus in the spring, berries in the summer, potatoes in the fall and winter).
The scoop: Provides variety in the kitchen. Some feel seasonal crops encourage more natural agricultural methods.

LOCAVORE: Someone who eats only foods grown within a certain distance of his/her home.
The scoop: Some feel it's environmentally and economically responsible to support local farmers and purveyors.

ALL-NATURAL: A listing on labels indicating that a product is less processed or chemical-packed.
The scoop: All-natural can mean different things to different people, and even many lab-created ingredients are considered "natural" if they don't contain certain chemicals. Does not mean organic.

NO SUGAR ADDED: This term means there is no table sugar in the food, but there may be other forms of sugar, such as corn syrup, dextrose, fructose, glucose, or maltose.
The scoop: Don't be fooled by this label … basically, there are many different ways to spell sugar! The product marked "no added sugar" can be loaded with sugar if it contains fruit juice concentrate, turbinado sugar, muscovodo sugar, or any of the terms mentioned above. The bottom line is, check the Nutrition Facts Panel on your food label to determine the number of grams of sugar that are actually in the food you're choosing.

Flour

ENRICHED WHITE FLOUR: Often bleached, enriched flour is stripped of the bran and germ — which contain most of the fiber, nutrients, and vitamins. Enriching is necessary to put back some vitamins but you still don't get nearly the same nutritional value that you get from whole wheat flour. Hard to give up since it is the main ingredient in most cakes, cookies, and breads, but try working in some whole grains by replacing portions of white flour in your favorite recipes and see how far you can take it without affecting flavor and texture.

WHOLE WHEAT FLOUR: Ground wheat that has not been processed, removing its hull and germ. High in fiber. Denser than white flour and with lower gluten (which gives breads and cakes elasticity), so often gets mixed in equal parts with conventional white flour.

WHOLE WHEAT PASTRY FLOUR: A more refined form of whole wheat flour made from softer strains of wheat. Helps make baked goods tender and flaky; great for pie crusts and softer cookies. Not great in crispy cookies.

WHITE WHOLE WHEAT FLOUR: Made from hard winter wheat, it has almost the same nutrional profile as whole wheat flour but is lighter in color and sweeter in taste. This finer grind of flour acts more like all-purpose flour in baking than regular dark whole wheat.

RICE FLOUR: Made from either white rice or brown rice. Very common in India. Starchy; makes great crispy-edged crepes and other crispy foods like crackers, chips, and shortbreads. Gluten-free. Brown rice flour is slightly sweeter and nuttier and is higher in fiber.

BRAN FLOUR: Very high in fiber, and very dense. A great way to incorporate fiber into your diet. Not interchangeable with regular flour. Great used in muffins and incorporated into quickbreads and heavier pastry recipes.

SEMOLINA: Made from the inner hull of a wheat kernel, semolina is the wheat equivalent of corn grits. Higher in fiber, great for making hot breakfast cereal, pastas, cakes, and some cookies.

FLAXSEED MEAL: Made from ground flaxseeds. Very high in fiber, low in carbohydrates, full of omega-3 fatty acids, B vitamins, and other nutrients. Though flaxseed has a nutty flavor, it can also taste mildly fishy, so integrate only a few tablespoons into other dishes, such as hot cereal, meatloaf, and muffins.

BARLEY FLOUR: Same nutritious properties as barley, including high fiber and the ability to lower glycemic index in diabetics. Can replace white flour in cookies and muffins. In risen desserts, must be mixed with a flour containing gluten, such as white flour or even whole wheat pastry flour.

Grains

Leave the white pasta and rice

in the box and choose one of these healthy grains instead —

— they're full of fiber and other good stuff, easy to find in most supermarkets and health-food stores, and are shelf-stable, meaning you can pull them off the shelf whenever you need them.

QUINOA: Native to South America, only available in the U.S. in the last 20 years. Actually a member of the beet family, it is the only non-meat food that is a "perfect protein," containing all 9 essential amino acids. Kosher for Passover, quinoa also contains lots of dietary fiber. Quinoa also contains iron and phosphorous, which give us energy to get through the day.

MILLET: Popular in Africa, where it's a staple, you can find millet at any health-food store. The manganese and phosphorous in millet contribute to bone health, and it is gluten-free. It's a great source of fiber and protein, as well as lutein, which promotes good vision and eye health.

BARLEY: A good source of soluble fiber, barley also contains beta-glucans, which can aid in controlling cholesterol levels. The glucose in barley helps regulate blood sugar levels — making it a good choice for diabetics — and its antioxidants help regulate free radicals in the body. Pearled barley is not as healthful as hulled. In pearled barley, the barley is "polished," which literally sands away a lot of the nutrients and fiber. It is still healthy, but hulled is better.

OATS: Unlike other forms of processed grains, oats maintains their bran and germ, which means they're fiber-rich. A special type of fiber in oats may help lower cholesterol and promote heart health. The insoluble fiber in oats helps us digest food (that's why it's good if you're feeling sick), and the soluble fiber helps absorb cholesterol and flush it out of the body. Steel-cut oats are even less processed and take longer to cook, but their nutritional value is the same as old-fashioned and quick-cooking varieties.

BROWN RICE: It may come from Asia originally, but brown rice is now a staple in our diets. White rice is processed, so it loses most of its B-vitamins and up to 11 other vitamins and minerals. Brown rice also contains tryptophan, also found in turkey, which can help you sleep better.

WHOLE WHEAT: Like rice, wheat is often processed beyond recognition — that's why whole wheat is so vital to good health. The bran and germ in whole wheat contain fiber, iron, and folic acid, as well as B-vitamins. Types of available whole wheat include whole wheat flour, wheat berries (unprocessed wheat kernels), bulgur (also known as cracked wheat or tabouli), and whole wheat couscous.

SPELT and FARRO: Spelt is a high-protein grain that is related to wheat and can be used in similar ways. Many people who are allergic to wheat have found solace in spelt. It has a mellow taste and chewy texture; try it instead of rice, potatoes, or couscous. It is great warm or cold in salads. Italian whole grain farro is often confused with spelt. They are related but not the same. Farro retains a firmer texture than spelt when cooked.

FARRO

OLD-FASHIONED OATS

MILLET

SPELT

PEARLED BARLEY

QUINOA

WHEAT BERRIES

SHORT GRAIN BROWN RICE

STEEL-CUT OATS

LONG-GRAIN BROWN RICE

Oils

There's a world of other oils

out there, perfect for lending a healthy dose of flavor to your healthy cooking.

But so many people are carrying around more pounds than they need because they consider oils to be "healthy," without considering their effect on body weight. As with most foods, the portions we consume could determine how we look and feel. At almost 2,000 calories per cup, cooking oils are rich in flavor, but could weigh heavily (literally) on your calorie budget.

The recipes within this book utilize oils appropriately, but sparingly, without sacrificing taste or aesthetics. Oils are added at just the right time to create the ideal blend of flavor and, when used in baking, fat substitutes (like applesauce, for example) provide just the right texture and consistency.

SESAME OIL: For adding great flavor to Asian-inspired dishes, sesame oil is unmatched. Because it's heavy with a low smoke point (the temperature at which the oil breaks down), use it as an accent with a lighter, more neutral oil, such as canola.
Good for: Asian accents in stir fries, dumplings, and soups. Stir in at end of cooking, or drizzle on afterward.

WALNUT OIL: Delicate flavor of walnuts, fairly neutral. Avoid cooking with it, since it loses nutrients and antioxidant power, and becomes bitter at higher temperatures.
Good for: Salad dressings, drizzling on cooked veggies, pasta salads.

CANOLA OIL: The most popular cooking oil in the U.S. Actually made from rapeseeds, canola is considered a healthy, neutral oil; it is rich in monounsaturated fats, with a high smoke point (the temperature at which the oil breaks down). Some claim that when the oil breaks down, it becomes unhealthy (see coconut oil).
Good for: Sautéing, frying, diluting stronger oil such as sesame oil.

BUTTER: Made from churned heavy cream, butter is high in saturated fat and cholesterol. However, it contains no trans fats, making it healthier, in some ways, than hard stick margarine, which is made with hydrogenated fats. Butter burns at high temperatures.
Good for: Dairy desserts, sauces, medium-temperature sautéing.

CORN OIL: Low in saturated fat and cholesterol-free (only animal fats contain cholesterol), corn oil is considered a great frying oil because of its high smoke point (the temperature at which the oil breaks down).
Good for: Frying, cooking when you want the taste of corn.

OLIVE OIL:
If there is one oil you should be using most, it's olive oil. In contrast to most oils, whose best health claims are that they don't damage your health, olive oil can actually improve your health. Olive oil contains monounsaturated fat, which is thought to lower the risk of heart disease, as well as some antioxidants that also have heart-healthy properties. The gold standard when needing raw oil, as in dressing, marinades, dips, etc., is extra-virgin first-cold-pressed oil, which preserves the most nutrients and undergoes the least amount of filtering and processing.

Good for: Low-temperature sautéing (not wok-frying or deep-frying), drizzling on vegetables, salad dressings, pasta sauces — just about anything except deep-frying!

SUNFLOWER OIL:
It makes sense that sunflower oil is one of the healthiest, since sunflower seeds are packed with nutrition. It has more Vitamin E per teaspoon than any other oil. It's low in saturated fat and helps lower "bad" cholesterol levels.

Good for: Sautéing, frying.

COCONUT OIL:
Although high in saturated fats, coconut oil is undergoing a kitchen renaissance. Many believe that it is the only oil that does not break down at high temperatures and therefore maintains its antioxidant properties. It's also shelf-stable and doesn't go rancid. I recommend trying it only in moderation if you're concerned about saturated fats. Until all the facts are in, I'd proceed with caution with this oil.

Good for: Baking, frying, sautéing.

Sugars

Americans sure do have a

national sweet tooth — each of us consumes an average of 74 pounds of sugar per year! Why is it important to limit your sugar? The answer is not only because of the calorie content, but also because of the highs and lows in blood sugar that it causes. Sugar starts cravings for more high-calorie foods. In moderation, sugar can be incorporated into most of our diets, but a crop of new options and substitutes have been flooding the market. Here, the skinny on the sweet stuff:

WHITE TABLE SUGAR: This is the most popular sweetener in the world. It's got 16 calories per teaspoon and can be used in both cooking and baking. It's no less healthy than "raw" sugars like demerrara and muscovado sugar — they're just processed differently, and contain more or less molasses and moisture.

BROWN SUGAR: Brown sugar is white table sugar with the molasses added back in to the crystals. It comes in either light or dark versions. Dark brown sugar contains more molasses and is therefore slightly more moist and has a stronger flavor. Brown sugar can add moisture to cookie and cake recipes.

AGAVE NECTAR: Did you know that agave nectar (also known as blue agave) is actually made from the same cactus used to make expensive tequilas? It's much sweeter than natural sugar, and it has a lower glycemic index (meaning the body absorbs it more slowly) than sugar. To replace 1 cup of sugar with agave in a baking recipe, substitute ¾ cup syrup and reduce liquid in recipe by 3 tablespoons. New, crystallized versions have recently hit the market — they can be used in place of sugar in a one-to-one ratio.

SPLENDA: The new kid on the block, Splenda is the commercial name for sucralose, a sugar derivative that was accidentally discovered in a chemistry lab. In its powdered form, it's used for sweetening drinks, but in its granulated form it can be substituted for sugar in a one-to-one ratio. I have chosen to avoid it in this book, as well as other sugar substitutes, as the health effects are unknown.

HONEY: Honey and sugar actually contain the same natural sweeteners, glucose and fructose. Honey has more calories per teaspoon than sugar (22 vs. 16) and is actually a little sweeter than sugar. In its natural form, honey is an unprocessed food, and contains enzymes that aid digestion, but it is still not suitable for diabetics. To replace 1 cup of sugar with honey in a baking recipe, substitute ¾ cup honey and reduce liquid in recipe by 3 tablespoons.

MAPLE SYRUP: Maple syrup is the sap of the maple tree. Try to get darker, Grade B syrup instead of lighter Grade A. To replace 1 cup of sugar with maple syrup in a baking recipe, substitute ¾ cup syrup and reduce liquid in recipe by 3 tablespoons.

Seeds and Nuts

Although they many be high in

calories, seeds and nuts are loaded with healthy oils, protein, and lots of other great things. Super-versatile, seeds and nuts can be integrated into any course of a meal.

SUNFLOWER SEEDS: When it comes to heart-healthy nuts, nothing beats sunflower seeds. Aside from protein and fiber, their antioxidant qualities come from high levels of Vitamin C, which promotes heart health. Vitamin E helps stimulate brain activity and also neutralizes harmful free radicals. Lightly toast and sprinkle onto a salad or integrate into a healthy trail mix.

FLAXSEEDS: A great source of omega-3 fatty acids, flaxseeds are an excellent anti-inflammatory. Often ground for their oil, but can be used whole in lots of recipes. Certain properties in flaxseeds are believed to help prevent breast cancer, and phosphorous helps build strong bones. Scatter over cereal, sneak some into your kid's granola, or top fresh fruit with a teaspoon or two.

WALNUTS: The monounsaturated fats and amino acids in walnuts help lower "bad" LDL cholesterol and contribute to heart health. Walnuts also contain antioxidant and cancer-fighting properties, as well as melatonin, which helps us sleep. Eat them before changing time zones! Lightly toast walnuts and use in healthy cookies and bars, or to add crunch and richness to a salad.

ALMONDS: Almonds contain heart-healthy monosaturated fats, plus a lot of protein and fiber, which makes a handful of them a filling snack. The antioxidants in almonds are also thought to help prevent certain types of cancer. Spread almond butter on bread; toast them and sprinkle on steamed veggies; or eat with hot breakfast cereal.

PEANUTS: What do peanuts and grapes have in common? Resveratrol, an antioxidant recently discovered to help prevent heart disease and cancer! Niacin found in peanuts is thought to help with memory retention, and — like most nuts — peanuts are high in heart-healthy monounsaturated fats. Use peanuts and natural peanut butter in pasta dishes, as an accent to rice and other grains, and in healthy trail mixes.

PECANS: Contain thiamine, Vitamin E, magnesium, protein, and fiber. Two properties in pecans — oleic acid and beta-sitosterol — make them heart-healthy.

PISTACHIOS: A combination of four nutrients in pistachios contribute to heart health, and they also contain lots of lutein, which helps prevent macular degeneration.

Gadgets for healthy cooking

Want to stay light on your feet

in the kitchen? The right tools really help! Stock your kitchen with these implements — they'll help you keep you (and your cooking) healthy.

SALT CELLAR and PEPPER GRINDER: Good-quality sea salt and fresh ground pepper pack a real flavor wallop, so give these spice stalwarts their due by keeping them handy at all times.

SILICON SPATULAS: Usually heat-proof up to 600 degrees, these flexible wonders help cook foods with less oil by making it easier to maneuver items around a sauté pan or soup pot. These spatulas do absorb flavor, so have one each for sweet and savory cooking.

KITCHEN SCALE: Great for weighing portions to help limit calorie intake, a digital scale doesn't take up a lot of room but is invaluable in the kitchen. The digitals can also be reset to zero as you add each new item to the bowl.

NONSTICK SKILLETS: Eggs, crepes, and proteins slide right out of the pan, allowing you to use less fat in the cooking process. Make sure to stir with a silicon spatula or wooden spoon rather than with sharper metal items, which can scrape the nonstick surface.

GEL MATS: While taking care of your body, remember to watch your back! Take the pressure off it during long hours in the kitchen on these gorgeous ergonomic mats that are filled with shock-absorbing gel. Check out the website: www.letsgel.com

MICROPLANE GRATER: This rasp-like instrument is great for shaving chocolate and cheese into fine shreds, allowing you to get a lot of volume and flavor bang for the buck — grate high-calorie items as flavor garnish for the most impact. Also great for citrus! I also like the Zyliss julienne peeler for long, thin strips.

BAMBOO STEAMER or METAL STEAMER: If you're looking to steam instead of fry, invest in one of these. You can steam dumplings, fresh vegetables, even chicken, without additional fat. Use wine and herbs in your steaming liquid for additional flavor.

LEMON/LIME PRESSES: Fresh citrus juice is essential for brightening the flavor of many of my dishes. Originally from Mexico, these clamp-style juicers take the elbow grease out of extracting fresh juice from lemons and limes — and remove the pits at the same time!

NONSTICK SPRAY: Now available in different flavor varieties, these sprays can save you literally hundreds of calories when frying, sautéing, and baking. Make sure to use a neutral flavor for baking, but opt for olive oil spray in cooking for additional depth of flavor and richness. High-heat or professional sprays burn less for grilling and high-heat cooking, like stir fries.

SMALL PLATES: Studies have shown that appetite is partially visual, and serving smaller portions in smaller plates will satisfy your brain (and your hunger, too).

SPRITZ BOTTLES: Use these to dress your salads. They evenly distribute your dressing with a minimum of calories. Just make sure the dressing is more of a vinaigrette than a heavy dressing and that it doesn't have large flakes of spicing — they may clog the spritzer.

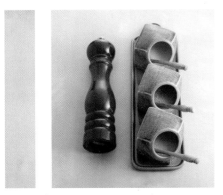
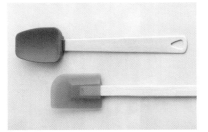

Ideas for Entertaining

Hold the roast beef and host a tasting party!

Bringing your friends and family together does not always have to be focused around a huge meal. Next time you are in the mood to play host or hostess, think of this fun, inexpensive way to both **entertain** and **educate**.

Themed tasting parties are all the **rage** right now. The party can be as uncomplicated as grabbing six bottles of wine and some **tidbits of information** from your local liquor store or as fussy as hiring a consultant to teach your guests about a particular food topic. Some of the more popular choices for tasting parties are wine, tomatoes, cheese, chocolate, and the one I show here, extra-virgin olive oils. Perhaps you can even think seasonally. Hold a pre-Rosh Hashanah apple tasting with a variety of apples, store-bought or picked from a local orchard. A pre-Shavuot cheese tasting could be educational and inspirational as your friends go home to plan their holiday menus. On a cold winter night, a coffee tasting could be a welcoming way to gather friends. Tomatoes are timely for a summer get-together, as this is when they are at their best. If kids are involved, host a vanilla ice-cream tasting party. Four or five spoonfuls of ice-cream can be just as much fun as downing ice cream sundaes.

Don't overload your guests. Depending on your tasting, select no more than six varieties of your item. Some foods lend themselves to more variety. People may be more apt to sample six cheeses than six oils or

honeys. When I hosted an olive oil tasting, I kept it to four varieties. One way to vary your **samples** is by country of origin. Just like wine, olives grown in different regions yield different-tasting oils and have their own character. This has a lot to do with climate and soil. For example, at my olive oil tasting we had bottles from Italy, Greece, Israel, and California. They could not have been more different from each other. You can also focus on just one part of the world and have three or four bottles from that area. Four bottles of oil from California can taste completely different, due to olive varieties and climate changes within the state.

Let the labels help guide you when making your **selections**. Words like "hand-picked" and "stone-ground" are good and show care by the producer. When I was in Israel, I visited an olive-oil producing farm and was treated to a run-through of how the oil is produced the old-fashioned way, utilizing hand-picking and large stones for mechanical grinding. The end result was an **artisanal batch** of incredible oil.

You can give out scorecards or notepads to have your guests **rank** what they taste. For any of these foods, you can rank based on appearance, smell, taste, and overall preference. A tasting can be done "blind," during which the labels are covered to prevent prejudice; or open, allowing bottle or packaging to come into the evaluation.

You will need some supplemental foods, but try to keep these to a minimum. True connoisseurs would not serve bread at an olive oil tasting, as bread imparts its own flavor, but my party was more for fun and I

can't see downing shots of oil as a festive mini-meal. I served slices of good, crusty bread; small plates of chummos with vegetables; assorted cheeses; and a variety of olives. Green apples serve nicely as palate cleansers. I had plenty of water and a bottle of red wine handy.

Finish off the night with some dark chocolate and nuts or fresh fruit.

Remember to **savor** and **enjoy** the party. A tasting should not be rushed — take your time discussing and comparing notes.

Enjoy the fruits of your labor...

Let fresh fruit be the show stopper of your next barbecue or party. Fresh fruit is **sweet**, colorful, and **good** for you. When it comes to dessert, it can be just as **exciting** as cake, candy, and cookies — it's all in the presentation. Wooden skewers, glass bowls, tall vases, and some wheatgrass are all you will need to put this divine table design together.

Fill tall glass vases with whole fruits. In front of the **vases**, assemble bales of wheatgrass. In the quantities needed for a large display as shown, you may need to order it in advance from a florist or health-food store. Some upscale organic supermarkets carry it as well, in smaller quantities.

Select an assortment of fruit, berries, and melons. Cut each into a different shape. Slide the cut fruit or whole berries onto wooden skewers. Arrange as desired. Varied **heights** offer great visual appeal. Bowls of grapes and smaller berries can be tucked into the table layout. The only other thing you will need is plenty of napkins. Be prepared for a shower of compliments. This **sensational ending** to a meal will be appreciated by people of all ages.

Pack up your leftovers instead of packing on the pounds!

I have always been an advocate of opening your home for all occasions. From small Shabbos lunches to large family parties, I love to cook for my loved ones and have them surround me in my home, my favorite place to be. There is usually an abundance of **chatter**, **fun**, and, of course, **food**.

As the party breaks up, I often find myself picking at the platters as I clean up and pack away the remaining food, or returning multiple times to the refrigerator to snack on the **yummy morsels** that were left over. By "**grazing**" that way, you can eat the equivalent of a meal, without ever sitting down and even if you are not hungry. Don't let leftovers become a portion pitfall.

My solution is the equivalent of a goody bag at a kid's party. Supply your company with colorful **to-go boxes**. The containers can be of varied sizes and colors. The material can be plastic, metal, or coated paper; just make sure they are leak-proof. The ones I show here are from The Container Store. They are a combination of plastic pails, metal lunch boxes, and plastic totes. Even Chinese take-out containers will work. Let your friends fill them like **goody bags** with the leftover food. That way your guests will still be thanking you as they eat their delicious lunches the next day, and all the temptation will have gone with your last guest.

Be the toast of the town with a spritzer bar.

We keep hearing how bad soda is for you. The high fructose corn syrup in regular soda has been fingered as one of the largest culprits in causing childhood obesity. Diet soda has recently taken the rap for causing possible damage to body organs and impeding weight loss. The **good news** is that healthy drinks need not be boring. Set up a seltzer station and allow your guests to mingle as they mix up their own spritzers. Provide plenty of berries, citrus, and fruit for garnish, and zest or fruit juice for flavor. You can slide berries onto skewers and use them as **swizzle sticks** in the drinks for **flavor** and **whimsy**.

Cranberry, **lime**, and **lemon** are my favorite seltzer flavors, but let your friends and family experiment. You can even purée watermelon, drain the juice, discard the pulp, and make watermelon spritzers. Supply plenty of assorted glasses and pitchers or bottles of water and seltzer. Load up on ice as well.

To get in the **spirit**, I put out my Penguin, a product made in Israel by the Soda Club company. It turns bottled water into fizzy, bubbly seltzer. It is a real conversation piece and the kids love it. **They don't even ask for soda anymore.**

Bouquet of
Smoked Salmon and Beets

PARVE ■ MAKES 6 SERVINGS

3 medium-large beets, rinsed, roots and stems trimmed

1 tablespoon extra-virgin olive oil

1 teaspoon prepared white horseradish

⅛ teaspoon fine sea salt

1 teaspoon red-wine vinegar

12 ounces smoked salmon, pre-sliced

2 cups arugula leaves, rinsed

1 tablespoon chopped fresh dill, for garnish

Although arugula looks like a type of lettuce, it's actually a member of the cruciferous family, like broccoli and cauliflower. It has similar potent health benefits, including reducing the risk of several types of cancer, in addition to providing only 2 calories for a ½-cup serving.

Beets are a low-calorie food and are an excellent source of folate. If your diet is poor in potassium, bananas are not the only rich food-source for that mineral — try beets.

This dish looks gorgeous as a Shabbos first course.

Preheat oven to 450°F.

Wrap the beets in foil and roast for 1½ hours. With paper towels to protect your hands from the heat and from staining, slip the skins off the beets and cut the beets into 1-inch chunks. Place into a medium bowl. Drizzle on the oil. Mix in the horseradish, salt, and vinegar. Toss to coat and set aside.

Take a slice of salmon and fold in half lengthwise. Roll it up. Pull back and open up the cut side to look like rose petals. Repeat with remaining salmon.

Arrange 3 salmon roses on each salad-sized plate. Arrange ⅓ cup arugula between the roses. Surround with beet chunks and garnish with dill. Repeat for remaining servings.

Wrapped Asparagus Radicchio

PARVE ■ MAKES 6 SERVINGS

4 sheets phyllo dough, defrosted

nonstick olive oil cooking spray

fine sea salt

freshly ground black pepper

dried thyme leaves

1 pound thick asparagus spears

1 tablespoon olive oil

2 cloves fresh garlic, chopped

¼ cup balsamic vinegar

1 tablespoon low-sodium soy sauce

1 tablespoon honey

2 teaspoons canola oil

2 shallots, thinly sliced

1 clove fresh garlic, minced

10 ounces sliced shiitake mushroom caps

½ small head radicchio, thinly sliced

There are times when I entertain that I like the idea of serving a vegetarian appetizer and saving the protein for the main dish. Asparagus, known as the aristocrat of vegetables, is an excellent source of folic acid and a good source of Vitamin C, thiamin, and B_6. That odd smell you may notice upon urination after eating asparagus is a harmless, temporary reaction and it happens to 40% of the population.

When shopping for asparagus, look for a deep green color, tips that are tight and closed, and ends that don't look too dried out or thorny.

Preheat oven to 350°F.

Cover a cookie sheet with parchment paper. Set aside.

Place one phyllo sheet horizontally on your cutting board. Spray with nonstick spray. Season with salt, pepper, and thyme. Top with a second sheet. Repeat until all 4 sheets are stacked and the top sheet is sprayed and seasoned. Cut into 6 (2-inch wide) strips.

Trim the rough ends from the asparagus. Wrap a phyllo strip around 3–4 spears. Place on prepared sheet. Repeat with remaining asparagus. Bake for 20–25 minutes.

Meanwhile, prepare the balsamic glaze: Heat the olive oil in a small pot over low heat. Add the garlic and caramelize it slowly, about 3–4 minutes. Add the vinegar and soy sauce. Reduce by half over medium-low heat. Add the honey and stir to combine.

Prepare the radicchio: Heat the canola oil in a medium skillet. Add the shallots and minced garlic. Sauté 4 minutes, until the shallots are shiny and translucent. Add the mushrooms, salt, and pepper. Sauté 3 minutes, until the mushrooms wilt. Add the radicchio and sauté 1 minute.

Spray a ¼-cup measure with nonstick cooking spray. Pack with the mushroom-radicchio mixture. Shake the mound onto a plate; repeat with remaining mixture. Lay an asparagus bundle over each mound. Drizzle each with balsamic glaze and pool some on each plate.

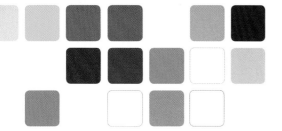

Steamed Veal Dumplings

MEAT ■ MAKES 6 SERVINGS

½ pound ground veal
or ground chicken

2 scallions, ends trimmed,
cut into 2-inch pieces

2 tablespoons loosely
packed fresh cilantro

3 white button mushrooms

½ teaspoon ground ginger

1½ teaspoons honey

½ teaspoon garlic powder

¼ teaspoon freshly ground
black pepper

juice of 1 lime

2 tablespoons low-sodium
soy sauce

1 tablespoon mirin

½ jalapeño pepper,
very finely chopped

1 teaspoon finely chopped
fresh parsley

18-20 wonton wrappers

Steaming is a healthy, delicious cooking method that adds no fat or grease and brings out the intensity of food's natural flavors. For many foods, vegetables in particular, steam cooking preserves the food's texture, color, taste, and nutritional value. The steamer sits right in a pot or wok. You can put aromatics like white wine, whole herbs, or citrus slices into the pot to infuse more flavor. Just make sure there is enough water to keep the steamer from burning — but not enough to touch the food within. Spray the bamboo with nonstick cooking spray; it will season over time. You can place a ceramic plate right in the steamer, or use parchment paper to help prevent sticking.

Bamboo is a grass, not wood, so it is environmentally friendly and inhibits condensation. If you do not have a bamboo steamer, you can use a pasta pot with a strainer insert as a steamer.

To freeze: Freeze the uncooked dumplings on a baking sheet. When frozen, transfer to an airtight container, setting parchment paper between the layers, or seal in a ziplock bag. They can be stored for a month. Steam for 10–12 minutes right from the freezer; do not defrost.

Place the ground veal into a medium bowl. Place the scallions, cilantro, mushrooms, ginger, honey, garlic powder, and pepper into the bowl of a food processor fitted with a metal blade. Pulse to finely chop; don't overprocess or the mushrooms will become a paste.

Toss the mushroom mixture with the veal. Stir to fully combine.

Prepare the dipping sauce: In a medium bowl mix the lime juice, soy sauce, mirin, jalapeño, and parsley. Set aside.

Working with a few wontons at a time, lay the wonton wrappers on a parchment paper-lined countertop. Place a scant tablespoon of filling in the center of each wrapper. Fill a small bowl with water. Dip your finger in water and wet the 4 edges of each wrapper. Bring opposite (diagonal) corners together over the filling and pinch, using more water if necessary to seal. Bring the other 2 corners to the center and pinch all along the seams to seal. Keep a wet cloth handy to wipe your hands between wontons.

Select a pot that the steamer can fit into. Add ½-inch of water to the pot. Spray each layer of the steamer basket with nonstick cooking spray and place a small square or round of parchment paper into each layer of the basket. Place the steamer into the pot and bring the water to a boil. Being careful not to get steam in your face, carefully open the top lid to make sure steam is coming out. When it is, add the dumplings, making sure they don't touch each other, and re-cover the steamer and the pot. Steam for 5–6 minutes. Serve 3 wontons per plate with dipping sauce.

Vegetarian Pâté Bundles

PARVE ■ MAKES 10 SERVINGS

nonstick cooking spray

2 large onions, cut into ¼-inch pieces

3 ounces portobello mushroom slices

1 cup walnut pieces

1 (15-ounce) can green peas, drained

1 (15-ounce) can chickpeas, rinsed and drained

½ cup canned red kidney beans, rinsed and drained

fine sea salt, optional

freshly ground black pepper, optional

ice cubes

water

6 very long chives or scallions sliced into long thin strips

Bibb lettuce

smoked paprika, such as McCormick®

I have written about my father's love affair with chopped liver many times before. To illustrate the point, my mother's butcher sent her a case of it as a Rosh Hashanah present last year.

This pâté, which my mom carefully consulted on, is similar to vegetarian liver but is a little creamier. It has far less fat and cholesterol than the original. The canned peas lend a more authentic color, but canned green beans or fresh steamed green beans work fine too. Vegetarian or nonvegetarian eating — these types of foods can nourish you, taste great, and prevent health problems.

Spray a large skillet with nonstick cooking spray. Place over medium-low heat. Add the onions. Sauté for about 15 minutes, until the onions are caramelized. Add the mushrooms and sauté for about 5–6 minutes until tender, turning once during cooking.

Meanwhile, place the walnuts into the bowl of a food processor fitted with a metal blade. Process until finely ground. Add the onion/mushroom mixture along with the peas, chickpeas, and kidney beans to the food processor. Process until creamy. If your peas were unsalted, season with salt. Season with black pepper if desired.

Fill a large bowl with ice cubes and water. Set aside.

Fill a pot halfway with water. Bring to a boil. Drop the chives or scallions into the pot to blanch or soften for 30 seconds–1 minute. Remove and place into the ice water to stop the cooking.

Separate the head of lettuce into individual leaves; select the 12 largest. Spoon a scant ¼ cup pâté into each lettuce cup. Sprinkle each with a pinch of smoked paprika and roll the sides to form a packet. Trim the lettuce leaves as necessary. Tie each packet with a chive or scallion strip. Serve 2 to a plate.

Tex-Mex Turkey Meatballs

MEAT ■ MAKES 6 SERVINGS

1½ pounds ground turkey

½ teaspoon garlic powder

½ teaspoon onion powder

½ teaspoon dried oregano
   leaves

½ teaspoon fine sea salt

¼ teaspoon freshly ground
   black pepper

¼ teaspoon smoked paprika,
   such as McCormick®

¼ teaspoon ground cumin

1 tablespoon olive oil

nonstick cooking spray

½ medium onion,
   cut into ¼-inch dice

3 cloves fresh garlic,
   finely chopped

1 (28-ounce) can crushed
   tomatoes flavored with
   basil

1 (15.5-ounce) can black
   beans, rinsed and drained

2 teaspoons hot sauce, such
   as Frank's® or Tabasco®

fresh cilantro, chopped,
   for garnish

Meatballs are a staple food for people who have kids. Substituting turkey for ground beef lightens them and makes them a healthy choice. Make sure your ground turkey is very fresh or it will impart a strange flavor to your dish. When rolling the meatballs, the meat will be sticky. Spray your hands with nonstick cooking spray to make the meatballs easier to roll.

Smoked paprika is an incredible spice. It has a sweet-smokey flavor and is sold with kosher certification by McCormick in their gourmet collection. If you can't find smoked paprika, mix regular paprika with 2 drops liquid smoke.

Originating in Hungary, paprika contains Vitamin C and has been shown to normalize stomach acid to assist in digestion. Paprika also regulates blood pressure and may improve circulation by providing a blood-thinning agent.

Place the ground turkey into a large mixing bowl. Add the garlic powder, onion powder, oregano, salt, pepper, paprika, and cumin. Mix to distribute the spices evenly.

Heat the olive oil in a large skillet over medium heat. Form the turkey mixture into 18 balls, about the size of golf balls. Sear the meatballs, about 2 minutes per side, rotating to make sure all the sides of each meatball become brown.

Meanwhile, spray a medium pot with nonstick cooking spray. Heat over medium. Add the onion and sauté for 3–4 minutes, until the onions are shiny and translucent. Add the garlic and cook, stirring so the garlic does not burn. Pour in the crushed tomatoes and simmer for 10 minutes. Add the turkey balls and gently coat them with the sauce. Cook for 5–7 minutes. Depending on the brand of tomatoes, you may need to add some water if the sauce is too thick and stew-like. Add the black beans and hot sauce. Stir. Heat through, about 3 minutes.

Serve 3 turkey meatballs in each bowl, making sure to scoop up some of the sauce with the beans.

Garnish each bowl with chopped cilantro.

Vegetarian Chili

PARVE ■ MAKES 16 (1-CUP) SERVINGS

2 tablespoons ground cumin

2 tablespoons chili powder

1 tablespoon paprika

1 tablespoon garlic powder

½ teaspoon fine sea salt

½ teaspoon freshly ground black pepper

dash of cayenne pepper

1 tablespoon olive oil

1 small Vidalia onion, cut into ¼-inch pieces

1 small red bell pepper, cut into ¼-inch pieces

½ small frying pepper, minced

1 small jalapeño pepper, minced

12 ounces ground veggie protein crumbles, such as Smart Original®

2 (28-ounce) cans crushed tomatoes with basil

16 ounces unpeeled sweet potatoes, cut into ⅓-inch pieces (about 2½–3 cups)

1 (15-ounce) can black beans

1 (15-ounce) can navy beans or small white beans

1 (15.5-ounce) can chick peas

1 (15.5-ounce) can red kidney beans

2 medium zucchini, unpeeled, cut into 1-inch chunks

baked tortilla chips

fresh cilantro leaves, for garnish

My photographer, John Uher, developed this recipe when his daughter became a vegetarian. He figured it was so healthy compared to the meat chilis he usually whipped up that he just kept adding ingredients until he discovered that he had written a recipe for the world's largest batch of vegetarian chili. When he gave me the recipe, I had to work this down from a 25-quart batch to something more manageable. This stands in as a great and filling main course and makes 8 (2-cup) portions. The blend of colors and flavors in this dish also provides a blend of vitamins and minerals. In addition to a wealth of nutrients, the rich protein value of the beans will help keep you feeling satisfied while lowering your cholesterol at the same time.

In a small bowl, mix the cumin, chili powder, paprika, garlic powder, salt, pepper, and cayenne. Set aside.

In a large pot, heat the oil over medium-high heat. Add the onion and red pepper. Sauté about 5–7 minutes, until translucent and aromatic. Add the frying and jalapeño peppers. Sauté another 3–5 minutes, until the mix starts to brown.

Add the spices and toast until darkened and aromatic, about 2–3 minutes. Add the crumbles, stirring constantly; cook until they start to stick to the bottom. Add both cans of crushed tomatoes (save one empty can), and scrape the bottom of the pot with a wooden spoon. Continue to cook the tomatoes, stirring and scraping periodically. The chili should be getting slightly darker and caramelized. Simmer for about 5–7 minutes.

Add 1 tomato-can full of water and the sweet potatoes. Drain and rinse the black beans, navy beans, chick peas, and kidney beans. Add to the pot. Reduce the heat to medium, and simmer for about 30 minutes or until the sweet potatoes are tender. Stir occasionally.

When the potatoes are done, add the zucchini, and simmer until the zucchini is just cooked through, about 20 minutes. Season with additional salt and pepper if desired.

Serve in bowls with 3 tortilla chips and garnish with a sprig of cilantro.

Summer Rolls

2 boneless, skinless chicken breast halves

⅛ teaspoon fine sea salt

⅛ teaspoon freshly ground black pepper

nonstick cooking spray

½ cup rice vinegar

1 tablespoon sugar

1 tablespoon mirin

1 tablespoon low-sodium soy sauce

2 cloves fresh garlic, minced

1 scallion, thinly sliced on the diagonal

1 tablespoon lime juice

¼ teaspoon hot sauce, such as Frank's® or Tabasco®

2 ounces dry rice sticks, also known as rice vermicelli or rice noodles

hot water

1 (12-ounce) package rice paper rounds

12 large basil leaves

1 large carrot, julienned, or 1 cup grated carrot

12 large mint leaves

This delicacy is always served cold or at room temperature. Unlike its relatives, the spring roll and egg roll, summer rolls are never fried. Preparing this tasty appetizer in this fashion saves you 120 calories for every tablespoon of oil that you have avoided by not frying.

The traditional woven pattern pressed into the rice paper rounds harkens back to a time when Vietnamese women dried homemade rice paper on baskets. Rice paper is fragile. If you are having trouble with tearing, use a double thickness of rice paper until you get the hang of it. The key is being prepped with all your ingredients and then putting the dish together assembly-line style.

Zyliss makes a great julienne peeler, which will leave you with spaghetti-like strands of carrot or other vegetables. Willi-Food, an Israeli company, packages the rice sticks with a kosher certification. Get them in a kosher supermarket or do an online search.

Season the chicken breasts with salt and pepper. Spray a skillet with nonstick cooking spray and heat over medium heat. Pan sear the chicken for 4–5 minutes per side, or until cooked through. Thinly slice the chicken into strips. Set aside.

In a medium bowl, whisk the vinegar, sugar, mirin, soy sauce, garlic, scallion, lime juice, and hot sauce. Set aside in a bowl for dipping.

Cook the rice sticks for 2–3 minutes in a pot of boiling water. Drain. Rinse in cold water to stop the cooking process.

Use hot water to fill a pan large enough to hold a rice paper round. Dampen a clean kitchen towel with water; spread the towel on your work surface. Immerse one rice paper in the hot water until softened and flexible (the pattern will be less visible), about 1 minute. Transfer to the dampened towel and smooth out. Place a second rice paper in the pan to soften while working with the first. If the water gets too cool after working with a few, replace with warm water.

Lay two basil leaves 2 inches from the bottom edge of a rice paper round. Top with 2–3 slices of the chicken and then some of the carrot. Place a ¼ cup of the cooked rice sticks on top. Cover with 2 mint leaves. Roll the rice paper over twice. Fold in the sides, then roll up completely. Continue with remaining ingredients.

Serve the summer rolls with the dipping sauce pooled on the plate and some extra to dip on the side.

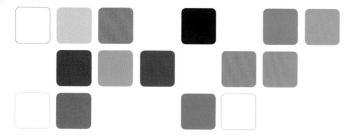

Roasted Pepper Crostini

PARVE ■ MAKES 8 SERVINGS

1 red bell pepper

1 orange bell pepper

1 yellow bell pepper

1 tablespoon extra-virgin olive oil

1 tablespoon balsamic vinegar

2 cloves fresh garlic, minced

½ French or Italian bread, cut into 8 (½-inch) slices

2 cloves fresh garlic, halved

In Italian, crostini means "little toasts," and that is exactly what they are. They are used in this recipe as a base to catch all the wonderful flavors of the roasted peppers and dressing. To keep this light, make sure you slice your crostini thin. They make a very filling appetizer or pass-around hors d'oeuvre. I sometimes serve them as a side to a salad. Any way you serve them, be sure to make extra peppers. They are great over chicken, burgers, and fish.

Peppers are loaded with Vitamin C, and the various colors provide a variety of other nutrients. Their anti-inflammatory properties may help relieve arthritis.

Preheat the broiler to high. Cut each of the peppers in half down the center. Scoop out and discard the seeds. Place the peppers, cut-side-down, on a jellyroll pan. Press each to flatten slightly. Broil 6 inches from heat for about 5–8 minutes, until the skin is blistered and completely blackened. If the sides are not getting black, once you have removed the peppers from the oven, use tongs to hold the pepper directly over a gas burner. Any skin that is not blackened will not remove easily.

While the peppers are roasting, in a medium bowl, whisk the olive oil, vinegar, and minced garlic. Set aside.

When the peppers are blackened, place them into a heavy-duty zip-top bag to steam for 5–10 minutes. Rub the skin off. It is okay if a few of the blackened bits remain; they will add flavor. Do not wash under water.

Thinly slice the peppers and place into the balsamic marinade in the bowl. Allow to marinate for at least a few minutes. Can be made 2–3 days in advance.

Preheat oven to 375°F.

Place the bread slices onto a cookie sheet. Rub each slice with the cut side of a garlic clove. Bake for 8–10 minutes, until golden brown and slightly dried out.

Top each crostini with the marinated peppers.

Chummos Canapés

PARVE ■ MAKES 12 CHUMMOS CANAPÉS

1 (15-ounce) can chick peas (also known as garbanzo beans), rinsed and drained

3 tablespoons tahini paste (also known as Middle Eastern sesame paste)

3 tablespoons fresh lemon juice

2 cloves fresh garlic

1 teaspoon ground cumin

½ teaspoon fine sea salt

¼ teaspoon freshly ground black pepper

2 tablespoons good-quality extra-virgin olive oil

3-6 tablespoons water

3 slices whole wheat bread, toasted

1 kirby cucumber, sliced paper-thin

½ cup romaine lettuce, shredded

1 plum tomato, thinly sliced

alfalfa sprouts

Right after Superbowl 2008 (yay, Giants!), I read an article that claimed chips and dip were being replaced by chummos as the snack food of the year. Americans, growing more aware of healthier eating as well as developing a growing openness to international foods, have sparked a chummos renaissance. It is a fiber-rich snack, but be careful — some store-bought versions are very high in fat and preservatives. This homemade version serves up all the good stuff, while keeping the fats to a minimum. Be sure to make extra chummos; it makes a great lunchbox snack with baby carrots or pretzels.

The benefits of beans, such as chick peas, can't be emphasized enough. Add that to the iron and blood-glucose-lowering effect of cumin and you've got a recipe for good health! Dip with ease at this tasty favorite for all ages. Although chummos is found in many supermarkets today, it's a dish that's so easy to make at home.

Place the chick peas, tahini, lemon juice, garlic, cumin, salt, and pepper into the bowl of a food processor fitted with a metal blade. Pulse until smooth and creamy. With the machine running, pour in the oil. If the consistency is too thick, drizzle in water, a little at a time, to thin as desired.

Spread a thin layer of chummos on the toasted bread slices. Top with 3–4 slices of cucumber. Top with some of the lettuce; drizzle with a little more chummos. Top with 2 slices of tomato and some sprouts. Press down to compact. Cut the crusts from the toast. Cut each slice of bread to form 4 small squares.

Pickled Vegetables

PARVE ■ MAKES 10-12 SERVINGS

3 sprigs fresh dill

3 sprigs fennel fronds

10 sprigs fresh thyme

1 bay leaf

½ head cauliflower, broken into medium florets

½ small red onion, thinly sliced

10 baby carrots

4 red radishes, with skin, each cut in half

4 cloves fresh garlic, each cut in half lengthwise

¾ teaspoon whole black peppercorns

½ teaspoon juniper berries, optional

⅛ teaspoon fennel seeds

1 cup water

1 cup rice vinegar

1 tablespoon fine sea salt

1 tablespoon sugar

This lovely dish makes a thoughtful hostess gift. Old-fashioned Ball jars or other pretty glass jars with lids are perfect containers for this recipe. Besides being a nice appetizer, the vegetables are great to snack on. Keep them visible in your refrigerator so you will go for them instead of a less-healthy choice when looking for a munchie. The pungent flavor of this dish will last on your palate and perhaps create less of a desire for sweets. This healthy, nutrient-rich dish is great to pick on when the kids come home from school, too. Even kids who say they don't like vegetables may like the taste of this colorful treat.

As a change, try alternating layers of peeled and quartered baby beets, peeled turnips trimmed to ½-inch moons, red onions, mint leaves, and ¼ teaspoon whole black peppercorns. The beets turn everything pink, so you may want to keep them out of other mixtures.

Place the dill sprigs and fennel fronds into your selected container. Add the thyme sprigs, standing them around the sides. Add the bay leaf.

Layer the cauliflower, red onion, carrots, radish, and garlic. Add the peppercorns, juniper berries if using, and the fennel seeds. Tap lightly to get some of the seeds to the bottom of the container.

In a small pot, bring the water, vinegar, salt, and sugar to a simmer. Stir until the sugar dissolves. Remove from heat and pour into the container of vegetables. Make sure the vegetables are submerged. Allow the container to cool and then place into the refrigerator. The vegetables will be ready in 1–2 days and will keep for a week in the refrigerator.

Honey Oat Challah

PARVE ■ MAKES 4 CHALLAHS

2 (¼-ounce) packages active dry yeast (½-ounce or 2 tablespoons total)

1 teaspoon sugar

2 cups lukewarm water

3½ cups unbleached bread flour, plus a little more for kneading

1½ cups whole wheat flour

1⅓ cups oat flour

2 tablespoons flax meal

3 tablespoons old-fashioned oats, divided

1 tablespoon vital wheat gluten

½ teaspoon kosher salt

¼ cup sugar

¼ cup light brown sugar

½ cup honey

2 large eggs

¼ cup grapeseed oil or extra-virgin olive oil

nonstick cooking spray

1 tablespoon sesame seeds

1 tablespoon golden flax seeds

1 egg, beaten, for egg wash

This is not your grandmother's challah! It's a new, healthier way to bring warmth to your table, Shabbos or any day, while bringing whole-grain goodness along with it.

If you are using a Bosch or Magic Mill mixer, and want to be able to make a bracha, just double the ingredients and add two extra cups of bread flour and 1 extra cup of whole wheat flour. Follow the instructions of your machine. The single 1½ hour rise will be enough. There is no need for a second rise when using a machine.

People who consume whole grains are less likely to develop type-2 diabetes and they have less chance of becoming obese, because whole grains are so satisfying and filling. The added bonus is that you don't even need a big portion to reap big benefits from this emotionally and physically pleasing recipe.

Gluten is the natural protein of a grain. It is responsible for stretchiness of dough and helps hold the shape of baked goods. Vital wheat gluten is not gluten flour. It is just the gluten of whole wheat flour. It is more of a flour conditioner that helps with elasticity. It helps to avoid the dense heavy loaves that are associated with whole grain challahs.

Place the yeast, 1 teaspoon sugar, and lukewarm water into a large glass measuring cup or bowl. Set aside in a warm place for 5–10 minutes. (If your kitchen is cold, put in on the opened oven door with the oven temperature set at 300°F.)

In a large bowl, whisk together the bread flour, whole wheat flour, oat flour, flax meal, 2 tablespoons oats, wheat gluten, and kosher salt. Set aside.

Place the sugar, light brown sugar, honey, 2 eggs, and oil into the bowl of a stand mixer. Whisk until blended. When yeast is bubbly, add it to the egg mixture, and whisk until well blended. (If the yeast does not get bubbly, it is dead and you must discard it and make the yeast mixture again with fresh yeast.)

Add the flour mixture to the yeast base. Mix with a wooden spoon until incorporated, scraping sides with a rubber spatula as needed.

Place the bowl on the mixer and attach the dough hook. On medium speed, knead the dough for 1 minute. Stop the mixer, scrape the dough off the hook and down the sides. Knead again on medium for one minute. Dough will be a little sticky at the bottom, but will pull from the sides and form up at the top, around the hook. If the dough is really wet and sticking to the sides everywhere, add more bread flour, 1 tablespoon at a time, kneading between additions, until it is no longer sticky. (The dough can also be kneaded by hand for 5–8 minutes until smooth and elastic.)

Remove the dough from the bowl and knead on a lightly bread-floured surface until smooth and elastic, about 2 more minutes. Coat the bowl with oil, and put the

dough back into the bowl. Spray a piece of plastic wrap with nonstick cooking spray and place it on the top of the bowl, oil-side-down.

Let the dough rise in a warm place for one hour. Punch down, and let the dough rest for 10 minutes. Line 2 large baking sheets with parchment paper. Divide the dough into four equal portions; braid each as desired. Place 2 loaves at least 6 inches apart on each sheet. Spray pieces of plastic wrap with nonstick cooking spray, and place them over the shaped loaves. Let rise in a warm place for 1 hour.

Preheat oven to 350°F. In a small bowl, mix the remaining tablespoon oats with flax seeds and sesame seeds. Brush the loaves with the beaten egg. Sprinkle with the seed mixture, and bake for 25–30 minutes, until golden brown. Remove loaves from the parchment paper and place on racks to cool, or serve immediately with honey.

Lamb Patties with Green Techina

GREEN TECHINA:

- ½ cup tahini paste (also known as Middle-Eastern sesame paste)
- ¼ cup parsley leaves, stems removed
- ¼ cup baby spinach leaves
- 2 cloves fresh garlic

juice of 1 lemon

- ½ teaspoon dried rosemary
- ½ teaspoon ground cumin
- ½ cup water
- ¼ cup extra-virgin olive oil

LAMB PATTIES:

- 1 pound ground lamb
- 1½ teaspoons oregano
- 1 teaspoon paprika
- 1 teaspoon garlic powder
- 1 teaspoon freshly ground black pepper
- ½ teaspoon cayenne pepper
- ½ teaspoon ground cumin
- ¼ teaspoon red pepper flakes
- 2 teaspoons olive oil

Ground lamb is a good source of protein, and the bite-sized portion keeps the saturated fats to a minimum while allowing the indulgence of lamb. By serving foods in these smaller portions, all foods can fit into your diet to help you enjoy and appreciate everything.

Tahini is raw sesame paste. It is an ingredient in techina and other Middle Eastern dressings.

Prepare the green techina: Place tahini, parsley, spinach, garlic, lemon juice, rosemary, cumin, and water into the bowl of a food processor fitted with a metal blade. Process for 1 minute.

Drizzle in the olive oil. Process again. Transfer the techina to a plastic or glass container and cover. Chill in the refrigerator.

Prepare the lamb patties: In a medium mixing bowl combine the lamb, oregano, paprika, garlic powder, pepper, cayenne, cumin, and red pepper flakes. Mix to evenly distribute the spices. Form into 18 small patties.

Heat the 2 teaspoons olive oil in a large skillet over medium heat. Cook the patties for 4–5 minutes per side, until just done; do not overcook.

Serve 3 patties per plate, drizzled with the green techina.

White Portobello Pizzas

DAIRY ■ MAKES 6 SERVINGS

2 teaspoons olive oil

3 shallots, thinly sliced

6 medium (4-inch diameter) portobello mushroom caps, gills removed

olive-oil flavored nonstick cooking spray

1½ cups low-fat ricotta cheese

2 cloves fresh garlic, minced

1 teaspoon dried oregano

¼ teaspoon dried basil

¼ teaspoon fine sea salt

⅛ teaspoon white pepper

6 tablespoons part-skim shredded mozzarella cheese, divided

1 plum tomato, cut into paper-thin slices

6 small basil leaves

freshly ground black pepper

I have always loved pizza, all pizza on all continents. My high school ID read, "In case of emergency, contact Sabra Pizza." When I got to college, I just crossed it out and penciled in "Shimon's Pizza." I spent a year in Israel after college and ate at Big Apple Pizza often. I guess really often. I had not been back to Israel until my honeymoon seven years later. My husband and I walked into Big Apple Pizza and the owner jumped over the counter. "Hey!" he yelled, "Where have ya been?"

This dish is a twist on traditional white pizza, although the concept of assembling pizza ingredients in a portobello cap instead of on dough works for regular sauce-and-cheese pizza as well. Cutting out the dough cuts out lots of calories. Pizza is one of the healthiest fast foods … especially prepared in this fashion, with the addition of nutrient-rich portobellos. The cheese is a great source of calcium and the sauce contributes Vitamins A and C and phytonutrients. Most of all … the kids will love it!

Preheat oven to 425°F.

Heat the oil in a medium skillet over medium-low heat. Add the shallots and cook slowly, stirring occasionally, and allow the shallots to caramelize, about 10 minutes. If they are getting too brown, lower the heat.

Meanwhile, place the mushrooms caps, gill-side-up, on a parchment-lined cookie sheet. Spray the mushrooms with nonstick cooking spray. Bake the mushrooms for 5 minutes. Remove from oven.

In a medium bowl, mix the ricotta cheese with the garlic, oregano, basil, salt, white pepper, and caramelized shallots. Stir to combine. Mound ¼ cup of the cheese mixture into each mushroom cap. Top with 1 tablespoon shredded mozzarella. Place a tomato slice in the center and a basil leaf off-center.

Return the "pizzas" to the oven and bake for 5–6 minutes, until the mozzarella cheese is melted. Sprinkle with black pepper. Serve immediately.

Healthy Deli Rolls

MEAT ■ MAKES 6 SERVINGS

TURKEY-SWEET POTATO ROLL:

- 1 large sweet potato (about ¾ pound)
- 1 (8-ounce) can jellied cranberry sauce
- ¼ teaspoon dried rubbed sage
- ½ box phyllo dough, defrosted
- nonstick cooking spray
- 8 ounces thinly sliced turkey breast
- 1 egg, lightly beaten
- 1 tablespoon pumpkin seeds

ROAST BEEF DELI ROLL:

- 2 teaspoons canola oil
- 2 red onions, very thinly sliced
- ½ box phyllo dough, defrosted
- nonstick cooking spray
- ½ cup stone-ground honey mustard, such as Honeycup®
- 8 ounces cooked very rare roast beef, very thinly sliced
- ¼ cup prepared white horseradish
- 1 egg, lightly beaten
- 2 teaspoons caraway seeds

Deli roll is where it all began for me and this book. Deli roll is not in my usual repertoire nor has it been in any of my cookbooks, but it is and has been all the rage for years on Shabbos tables across this country. My kids requested it one Shabbos. As I began to assemble the dish on Friday morning it struck me, "This represents everything wrong with how we cook today." Enraged, I called my girlfriend Estee Stein and ranted, "Layers of puff pastry, spread thick with mayonnaise and layered with pounds and pounds of salami, pastrami, corned beef! No wonder obesity and diabetes are rampant!" "Do something," she said. "Your cookbooks have made a dent toward healthier eating, make a bigger dent." That was it. I began jotting down ideas that afternoon. The ideas included a healthier version of the deli roll that won't make such a big dent on your scale. Not only is this dish lower in fat, cholesterol, and calories, but it also provides vitamin-packed sweet potato. You can have Thanksgiving any day of the year. I hope you enjoy it.

TURKEY-SWEET POTATO ROLL:

Preheat oven to 350°F.

Cover a cookie sheet with parchment paper. Set aside.

Wrap the sweet potato in a paper towel and microwave for 8–10 minutes, until soft. Peel and mash in a small bowl. Set aside.

In a small bowl, whisk the cranberry sauce with the sage.

Open the phyllo dough. Lay one sheet of the dough on the prepared cookie sheet. Spray on a light, even coating of nonstick cooking spray. Top with another sheet of phyllo dough and nonstick cooking spray. Repeat for a total of 5 sheets of dough.

With an offset spatula, spread a thin layer of cranberry sauce. Top with an even layer of turkey. Spread the sweet potato over the turkey. From a long side end, roll up the dough.

Brush the top of the roll with beaten egg and sprinkle with pumpkin seeds. Bake, uncovered, for 35 minutes. Slice and serve hot.

ROAST BEEF DELI ROLL:

Preheat oven to 350°F.

Cover a cookie sheet with parchment paper. Set aside.

Heat the canola oil in a medium skillet over medium heat. Add the sliced onions and sauté for 10–15 minutes, until soft and caramelized.

Open the phyllo dough. Lay one sheet of the dough on the prepared cookie sheet. Spray on a light, even coating of nonstick cooking spray. Top with another sheet of phyllo dough and nonstick cooking spray. Repeat for a total of 5 sheets of dough.

With an offset spatula, spread a thin layer of honey mustard. Top with an even layer of roast beef. Spread the horseradish over the roast beef and top with caramelized onions. From a long side end, roll up the dough.

Brush the top of the roll with beaten egg and sprinkle with caraway seeds. Bake, uncovered, for 35 minutes. Slice and serve hot.

Ambrosia

PARVE ■ MAKES 8 SERVINGS

½ cup mango or papaya, peeled, seeded, and cut into ⅓-inch pieces

small Granny Smith apple, with skin, cut into ⅓-inch pieces

10 ounces frozen raspberries, not in syrup

1 (11-ounce) can mandarin oranges, drained

1 (20-ounce) can crushed pineapple, drained in a strainer

¾ teaspoon pure vanilla extract

1 tablespoon honey

7-8 large mint leaves, thinly sliced

juice of ½ lime

¾ cup fresh raspberries

4 teaspoons flaked coconut, divided

8 mint leaves, for garnish

My husband and I both lay claim to the old version of this recipe. He claims it is based on "Fruits Fishbein," a staple at all of his mother's dinner parties in the 70's and early 80's. I, however, maintain it is "Happy Fruit," named for my Aunt Happy who served it as an opener at all of my childhood Succot meals. Either way, we have distanced ourselves from the original, which was loaded with sugar. Even the berries were packed in a heavy, sugary syrup. This version is lighter and really highlights the freshness of the fruit. It looks gorgeous in a wine glass. This colorful blend of fruit can double as a dessert.

In a large bowl, combine the mango or papaya, apple, frozen raspberries, oranges, and pineapple. Mix in the vanilla, honey, sliced mint, and the juice from the lime half. Gently fold in the fresh raspberries, trying to keep their shape.

Divide the ambrosia into parfait or wine glasses. Top each with ½ teaspoon coconut and garnish with a fresh mint leaf.

Soups

Roasted Beet Soup
with Pumpernickel Croutons

MEAT, DAIRY, OR PARVE ■ MAKES 8 SERVINGS

4-5 large beets, scrubbed but not peeled

olive oil

3 slices pumpernickel bread

18 walnut halves

½ teaspoon ground or rubbed sage

1 large red onion, cut in half and thinly sliced

2 cloves fresh garlic, thinly sliced

1 cup apple cider

2 cups chicken or vegetable stock

1 cup water

¼ teaspoon fine sea salt

low-fat sour cream or nondairy sour cream, such as Tofutti brand Sour Supreme®

Many beet soup recipes begin with boiling the beets. When you do that, you lose nutrients, color, and flavor. I prefer roasting the beets — and I always make extra. The natural sugars in the beet caramelize and the texture is wonderful. Beets contain a wealth of fiber and are rich in folic acid, essential for preventing some anemias and neural-tube birth defects. Aside from their gorgeous color, roasted beets are delicious in salads with a sprinkle of goat-cheese crumbles, walnuts, and a light olive-oil vinaigrette.

Preheat oven to 400°F.

Rub each beet with 1 teaspoon of olive oil, coating all sides. Wrap individually in aluminum foil and place onto a cookie sheet. Place into the oven and roast for about 1 hour, 15 minutes or until tender.

Remove from oven and allow to stand until no longer hot to the touch. Using a paper towel, rub off the skins and discard. Cut the beets into quarters and set aside.

Meanwhile, prepare the roasted walnuts and croutons: Using a canape cutter or mini cookie cutter of any shape, cut 6 shapes out of each slice of pumpernickel bread. Place the cut-out pumpernickel shapes into a medium bowl with the walnuts. Add 1 tablespoon olive oil and the ground sage. Toss to coat. Place in a single layer on a parchment-lined cookie sheet and place in the hot oven for 5 minutes, until slightly toasted and fragrant. Set aside to cool.

Heat 1 teaspoon olive oil into a large soup pot over medium-low heat. Add the red onion slices and cook; try not to get any color on the onion, just allow it to "sweat." Add the garlic slices and cook for 2 more minutes, until the garlic is fragrant. Pour in the apple cider, stock, and 1 cup water. Add the beets. Simmer for 5 minutes, until heated through.

Using an immersion blender, purée the soup. This can also be done in batches in a blender or food processor fitted with a metal blade. Season with salt.

To serve, divide the soup among 8 ramekins or small bowls. Top each with a teaspoon-size dollop of sour cream, 3 pumpernickel croutons, and 3 walnut halves.

Zucchini Lentil Soup

3 egg roll wrappers,
   such as the Nasoya® brand

1 egg white (from large egg)

1 tablespoon water

¼ teaspoon dried dill

¼ teaspoon dried basil

1 tablespoon olive oil

1 large sweet onion, such
   as Vidalia, cut into ¼-inch
   pieces

4 cloves fresh garlic, coarsely
   chopped

½ teaspoon dried sage

¼ teaspoon dried thyme

2 large or 3 medium zucchini,
   with skin, cut into ¼-inch
   pieces

¼ cup fresh dill, stems
   trimmed, loosely packed

6 cups chicken or vegetable
   stock

1 cup dried red lentils

Red lentils add an earthy tone to this soup and are one of the fastest cooking legumes. Lentils are even mentioned in the Bible, as Esau traded his birthright to Jacob for "a potage of lentils"! This historic legume is rich in fiber, niacin, potassium, and zinc. Don't overcook the lentils or they will start to come apart.

The spiced egg roll wrappers are a crisp garnish and sub in nicely for crusty bread or soup nuts.

Preheat oven to 425°F.

Cover a cookie sheet with parchment paper.

Lay the egg roll wrappers on the prepared cookie sheet. In a small bowl, whisk the egg white and water. Brush each egg roll wrapper very lightly with the egg white mixture. Sprinkle with dried dill and dried basil. Place into the oven and bake for 5 minutes or until just golden brown. Set aside.

Meanwhile, heat the olive oil in a large soup pot over medium-low heat. Add the onion, garlic, sage, and thyme. Cook until the onion is translucent; do not allow it to brown.

Add the zucchini and dill. Sauté for 4–5 minutes, until zucchini is a little shiny.

Add the stock. Simmer for 15–20 minutes, or until the zucchini is soft.

Using an immersion blender, right in the pot, purée the soup until creamy. This can also be done in batches in a blender.

Add the lentils. Simmer, stirring occasionally, for 8 minutes.

Ladle the soup into bowls. Holding a spiced egg roll crisp over the pot to catch the spices that may fall off, break each into uneven shards and stand a few in the center of each bowl.

Mexican Turkey Albondigas Soup

MEAT ■ MAKES 6 SERVINGS

1 pound ground turkey

2 teaspoons olive oil, divided

1 onion, cut into ¼-inch pieces

1 clove fresh garlic, minced

½ teaspoon ground cumin, divided

¼ teaspoon cayenne pepper

¾ teaspoon dried oregano

½ teaspoon fine sea salt

1 small red onion, cut in half and thinly sliced

1 carrot, peeled, cut into ¼ inch pieces

2 stalks celery, cut into ¼ inch pieces

1 small jalapeño pepper, seeds and ribs removed, finely chopped

3 cloves fresh garlic, sliced

½ teaspoon paprika

1 cup tomato sauce

8 cups chicken stock

2 slices whole wheat bread

3 tablespoons egg substitute, such as Egg Beaters®, or 1 large egg

2 scallions, thinly sliced on a diagonal

¼ cup fresh cilantro, leaves coarsely chopped

Albondigas is the Spanish word for "meatball." This meatball soup is a Mexican favorite. The egg replacement, ground turkey, and whole wheat bread lighten up this filling dish.

By using egg replacement or 2 egg whites instead of one whole egg, you can save around 220 milligrams of cholesterol. By using the ground turkey instead of beef, you can cut the cholesterol by one-third.

Place the ground turkey into a medium mixing bowl. Set aside.

Place one teaspoon of the olive oil into a large pot over medium heat. Add the onion and the garlic and sauté until the onion is translucent, about 5–6 minutes. Add ¼ teaspoon cumin, cayenne, oregano, and salt. Toast until the spices are fragrant, about 1 minute. Add the spiced onions to the turkey.

Pour the remaining teaspoon of olive oil into the pot. Heat over medium. Add the red onion slices, carrot, celery, jalapeño pepper, and sliced garlic. Sauté for 4–5 minutes, until vegetables are fragrant. Add the paprika and remaining cumin. Stir to coat the vegetables. Pour in the tomato sauce and chicken stock. Bring to a simmer.

Meanwhile, cut the crusts from the bread and discard. Place the bread into a food processor fitted with a metal blade. Pulse until coarse bread crumbs form. Add the bread crumbs to the turkey, along with the egg product. Gently mix with your hands. The mixture will be very soft. This will keep the turkey from toughening. Wet your hands to keep the turkey from sticking. Form into walnut-sized meatballs and carefully drop the meatballs into the soup. Cover the pot and allow the soup to simmer for 15 minutes (do not boil), or until the meatballs are cooked through.

Ladle the soup into bowls. Garnish each bowl with scallions and cilantro.

Kale, Sausage, and White Bean Soup

MEAT ■ MAKES 10-12 SERVINGS

2 teaspoons olive oil

3 shallots, minced

2 cloves fresh garlic, coarsely chopped

1 (12-ounce) package of andouille chicken/turkey sausage (4 links)

½ teaspoon dried oregano

4 plum tomatoes, from a 28-ounce can with basil, drained, coarsely chopped

6 cups chicken stock

12 fresh kale leaves, stems removed, washed and drained, stacked and chopped into 2-inch pieces; about 4 cups

2 (15-ounce) cans small white beans, rinsed and drained

¼ teaspoon freshly ground black pepper

Sausage is available at most kosher butchers. In kosher supermarkets look for my favorite brand, Neshama®. The sausages are also available at www.neshama.us and are low in fat and MSG-free. Buy an extra pack to grill on the barbecue or toss into a sauté of caramelized onions and peppers.

Although all leafy greens help ward off cancer and heart disease, kale leads the pack and is also one of the best sources of Vitamin A, in the form of beta-carotene.

Kale stems are tough, even when cooked, so they must be trimmed. To do this, turn each leaf over. Use a knife to cut a v-shape along both sides of the rib, cutting the stem free from the leaf but preserving most of the leaf.

Heat the olive oil in a large soup pot over medium-low heat. Add the shallots and garlic. Cook until the shallots are shiny and translucent, about 4 minutes; do not allow to brown. Chop the sausage into 1-inch chunks and add to the pot. Sprinkle in the oregano. Cook until the sausage is starting to brown, about 5 minutes.

Add the chopped tomatoes, stock, kale, beans, and black pepper. Bring to a boil. Cover the pot, lower the heat, and simmer for 15 minutes.

Thai Chicken Soup

MEAT ■ MAKES 6 SERVINGS

1 tablespoon olive oil

1 medium onion, cut in half, and then into thin strips

2 cloves fresh garlic, thinly sliced

4 chicken drumsticks, skin discarded

1 serrano chili pepper or 3 Thai chilies; poke holes in the chilies with a fork

1 teaspoon fresh minced ginger

6 cups chicken stock

1 carrot, julienned

1 yellow bell pepper, seeded and cut into thin matchsticks, 1-inch in length

8 shiitake mushroom caps, thinly sliced

1 jalapeño pepper, thinly sliced

4 scallions, thinly sliced on the diagonal

¼ cup fresh cilantro leaves

1½ limes, quartered

¼ cup unsalted peanuts or soy nuts, coarsely chopped

Aside from adding zest to your dish, chili peppers can help fight inflammation and arthritis pain. The active ingredient, known as capsaicin, may also help your heart. And keep a glass of water handy, because the hotter the pepper … the greater the capsaicin content!

Poking holes in the chili peppers allows flavor to infuse into the soup without adding overwhelming heat.

Heat the olive oil in a large soup pot over medium-low heat. Add the onion and garlic. Cook until the onion is shiny and translucent, about 4 minutes; do not allow it to brown. Add the chicken, serrano or Thai chilies, and ginger. Stir in the chicken stock and bring to a simmer.

Add the carrot and yellow bell pepper to the pot. Allow the soup to simmer on medium for 10 minutes.

Carefully remove the chicken legs and the chilies from the pot. Discard the chilies. Take the meat off the chicken bones, discarding bones, and return the chicken to the soup. Stir in the shiitake mushrooms, jalapeño pepper, scallions, and cilantro leaves. Heat through.

Ladle into bowls. Squeeze ¼ lime over each bowl. Garnish with a sprinkle of chopped peanuts or soy nuts.

Peasant Soup

8 ounces collard greens (about 2 bunches)

2 teaspoons olive oil

1 large onion, cut into ¼-inch pieces

3 cloves fresh garlic, coarsely chopped

1 bay leaf

½ teaspoon dried thyme

¼ teaspoon red pepper flakes

1 large beef marrow bone

8 cups beef stock (can be made from consommé powder dissolved in water)

2 russet potatoes, peeled and cut into ¾-inch chunks

3 thick slices of sourdough or other crusty bread, crusts removed

Every culture has a version of this hearty soup. It fills you up using meager ingredients. So even if you are not a serf, go ahead and whip up a batch. Some markets sell collards pre-chopped in bags. This is a nice time-saving option. Collards are inexpensive and yet rich in disease-fighting beta-carotene and Vitamin C.

Sourdough croutons will give you the bread for sopping up the soup without the temptation of a huge crusty loaf on the table.

Preheat oven to 400°F.

Prepare the collard greens: Turn each leaf over. Rip the leaves off each side of the spine, discarding the spine. Chop the leaves into bite-sized, 2-inch pieces. Wash and drain. Set aside.

Heat the olive oil in a large soup pot over medium-low heat. Add the onion and garlic. Cook until the onion is translucent, about 4 minutes; do not allow it to brown. Add the bay leaf, thyme, and red pepper. Stir to distribute the spices.

Add the collard greens and the marrow bone. Cook for 10–12 minutes, uncovered, to give the greens a chance to cook down a bit.

Add the stock and the potatoes. Raise the heat to medium. Bring the soup to a simmer. Cook for 30 minutes.

Meanwhile, prepare the croutons: Cut the bread into 1-inch dice. Place on a cookie sheet and toast in the oven for 7 minutes, until crisp.

Serve each bowl of soup with 3 bread cubes.

Cabbage Soup

MEAT OR PARVE ■ MAKES 6 SERVINGS

1 tablespoon olive oil

1 large onion, cut into ¼-inch pieces

3 cloves fresh garlic, chopped

1 tablespoon tomato paste

⅛ teaspoon red pepper flakes

6 cups beef stock (can be made from beef consommé powder dissolved in water)

½ teaspoon dried basil

½ teaspoon dried oregano

¼ teaspoon freshly ground black pepper

3 cups fresh green cabbage, roughly ¼ of a small cabbage, thinly sliced

1 (14.5-ounce) can stewed tomatoes, coarsely chopped, reserve juices

1 cup canned crushed tomatoes

Who remembers an entire diet craze that centered around cabbage soup? Some fads are meant to pass, but there is no need for the soup to pass with it. Vegetables in the cabbage family, like broccoli, cauliflower, and Brussels sprouts, may even protect against certain cancers. Here is my version of a really flavorful cabbage soup that is sure to fill you up and satisfy with its sweet-tangy flavor. For a heartier touch, add some sliced turkey or chicken sausage. All you need is a piece of crusty whole-grain bread and you have a full meal.

Heat the olive oil in a large soup pot over medium-low heat. Add the onion and garlic. Cook until the onion is translucent; do not allow it to brown. Add the tomato paste and red pepper flakes. Stir to combine.

Pour in the stock. Season with the basil, oregano, and black pepper. Raise the heat and bring to a simmer. Stir in the cabbage. Simmer until the cabbage wilts, about 10 minutes.

Add the stewed tomatoes with their liquid, and the crushed tomatoes. Stir. Continue to simmer for 10–15 minutes. Serve hot.

Vegetable Hot Pot

PARVE ■ MAKES 6 SERVINGS

My husband claims he can hear his body thanking him when he eats a bowl of this soup. It is bursting with vitamins, has close to no fat, and is so satisfying.

So here's why every cell in your body applauds when you swallow this savory dish: spinach and carrots can help protect your eyes; ginger helps put a halt to morning and motion sickness; bok choy, leeks, and zucchini fight cancer; cilantro is an antibacterial agent; hot chilies can soothe arthritis aches; and garlic and mushrooms might help give your immune system a boost! Wow … you won't want to put your spoon down!

Place the ginger, garlic, chilies, and cilantro into a cheesecloth or mesh bag to make a bouquet garni. Place into a large soup pot.

Add the bok choy, leeks, carrot, spinach, zucchini, mushrooms, water, and 2 teaspoons salt. Cover and bring to a boil over medium-high heat. Reduce heat to low and simmer for 10 minutes. Add the snow peas during the last 3 minutes. Remove and discard the bouquet garni. Stir in the sesame oil. Add salt to taste.

2 inches fresh ginger, peeled, halved lengthwise

3 cloves fresh garlic, peeled

3 hot chilies, poked with a fork along the length of each chili pepper

handful fresh cilantro sprigs

3 heads baby bok choy, halved lengthwise

2 leeks, bottom 4 inches, quartered lengthwise

1 small carrot, peeled, thinly sliced lengthwise into ⅛-inch slices, then cut into 1½-inch pieces

2 cups fresh baby spinach leaves

½ zucchini, with skin, thinly sliced lengthwise into ⅛-inch slices, then cut into 1½-inch pieces

2 bunches oyster mushrooms, coarsely chopped, or 1⅔ cup (3.2 ounces) sliced assorted mushrooms

6 cups water

2 teaspoons fine sea salt, or more to taste

½ cup snow peas

½ teaspoon roasted or toasted sesame oil

Velvety Roasted Vegetable Barley Soup

MEAT OR PARVE ■ MAKES 8 SERVINGS

2 tablespoons olive oil, divided

1 large sweet potato, with skin, scored

1 medium acorn or butternut squash, with skin, quartered, seeded

1 large parsnip, peeled and cut into chunks

4 plum tomatoes, each cut in half

⅛ teaspoon fine sea salt

¼ teaspoon freshly ground black pepper

3 stalks celery, coarsely chopped

1 Spanish onion, cut in half, thinly sliced

2 cloves fresh garlic, chopped

6 cups chicken or vegetable stock

⅛ teaspoon cayenne pepper

1 cup pearled barley

4 cups water

Barley is a grain that is packed with fiber and low in fat. Hulled barley is more nutritious than pearled barley since it retains the outer bran. I use pearled barley, though, which is still healthful, because it cooks faster and has a nicer texture.

Barley contains the soluble fiber beta-glucan, the same cholesterol-lowering constituent that's in oat bran and beans. Did you know that the whole, hulled form of barley has even more insoluble fiber than wheat?

Although the barley adds nutrition and texture to this soup, it can be omitted. It is cooked separately because barley expands and expands as it cooks, absorbing all the liquid. It should also be reheated separately.

Preheat oven to 375°F.

Cover a jelly-roll pan with aluminum foil, leaving large flaps of foil on the sides to be able to fold over the top of the vegetables.

Rub one tablespoon of the oil on the outside and flesh of the sweet potato, squash, parsnip, and tomatoes. Sprinkle with salt and pepper. Place the vegetables, cut-side-down, on the prepared sheet.

Fold the foil flaps over the vegetables and roast for 1 hour. Check to make sure the vegetables are soft when poked with the tip of a knife. Uncover and broil on high for 5 minutes. Remove from oven.

During the last 20 minutes of the roasting process, heat the remaining tablespoon of olive oil in a large soup pot. Add the celery and onion. Heat over medium-low, and cook slowly for 8–10 minutes, stirring occasionally, to bring out the natural sugars. Do not allow the onions to brown. Add the garlic and continue to cook for 5 more minutes.

When the vegetables are done, add the parsnips, tomatoes, and flesh of the sweet potato and squash.

Add the stock and cayenne. Simmer for 20 minutes.

Meanwhile, place the barley and 4 cups of water into a pot. Bring to a boil over medium heat. Boil until al dente, about 15 minutes. The water will be absorbed. Set aside.

Using an immersion blender right in the soup pot, purée the soup until completely creamy, about 5–6 minutes.

Add a portion of barley to each bowl before serving.

Roasted Garlic Broth
with Vegetables

MEAT OR PARVE ■ MAKES 6 SERVINGS

1 tablespoon olive oil

2 shallots, sliced into thin
rings

2 heads garlic, roasted
as noted

⅛ teaspoon dried rubbed
sage

2 cups chicken or vegetable
stock

4 cups water

1½ cups broccoli florets,
trimmed into small pieces

1½ cups cauliflower florets,
trimmed into small pieces

1 yellow squash, with skin,
cut into ¼-inch dice

1 zucchini, with skin,
cut into ¼-inch dice

1 (15-ounce) can diced
tomatoes, strained
and rinsed

1 teaspoon fine sea salt

6 fresh sage leaves, chopped

white pepper, optional

Roasting garlic takes 45–60 minutes. Prep the rest of the vegetables while it cooks. Make sure to roast some extra heads — they keep for 5 days and add lots of fat-free flavor to stews, dressings, burgers, sauces, etc. Hold the head on its side. Slice off ¾-inch to expose the cloves. Spray with nonstick cooking spray and season with salt and pepper. Wrap in foil. Bake at 350°F until golden, fragrant, and soft, about 45–60 minutes. You can store extra heads in the foil in an airtight container or ziplock bag to contain the smell.

Garlic has been applauded through the centuries for its medicinal qualities. Aside from adding amazing flavor and aroma to your meal, garlic has a host of other benefits. The chemicals in garlic, called allium compounds, boost levels of naturally occurring enzymes that stimulate cancer-fighting immune cells and help to fight off infection.

Heat the olive oil in a large soup pot over medium heat. Add the shallots and cook for 3 minutes, until translucent and shiny. Squeeze the roasted garlic cloves out of the heads. Using the back of a chef's knife or a spoon, smash the garlic against the cutting board to smear it into a paste. Add it to the shallots, along with the rubbed sage. Add the stock and water. Bring to a boil.

Add the broccoli and cauliflower. Cook for 8 minutes, until they are soft. Add the squash, zucchini, tomatoes, and salt. Cook for 3 minutes, until squash is soft.

Sprinkle in the chopped sage leaves. Heat through for 1 minute. Season with salt and white pepper if desired.

Japanese Udon Noodle Soup

MEAT OR PARVE ■ MAKES 6 SERVINGS

8 ounces udon noodles, cooked according to package directions

4 cups chicken or vegetable stock

4 cups water

½ ounce dried kombu

1 cup baby carrots, cut into ¼-inch slices

2 tablespoons mirin

2 tablespoons low-sodium soy sauce

1 small knob fresh ginger peeled and grated on a microplane to yield 1 teaspoon

Udon is a thick Japanese noodle found in most supermarkets. I discovered big differences in sodium and fat content in varied brands of udon. As far as taste and texture, however, I like the Eden Organic brand, wheat-and-rice udon. It is an 80% wheat flour–20% short-grain brown rice flour blend.

Udon noodles are typically paired in Asian soups with a lean protein like chicken, but I kept the protein out of this recipe so it can be made parve. Feel free to add cooked chicken back in, or break apart grilled salmon and add it into the soup.

Kombu draws a long list of elements from the sea, including sodium, calcium, magnesium, potassium, chloride, sulfur, phosphorous, iron, zinc, copper, selenium, molybdenum, fluoride, manganese, boron, nickel, and cobalt! Kombu is extremely rich in iodine and is used in Japan to make over 300 products, such as condiments and teas. Its addition in soups and stews imparts flavor and boosts nutritional value.

Prepare the udon noodles.

Meanwhile, bring the stock along with 4 cups of water to a boil. Add the kombu and simmer for 1 minute. Add the carrots, mirin, soy sauce, and ginger. Gently simmer 3–4 minutes.

Divide the udon noodles between the serving bowls. Remove the kombu and ladle the broth over the noodles.

Curried Cauliflower Soup

2 ribs celery

1 head cauliflower

2 teaspoons olive oil

1 large onion, coarsely chopped

1 large Granny Smith apple, with skin, cored, cut into ½-inch pieces

1 teaspoon curry powder

½ cup dry white wine

5 sprigs thyme

1 bay leaf

6 cups chicken stock or consommé powder dissolved in 6 cups water

GARNISH:

½ Granny Smith apple, with skin, cut into ¼-inch pieces

1 lemon

6 cilantro leaves

Cauliflower is a cruciferous vegetable, part of the same family as broccoli, kale, cabbage, and collards. This group is being studied for its role in reducing cancer. What we know for sure is that it is very high in Vitamin C and fiber. More importantly, it is delicious.

Split each rib of celery down the center, lengthwise. Chop into ½-inch pieces. Set aside.

Cut the cauliflower in half and remove the core. Pull into florets. Reserve 1 cup of small florets for garnish and pull these apart into tiny florets. Set aside.

Heat the olive oil in a large soup pot over medium heat. Add the celery and onion. Cook together for 4–5 minutes, until shiny and translucent. Make sure not to get any color on the onion; if it starts to brown, lower the heat.

Add the apple and sauté for 5 minutes longer. Add the curry powder and wine. Cook for 2 minutes to cook off some of the alcohol. Add the cauliflower, reserving the tiny florets for garnish. Add the whole sprigs of thyme, bay leaf, and stock.

Simmer for 20 minutes or until the cauliflower is tender. Remove the thyme sprigs and bay leaf and discard.

Meanwhile, prepare the garnish: Place the small pieces of apple into a bowl and cover with water and the juice of the lemon.

Bring a small pot of water to a boil. Add the reserved cauliflower and cook until soft.

Carefully transfer the soup in batches to a blender. Holding the top of the blender with a towel, purée the soup for 3–4 minutes. You will get a better result in a blender but if you don't have one, you can also use an immersion blender right in the pot, but blend for a full 6–7 minutes, until the soup is velvety smooth.

Drain the lemon water from the apples and drain the cauliflower. Ladle the soup into bowls and garnish with a small mound of apple and cauliflower. Finish each bowl with a cilantro leaf.

Three Sisters Soup

PARVE ■ MAKES 6 SERVINGS

1 tablespoon olive oil

1 large onion, cut into ¼-inch dice

1 stalk celery, halved lengthwise and cut into ¼-inch dice

½ teaspoon dried oregano

1 teaspoon garlic powder

¼ teaspoon ground cumin

2 cups frozen butternut squash cubes

1 (15-ounce) can black beans, rinsed and drained

1 cup frozen corn kernels

2 cups canned crushed tomatoes

3 cups water

½ cup frozen shelled edamame

¼ teaspoon cayenne pepper

fine sea salt

freshly ground black pepper

In the school that my children attend, a unit on Native Americans is studied in 4th grade. I have twice been lucky enough to be the parent chaperone on the end-of-unit trip to Waterloo Village, a recreated Lenape Indian village. The Lenapes inhabited New Jersey long before the Europeans arrived and led a very well-organized, peaceful lifestyle. One of the highlights for me is the farming area where the symbiotic style that governs so much of their traditions is put to good use. They planted what they called "the three sisters" — squash, corn, and beans — because the three grew so well together. These sisters are also laden with fiber, and their multiple colors provide the benefits of multiple vitamins and minerals as well.

As a mother of "three sisters" who share their own symbiotic relationship as they grow, I always loved that concept and developed this soup with that in mind.

Heat the olive oil in a large soup pot over medium heat. Add the onion and celery. Cook together for 4–5 minutes, until shiny and translucent. Make sure not to get any color on the onion; if it starts to brown, lower the heat.

In a small bowl mix the oregano, garlic powder, and cumin. Stir and add to the onions. Sauté for 2 minutes to toast the spices.

Add the butternut squash, beans, corn, and tomatoes. Cook for 5 minutes. Add 3 cups water, or more if needed to cover the vegetables. Add the edamame and cayenne and simmer for 15 minutes. Season with salt and pepper to taste.

Miso Soup

6 cups chicken stock or water

½ cup light miso

2 tablespoons low-sodium soy sauce

3 ounces firm tofu, cut into ¼-inch dice (¼ of a 14-ounce block)

4 medium shiitake mushroom caps, thinly sliced

3 scallions, thinly sliced on the diagonal

Miso is a fermented paste of soybean, grains, and yeast. Except for the salt content, it is virtuous in its health benefits. It's high in the minerals iron, copper, and manganese, and is also a favorite of vegans because of its naturally high protein, Vitamin K, and B_{12} content.

This recipe calls for white or light blond miso. Darker misos, sometimes called red, brown, or barley miso, are fermented longer and have a very strong flavor.

If using chicken stock, make sure it is not too salty. If it is, use only 4 cups stock and dilute with 2 cups water so the salt doesn't overpower the miso flavor. Some say boiling miso kills off some of its nutrients, so make sure to turn the heat down when you are ready to add it.

Bring the water or chicken stock to a boil over medium heat. Lower the heat. Add the miso and stir to help it dissolve. Add the soy sauce and the tofu. Stir. Add the shiitake mushrooms and scallions and heat through.

Salads

Mile-High Chinese Chicken Salad

MEAT ■ MAKES 6 SERVINGS

4 boneless, skinless, chicken breast halves

¼ teaspoon cayenne pepper

1 lime

1 head Bibb lettuce

½ box sprouts, any kind, rinsed and trimmed

1 carrot, julienned

½ English (hothouse) cucumber, unpeeled, seeded and cut into half-moons

3 scallions, thinly sliced on the diagonal

⅓ cup fresh cilantro leaves, chopped

⅓ cup extra-virgin olive oil

¼ cup rice vinegar

2 tablespoons low-sodium soy sauce

GARNISH:

canola oil

2½ ounces (2 large handfuls) rice sticks or rice vermicelli

Adeena Sussman is a fabulous food writer and recipe developer who has her finger on the pulse of the kosher food industry. She worked with me on a few recipes for this book. Between our common love for our jobs and a few good rounds of "Jewish geography," we became fast friends. Generous in spirit and deed she always came baring gifts. One of my favorites was the julienne peeler by Zyliss. It is great here for making spaghetti-thin strands of carrot.

The juices from the chicken packets add great fat-free flavor to this salad and voluminous rice sticks add a fabulous and fun visual appeal. This salad makes a tasty and satisfying lunch or dinner, providing lots of color without lots of calories.

Preheat oven to 400°F.

Place two chicken breast halves onto a large square of tin foil. Repeat with the other two chicken breasts and a second piece of foil. Sprinkle the chicken with the cayenne and squeeze ½ lime over each packet. Close up the packets and place onto a cookie sheet or jelly-roll pan. Place into the oven and bake for 20 minutes or until the chicken is done. Larger breasts can take up to 10 minutes longer. Reserve the juices from the foil packets.

Separate the head of lettuce into individual leaves and place the leaves into a bowl. Place the sprouts, carrot, cucumber, and scallions into a separate bowl.

In a quart-sized container, whisk the cilantro leaves, olive oil, rice vinegar, and soy sauce.

Pour some of the dressing into each bowl and toss to coat.

On each of six plates, set out a bed of dressed lettuce. Top with the carrot mix.

When the chicken has cooled for a few minutes, slice on the diagonal and lay six strips over each salad. Drizzle the juices from the foil packets and any remaining dressing over the salads.

For the garnish, heat ½-inch of canola oil in a large skillet over medium heat. When the oil is hot, test with one rice stick. In 1 second, it should puff and turn white. If the oil temperature is right, add rice sticks, a small handful at a time. Top each salad with some of the rice sticks. The puffed rice sticks can be stored separately in a ziplock bag until ready to use and can be prepared up to 2 days in advance.

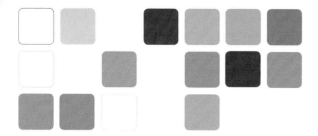

Rice Cracker Slaw

PARVE ■ MAKES 8 SERVINGS

1 (16-ounce) bag coleslaw mix (mix of shredded green cabbage and carrots)

⅓ cup seasoned rice vinegar

1 tablespoon hoisin sauce

1 tablespoon honey

1 teaspoon coarse sea salt

1 teaspoon dried mustard powder

1 teaspoon dried ground ginger

1 teaspoon freshly ground black pepper

⅓ cup canola oil

¼ cup roasted or toasted sesame oil

2 tablespoons water

1 cup rice cracker snacks, with wasabi peas if possible

I love crunchy things in my salads. From croutons to nuts, I usually grab for something to top a plate of greens. In looking for something lower in calories and fat, I discovered rice cracker mix. Notice the wasabi peas in the picture. For a great kick, try to find the kind of snack mix that includes them.

Cabbage and its relatives, the cruciferous vegetables, are not only cancer fighters, but they're also filled with fiber and they may reduce blood pressure.

You can make the salad in advance and store it in a large ziplock bag, but toss the rice snacks in right before serving or they will get mushy.

Empty the bag of coleslaw mix into a large bowl.

In a quart-sized container, prepare the dressing: combine the rice vinegar, hoisin sauce, honey, salt, mustard powder, ginger, pepper, canola oil, sesame oil, and water. Use a whisk or immersion blender to combine.

Pour the dressing over the coleslaw. Allow to marinate at least an hour to give the cabbage a chance to soften and for the flavors to mingle. Right before serving, toss the rice crackers on top.

Bok Choy Slaw

PARVE ■ MAKES 6 SERVINGS

½ large head bok choy

2 scallions, thinly sliced
   on the bias

⅓ cup pumpkin seeds

⅓ cup slivered almonds

½ cup sweetened dried
   cranberries, like Craisins®

¼ cup canola oil

1 tablespoon creamy
   peanut butter

½ cup apple-cider vinegar

⅓ cup honey

1 teaspoon fine sea salt

1 cup thin chow mein
   noodles

When I taught a show at the Chabad of Bedford my hostess, Sara Wolf, and I chatted about how we both love salad with lots of "stuff" in it. She kindly shared this recipe from her Australian mother-in-law.

Although they have the healthy kind of fat, nuts bring the fat content of salads way up, so measure carefully. By using nuts in their chopped, sliced, or slivered versions, you can significantly cut back on calories while jazzing up your favorite dishes.

Bok choy is an Asian cabbage that is loaded with health benefits. It is high in vitamins, folic acid, beta-carotene, calcium, and fiber. It is often used in stir fries or soups at Chinese restaurants. The bitterness in bok choy varies, so you may add a touch of sugar to balance the dressing.

Cut a small slice from the base of the bok choy and discard. Separate the leaves. Thinly slice ½ of the bok choy, including the leaves. Place sliced bok choy into a mixing bowl. Toss in the scallions, pumpkin seeds, almonds, and cranberries.

In a quart-sized container, combine the canola oil, peanut butter, vinegar, honey, and salt. Use a whisk or immersion blender to combine.

Pour the dressing over the bok choy mixture. Toss to combine.

Sprinkle on the chow mein noodles right before serving or they will get soggy.

Fat-free Tuna Salad with Potato Crisps

PARVE ■ MAKES 6 SERVINGS

2 large red potatoes
(4-inch diameter),
scrubbed, skin intact

nonstick cooking spray

coarse sea salt

2 teaspoons dried rosemary

3 (6-ounce) cans (18-ounces
total) chunk light tuna in
water

3 tablespoons sweet pickle
relish

2 tablespoons yellow
or honey mustard

8 ounces mesclun lettuce

¼ cup balsamic vinegar

¼ cup water

1 tablespoon yellow mustard

½ teaspoon garlic powder

When the ladies come for lunch, a great tuna salad is always a welcome sight. This recipe is reminiscent of the "tuna sandwich and french fry" lunches of my younger days but far more elegant, delicious, and healthful.

Current studies show that "solid white" tuna contains roughly 3 times more mercury than "chunk light" tuna. The reason for that is that albacore is a much larger fish than the smaller, less flavorful fish used for light tuna. Pregnant women are usually warned of this danger. If this issue concerns you, try switching to canned wild salmon; it is lower in mercury and higher in omega-3 fatty acids and calcium.

On the positive side, numerous studies have shown that children born to (and breast-fed by) women who consume a diet high in fish oils (rich in omega-3's) have been found to have higher IQ's than those born to mothers whose diets lack these essential fatty acids. Deficits of these substances have also been linked to postpartum depression. When it comes to fish and pregnancy … proceed with caution, but proceed!

Preheat oven to 400°F.

Line two cookie sheets with parchment paper. Set aside.

Using a handheld mandoline, slice the potatoes into 3-mm. slices. You want them even and thin, but not paper-thin. Spread them in a single layer on the prepared sheets. Pat them dry with paper towels. Spray a heavy coating of nonstick cooking spray over the potatoes. Sprinkle on the salt and crumble on the rosemary. Bake for 10 minutes, then flip the potatoes and rotate the two sheets until the potatoes start to crisp but not burn, about 5–10 minutes. They bake a bit unevenly, so watch carefully and take the chips out as they are done.

Meanwhile, drain the tuna and transfer to a shallow container. Using the back of a fork, thoroughly mash the tuna. Mix in the relish and mustard and mash again.

Arrange a mound of lettuce on each plate.

In a jar or cruet, shake or whisk the vinegar, ¼-cup water, yellow mustard, and garlic powder. Dress the lettuce with the dressing. Place a 3-ounce scoop of tuna over each salad.

Place some potato crisps alongside each salad.

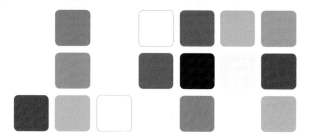

Sweet Potato Salad

PARVE ■ MAKES 6 SERVINGS

2 large sweet potatoes, unpeeled

3 tablespoons light pancake or maple syrup

1 tablespoon chopped fresh cilantro leaves

¼ teaspoon coarse sea salt

¼ cup chopped pecans

The sweet potato is a nutrition powerhouse! One baked sweet potato can give you 2.5 times your daily need for Vitamin A (from beta-carotene) and one third of your daily requirement for Vitamin C. Vitamins A and C are antioxidants that help eliminate substances that destroy cells in the body.

This recipe is nice at room temperature the next day, so be sure to make a double batch.

Place the whole potatoes into a pot and cover with water. Cover the pot and bring to a boil. Boil for 30–40 minutes until fork-tender but not mushy. The time will vary based on size of the sweet potatoes. Remove from water.

When the potatoes are cool enough to handle, peel and cut into 1-inch chunks.

In a small bowl, whisk the syrup, cilantro leaves, and salt.

Pour the syrup over the sweet potatoes and toss to combine. Sprinkle with the pecans.

Cranberry Couscous Salad

PARVE ■ MAKES 16 SERVINGS

1 tablespoon olive oil

2 (8.8-ounce) boxes or bags of Israeli couscous

4 cups boiling water

⅓ cup canola oil

3 tablespoons apple cider vinegar

1 tablespoon water

1 tablespoon honey

2 tablespoons orange juice

4 cloves fresh garlic, minced

juice of ½ lemon

½ teaspoon turmeric

½ teaspoon dried thyme

½ teaspoon fine sea salt

½ teaspoon freshly ground black pepper

¼ teaspoon dried tarragon

½ cup sweetened, dried cranberries, such as Craisins®

¾ cup coarsely chopped pecans

5 scallions, thinly sliced

4 sprigs of fresh thyme, leaves removed; discard stems

Loads of colors, textures, flavors, vitamins, minerals, and fiber in this one! Cranberries help to fight off bladder infections by blocking the ability of bacteria to stick to the surface of the bladder. Cranberries are also a good source of vitamin C.

This salad can be made in advance and kept in a heavy-duty ziplock bag for up to 3 days.

Heat the olive oil in a large soup pot over medium heat. Add the couscous and toast until slightly browned. Add 4 cups boiling water. Cover and simmer on low for 8–10 minutes, until the water is absorbed.

Meanwhile, prepare the dressing: In a quart-sized container, combine the canola oil, cider vinegar, water, honey, orange juice, minced garlic, lemon juice, turmeric, thyme, salt, pepper, and tarragon. With a whisk or immersion blender, blend until fully combined.

When the couscous is done, fluff with a spoon or fork. Pour in the dressing. Add the cranberries, pecans, and scallions. Toss to fully combine.

Garnish with fresh thyme leaves.

Mexican Citrus Salad

PARVE ■ MAKES 6 SERVINGS

SPICED PEPITAS:

⅓ cup pumpkin seeds

1 teaspoon canola oil

¼ teaspoon chili powder

¼ teaspoon ground cumin

1 teaspoon sugar

pinch of fine sea salt

SALAD:

1 (11-ounce) can mandarin oranges, drained

¼ small red onion, cut into paper-thin slices

¼ cup fresh cilantro or parsley leaves, stems discarded

1 Haas avocado, halved, pitted, cut into cubes

1 shallot, very finely minced

2 tablespoons lemon juice (from about ½ large lemon)

¼ teaspoon ground mustard powder

pinch of fine sea salt

pinch of ground white pepper

¼ cup walnut oil

1 teaspoon honey

3 cups frisée lettuce

1 pink grapefruit, peeled and sliced horizontally into 6 (½-inch) slices

Walnut oil is nutty, rich in antioxidants (as long as it is not heated), and rich in flavor, which means you can use less of it and still get great taste. When whisked, walnut oil gets a creamy quality. Nut oils get rancid quickly, so they are best bought in small amounts and kept in the refrigerator.

Did you know that 1½ ounces of pepitas (pumpkin seeds) have as much potassium as a banana? Potassium helps us maintain normal blood pressure and helps our muscles contract.

Preheat oven to 350°F.

Prepare the Spiced Pepitas: In a small bowl, toss the pumpkin seeds with the oil, chili powder, cumin, sugar, and salt. Spread in a single layer onto a parchment-lined baking sheet. Toast for 10 minutes.

Meanwhile, prepare the salad: Place the oranges, onion slices, cilantro leaves, and avocado cubes into a large mixing bowl. Set aside.

In a jar or cruet, whisk the shallot, lemon juice, mustard powder, salt, pepper, oil, and honey until an emulsion forms. Add the dressing to the bowl and toss to coat.

Place ½-cup of frisée in the center of each plate. Rest a grapefruit slice on the frisée. Top with the citrus mixture. Sprinkle with the spiced pepitas.

Lebanese Salad

MEAT OR PARVE ■ MAKES 8 SERVINGS

nonstick cooking spray

2 medium zucchini, with skin

1 medium red onion, papery skin removed, cut in half

2 (15-ounce) cans chick peas (also known as garbanzo beans), drained, rinsed, patted dry

¼ cup fresh minced parsley leaves

2 tablespoons fresh chopped mint leaves

¼ cup olive oil

5 large cloves fresh garlic, peeled

DRESSING:

½ cup tahini paste (also known as Middle Eastern sesame paste)

juice of 1 lemon

½ cup water

1 teaspoon low-sodium soy sauce

1 teaspoon balsamic vinegar

½ teaspoon fine sea salt

¼ teaspoon freshly ground black pepper

Chick peas and other varieties of beans are much more than just vegetables; they are the only vegetables loaded with protein. The special soluble fiber in beans can significantly lower cholesterol levels.

Tahini paste is high in fat. Although it is unsaturated fat, tahini should still be used in moderation.

Spray a grill pan with nonstick cooking spray. Place over medium heat. When pan is hot, add the zucchini and onion, placing the onion cut-side-down. Using tongs, rotate the zucchini as it blisters. Cook for a total of 15 minutes; parts of the onion and zucchini will blacken. When they are done, slice the zucchini lengthwise, and then again. Cut the zucchini and onion into ½-inch pieces and place into a mixing bowl. Add the chick peas, parsley, and mint.

Place the olive oil into a small pot over medium until it shimmers. Add the garlic cloves. Remove from heat and allow the garlic to remain in the hot oil.

Meanwhile, in the bowl of a food processor fitted with a metal blade, place the tahini paste, lemon juice, water, soy sauce, vinegar, salt, and pepper. Pulse 5–6 times. Add the garlic and olive oil it was in. Pulse until a smooth dressing forms.

Drizzle dressing over the salad and toss.

Season with salt and pepper as needed.

Portobello and Asparagus Salad

PARVE ■ MAKES 6 SERVINGS

¼ cup balsamic vinegar

2 tablespoons extra-virgin olive oil

1 tablespoon honey

nonstick cooking spray

4 large portobello mushroom caps

1 pound asparagus, stem ends removed

water as needed

1 small Belgian endive

⅓ cup chopped, sun-dried tomatoes

⅓ cup loosely packed shredded basil

3 tablespoons pine nuts

½ medium head romaine lettuce, cut into 1-inch pieces

fine sea salt to taste

freshly ground black pepper to taste

Portobello mushrooms are meaty and filling. Grilling them really enhances their flavor.

Although mushrooms may not be the first vegetable that comes to mind when you think of great sources of vitamins and minerals, you'd be surprised to know that mushrooms are among the richest sources of selenium, a mineral that helps to protect cells from damage and helps to boost the immune system.

In a medium bowl, whisk together the vinegar, olive oil, and honey. Set aside.

With a damp paper towel, wipe any dirt from the portobello caps. Use a melon baller to scoop out and discard the gills. Heat grill pan, sauté pan, or outdoor grill over medium-high heat. Lightly grease the pan with nonstick cooking spray and grill the portobello caps, flipping them twice and cooking each time about 3–4 minutes per side, or until they are tender and juicy. Immediately dice into 1-inch cubes, toss with the dressing, and season with salt and pepper. If juices seeped out on the plate, add them to the bowl. Let rest about 10 minutes.

Place the asparagus into a skillet and add water to come halfway up the asparagus. Heat over medium heat and steam until the asparagus is bright green and slightly tender, about 3 minutes. Drain, chop into 2-inch pieces, and set side.

Meanwhile, slice the Belgian endive in half, then into ¼-inch-thick half-moons. Add the endive to the mushrooms, along with the asparagus, tomatoes, basil, pine nuts, and romaine. Toss gently to coat everything with the dressing. Season to taste.

Serve warm or chilled. If serving chilled, omit the romaine until ready to serve.

Sunshine Salad

6 medium yellow beets

olive oil

1 cup walnut halves, chopped

8 fresh pineapple rings, cut into ¾-inch pieces (can use ½ medium pineapple, peeled, cored, and cut)

¼ cup pineapple juice

3 tablespoons apple cider vinegar

½ teaspoon fine sea salt

⅓ cup extra-virgin olive oil

One of the things I love about going to bar mitzvahs and weddings is how up-to-date most kosher caterers are becoming in trying not to serve the "same old, same old."

At my friends the Silberfarbs' son's bar mitzvah, I had an incredible yellow beet-golden raisin-pineapple salad. I remember thinking how it looked like a breath of sunshine with its bright yellow colors. While I was not able to get the caterer to divulge the recipe, and it has been over a year since I ate the thing, here is my version from the memory banks of my taste buds. I remember liking their version — but hold the raisins, add the walnuts and the lightest dressing, and this one rocks!

Beets build blood! It's easy to remember … and it's true because this vegetable is high in iron and could prevent anemia. Beets are naturally sweet, yet low in calories, and they're loaded with the type of fiber that can help reduce cholesterol levels as well as help reduce the incidence of colon cancer. The rich color of purple-crimson beets is caused by the pigment betacyanin, which, in itself, is a powerful cancer-fighting agent. In beets you'll also find magnesium, calcium, phosphorus, potassium, and Vitamins A, C, and niacin. The folic acid in beets helps protect from heart disease and guards against birth defects.

Preheat oven to 400°F.

Trim both ends from each beet. Wash the beets and pat dry. Cut six squares of aluminum foil. Place 1 beet onto each square. Rub the outside of each beet with a tiny bit of olive oil. Close up each foil into a bundle and place the wrapped beets on a cookie sheet. Roast for 1 hour, 15 minutes or until the beets yield to pressure when pressed. When cool enough to handle, use a paper towel to remove the skins and discard them.

Cut the beets into ¾-inch pieces and place into a medium bowl. Add the walnuts and pineapple. Mix.

In a small bowl, whisk the pineapple juice, vinegar, and salt. Whisking constantly, pour the oil into the mixture in a steady stream to form an emulsion. Pour the dressing over the salad.

Serve at room temperature.

Deli Salad

3 large eggs

1 small head iceberg lettuce, chopped

4 ounces sliced turkey, each slice rolled

2 ounces sliced salami, sliced into narrow strips

2 ounces veggie ham, cut into small squares

2 plum tomatoes, seeded and chopped

½ English (hothouse) cucumber, decoratively peeled, sliced into thin circles

½ cup light mayonnaise

2 scallions, top dark green part only, each cut in half

3 tablespoons tarragon vinegar

10 baby spinach leaves

1 tablespoon plus 2 teaspoons water

⅓ cup fresh parsley, packed

¼ teaspoon freshly ground black pepper

¼ teaspoon fine sea salt

"Veggie ham" is a soy product sold in most supermarkets. It is a tofu product, which makes it a good source of protein, and usually sold in the produce section with the soy. I like the Lifelight® brand, although there are many others. I found that when I mixed it with real deli meats, it was hard to detect. I appreciate the added protein and the big savings in fat. You may notice that some brands have the words "no GMO's." That means they contain no genetically modified organisms. Genetically modified soy is controversial and some health-conscious consumers feel it is less desirable. Basically, you are assured that seeds, produce, or meats labeled "GMO's" have not been genetically altered.

Slipping spinach into the creamy dressing is another great trick. It packs it full of vitamins and lends a pretty color.

Either drizzle the dressing over the salad or, for portion control and a cute presentation idea, measure out 1 tablespoon of dressing into 6 shot glasses and serve alongside the salad.

Place the eggs into a small pot. Cover with cold water. Bring to a boil. Cover. Remove from heat and let stand for 18 minutes. Cool. Peel the eggs and slice each egg in half; discard 2 of the yolks. Coarsely chop the remaining yolk and the whites.

Arrange the chopped lettuce on a large platter. Over the lettuce, arrange columns of the turkey, salami, veggie ham, tomatoes, cucumbers, and chopped eggs.

In the bowl of a food processor fitted with a metal blade, pulse the mayonnaise, scallions, vinegar, spinach, water, parsley, pepper, and salt. Process until smooth and creamy.

Serve the salad with the dressing.

Shaved Brussels Sprouts Salad

PARVE ■ MAKES 6 SERVINGS

½ pound Brussels sprouts, about 10 small; discard outer layers

½ cup blanched hazelnuts or raw cashews, toasted if possible, coarsely chopped

1½ heaping cups red grapes, each cut in half

1 teaspoon zest and 2 tablespoons juice of a lemon

½ cup extra-virgin olive oil

½ teaspoon fine sea salt

¼ teaspoon freshly ground black pepper

juice of ½ navel orange

You can shred the Brussels sprouts by cutting paper-thin slices with a knife, but a hand-held mandoline makes this preparation a snap. If your hazelnuts were not toasted, just place them onto a jelly-roll pan and toast them for 10–12 minutes at 375°F until they are fragrant. If they had the skins, rub them off in a kitchen towel.

The sweet taste of the grapes beautifully accompanies the strong flavor of the Brussels sprouts. Grapes are filled with an antioxidant called resveratrol that helps our hearts by slowing the buildup of "bad" LDL cholesterol.

Using a standard or hand-held mandoline, shave the Brussels spouts. Transfer to a mixing bowl.

Toss most of the hazelnuts into the bowl, reserving 1 tablespoon for garnish. Add the grapes and the 1 teaspoon of lemon zest.

In a small bowl, whisk 2 tablespoons of the fresh lemon juice with the oil, salt, and pepper. Pour over the salad and toss to combine. Squeeze the orange half over the salad and toss again. Transfer to a salad bowl and toss with remaining chopped hazelnuts.

House Salad

PARVE ■ MAKES 6 SERVINGS

With all the fancy salads I know how to make, when my sister, mom, and I get together we always pull together this salad. My Grandma Mollie was the original creator of the dressing, which she would whip up at every holiday.

You can toss anything into this salad, including carrots, snap peas, and olives. I use a hand-held mandolin for the cucumbers and red onion to get them paper-thin. Remember, the darker the greens, the greater the nutrient value.

Place the lettuce leaves into a large salad bowl.

In a jar or cruet, whisk or shake the oil, vinegar, water, garlic powder, onion powder, and salt. Toss some of the dressing with the lettuce to coat the leaves. Don't overdress. Reserve remaining dressing for another use. Add the tomatoes, cucumbers, and onion.

6 cups baby romaine lettuce or mesclun leaves

⅓ cup canola oil

¼ cup white vinegar

⅓ cup water

2 teaspoons garlic powder

1 teaspoon onion powder

¼ teaspoon fine sea salt

½ cup yellow grape tomatoes, halved

½ cup red grape tomatoes, halved

¼ English (hothouse) cucumber, unpeeled, very thinly sliced

¼ cup very thinly sliced red onion

Curry Chicken Salad

1 teaspoon ground ginger

2 teaspoons curry powder

1½ teaspoons ground cumin

¼ teaspoon fine sea salt

¼ teaspoon freshly ground black pepper

3 boneless, skinless chicken breast halves

3 tablespoons lime juice, divided

¼ cup light mayonnaise

1 teaspoon honey

1 ripe mango, cut into ½-inch dice

½ cup seedless red grapes, halved

⅓ cup raw cashews

2 ripe avocados

chopped cilantro leaves, for garnish

To create the tower effect as seen in the photo, mold the salad in ring molds. If you don't have ring molds, you can use a clean 8-ounce tomato-sauce can. Use a can opener to remove the top and bottom. The salad molds together beautifully but to be able to transport it with ease to a plate, use the ring mold to cut out the same size circle of whole-grain bread. Toast the bread circles at 350°F for 10 minutes or until golden brown. This will shrink them just a touch and the can will fit right over them. Fill the can two-thirds of the way with the salad, slightly packing it. Lift the can and the tower will stay. You can also serve this salad in hollowed-out avocado halves.

Light mayonnaise has one-third the calories of regular mayonnaise. It's better to spend your fat calories on the omega-rich fat of the avocado in this recipe.

One mango has about 4 grams of fiber and all the Vitamin C an adult needs in a day.

Preheat oven to 400°F.

Line a cookie sheet with aluminum foil.

In a small bowl, whisk together ginger, curry powder, cumin, salt, and black pepper. Divide in half, placing one half in a medium bowl.

Cut each chicken breast in half, to make six pieces about 3- by 3-inches square.

Toss the chicken in the spices in the medium bowl. Place the chicken on the foil and drizzle with 1 teaspoon lime juice. Fold the foil sides up and over to create a packet.

Bake for 25–30 minutes, until the chicken is cooked through. Open the packet and let the steam escape. Pour the juices into a medium bowl. Cool for one minute, then cut the chicken into ½-inch pieces. Place into the bowl. With a wooden spoon, immediately toss the warm chicken with the remaining spices, remaining lime juice, mayonnaise, and honey. Let sit for 1–2 minutes so the chicken absorbs the mayonnaise mix. Gently stir in the mango, grapes, and cashews.

Slice each avocado in half and remove the pits. Score the flesh. Using a large spoon, scoop the flesh out, and spoon the diced avocado into the chicken and mango salad. Gently fold until well mixed.

Place a ring mold on a salad-sized plate. Pack the salad into the mold. Lift the mold and garnish the top with a cilantro leaf. Repeat. Garnish each with chopped cilantro, if desired. Serve immediately or chill until ready.

Wheat Berry Mushroom Salad

PARVE ■ MAKES 6 (3/4 CUP) SERVINGS

1½ cups hard winter wheat berries (red) (soaked overnight in cold water, optional, see note)

5 cups vegetable stock or water flavored with 5 teaspoons parve chicken-flavored consommé powder

2 tablespoons olive oil

2 ounces sliced crimini mushrooms

3.5 ounces oyster mushrooms, trimmed

3.5 ounces enoki mushrooms, trimmed

2 tablespoons white wine

¼ cup red-wine vinegar

1 clove fresh garlic, minced

1 teaspoon Dijon mustard

¼ teaspoon fine sea salt

¼ teaspoon freshly ground black pepper

2 teaspoons honey

¼ cup extra-virgin olive oil

2 scallions, very thinly sliced on the diagonal

leaves from 2 sprigs fresh thyme

Wheat berries are the whole grain of wheat before it is ground and before so much of the nutritional value is stripped sway. They can be a blank slate for almost anything. Try tossing them with greens, tuna salad, or vegetables. Serve in place of rice or potatoes, as a side dish to poultry or meat; the possibilities are endless for this grain.

Wheat berries and other grains, including bulgur, cracked wheat, rolled wheat flakes, and wheat germ, are all whole grains. It's hard to believe that Americans consume only one-third of the minimum amount of whole grains recommended when they can taste so good!

My family loves this dish firm and almost a little crunchy-chewy. If yours likes a bit of a chewier texture, place the wheat berries into a medium bowl, cover with water, and soak overnight. Drain the water and begin the recipe.

You can use any combination of exotic mushrooms in this salad.

Place the wheat berries into a pot. Add the stock. Add water if necessary to just cover the grains. Bring to a boil. Lower the heat, cover, and simmer on low for 50–55 minutes. If the water boils out before the wheat berries are soft, add more during the cooking process. If water is left at the end of cooking, drain.

Meanwhile, heat 2 tablespoons olive oil in a large skillet over medium heat. Add the crimini mushrooms and sauté for 4 minutes. Add the oyster and enoki mushrooms with the wine and sauté for 3 minutes, until the mushrooms are wilted. Set aside.

In a medium bowl, whisk the vinegar, garlic, mustard, salt, pepper, and honey. While whisking, drizzle in ¼ cup olive oil. Add the wheat berries and the mushrooms. Toss to distribute the dressing.

Garnish with the scallions and thyme leaves.

Salmon Salad
with Carrot-Ginger Dressing

PARVE ■ MAKES 6 SERVINGS

1½ pounds salmon fillet, with skin and pin bones removed

⅛ teaspoon fine sea salt

8 sprigs fresh cilantro

1 tablespoon white wine

2 (1-inch) pieces of fresh ginger, peeled, thinly sliced, divided

1 lemon, thinly sliced

1 carrot, shredded

3 tablespoons canola oil

2 tablespoons apple cider vinegar

1 tablespoon mirin

⅓ cup water

3 ounces mesclun lettuce

1 cup watercress, break off and discard thicker stems

leaves from 2 sprigs cilantro, chopped

¼ cup soy nuts, for optional garnish

This main-dish salad is a complete meal. Salmon is an incredibly healthy food. It is rich in omega-3 fatty acids. Wild salmon is healthier than farm-raised salmon but it tastes gamier. My family prefers the taste of farm-raised and I buy it from a reputable fish store. I trim the fat, as many of the cancer-causing contaminants that are a source of concern in farm-raised salmon are stored in the fat. But farm-raised salmon has its benefits too — believe it or not, because farm-raised salmon gets less exercise than wild salmon, it may actually contain more of the protective omega-3 fatty acids. The salmon industry has taken steps in recent years to ensure the healthfulness of the farm-raised variety, and certainly experts agree that the health benefits of salmon outweigh the risks. That said, if you like wild salmon, it is a healthier way to go.

Preheat oven to 375°F.

Prepare a large rectangle of aluminum foil. Lay the salmon in the center of the foil.

Season with salt. Arrange the cilantro sprigs over the top. Drizzle with wine. Toss on half the ginger slices and the lemon slices. Seal the foil package. Place onto cookie sheet and bake for 30 minutes.

Meanwhile, prepare the dressing: Place the shredded carrot, remaining ginger, oil, vinegar, mirin, and water into the bowl of a food processor fitted with a metal blade. Process until smooth.

Arrange the mesclun on the serving platter. Top with most of the watercress.

After removing the salmon from the oven, open the packet. Scrape off and discard the cilantro, ginger, and lemon. Break the salmon into bite-sized chunks and place on mesclun. Scatter with chopped cilantro leaves. Drizzle with the dressing. Top with more watercress. If using, scatter with soy nuts.

Greek Farro Salad

DAIRY ■ MAKES 6 SERVINGS

2 cups farro

8 cups water whisked with 2 tablespoons parve chicken-flavored consommé powder

¼ cup red-wine vinegar

4 cloves fresh garlic, minced

juice of 1 lemon

1 tablespoon fresh chopped parsley

½ teaspoon dried oregano

⅔ cup extra-virgin olive oil

2 tablespoons water

2 plum tomatoes, seeded, cut into ¼-inch pieces

10 Kalamata olives, pitted and chopped

½ small red onion, cut into ¼-inch pieces

3 ounces feta cheese, crumbled

After thousands of year, farro has made a comeback! Farro is the "mother grain" from which modern grains descend. It was first cultivated thousands of years ago in the Middle East and is still popular in Italy, but it has been discovered in a big way and is a hot item in restaurants right now.

Interestingly, although it belongs to the wheat family, many people who are sensitive to wheat are able to tolerate farro. A close cousin to spelt, farro is rich in fiber, magnesium, and Vitamins A, B, C, and E.

Farro is harvested by hand, so the soaking allows any debris to come to the top. Wheat berries, although darker and firmer, can be used as an alternative to the farro, as they too will stay firm and not get mushy. Pearled barley or spelt can also be used. For a parve version, omit the feta cheese and add 1 small kirby cucumber, seeded and cut into small dice.

Place the farro into a medium bowl. Cover with cold water and soak for 30 minutes. Drain and place into a pot. Cover with the consommé-flavored water. Whisk. Bring to a boil. Turn down to a simmer and cook, uncovered, for 30 minutes.

Drain the farro and return it to the pot. In a medium bowl or container, whisk the vinegar, garlic, lemon juice, parsley, and oregano. While whisking, drizzle in the olive oil and water.

Pour the dressing over the farro. Add the tomatoes, olives, and red onion. Mix well. Gently fold in the crumbled feta cheese. Transfer to a serving dish. Serve warm or at room temperature.

Marrakesh Carrot Salad

PARVE ■ MAKES 6 SERVINGS

6 carrots, peeled, sliced into ½-inch rounds

½ cup extra-virgin olive oil

juice of ½ lemon

2 cloves fresh garlic, minced

1 teaspoon ground cumin

1 teaspoon paprika

¼ teaspoon fine sea salt

¼ teaspoon freshly ground black pepper

⅛ teaspoon cayenne pepper

2 tablespoons fresh chopped parsley leaves

One of my favorite meat restaurants is Grill Time in Boca Raton, Florida. In addition to an interesting menu and perfectly cooked food, they welcome you in the most openhanded, generous way. As soon as your order is placed, they bring out an assorted sampler of small dishes of various dips and spreads to enjoy. One of my favorites was a carrot dish marinated in chermoula. Chermoula is a North African spice mixture used as a marinade for vegetables, seafood, or chicken. This is my version of that carrot salad.

Do you know where the saying, "carrots are good for your eyes," came from? Carrots are one of the richest sources of beta-carotene, a powerful antioxidant that helps protect against macular degeneration and the development of cataracts, the leading cause of blindness in the elderly.

Place the carrots into a medium pot. Cover with water. Bring to a boil over medium heat. Cook until the carrots are fork-tender, about 7–10 minutes. Drain and place into a mixing bowl.

Add the olive oil, lemon juice, garlic, cumin, paprika, salt, pepper, cayenne, and parsley. Toss to combine.

Serve warm or at room temperature.

Green Bean Salad with Garlic-Dill Dressing

PARVE ■ MAKES 8 SERVINGS

2 medium heads garlic

nonstick cooking spray

fine sea salt

¼ cup red-wine vinegar

1 tablespoon honey

2 sprigs fresh dill, stems removed, coarsely chopped

1 teaspoon Mrs. Dash® salt-free seasoning

½ teaspoon onion powder

cold water

½ cup good-quality extra-virgin olive oil

½ red bell pepper, seeded, cut into matchsticks

½ red onion, thinly sliced

1 pound green beans, trimmed

2 tablespoons sweetened dried cranberries

4 cups (6 ounces) baby spinach leaves

My sister-in-law Jessica and I always joke that in our spare time (ha-ha) we should produce a line of kosher food products. At the top of our list is her mom Betty's amazing salad dressing. It is featured here dressing green beans, but it is also incredible over any green salad.

Although only a touch of dill is added to this recipe, its soft, sweet taste adds a distinct flavor and lots of surprise health benefits. Dill got its name from the old Norse word "dilla," which means "to lull." Perhaps that explains why this herb is often thought of as a stomach soother and sleep inducer. Like garlic, dill's volatile oils have been shown to have antibacterial properties and, like parsley, dill is considered to be protective against certain types of cancers, especially those related to cigarette and charcoal-grill smoke.

Preheat oven to 375°F.

Prepare two squares of foil. Holding each head of garlic on its side, cut the top 1–2 inches off the bulb to expose the cloves. Place one head in the center of each foil square. Spray with nonstick cooking spray and season with a pinch of salt. Close the foil packets and place on a baking sheet. Roast for 45 minutes–1 hour, until garlic is caramelized and easily squeezes like a paste from the head.

When the garlic is cool enough to handle, squeeze the cloves into the bowl of a food processor fitted with a metal blade. Add the vinegar, honey, dill, Mrs. Dash, onion powder, and ½ teaspoon salt. Pulse until combined. Thin with 3–4 tablespoons cold water. With the motor running, drizzle in the olive oil. Dressing can be made in advance. Set aside.

Spray a large skillet with nonstick cooking spray and set it over medium heat. Add the red pepper and onion. Sauté until limp, about 6 minutes. Add the green beans and 2–3 tablespoons water to steam lightly; cook until tender and bright green, about 3–4 minutes.

Remove the pan from the heat and dress lightly with the garlic-dill dressing (you may have extra). In the pan, toss with cranberries and spinach. Transfer to a serving bowl. Serve warm or at room temperature.

Creamy Garlic Salad

PARVE ■ MAKES 8 SERVINGS

5 tablespoons low-fat mayonnaise

2 tablespoons sugar

3 tablespoons white vinegar

1 tablespoon water

3 cloves fresh garlic, minced (you may use 3 frozen garlic cubes)

¼ teaspoon fine sea salt

¼ teaspoon freshly ground pepper

1 large head romaine lettuce, cut into bite-sized chunks

2 small kirby cucumbers, peeled, cut into ¼-inch rounds

1 cup sliced button mushrooms

1 cup croutons

Another Simchat Torah, another trek to our friends the Fuchs family in Teaneck! Rina is a great cook and serves meal after meal of delicious food. This salad was so good, the kids at the table were asking for the recipe!

Garlic helps thin the blood to help reduce the incidence of heart attacks and strokes. Garlic lowers LDL, or "bad" cholesterol, and raises HDL, or "good" cholesterol.

At my cooking classes, with a wink and a smile, I ban the use of frozen garlic cubes since they do not give the fresh bright flavor or aroma of fresh minced garlic. However, in this recipe, their muted flavor is perfect. You can learn something new every day!

In a medium bowl, whisk the mayonnaise, sugar, vinegar, water, minced garlic, salt, and pepper. Set aside.

In a large salad bowl, toss the romaine with the cucumbers and mushrooms. Lightly dress. Top with the croutons.

Poultry

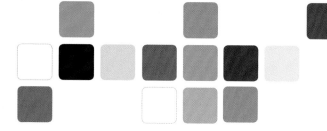

Chicken Skewers with Ponzu Dipping Sauce

MEAT ■ MAKES 6 SERVINGS

4 (7-ounce) boneless, skinless chicken breast halves

⅓ cup low-sodium soy sauce

4½ tablespoons black sesame seeds

4½ tablespoons white sesame seeds

4½ tablespoons flax seeds

2 teaspoons canola oil

nonstick cooking spray

PONZU SAUCE:

½ cup mirin

¼ cup fresh lemon juice

¼ cup rice vinegar

¼ cup low-sodium soy sauce

Flax seeds pack a wallop of omega-3 fatty acids, fiber, and a whole host of other vitamins, all coming together to help control cholesterol, digestion, and blood-sugar levels. Although used whole in this recipe, ground flax offers even more health benefits, since it is easier to digest and the body can reap the nutritional benefits more easily. Ground flax seeds become rancid quickly — it's better to buy the shelf-stable whole ones and use a coffee grinder to grind some only as you need it.

Sprinkle some in your cooked vegetable dishes or into your hot cereal to add the wholesome goodness of fiber combined with a crunchy, nutty flavor.

And don't think sesame seeds are just silent partners … they have many health benefits too. Sesame seeds are rich in phytosterols, thought to help fight heart disease and certain cancers, particularly prostate cancer.

You will need 24 wooden skewers. Soak them in water while prepping the chicken.

Cut each chicken breast on a slight diagonal into 6 (¾-inch-wide) strips. Pour soy sauce into a shallow plate. Pour a mix of the black sesame seeds, white sesame seeds, and flax seeds into a second shallow plate.

Dredge each chicken strip in the soy sauce and coat with the seed mixture. Thread, accordion style, onto a wooden skewer. You can thread two smaller strips on one skewer.

Heat the oil in a large skillet or grill pan over medium heat. Add the skewers and sear for 3–4 minutes per side, until cooked through. If doing in batches, wipe seeds out of pan with a paper towel and spray with nonstick spray between batches.

Meanwhile, prepare the ponzu sauce: In a medium bowl, whisk the mirin, lemon juice, vinegar, and soy sauce.

Serve four skewers per plate with a small bowl of ponzu sauce.

Braised Turkey

13-pound turkey, cleaned

3 large onions, thinly sliced into rings

5 cloves fresh garlic, each cut in half lengthwise

3 tablespoons garlic powder, divided

6 tablespoons paprika, divided

1 cup ketchup

5 cups water

1 teaspoon fine sea salt

I love a crisp-skinned centerpiece roast turkey, and my favorite recipe for this is in the original Kosher by Design. But on the other end of the turkey spectrum is my mom's turkey. It is a very soft, falling off the bone, kid-friendly, no-maintenance, no-basting, comfort-food recipe. My kids and all my nieces and nephews request it constantly from her. She serves it at many holidays, because, unlike roast turkey, it remains moist and flavorful even when reheated for a few meals. Anyone who has ever attended my live cooking shows knows that I am very upfront about my freezer phobia, so, dare I say it, this recipe freezes well and may be even better after it has been frozen, defrosted, and reheated.

This "foundation" dish can be embellished in a variety of ways. Whether you serve it beside a medley of colorful vegetables, cut it into smaller pieces and toss it over your favorite salad, or serve it cold and chopped with apples, parsley, and light mayonnaise, this staple is a great way to add lean protein with lots of flavor.

Preheat oven to 350°F.

Place the onion rings and fresh garlic in a single layer into the bottom of a heavy roasting pan. Sprinkle with 2 tablespoons garlic powder and 2 tablespoons of paprika.

Place the turkey on the onions. Rub 2 tablespoons paprika all over the outside and inside the cavity of the turkey.

In a medium bowl, whisk the ketchup, water, salt, remaining tablespoon garlic powder, and remaining 2 tablespoons paprika. Slowly, to prevent splattering, pour over the turkey and onto the onions.

Cover tightly, with a lid if possible. Roast for 3½ hours.

Remove the turkey to a cutting board. Carve it and remove skin as desired. Transfer the turkey pieces to a serving dish.

Cover the roasting pan with foil to prevent splattering. Fold up the far right corner of the foil. Using a towel to protect your hand, tilt the pan away from you and, right in the pan, use an immersion blender to purée the onions into the sauce. If you do not have an immersion blender, scoop out the onions and transfer them with 1–2 cups of the liquid to the bowl of a food processor fitted with a metal blade. Purée. Pour this purée and remaining gravy over the carved turkey.

Curry Chicken

MEAT ■ MAKES 6 SERVINGS

6 chicken pieces, breasts and thighs, skinless, with bone

2 tablespoons plus 2 teaspoons honey, divided

2 tablespoons Dijon mustard

2 tablespoons chicken broth or water

¼ cup light mayonnaise

1 teaspoon curry powder

1 navel orange, quartered, very thinly sliced

5 cloves fresh garlic, coarsely chopped

Did you know that curry powder is a blend of 20 spices, herbs, and even some seeds? Some of these ingredients are black pepper, cayenne, chilies, cloves, coriander, fennel seed, mace, nutmeg, saffron, sesame seeds, and turmeric. Although curry is found on many spice racks … some may feel it belongs in the medicine cabinet too! Curcumin, the active ingredient in turmeric, has been used as an anti-inflammatory remedy for centuries. Researchers have shown that curcumin may help combat cancer and protects against arthritis, Alzheimer's, and other diseases.

This is one of those simple mix-and-dump chicken dishes to turn to when you have no time to fuss. Removing the skin from the chicken eliminates a lot of fat calories, and in this recipe the flavor does not suffer.

Preheat oven to 350°F.

Place the chicken pieces into a roasting pan.

In a small bowl, whisk the 2 tablespoons honey, mustard, broth, mayonnaise, and curry powder.

Brush the curry mixture over the chicken. Scatter the oranges and garlic over the chicken.

Bake, uncovered, for 1 hour.

Baste the chicken with the pan juices and drizzle with 2 teaspoons honey.

Turn the oven to broil and broil for 2 minutes, until the chicken is golden.

Balsamic Glazed Chicken

⅔ cup good-quality balsamic vinegar

2 tablespoons honey

2 teaspoons garlic powder

½ teaspoon onion powder

fine sea salt

1 tablespoon extra-virgin olive oil, divided

6 boneless, skinless chicken breast halves

6 sprigs fresh rosemary

This recipe uses one of the healthful cooking techniques that I learned from my favorite chef and teacher, Damian Sansonetti. By cooking the chicken in closed packets, you seal in the juices and flavors while keeping the chicken moist; a real feat for cutlets.

Balsamic vinegar is savory and delicious and it also happens to be quite nutritious! Vinegar is high in acetic acid, which helps increase the body's absorption of minerals from the foods we eat. Vinegar could play a role in increasing the absorption of calcium in vegetables, particularly for women who have a hard time getting all the calcium they need on a daily basis to prevent the bone-thinning disease, osteoporosis.

Preheat oven to 400°F.

Place the vinegar into a small pot. Heat over medium for 8–10 minutes, until reduced by half. Remove from heat. Stir in the honey, garlic powder, and onion powder. Divide into two bowls. Set aside. The glaze will thicken as it cools.

Cut two large rectangles of aluminum foil, each large enough to enclose three chicken-breast halves.

Season both sides of each chicken breast with a pinch of salt. Rub ½ teaspoon of olive oil into both sides of each chicken breast. Place 3 breasts onto each of the two pieces of aluminum foil. Lay a rosemary sprig over each chicken breast. Close up the foil to form two packets. Place the packets onto a cookie sheet and into the oven for 20 minutes.

Open the packets and discard the rosemary. Brush each breast with glaze from one bowl. Return the packets, opened, to the oven for 5 minutes.

Put one breast on each plate and slice. Drizzle with the second batch of balsamic glaze.

Honey-Thyme Glazed Chicken with 3-Onion Jam

MEAT ■ MAKES 6 SERVINGS

nonstick cooking spray

¾ cup honey

5 sprigs fresh thyme, divided

½ large Vidalia or other sweet onion, thinly sliced

1 large red onion, halved and thinly sliced

2 shallots, thinly sliced

2 tablespoons apple-cider vinegar

4 whole black peppercorns

fine sea salt

freshly ground black pepper

6 boneless, skinless chicken breast halves, pounded to an even thickness

For centuries, thyme has been used in the pharmacy as well as the kitchen. Its pungent, minty leaves contain an active ingredient called thymol, known to have antibacterial, antifungal properties. The oils from the leaves of this plant have an effect on the respiratory tract, helping to relieve coughs.

Before measuring honey, spray your measuring cups with nonstick cooking spray to keep it from sticking.

Pour honey into a ramekin. Fold 2 sprigs of the fresh thyme to fit into the ramekin. Microwave on high for 1 minute. Set aside.

Spray a large nonstick skillet with nonstick cooking spray. Add the sweet onion, red onion, and shallots. Sauté for 10 minutes over medium heat. Add remaining 3 sprigs fresh thyme. Continue to cook the onions until they are caramelized, about 10 minutes longer.

Drizzle ¼-cup of the reserved thyme-infused honey into the onions. Add the vinegar and the peppercorns. Cook for another 10 minutes, stirring occasionally.

Meanwhile, spray a grill pan with nonstick cooking spray. Heat over medium. Season the chicken breasts with salt and pepper. When the pan is hot, add the chicken breasts. Sear for 3–5 minutes per side, depending on thickness.

Pull the thyme sprigs out of the honey and discard. Reserve ¼-cup honey to finish the dish. Baste the top of each breast with remaining honey. Glaze carefully, trying not to drip; anything that drips on the pan will burn.

Serve the chicken with a dollop of the 3-onion jam. Drizzle some honey over each plate.

Wheat Germ Crusted Chicken Cutlets

MEAT ■ MAKES 6 SERVINGS

6 boneless, skinless chicken breast halves, tenders separated, pounded to an even thickness

2 cups wheat germ

4 teaspoons dark brown sugar

2 teaspoons coarse sea salt

2 teaspoons freshly ground black pepper

2 teaspoons dried minced onion

2 teaspoons dried basil

2 teaspoons paprika

1 teaspoon garlic powder

1 teaspoon dried thyme

¾ cup egg substitute, such as Egg Beaters®, or 4 large eggs, lightly beaten

nonstick cooking spray

My kids, like so many, look forward to schnitzel on Shabbat. In trying to lighten up this breaded and fried dish, I added in wheat germ, the vitamin-packed, high-fiber part of the wheat kernel that is stripped away during the flour-making process. The germ is the nutrient-rich inner part of the grain. One ounce (¼ cup) of wheat germ provides 4.4 grams of fiber, in addition to protein, B-vitamins, and Vitamin E.

To keep the crunch without the frying, place a cookie cooling rack into a jelly-roll pan. Bake the chicken on this rack. This will allow the hot air in your oven to circulate and crisp up the coating on all sides.

Preheat oven to 350°F.

Line a jelly-roll pan with a cooling rack. Set aside.

Pour the wheat germ into a shallow container. Season it with the sugar, salt, pepper, minced onion, basil, paprika, garlic, and thyme. Mix to distribute the spices. Place the beaten eggs or egg substitute into a shallow container.

Dip a chicken breast into the wheat germ mix to lightly coat. Shake off the excess. Dip into the beaten egg, shaking off excess, and then back into the wheat germ mixture. Place onto prepared rack and repeat until all the chicken and tenders are coated.

Spray the coated chicken with a quick, even spray of nonstick cooking spray. Flip each piece over and spray the other side. Place into the oven and bake for 25–30 minutes until chicken is cooked through.

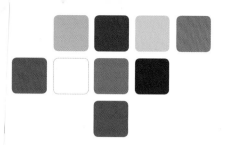

Spanish Chicken Paella

MEAT ■ MAKES 8 SERVINGS

2 tablespoons olive oil

1 teaspoon turmeric

1 teaspoon smoked paprika, such as McCormick®

½ teaspoon ground cayenne pepper

8 chicken thighs, bone-in, skin removed, excess fat trimmed

1 large Spanish onion, cut into ¼-inch pieces

4 cloves fresh garlic, coarsely chopped

1½ cups Carnaroli, Arborio, or risotto rice

½ ounce (large pinch) saffron threads

½ cup dry white wine

1 (14.5-ounce) can diced tomatoes, drained

1 cup frozen garden peas

3 cups chicken stock

Smoked paprika, also known as Pimenton de la Vera, Dulce, is one of my new favorite food finds. I consider it a magic ingredient that I use all the time and call for in a number of recipes in this book. The first time I smelled the spice, it brought me right back to the bags of barbecue potato chips I enjoyed as a kid. McCormick sells it with kosher certification in their gourmet collection. It is a Spanish specialty produced by slowly smoking sweet (dulce) peppers over wood planks. The result is a smoky, woody flavor, gorgeous color, and a flavor completely unlike the regular paprika that we are all so used to cooking with.

A paella pan has a diameter of at least 16 inches — I have even seen them as large as 26 inches! Most cookware sets come with a 10- or 12-inch frying pan, to give you a comparison. The huge, flat cooking surface enables you to cook a large batch of chicken, fish, really anything, without having to do it in batches. It is important in paella, as it helps the rice cook evenly. You can get an inexpensive one. I like a nonstick surface. If you don't have a paella pan, sear the chicken in batches. When it comes time to spread the rice in an even layer, do this in a full-sized roasting pan and top with the chicken. Cook as directed.

Aside from enjoying the rich color of paprika, you can also rest assured that you'll benefit from its solanine content. Solanine is a chemical that has been associated with relieving arthritis pain.

Preheat oven to 350°F.

In a paella pan or other large, wide-bottomed, sided oven-proof skillet with lid, heat the olive oil over medium heat.

In a small bowl mix the turmeric, smoked paprika, and cayenne. Remove 1 teaspoon of this mixture and reserve. Sprinkle the remaining spice mix over the chicken thighs. When the oil is hot, add the chicken, skinless-side-down, and brown for 3–4 minutes. When browned, remove the chicken and set aside. Add the onion to the pan and sauté for 2 minutes in the chicken drippings. Add the garlic, stirring frequently to keep the onions from burning.

Add the rice to the pan with the saffron and the reserved spice mixture. Add the wine and stir. Spread the rice into an even layer. Place the chicken on top of the rice, skinless-side-up. Sprinkle with the tomatoes and the peas. Cook for 1 minute. Add the stock.

Place into the oven and cook, uncovered, for 45 minutes. The edges of the rice will get nice and crusty. Serve the chicken with the rice.

Harissa-Style Turkey London Broil

MEAT ■ MAKES 6-8 SERVINGS

3 red bell peppers, cut in half, seeded

1 (3-pound) turkey London broil

4 cloves fresh garlic, minced

½ teaspoon smoked paprika, such as McCormick®

½ teaspoon ground cumin

1 teaspoon garlic powder

1 teaspoon dried oregano

½ teaspoon fine sea salt

⅛ teaspoon cayenne pepper

1 tablespoon olive oil

½ teaspoon onion powder

2 drops hot sauce, such as Frank's® or Tabasco®

⅛ teaspoon smoked paprika

¼ teaspoon fine sea salt

This lean, white-meat turkey recipe counts on a variety of spices to enhance flavor, add heat, and marry well with the harissa. Authentic harissa is a North African red-hot pepper paste typically served with couscous and made with dried chilies, garlic, and spices. Pereg makes a nice jarred one that, in moderation due to the heat, is great on pita, turkey, vegetables, or chicken.

Place the peppers, cut-side-down, on a cookie sheet. Place under the broiler, 6–8 inches from the heat, and roast until the skins are blackened, about 6–7 minutes. Place the peppers into a heavy-duty ziplock bag to steam. Set the oven to 375°F.

In a small bowl, mix the minced garlic, smoked paprika, cumin, garlic powder, oregano, salt, and cayenne. Rub it all over the turkey. If the London broil is too large to fit in a skillet, cut it in half.

Heat the olive oil in a large skillet over medium heat. Add the turkey and sear for 2–3 minutes on one side; flip and sear for 1 minute on the other.

Place the turkey into a roasting pan and bake, uncovered, for 20–25 minutes or until cooked through. Do not overcook, as turkey dries out very easily.

Meanwhile, remove the peppers from the bag and remove the skins. It is okay if a little bit of blackening remains; it will add smoky flavor. Place the peppers into a food processor (this can also be done in a quart-sized container with an immersion blender) and process until liquidy and smooth. Add the onion powder, hot sauce, smoked paprika, and salt. Pulse to distribute spices.

After removing the turkey from the oven, allow it to rest for 5–7 minutes. Slice the turkey and serve with the red pepper harissa.

Healthy Un-fried Chicken

MEAT ■ MAKES 6 SERVINGS

6 pieces chicken, skinless, with bone; can be breast, thigh, or leg

2 tablespoons nondairy sour cream, such as Tofutti brand Sour Supreme®

4 cups parve corn flake cereal

1 teaspoon cayenne pepper

1 teaspoon dried oregano

The ancient Greeks used oregano leaves to treat sores and aching muscles, and traditional Chinese doctors use oregano to relieve fever, gastrointestinal problems, and itchy skin. Like thyme, oregano contains thymol, and it also has caravol, both of which relieve respiratory problems.

Like in real deep-fried Southern-fried chicken, this dish has some tang that comes from the tiniest bit of soy sour cream and gets its crunch from corn flakes. The rack is of vital importance to this dish. It will allow air to circulate around all sides of each chicken piece to keep the coating crunchy and dry.

Preheat oven to 400°F.

Place a cookie cooling rack or a meat rack into a large roasting pan.

Rub 1 teaspoon of the parve sour cream on each piece of chicken.

Place the corn flakes, cayenne, and oregano into a large, heavy-duty ziplock bag. Crush the corn flakes, being careful not to mush into fine crumbs; you want some texture on the chicken so it ends up having the authentic texture of batter when it is cooked.

Drop the chicken, 1 piece at a time, into the bag . Shake bag to completely coat. Place each piece on the rack and repeat until all are coated.

Bake, uncovered, for 45 minutes, until chicken is no longer pink inside. Transfer to a serving platter.

Bruschetta Chicken

MEAT ■ MAKES 6 SERVINGS

6 boneless, skinless chicken breast halves, pounded thin

olive-oil flavored nonstick cooking spray

2 slices whole wheat or multi-grain bread, roughly torn

1½ tablespoons pine nuts

23 fresh large basil leaves, divided

¾ tablespoon olive oil

10 sun-dried tomato halves

3 large cloves fresh garlic

1 (14.5-ounce) can diced tomatoes, drained, divided

1 large tomato, seeded and diced into 1-inch cubes

½ cup white wine, such as Pinot Grigio

8 cloves fresh garlic, minced

¼ teaspoon fine sea salt

¼ teaspoon freshly ground black pepper

This recipe is my family's current favorite chicken dish. We all love the familiar taste of bruschetta that is wrapped in the low-fat, protein-rich chicken breasts. The fragrance alone will have your family at the table before dinner is even served.

Pignoli, or pine nuts, often used in Italian cooking (like pesto sauce), offer heart-healthy benefits. As a matter of fact, pine nuts, along with almonds, pecans, hazelnuts, peanuts, pistachios, and walnuts, were given a thumbs-up through a Food and Drug Administration (FDA) health claim that these nuts contain less than 4 grams of saturated fat per 50 grams. (As with any nut, though, it's easy to overeat, so be mindful of portion sizes.)

Preheat oven to 400°F.

Spray the bottom of a 9- by 9-inch pan with cooking spray.

In a food processor, pulse the bread slices with the pine nuts and 3 basil leaves to make coarse crumbs. Add salt and pepper if desired. With the machine running, drizzle in olive oil and process just to coat the crumbs. Remove to a bowl.

Place the sun-dried tomatoes, 10 basil leaves, 3 cloves garlic, and ¼-cup canned tomatoes into the bowl of the food processor. Process to form a paste. Using a spatula, spread a thin layer of this mixture over each chicken breast. Roll each breast.

Thinly slice the remaining 10 basil leaves and place into the prepared pan. Add the fresh tomato, remaining canned diced tomato, wine, 8 minced garlic cloves, salt, and pepper. Mix and spread the mixture over the bottom of the pan. Place the chicken rolls over the tomato base.

Sprinkle the bread crumbs over the top. Bake uncovered for 45 minutes, or just until chicken is cooked through.

Turkey Tagine

3 pounds dark meat turkey roast or skinless thighs

1¼ teaspoons turmeric

¾ teaspoon ground cumin

¾ teaspoon garlic powder

¾ teaspoon cayenne pepper

½ teaspoon onion powder

½ teaspoon fine sea salt

½ teaspoon freshly ground black pepper

2 tablespoons extra-virgin olive oil

1 medium sweet potato, peeled and cut into ½-inch chunks

2 tablespoons white wine

1 cup coin-cut carrots

4 cloves fresh garlic, chopped

1 red onion, cut into ½-inch chunks

1½ cups chicken stock, divided

chopped fresh parsley, for garnish

chopped fresh mint, for garnish

Unless you want the "Midas touch" (yellow hands from the turmeric), remember to wear gloves when working with this gorgeous yellow spice.

Did you know that turmeric contains essential vitamins and minerals, including Vitamins B_6 and C, iron, potassium, and manganese? Its strong antioxidant properties come from curcumin, a phytochemical that has been proven to reduce the incidence of heart disease, cancer, and Alzheimer's disease.

This dish is great served over whole-wheat couscous that has been flavored with a touch of honey and cinnamon.

Preheat oven to 375°F.

Untie the turkey roast if it is tied. Remove and discard any excess skin that has no meat attached. Cut out any bone fragments. Cut the turkey into large, 1½-inch chunks. Place into a large bowl. Add the turmeric, cumin, garlic powder, cayenne, onion powder, salt, and pepper. Toss to coat the turkey.

Heat the olive oil in a large skillet over medium heat. Place the turkey in the hot oil. You will have to do this in batches; do not crowd the pan. As the pieces are seared, about 2 minutes until golden brown, place them into a casserole dish; do not sear on the other side. Once all the turkey is seared, add the sweet potato, white wine, carrots, garlic, and onion to the skillet. Sauté for five minutes until shiny. Add ½ cup chicken stock. Scrape up the flavors from the bottom of the pan. Add the contents of the skillet to the casserole dish. Add the remaining cup of stock.

Roast, uncovered, for 45 minutes. Garnish with chopped parsley and mint.

Cajun Chicken

2 tablespoons olive oil, divided

2 stalks celery, reserve leaves; halved lengthwise, then cut into ¼-inch pieces

1 medium onion, quartered and thinly sliced

1 green bell pepper, seeded, cut into ¼-inch dice

1 bay leaf

5 sprigs fresh thyme

1 cup dry white wine

2 cups raw brown basmati rice

3 cups water

2 tablespoons Cajun blackening spice, such as Paul Prudhomme's Magic Barbecue Spice Blend®

6 boneless, skinless chicken breast halves, tenders removed

1 lemon

Paul Prudhomme is the chef who really brought Cajun-Creole cooking to the attention of the foodie public. He says that the celery, onions, and bell pepper in this recipe are the cornerstone to most dishes from that region. Like a mirepoix in French cooking (onion, carrots, and celery), they get treated almost as one ingredient and cook down together to form a base layer in a dish.

Some Cajun dishes are mean but not lean! The spices are great for fighting inflammation and pain, but traditionally, many dishes include fat from butter, sausage, and fatty meats; and they often focus on frying as a common cooking method. This dish combines a heart-healthy base and keeps fats to a minimum.

The celery leaves are nice yellow color and they make a beautiful, simple garnish.

Heat 1 tablespoon olive oil in a large pot. Add the celery, onion, and green pepper. Cook over medium-high for 5 minutes, stirring occasionally. Toss in the bay leaf and thyme sprigs. Cook for 4–5 minutes. The vegetables will become shiny and soft, and the onions will start to caramelize.

Stir in the wine, scraping the bottom of the pot to deglaze it. A wooden spoon works well here to scrape up the browned bits. Cook until most of the wine is evaporated and you are left with a little bit of thick, golden-brown syrup on the bottom of the pot.

Add the rice and the water. Stir. Bring to a boil. Cover the pot and turn the heat down to simmer for 45 minutes. Allow the pot to stand uncovered for 10 minutes.

Meanwhile, rub one teaspoon of the Cajun spice into each chicken breast, coating both sides.

Heat the remaining tablespoon of olive oil in a skillet or grill pan. Get the pan very hot over medium-high heat. Sear the chicken for 4–5 minutes per side, until cooked through. Squeeze the lemon evenly over all the chicken.

Serve the chicken over the rice. Garnish with the yellow celery leaves.

Confetti Chicken

6 boneless, skinless chicken breast halves

3 tablespoons light mayonnaise

1 tablespoon hot sauce, such as Frank's® or Tabasco®

1 cup red grape tomatoes, finely chopped

1 cup yellow grape tomatoes, finely chopped

1½ cups sliced mushrooms, finely chopped

6 fresh sprigs oregano

fresh parsley, finely chopped for garnish

People are always looking for new chicken dishes. This one is simple, low-fat, and delicious. The colors make it eye-appealing as well as palate-pleasing, and these colorful veggies will be enjoyed both inside and out: the Vitamin C-rich tomatoes and parsley may help reduce the duration of the common cold. The active ingredient in parsley, myristicin, has been shown to inhibit tumor formation, making it chemoprotective, and it is rich in antioxidants. So although parsley makes a pretty decoration … remember to chop it into your food and don't just place it on the dish.

Preheat the oven to 400°F.

Cover a jelly-roll pan with parchment paper. Set aside.

Slice each breast horizontally to make a pocket, being careful not to cut all the way through.

In a small bowl, mix the mayonnaise and hot sauce. Set aside.

In a small bowl, mix the chopped red tomatoes, yellow tomatoes, and mushrooms. Stuff 2 teaspoons of the mixture into the pocket of each breast. Slide one fresh oregano sprig into each pocket. Brush ½ tablespoon of the mayonnaise mixture over each breast. Pat remaining tomato-mushroom mixture evenly over each breast to form a crust.

Bake for 18–20 minutes. Transfer to a platter and drizzle with the pan juices. Sprinkle with chopped parsley right before serving.

Cuban Chicken Stew

MEAT ■ MAKES 8 SERVINGS

2 teaspoons olive oil

2 medium onions, cut into
½-inch pieces

8 cloves fresh garlic, sliced

3 medium red potatoes,
unpeeled, cut into ½-inch
pieces

2 red bell peppers, seeded,
cut into ½-inch pieces

6 plum tomatoes, cut into
½-inch chunks

2 bay leaves

4 whole chicken leg quarters,
skinless, with bone

4 whole chicken breasts,
wing removed, skinless,
with bone

1 teaspoon ground cumin

¼ teaspoon cayenne pepper

8 cups chicken stock

1 cup pitted green olives,
sliced

The main ingredient in most Cuban main dishes is sofrito. Sofrito is a fragrant mixture of garlic, onion, peppers, and bay leaf sautéed in olive oil until very soft. This heavily concentrates the flavors. Cuban side dishes usually include black beans and white rice. Switch it out for brown rice and you have a fabulous and healthy Cuban meal of which even Castro would be proud!

As a member of the parsley family, cumin's health benefits and natural healing properties include relieving digestive disorders from flatulence to morning sickness. Cumin is also said to help alleviate symptoms of the common cold.

Heat the olive oil in a large soup pot over medium-low heat. Add the onions and garlic. Cook until the onion is translucent; do not allow it to brown. Add the potatoes, red peppers, and tomatoes. Sauté for 3–4 minutes.

Add the bay leaves and the chicken pieces. Sprinkle with the cumin and cayenne.

Add the chicken stock. Cover and simmer on medium for 30 minutes.

Remove the cover. Discard the bay leaves. Add the olives and simmer for 5 minutes longer. Remove from heat and allow to cool for 15 minutes. Remove the chicken from the bones, discarding the bones. Using two forks, shred the chicken and add it back to the stew. Serve hot.

Whole Roasted Chicken Tikka Masala

MEAT ■ MAKES 6 SERVINGS

1 whole (3-5 pound) chicken, skin removed, legs tied

1 (6-ounce) container lemon-flavored soy yogurt

2 teaspoons ground cumin

2 teaspoons cayenne pepper

2 teaspoons cracked black pepper

1 teaspoon fine sea salt

1 teaspoon minced fresh ginger

½ teaspoon ground coriander

½ teaspoon ground cinnamon

1 tablespoon olive oil

3 cloves fresh garlic, chopped

½ jalapeño pepper, chopped

2 teaspoons ground cumin

2 teaspoons paprika

1 (8-ounce) can tomato sauce

1 cup plain or unsweetened soy milk

1 tablespoon nondairy sour cream, such as Tofutti brand Sour Supreme®

fresh cilantro, chopped, for garnish

Tikka masala is often attributed to Indian cuisine. However, it was truly invented in England by a chef from Bangladesh. I took some liberties with this traditional Indian dish. It is normally made with chunks of chicken that are marinated in curry spices, simmered in a spicy tomato sauce, and served over basmati rice. It usually contains the Indian spice, garam masala. I left it out since I had a hard time finding it kosher and the dish had tons of spice already. If you want to be closer to the authentic dish, you can find it at koshergourmetmart.com and add it to the spice mixture.

Soy yogurt has all the benefits of dairy yogurt, plus the benefit of being able to be eaten with meat dishes. It also makes a great alternative for people with lactose intolerance.

By removing the skin, you cut the calories in a chicken dish by a large percentage. This dish is cooked in a sauce, so I remove the skin at the start. If a chicken dish is not in a sauce or liquid, leave the skin on during cooking, for moisture; then remove it before eating.

Preheat oven to 350°F.

Place a rack into a baking pan large enough to hold it. Place the chicken on the rack.

In a small bowl, whisk the soy yogurt, cumin, cayenne, black pepper, salt, ginger, coriander, and cinnamon. Rub all over the chicken. Bake for 1½ hours, uncovered.

Meanwhile, heat the oil in a medium skillet until hot but not smoking. Add the garlic and jalapeño pepper. Sauté for 1 minute. Mix in the cumin and paprika; toast until fragrant, about 10 seconds. Add the tomato sauce and soy milk. Stir, then simmer for 10 minutes until it begins to thicken. Whisk in the sour cream.

Transfer the chicken to a serving platter. Pour the sauce over the chicken and garnish with cilantro.

Glazed Turkey Roast
with Cranberry Chutney

MEAT ■ MAKES 6-8 SERVINGS

1 (3-pound) boneless, skinless white meat turkey roast, tied

3 red onions, cut into 1-inch chunks, separate the layers

1 bay leaf

¼ teaspoon fine sea salt

¼ teaspoon freshly ground black pepper

1 (8-ounce) can jellied cranberry sauce

3 ounces pineapple juice

½ cup white wine

water

2 cups whole cranberries, (can be frozen)

juice and zest of 1 orange (½ cup juice)

¼ cup honey

orange slices, for garnish

Turkey is one of the leanest protein foods you can find. A 3½-ounce portion of turkey breast (without the skin, of course) provides only 115 calories and just 3 grams of fat. That's less fat than in a teaspoon of oil.

Turkey is the perfect match for the cranberries in this recipe. The Native Americans turned to cranberries as a food and medicinal source. Today's research shows that they are not only a healthy fruit rich in Vitamin C and fiber, but they have myriad health benefits. It is thought that cranberries may prevent urinary-tract infections, reduce gum disease, and have other good health benefits in the fight against heart disease and cancer. This recipe packs a double wallop of them.

Preheat oven to 400°F.

Place the turkey roast into a roasting pan. Surround with the onions. Place the bay leaf in the onions. Season with salt and pepper. Set aside.

Place the cranberry sauce, pineapple juice, and white wine into the bowl of a food processor fitted with a metal blade. Process until smooth. Pour the sauce over the roast. Brush to coat all surfaces. Add 2 cups water to the pan. Roast for 1 hour or until no longer pink inside. Baste 2–3 times with the liquid from the pan during the cooking process, starting 30 minutes into the cooking time, to prevent the sugar in the sauce from burning. While basting, if you see the juices are starting to caramelize and dry up in the pan, add 1–2 additional cups water and use a wooden spoon to scrape the bottom and mix.

Meanwhile, prepare the chutney: Heat the cranberries, orange zest, and orange juice in a medium pot over medium heat for 12–15 minutes; the berries will start to release their liquid. Stir. Continue to cook for an additional 15 minutes and then add the honey. Simmer for 5 minutes longer.

Slice the turkey roast and serve with the chutney. Garnish with orange slices.

Whole Wheat
Couscous-Crusted Chicken

MEAT ■ MAKES 6 SERVINGS

olive-oil flavored nonstick cooking spray

6 boneless, skinless chicken breast halves

¼ teaspoon fine sea salt

¼ teaspoon freshly ground black pepper

1 (10-ounce) box whole wheat couscous

2 tablespoons finely chopped fresh chives

2 teaspoons ground cumin

3 cloves fresh garlic, minced

6-8 sun-dried tomatoes, minced

2 tablespoons olive oil

juice from ½ lemon

3 plum tomatoes, thinly sliced

2½ cups water mixed with 1 tablespoon chicken-flavored consommé powder

chopped fresh parsley, for garnish

In the Middle East, most families make couscous by hand, but in the U.S., we can find it in a box, ready to be cooked and enjoyed with much less effort. You can find this grain in a variety of flavors, with its whole wheat version containing the greatest amount of phosphorus, potassium, zinc, and fiber. As a complex carbohydrate similar to rice, couscous can be served as a side dish with meat, poultry, or fish. To keep calories down and enhance its value even further, combine it with a medley of colorful vegetables.

Preheat oven to 375°F.

Spray two 9- by 13-inch baking pans with nonstick cooking spray.

Arrange the chicken breasts in a single layer. If you had tenders, lay them in the pan as well. Season the chicken with the salt and pepper. Spray the tops of the chicken with the cooking spray.

In a large bowl, combine the couscous, chives, cumin, garlic, and sun-dried tomatoes. Stir in the olive oil and lemon juice. Cover the chicken with the couscous mixture, pressing to pat it on as a crust on each chicken breast. Arrange 3 tomato slices to overlap on each breast.

Pour the water around the chicken. Cover the pan tightly and bake until cooked through and the chicken is no longer pink inside, about 25–35 minutes.

Garnish with parsley.

Turkey Piccata

1½ pounds turkey cutlets for scaloppini

¼ teaspoon fine sea salt

¼ teaspoon freshly ground black pepper

all-purpose flour

2 tablespoons olive oil

1½ cups white wine

9 cloves fresh garlic, minced

2 teaspoons cornstarch

¼ cup water

3 cups chicken stock

juice of 3 lemons

¼ cup small capers, rinsed and drained

3 tablespoons nondairy sour cream, such as Tofutti brand Sour Supreme®

chopped fresh parsley, for garnish

Capers have been used for centuries in Mediterranean cuisine, providing a tangy taste and decorative touch to meat, pasta, and salad dishes. Unexpectedly, capers are a source of antioxidants, particularly flavonols. Capers may be especially beneficial when added to meat dishes, as researchers have found that caper extract helped prevent the formation of certain by-products of digested meat that have been linked by others to an increased risk of cancer and heart disease.

Season the turkey with salt and pepper. Dredge with flour, shaking off excess.

Heat the oil in a large skillet over medium heat. Add the cutlets. Be careful of splattering. Sauté for 4 minutes, flip, and sauté for 3–4 minutes on the other side until cooked through and no longer pink inside. Transfer the turkey to a platter.

Deglaze the pan with the wine and add the garlic. Cook until most of the wine has evaporated, about two minutes. Dissolve the cornstarch in a ¼-cup water and add to the pan. Add the stock, lemon juice, and capers. Bring to a simmer and cook for three minutes. Return the turkey to the pan and warm through, about one minute.

Transfer the cutlets to a platter. Whisk the sour cream into the pan. Pour the sauce over the turkey. Garnish with parsley.

Meat

Rib Eye Portobello Steaks

MEAT ■ MAKES 6 SERVINGS

6 medium portobello mushrooms; scrape out gills and discard

1 cup balsamic vinegar

½ cup olive oil

1 teaspoon garlic powder

1½ teaspoon fine sea salt, divided

nonstick cooking spray

3 (1½-inch thick) rib steaks

½ teaspoon freshly ground black pepper

3 plum tomatoes, seeded and cut into ¼-inch pieces

12 fresh basil leaves, minced

3 tablespoons fresh chopped parsley leaves

⅛ teaspoon coarse sea salt

My husband and I found even one more way we are compatible when we started eating healthier. I used to serve each of us our own rib steak, but that portion size is way too big. Luckily, I like the bone and he likes the eye, so we split it that way. You can also go down the middle if you prefer but note that the right serving size is 4 ounces. The portobello are meaty and will fill you up, especially if you are used to eating larger portions.

In general, both adults and children do not eat enough vegetables. Some figures show that only 20% of us are meeting our needs. Yet, there is no food group that hosts more superfoods than the vegetable group. By covering half your plate with vegetables and treating meat and whole grains as a side dishes, you'll move way ahead in keeping yourself and your family healthier.

Preheat oven to 375°F.

Slice each portobello into ½-inch-thick slices. Place in a single layer into the bottom of a baking pan. Add the vinegar, olive oil, garlic powder, and ½ teaspoon salt. Stir. Roast for 15–18 minutes, until the mushrooms are soft.

Spray a grill pan with nonstick cooking spray. Heat over medium. Season the rib steaks with remaining salt and pepper. Sear the steaks for 8–10 minutes per side. This can be done on an outdoor grill as well.

Remove the steaks to a platter as they are done. Slice the steaks. Top each portion with roasted mushrooms.

In a small bowl, mix the tomatoes, basil, parsley, and coarse sea salt. Arrange over the mushrooms and drizzle with the balsamic pan juices.

Korean Beef Kim Chee Skewers

MEAT ■ MAKES 6 SERVINGS

2 pounds London broil

1 small head Napa cabbage, separated into leaves

8 cloves fresh garlic, each cut in half

½ cup canola oil

⅓ cup white vinegar

2 teaspoons red pepper flakes

1 teaspoon onion powder

½ teaspoon coarse sea salt or kosher salt

½ teaspoon ground cumin

¼ teaspoon cayenne pepper

¼ teaspoon paprika

1 teaspoon lime juice

2 red bell peppers, seeded and cut into chunks

12 cherry tomatoes

2 bunches scallions, trimmed, use just bottom 2 inches

high-heat nonstick cooking spray

Make sure the wooden skewers can fit into your grill pan. If they are too long, thread them as per the recipe and then cut the excess with scissors. This dish was a huge hit, the runaway favorite at the tasting party where it made its debut. People really loved the spicy flavor.

But here's another benefit of eating meat (or chicken) on skewers: smaller portions of protein.

Soak 12 wooden skewers in water. Set aside. Skip this step if using metal skewers.

Cut the meat into 1½-inch chunks. Place into a large bowl. Place the Napa leaves into a shallow pan.

Place the garlic, oil, vinegar, red pepper flakes, onion powder, salt, cumin, cayenne, paprika, and lime juice into the bowl of a food processor fitted with a metal blade. Pulse to combine. This can also be done in a quart-sized container using an immersion blender. Pour half the marinade over the beef cubes and the other half over the cabbage leaves. Toss and smear to coat. Allow to stand for 10 minutes.

Crush and roll the Napa cabbage leaves to form 12 bundles. Thread a cabbage bundle onto a skewer. Add a red pepper chunk, beef cube, tomato, cabbage bundle, then a red pepper chunk, beef cube, tomato, and a scallion to cover the last 2 inches of the skewer. Repeat with remaining skewers.

Spray an outdoor grill or grill pan with nonstick cooking spray and heat over medium heat. When it is very hot, add the skewers, in batches if necessary, rotating so each side is grilled, for a total of 12–15 minutes. If the meat is still too rare, place on a cookie sheet and into a hot oven for 5 minutes.

Serve 2 skewers per plate.

Merguez Sausage on Whole Wheat Couscous

MEAT ■ MAKES 6 SERVINGS

1 tablespoon olive oil, divided

1 (10-ounce) box whole wheat couscous

6 sun-dried tomato halves, very finely chopped

½ bunch fresh mint (discard stems), leaves chopped, divided

3 cups water

6 merguez sausages

½ cup light mayonnaise

2 teaspoons lime juice

1 bunch watercress

Moroccan Merguez is nicely spiced North African delicacy. The casing is edible, so you just toss them into the pan or on a grill. You can skewer the sausages for a pretty presentation. You can also experiment with lower-fat sausages, like turkey and chicken varieties.

Tomatoes contain the powerful phytochemical lycopene, associated with reducing the risk of prostate cancer, digestive disorders, and heart disease. Did you know that sun-dried tomatoes could have 10 times the amount of lycopene as raw tomatoes? Although lycopene is available in concentrated capsule form, there is inadequate evidence to conclude that supplements are more, or as beneficial as lycopene consumed in foods.

Heat 1 teaspoon olive oil in a medium pot. Add the couscous and toast over medium heat, stirring, for 3 minutes. Add the sun-dried tomatoes and 2½ tablespoons chopped mint; stir to combine. Add 3 cups water. Bring to a boil, cover the pot, and remove from heat. Set aside.

Meanwhile, in a large skillet, heat remaining 2 teaspoons olive oil over medium heat. Add the sausages and sear for 5–7 minutes, until cooked through, rotating the sausages as they cook. This can be done on an outdoor grill as well.

In a small bowl, mix the mayonnaise, remaining chopped mint, and lime juice.

Uncover the pot and use a fork to fluff the couscous.

Place a large spoonful of couscous onto each plate. Top with a sausage, whole or sliced, and a small pile of watercress. Garnish with the mint sauce.

Grilled Reuben Sandwiches

MEAT ■ MAKES 6 SERVINGS

¼ cup light mayonnaise

2 tablespoons pickle relish

1 tablespoon ketchup

1 teaspoon Dijon mustard

1 clove fresh garlic, minced

1 teaspoon fresh lemon juice

6 large slices rye bread

6 teaspoons deli mustard
   or spicy brown mustard,
   divided

12 ounces thinly sliced
   deli-style turkey breast,
   divided

12 ounces thinly sliced lean
   deli-style corned beef,
   divided

6 tablespoons sauerkraut,
   drained, divided

nonstick cooking spray

This is my current favorite go-to, no time to cook, dinner needs to be on the table in five minutes, walked in from work starving, or need a nice midday lunch dish. True renditions of Reuben or Rachel sandwiches use fattier pastrami or all corned beef, coleslaw, lots of mayonnaise, and a smear of fat on the outside of the bread before putting it down in the pan or grill. I streamlined it by replacing half the meat with turkey, swapping in sauerkraut, lightening up the mayo, and using nonstick cooking spray to help toast the outside. The result is a fabulous hot deli sandwich that you can also try in a whole wheat wrap. (Although coleslaw and sauerkraut are both members of the cruciferous vegetable family and both have cancer-protective qualities, sauerkraut has only one-quarter the calories of coleslaw and contains virtually no fat. The sodium content is higher, however, so be mindful of portion sizes, as displayed in this recipe.)

In a medium bowl, whisk the mayonnaise, relish, ketchup, Dijon mustard, garlic, and lemon juice.

With the rye bread horizontal on your work surface, spread the left half of each slice with 2 teaspoons dressing. Spread the other half of each slice with 1 teaspoon deli mustard.

Place 2 ounces turkey and 2 ounces corned beef on the mustard side, piling it as necessary. Top each with 1 tablespoon sauerkraut.

Fold each piece of bread over the sandwich so the dressing side is on top.

Spray both sides of each sandwich with nonstick cooking spray.

Heat a grill pan over medium heat. Add the sandwiches. Grill for 2–3 minutes per side until bread is golden brown and the meat is warmed through. Try not to move the sandwiches around once they hit the pan, and gently press them down in place. This will give them nice grill marks. Serve hot.

Caribe Island Stir Fry

MEAT ■ MAKES 6 SERVINGS

1 pound shoulder London broil

2 tablespoons olive oil, divided

1 small onion, thinly sliced

6 ounces crimini mushrooms, sliced

1 cup frozen broccoli florets

1 yellow bell pepper, seeded and very thinly sliced

1 orange bell pepper, seeded and very thinly sliced

1 mango, not too ripe, cut into ½-inch cubes

1 teaspoon garlic powder

¾ teaspoon freshly ground black pepper

½ teaspoon onion powder

2½ tablespoons low-sodium soy sauce

2 scallions, sliced, for garnish

All the additional vegetables in this incredible stir fry make this a kaleidoscope of color and an all-in-one skillet meal.

And what is all this color providing? The lean beef is an excellent source of iron (which most women don't get enough of), the mushrooms provide vitamin D, peppers are filled with vitamin C, and broccoli fights to keep cancer at bay. This medley style of cooking helps to incorporate a variety of plant-based nutrients that have been proven to increase satiety and decrease obesity.

The instruction stating "pick up the beef fond" refers to the browned bits that are left behind in the pan. When they are deglazed or liquid is added, they add tremendous flavor to a dish.

If your steak is very thick, cut the thickness in half. Slice the steak into very thin strips.

Heat 1 tablespoon olive oil in a large skillet or wok over medium-high heat. Add the beef and cook all the way through, 2–3 minutes. Searing on 1 side should be enough to cook it through. Don't overcrowd the pan or the meat won't sear properly; it will steam. Do in batches if necessary. Remove the meat.

Add remaining tablespoon oil to the pot. Add the onion and use a wooden spoon to stir and pick up the beef fond from the bottom of the pot. Add the mushrooms, broccoli, and peppers. When the peppers are soft, about 6–8 minutes, add the mango cubes and return the beef to the pot.

Add the garlic powder, black pepper, onion powder, and soy sauce.

Remove to plates or a platter. Garnish with scallions.

Italian Pot Roast

1 tablespoon canola oil

1½ tablespoons all-purpose flour

1 (3-pound) shell roast, chuck roast, or brick roast

2 red onions, sliced

water as needed

6 cloves garlic, chopped

1 (0.6-ounce) packet Italian dressing mix, such as Good Seasons®

1 cup white wine

1 cup chicken stock

1 turnip, peeled, cut into 1½-inch chunks

1 large eggplant, peeled, cut into 1½-inch chunks

2 small parsnips, peeled, cut into 1½-inch chunks

2 carrots, peeled, cut into 1½-inch chunks

2 (5-inch) sprigs fresh rosemary

2 stems fresh basil

In developing this recipe I tried to remove onion soup mix from traditional pot roast without sacrificing flavor. Some onion soup mixes contain over 1,200 milligrams of sodium per packet! The amount of sodium recommended for the whole day is around 2,300 milligrams for the average, healthy person. Although you may not be consuming the whole packet of mix ... just think of the savings by not adding it. Be sure to check out the nutrition facts panel for information when choosing food ... you'll be shocked by some sodium values.

Heat the oil over medium heat in a large pot or Dutch oven that snugly holds the roast without it touching the sides. Sprinkle each side of the roast with flour. Sear the meat for 3–4 minutes per side in the hot oil.

Remove the roast from the pan, reduce heat slightly, and add the onions with 3 tablespoons water. Sauté in the drippings for 6–7 minutes, until soft. Add the garlic and sauté 2 minutes longer. Place the meat back into the pot. Sprinkle on the Italian seasoning. Surround the roast with the wine, stock, and water to come up three-fourths of the way on the meat. Bring to a boil.

Cover and lower to a simmer. Cook for 2 hours.

After 2 hours, uncover the pot, turn the roast over, and add the turnip, eggplant, parsnip, and carrots. Cover and cook for 1½ hours longer. During the last 20 minutes, add the rosemary and basil.

Hawaiian Veal Roast

MEAT ■ MAKES 6 SERVINGS

½ cup dried pineapple, chopped into ¼-inch pieces

⅓ cup walnuts, coarsely chopped

zest and juice of 1 orange, divided

1 teaspoon coarse ground black pepper

1 teaspoon kosher salt

⅛ teaspoon ground allspice

⅛ teaspoon ground cinnamon

tiny pinch of ground cloves

1 (3-pound) veal roast

1 tablespoon olive oil

1 (20-ounce) can pineapple rings, no-sugar-added type

½ cup white wine

water as needed

You will feel like you are in paradise when you sample this delicacy that combines both dried and canned pineapple, adding a sweet edge to offset the rich spices in this veal dish.

Walnuts are number one on the list of nuts, containing significantly higher amounts of omega-3 fats than any other. Aside from preventing the formation of blood clots, and therefore reducing the risk of heart disease, walnuts may also improve brain function. In addition, walnuts are rich in fiber, B-vitamins, magnesium, and vitamin E. The Food and Drug Administration (FDA) has even approved a health claim for walnuts because of their heart-healthy benefits.

Preheat oven to 375°F.

In a medium bowl, toss the dried pineapple with the walnuts, orange zest, and juice from half the orange.

In a small bowl, combine the black pepper, salt, allspice, cinnamon, and cloves. Stir.

Cut the strings from the veal roast and open it up; it may separate into pieces. Lightly season the veal with some of the spice mixture. Stuff the roast with the walnut filling, reserving the liquid in the bowl. Retie the roast; silicone bands work well here, but kitchen string will do as well.

Heat the oil in a small roasting pan over medium heat. Sear the veal, turning with tongs as each side turns golden. Remove from heat.

Place 4 pineapple rings into the bottom of the pan. Place the veal on the pineapple; this will elevate the roast out of its juices. Rub the veal on all sides with the remaining spice mixture. Pour wine, remaining juice from bowl, and juice of the remaining orange half over the roast. Arrange remaining pineapple rings to overlap on top of the roast. Add 1½ cups water to the pan.

Place the veal into the oven and roast, uncovered, for 1½ hours or until no longer pink inside. Check the veal during the roasting; if the pan looks dry add more water to the pan, ½ cup at a time, and scrape up the browned bits. Allow to stand for 10 minutes before slicing. Use a spatula to transfer slices to a platter, in order to keep the filling in the veal. Serve with pan juices.

Garlic Burgers

MEAT ■ MAKES 6 SERVINGS

1½ pounds lean ground beef

1 large shallot

2 cloves fresh garlic

6 ounces portobello mushroom caps

⅛ teaspoon crushed red pepper flakes

⅛ teaspoon cracked black pepper

2 teaspoons dried parsley

1 tablespoon low-sodium soy sauce

1 teaspoon Worcestershire sauce

nonstick cooking spray

1 teaspoon canola oil

4 cloves fresh garlic, sliced

¼ teaspoon garlic powder

¼ teaspoon onion powder

⅛ teaspoon chili powder

½ cup light mayonnaise

6 whole wheat buns

1 tomato, sliced, for garnish, optional

After high school, I spent a year in Israel at Machon Gold on a student's budget. It was always a treat when someone's parents came to visit and took us girls out to dinner. Norman's was one of my favorite haunts; I especially liked their burgers with garlic sauce. When my family was in Israel for my daughter's bat mitzvah, Norman's topped my list as a must-eat destination for that burger. We arrived to watch a teenage boy order and eat the "sumoburger," a 2½-pound burger. Finishing it qualifies you for a spot in Norman's record book and a T-shirt. So much for portion control!

Today we can find cuts of beef that are leaner than ever. So if you watch your portions, beef can be included as part of a healthy diet. Beef is a source of essential nutrients, including iron and vitamin B_{12}, and an excellent source of protein.

In my version, mushrooms and onion provide bulk and moisture to the burger, making this a must-try for your family.

Place the ground beef into a large mixing bowl. Place the shallot and garlic into the bowl of a food processor fitted with a metal blade and pulse until finely chopped. Add the portobello mushrooms and pulse until the mixture resembles ground beef; don't over-pulse or it will turn into a paste.

Add the mushroom mixture to the beef. Add the red pepper flakes, black pepper, parsley, soy sauce, and Worcestershire sauce. Use your hands to gingerly toss until the meat is all mixed and seasoned.

Spray a grill pan with nonstick cooking spray. Heat the pan over medium heat.

Make 6 patties (about 6-ounces each); they should be 1-inch thick and about 6-inches in diameter. Grill the burgers for 6 minutes per side for medium.

Over medium-low, heat the canola oil in a small pot. Add the sliced garlic and cook, stirring the whole time to make sure the garlic does not burn. Cook until the garlic is fragrant, about 3 minutes. Add the garlic powder, onion powder, and chili powder. Remove from heat and stir in the mayonnaise.

Serve the burgers, topped with the garlic spread, on whole wheat buns. Garnish with sliced tomatoes if desired.

A note about Worcestershire sauce: Most Worcestershire sauce contains anchovies. If the kosher certification mark stands alone, then the percentage of anchovies is less than 1.6% of the whole product. Many rabbinical authorities say that this is okay to use with meat. If the kosher certification on the label has a fish notation next to it, the level exceeds 1.6% and you should refrain from using it in meat dishes.

Veal Marsala

MEAT ■ MAKES 6 SERVINGS

6 veal cutlets, pounded very thin

¼ teaspoon fine sea salt, divided

¼ teaspoon freshly ground black pepper, divided

¼ cup white whole wheat flour, or sifted whole wheat flour

2 tablespoons olive oil

4 ounces sliced crimini mushrooms

½ cup marsala wine

6 ounces plain or unsweetened soy milk

chopped fresh parsley, for garnish

Veal is a relatively low-cholesterol meat, especially when using lean cutlets (around 95 milligrams of cholesterol for a 3-ounce portion.) By pounding the cutlets thin and topping them with nutrient-filled mushrooms, you can enjoy this savory dish without overdoing portion sizes.

It is spectacular in this classic preparation — definitely a cause to open a good bottle of vino and break out the wine glasses! And let's not forget the potential health benefits of drinking red wine; for some people, drinking wine may help lower the risk of heart disease. As with all food and beverages, moderation is the key.

Season both sides of each veal cutlet with salt and pepper. Place the whole wheat flour into a plate or shallow dish. Dredge both sides of each cutlet in the flour, shaking off the excess.

Heat the olive oil in a large skillet over medium heat until hot but not smoking. Add the veal cutlets, pressing the center of each one to make contact with the pan so the ends don't curl up. Sear for 2 minutes per side. Remove the veal to a plate or platter. Add the mushrooms and sauté for 4 minutes.

Add the marsala to the pan and cook until reduced by half, about 3 minutes. Lower the heat and stir in the soy milk. Pour the sauce over the veal. Garnish with fresh parsley and serve immediately.

Argentinean Bison Steaks

MEAT ■ MAKES 6 SERVINGS

6 bison rib steaks

fine sea salt

freshly ground black pepper

2 shallots, peeled

½ green bell pepper, seeded and coarsely chopped

4 cloves fresh garlic

1 bunch parsley, stems discarded

¼ cup fresh mint leaves

1 teaspoon ground cumin

⅓ cup extra-virgin olive oil

2 teaspoons red-wine vinegar

nonstick cooking spray

2 tomatoes, wedged, for garnish

The New York Times called bison "a steak without guilt," referring to the fact that it is widely praised by chefs, nutritionists, and environmentalists. It is a lean red meat that has less cholesterol than chicken with the skin removed and less fat than turkey. Due to the lack of fat, it cooks faster than beef — so watch your cooking times. Bison is grass-fed and free of growth hormones. A 3-ounce portion of bison supplies only 122 calories as compared with 3-ounces of beef, which could provide anywhere from 150 to 350 calories for the same portion, depending on the cut.

Argentina is known for beef, so I turned to a classic chimichurri to top this dish.

Season both sides of each steak with salt and pepper. Set aside.

In the bowl of a food processor fitted with a metal blade, use on-off pulses to chop the shallot, green pepper, and garlic. Do not over-process. Scrape down the sides. Add the parsley, mint, and cumin; pulse 5–6 times. Transfer to a bowl. Mix in the olive oil and vinegar. Set aside.

Spray a nonstick grill pan or skillet with nonstick cooking spray. This can also be done on an outdoor grill. Heat the pan over medium heat until very hot. Add the steaks and sear for 6–7 minutes per side for perfect medium-rare.

Serve each steak with a scoop of the chimichurri sauce and a tomato wedge.

Citrus London Broil

MEAT ■ MAKES 10 SERVINGS

3 pounds shoulder London broil

4 cloves fresh garlic, sliced

1 orange, thinly sliced

1 lemon, thinly sliced

1 lime, thinly sliced

1 tablespoon teriyaki sauce

¼ cup extra-virgin olive oil

¼ cup orange juice, not from concentrate

5 sprigs fresh basil

½ teaspoon fine sea salt

¼ teaspoon freshly ground black pepper

1 tablespoon olive oil

CITRUS DRESSING:

1 tablespoon roasted or toasted sesame oil

zest from 1 orange and juice from ½ orange

zest from 1 lemon and juice from ½ lemon

zest from 1 lime and juice from ½ lime

6 fresh basil leaves, minced

2 teaspoons teriyaki sauce

2 cloves fresh garlic, minced

½ teaspoon freshly ground black pepper

Bright citrus flavors complement the steak beautifully. Citrus is most commonly thought of as a good source of Vitamin C, but it also contains a remarkable list of other essential nutrients, including potassium, folate, calcium, thiamin, niacin, Vitamin B_6, phosphorus, magnesium, copper, riboflavin, pantothenic acid, and fiber. Wow! Moreover, citrus contains no fat, cholesterol, or sodium, so this citrus sauce adds a juicy topping that's not fat-laden, as many typical meat sauces are.

Add a bright green, like steamed asparagus, and some brown rice and you have a perfect meal.

Score the meat with a diamond pattern on both sides. Place into a large, heavy-duty ziplock bag. Scatter the sliced garlic over the meat. Layer the slices of orange, lemon, and lime on and under the meat.

In a medium bowl, whisk the teriyaki sauce, olive oil, and orange juice. Add to the bag along with the sprigs of basil. Seal the bag, pressing out all the air. Allow the meat to marinate overnight or for at least 4 hours.

Preheat oven to 450°F.

Remove the meat from the bag and discard the marinade. Season the meat on both sides with salt and pepper.

Heat the tablespoon of olive oil in a large skillet over medium heat. Sear the meat for 4 minutes per side to caramelize the outside. Transfer the meat to a baking pan and roast for 25–35 minutes, depending on thickness; do not overcook.

Allow the meat to rest for 10 minutes, then thinly slice on the diagonal.

While the meat is resting, prepare the citrus dressing: In a medium bowl, whisk the sesame oil; zest and juices from the orange, lemon, and lime; minced basil leaves; teriyaki sauce; minced garlic; and pepper. Drizzle over the meat.

Enchiladas

MEAT ■ MAKES 6 SERVINGS

1½-2 pounds (about 10 medium or 25 small) tomatillos; discard outer husks

1 jalapeño pepper, halved and seeded

2 teaspoons canola oil

1 large onion, finely chopped

3 cloves fresh garlic, chopped

¾ pound ground white turkey

¾ pound lean ground beef

1 (14.5-ounce) can diced tomatoes, with liquid

½ cup canned black beans, rinsed and drained

¼ cup nondairy sour cream, such as Tofutti brand Sour Supreme®

1 (1.25-ounce) packet taco seasoning

6 large (8-10 inch) whole wheat tortillas

water as needed

2 cloves fresh garlic

½ cup fresh cilantro

½ teaspoon ground cumin

½ small onion

½ teaspoon coarse sea salt or kosher salt

Tomatillos look like green tomatoes wrapped in a papery husk. They are actually more closely related to gooseberries and have a distinct citrusy flavor. They are a staple in Mexican and Latin American cooking and are the key ingredient in Mexican salsa verde (green salsa). Before using, remove the husks and rinse off the sticky resin on the skins. Store them in the refrigerator, in a paper or plastic bag in their husks, for up to one month.

The rich nutrient value of the tomatillo may surprise you. One medium raw tomatillo contains only 11 calories and is accompanied by potassium, vitamin C, beta-carotene, niacin, folic acid, and fiber. Then turn on the heat with the jalapeño pepper and its anti-inflammatory benefits. Add a few heart-healthy beans and you've got a pretty potent dish here!

This dish can double as a lovely appetizer. Sub in 6-inch tortillas and serve with a dollop of guacamole and some baked torilla chips.

Preheat the broiler to high.

Place the tomatillos onto a cookie sheet. Add the jalapeño halves, skin-side-down. Broil until blackened, about 10 minutes. Smaller ones may be blackened before larger ones; they can be taken out sooner while the larger ones continue cooking.

Meanwhile, heat the canola oil in a large skillet over medium heat. Add the onion and garlic. Sauté about 5–6 minutes, until translucent. Add the turkey and beef and cook until the beef is no longer pink, about 7–10 minutes, breaking up the meat with a wooden spoon as it cooks. Add the tomatoes, black beans, sour cream, and taco seasoning. Stir to combine. Heat through and remove from heat.

Preheat oven to 350°F.

Place a heaping cup of the filling on almost the bottom edge of one tortilla. Roll up the tortilla and place, seam-side-down, in a 9- by 13-inch glass or ceramic baking dish. Repeat with remaining tortillas.

Using a pastry brush, brush the top of the tortillas with a little bit of water.

Prepare the salsa verde: Place the blistered tomatillos and jalapeños (do not peel) into the bowl of a food processor fitted with a metal blade. Add the 2 cloves garlic, cilantro, cumin, onion half, and salt. Process until a smooth green salsa forms.

Pour the salsa verde over the enchiladas. Bake, uncovered, for 15 minutes.

Sliced Steak Provençal

MEAT ■ MAKES 8 SERVINGS

3 pounds filet split or London broil

½ teaspoon fine sea salt, divided

½ teaspoon freshly ground black pepper, divided

nonstick cooking spray

2 large yellow tomatoes, seeded, finely chopped

6 cloves fresh garlic, finely chopped

¼ cup fresh parsley leaves, minced

¼ cup fresh basil leaves, minced

⅓ cup extra-virgin olive oil

½ teaspoon balsamic vinegar

It may be hard to believe, but one of the most common nutrient deficiencies in the U.S. is iron deficiency, significantly affecting many women and children. Here's a quick course in helping you prevent that problem: the iron in meat, fish, and poultry is 30-60% in the form of heme iron. Nonheme iron is the form found in vegetables, beans, and dried fruit. If you combine both types of iron in the same meal, your body will absorb iron more efficiently.

Season both sides of the meat with ¼ teaspoon each salt and pepper.

Coat a grill pan or skillet with nonstick cooking spray. Heat over medium until very hot but not smoking. Sear the meat for 7 minutes per side, longer for the thicker London broil. Do not move it around once it hits the pan until it is time to flip it with tongs. Sear the second side. Remove to platter and allow to stand for 10 minutes.

Meanwhile, in a medium bowl, mix the tomatoes, garlic, parsley, basil, oil, vinegar, and remaining salt and pepper.

Pat an even coating of the tomato mixture over the steak. Slice the steak thinly on the diagonal and serve.

Buffaloed Burgers

MEAT ■ MAKES 6 SERVINGS

¾ pound ground bison

¾ pound ground beef

¼ cup plus 6 tablespoons hot cayenne pepper sauce, such as Frank's® or Tabasco®, divided

¼ teaspoon freshly ground black pepper

nonstick cooking spray

½ cup nondairy sour cream, such as Tofutti brand Sour Supreme®

3 tablespoons chopped fresh dill

6 whole wheat or whole-grain buns

1 small head Bibb lettuce, separated into leaves

1 beefsteak tomato, sliced

celery sticks, for garnish

It was important to me to experiment with ground bison since I use so much ground beef in my house and I was looking for a way to cut down while still giving my kids the dishes that they love — like meatballs, burgers, and meat lasagnas. When I tried all bison, it got the thumbs-down from my crowd, for tasting gamey. By all means, try it with your family. However, my solution swaps out half the beef for bison, a compromise that makes me and them happy. This process of "diluting down" calories and fat doesn't necessarily mean you're compromising taste.

Remember, eating healthier is a process. If you want the results to last and be integrated into the long-term, you have to like what you are eating.

It might be fun to let the kids make their own burgers … sort of a burger smorgasbord! Make platters of sliced tomato, sliced cucumber, different types (and colors) of lettuce, and a variety of condiments, so that they all can create their own favorites. It may even get the kids to eat more vegetables!

The sauce is a play on buffalo wing sauce, a nice spicy touch.

In a medium bowl, mix the ground bison and ground beef with ¼ cup hot sauce and black pepper. Form six patties. Set aside.

Spray a nonstick grill pan or skillet with nonstick cooking spray. This can also be done on an outdoor grill. Heat the pan over medium heat until very hot. Add the burgers and sear for 4 minutes per side.

In a small bowl, mix the nondairy sour cream with the dill. Set aside.

Place each burger into a bun. Top each with a tablespoon of hot sauce. Add a piece of lettuce and a slice of tomato. Smear the top half of the bun with dill sauce. Replace the top of the bun. Serve with celery sticks.

Fish

Sole en Papillote

PARVE ■ MAKES 6 SERVINGS

6 sole fillets, all bones removed

½ teaspoon smoked paprika, such as McCormick®

¼ teaspoon dried thyme

½ teaspoon fine sea salt

¼ teaspoon freshly ground black pepper

½ red onion, very thinly sliced

½ red bell pepper, seeded, very thinly sliced

2-3 plum tomatoes, sliced into ¼-inch-thick rounds

½ lemon

1½ cups baby spinach leaves

2 tablespoons white wine, divided

Cooking food "en papillote" means in parchment paper. It makes a for a dramatic presentation and is perfect for cooking delicate fish. But don't let the drama fool you — this is a simple cooking technique. By steaming in its own juices, the fish's moisture is locked in and flavor is boosted without any added fat. Working directly on the jelly-roll pan makes is easier than transferring the packets after they are filled. The paper even makes for a speedy clean-up! You can use flounder or turbot in place of the sole.

Here's a healthy tip about spinach: Spinach is an excellent source of iron; try to eat it at the same time that you consume something high in Vitamin C to enhance the absorption of iron. Some examples of Vitamin C-rich foods are oranges, strawberries, baked potatoes, and tomatoes. In this recipe, the red bell pepper is a source of Vitamin C.

Preheat oven to 400°F.

Cut six rectangles of parchment paper 2 inches longer than the fish on each side. Fold each in half lengthwise and open out again. Place one fish fillet against the center fold of one of the pieces. Repeat with remaining fish and parchment. Place the open packets on two jelly-roll pans.

In a small bowl or ramekin, mix the smoked paprika, thyme, salt, and pepper. Sprinkle the spices evenly over the 6 fillets. Scatter onion and red pepper over each. Top with 2–3 slices of tomato. Squeeze fresh lemon juice over each packet. Top each with ¼ cup spinach. Drizzle 1 teaspoon of wine over each packet.

Turn the pans so that the fish lay horizontally in front of you. Tuck the tail end of each fish under to help cook more evenly. Fold the parchment over on the fold to make rectangles. Starting at one end, seal the packets by folding and rolling the edges to crimp them together. It should look like a calzone. If you are having trouble, you can staple them.

Bake for 10–14 minutes, depending on thickness of the fish. The steam will force the packets into a dramatic dome shape. Move the packets to plates or a platter. Cut an "x" into the top of each packet to allow steam to escape. Open packets to serve.

Miso Glazed Cod

PARVE ■ MAKES 6 SERVINGS

1 large (1½-pound) cod fillet

¼ teaspoon fine sea salt

3 tablespoons blond, light shiro miso paste

1 teaspoon freshly grated ginger

2 tablespoons mirin

2 tablespoons dark brown sugar

1 teaspoon roasted or toasted sesame oil

2 scallions, thinly sliced on the diagonal

½ teaspoon black sesame seeds

Mirin is Japanese sweet cooking wine. The Mitoku brand is my favorite and more authentically thick than other brands that I have used. Mirin contrasts nicely with miso and harmonizes the flavors.

Miso is made from a combination of soybeans and a grain such as rice or barley. It adds a distinct flavor, but it can also add 900 milligrams of sodium per tablespoon … so proceed with caution.

Microplanes got their start in woodworking shops to shave wood. They crossed over to the kitchen to finely and easily grate chocolate, lemon zest, and ginger.

Preheat oven to 375°F.

Lightly season both sides of the cod with salt. Place on a parchment-lined cookie sheet.

In a medium bowl, whisk the miso, ginger, mirin, brown sugar, and sesame oil. Generously brush the miso glaze over the cod. Bake, uncovered, for 14 minutes. Turn the oven to broil, and broil for 1 minute.

Scatter the top of the fish with scallions and sesame seeds.

Salmon With Bok Choy and Tomatoes

PARVE ■ MAKES 6 SERVINGS

1 large head bok choy

1½ pounds salmon fillets, skin and pin bones removed, sliced into 12 long strips

nonstick cooking spray

2 tablespoons Billy Bee Honey Barbecue Seasoning®, divided

honey, optional if using homemade spice mixture; see note

2 (14.5-ounce) cans stewed tomatoes with Italian seasoning

⅛ teaspoon cayenne pepper

Chinese mustard cabbage, or bok choy, resembles a cross between celery and swiss chard. Bok choy is nutritionally superior to other types of cabbage because it is higher in calcium and provides 40% more Vitamin A in the form of beta-carotene.

Shari-Beth Susskind, a personal trainer I consulted for this book, shared this recipe. She has turned so many people on to this spice mix that she is known to some of her clients as Miss Billy Bee. She uses it on every kind of protein, from chicken to meat to fish. It is wonderful in this recipe; however, if you can't find the Billy Bee Honey Steak Seasoning you can make a spice mixture as follows: combine 1 teaspoon brown sugar, ½ teaspoon paprika, ½ teaspoon coarse sea salt, ½ teaspoon dried minced onion, ¼ teaspoon garlic powder, ¼ teaspoon fennel seeds, ⅛ teaspoon cayenne pepper. Stir to combine.

Trim off the very bottom root end of the bok choy and discard. Cut the remaining bok choy into bite-sized pieces, stems and leaves included. Set aside.

Place the salmon into a shallow oven-safe dish. Spray with nonstick cooking spray. Heavily coat the fish with 1 tablespoon of the Billy Bee honey steak seasoning or homemade spice mixture above. If using homemade spice mixture, drizzle a little honey over the top of each fillet. Place under the broiler and broil for 8–10 minutes, until fish is cooked through.

While the fish is cooking, spray a large skillet with nonstick cooking spray. Heat over medium and add the bok choy, tomatoes, and remaining tablespoon steak seasoning. Add the cayenne. The bok choy will cook down so it is okay if the pan is overflowing. Cook until the bok choy is tender but not wilted — you still want some crunch.

Divide the bok choy and tomatoes among six plates, placing them in a heaping mound in the center. Crisscross two salmon fillets over the top of each mound.

Stuffed Whole Roasted Bronzini

PARVE ■ MAKES 6 SERVINGS

nonstick cooking spay

6 whole bronzini, gills removed, gutted

1 tablespoon extra-virgin olive oil

1 small bulb fennel, thinly sliced

3 cloves fresh garlic, chopped

3 plum tomatoes, chopped

3 ounces baby spinach leaves

fine sea salt

freshly ground black pepper

6 sprigs fresh rosemary

2 tablespoons white wine, divided

2 lemons, thinly sliced

Bronzini, often referred to as Mediterranean sea bass, gets that name from the waters where it is harvested. A big hit in Europe, it has finally made its way here and is currently very popular in restaurants, where it is served whole and filleted at the table. I like how mild the taste is, similar to red snapper. It does not need any heavy saucing, just fresh ingredients to enhance its natural sweetness.

And there's a good chance that you'll digest this dish easily because of the addition of fennel. In the form of a tea, this gas-relieving agent may even be soothing for infants with colic. The leaves are also a good source of calcium and an excellent source of iron and potassium.

Preheat oven to 375°F.

Cover a jelly-roll pan with parchment paper. Spray with nonstick cooking spray.

Rinse the cavity of each fish and drain the liquid.

Pour the olive oil into a large bowl. Add the fennel and toss. Add the garlic, tomato, and spinach.

Season each fish inside and out with salt and pepper. Place a rosemary sprig into each cavity. Holding open one fish, pour 1 teaspoon white wine into the cavity. Fill the fish with one-sixth of the fennel mixture. Lay 3 lemon slices over the filling. Repeat with remaining bronzini.

Place the filled bronzini onto the prepared pan. Bake, uncovered, for 20 minutes. Most people serve the fish whole, but, if this is objectionable, either fillet it or cut off and discard the tail and head and before serving.

Wasabi Pea-Crusted Salmon

6 (4-ounce) salmon fillets, with skin, pin bones removed

1 cup wasabi-coated green peas

1 tablespoon sesame seeds

½ cup light mayonnaise, divided

¼ teaspoon wasabi powder

1¼ teaspoons hot sauce, such as Frank's® or Tabasco®

1 teaspoon roasted or toasted sesame oil

½ teaspoon cayenne pepper

Wasabi peas are dried green peas coated in wasabi powder. They offer great crunch and a very hot, spicy kick to this dish.

Wasabi, also known as Japanese horseradish, is a cancer- and bacteria-fighter. It's even been known to prevent tooth decay!

Preheat oven to 375°F.

Rinse the salmon fillets. Pat dry and place on a cookie sheet. Set aside.

Place the wasabi peas into the bowl of a food processor fitted with a metal blade. Process until most of the peas are crushed, but leave a little texture — don't grind to a powder. Transfer to a plate. Add the sesame seeds and mix with a spoon.

In a small bowl, mix ¼ cup mayonnaise with the wasabi powder. Spread a thin layer of mayonnaise on each fillet. Dip the coated side of each fillet into the wasabi peas. Use your palm to press the peas into the salmon to coat evenly.

Bake, uncovered, for 15 minutes.

Meanwhile, prepare the spicy mayonnaise: In a small bowl, mix the remaining mayonnaise, hot sauce, sesame oil, and cayenne. Stir well. Transfer the spicy mayonnaise to a heavy-duty ziplock bag.

Snip the very corner of the ziplock bag and drizzle each plate with spicy mayonnaise sauce. Place a salmon fillet in the center of the drizzle. You may have extra sauce.

Green Tea Poached Cod

PARVE ■ MAKES 6 SERVINGS

water, as needed

4 bags green tea

2½ teaspoons coarse sea salt or kosher salt, divided

½ teaspoon cayenne pepper

½ teaspoon paprika

1 teaspoon black sesame seeds

1 teaspoon white sesame seeds

1 teaspoon ground ginger

zest of ½ orange

¾ teaspoon freshly ground black pepper

6 (5-ounce) cod or hake fillets

1 shallot, cut in half

2 cloves fresh garlic

1 inch fresh ginger, peeled

2⅔ cups mashed potato flakes

¼ cup shredded carrots

¼ cup daikon radish, peeled, cut into matchsticks

1 tablespoon rice vinegar

¼ teaspoon sugar

The spicy inspiration in this dish is a Japanese seasoning called togarashi, a spicy combination that varies by maker.

Green tea is made of unfermented tea leaves and has the highest concentration of the powerful antioxidants called polyphenols. Green tea has a potpourri of health benefits, including combating cancer, alleviating rheumatoid arthritis, preventing heart disease, and boosting the immune system.

Pour 2 inches of water into a deep-sided skillet large enough to hold the fish. Bring to a boil. Turn off the heat. Add the tea bags and allow the tea to steep while preparing the rest of the ingredients.

In a small bowl, combine 1 teaspoon salt, cayenne, paprika, black and white sesame seeds, ginger, orange zest, and black pepper. Mix to combine.

Sprinkle about 1 teaspoon of the seasoning over each fillet. Set aside.

In the bowl of a food processor fitted with a metal blade, pulse together the shallot, garlic, and ginger until finely minced, about 45 seconds–1 minute.

Stir the shallot mix and the remaining 1½ teaspoons salt into the tea, and simmer over low heat for 7 minutes.

Adjust the heat to a gentle simmer; the tea should just be shimmering. If it is bubbling, turn down the heat. Add the cod and cook, covered, 8–10 minutes, or just until cooked through. Remove the fish with a slotted spoon and keep warm.

Pour the potato flakes into a bowl. Add 2 cups poaching broth from the fish plus 1 cup water. Stir to reconstitute the potato flakes.

To serve, combine the carrots, daikon, rice vinegar, and sugar. Place a dollop of potatoes in the center of each plate. Top with cod fillet and garnish with the carrot salad. Serve immediately.

Za'atar–Rubbed Halibut

PARVE ■ MAKES 6 SERVINGS

olive-oil flavored nonstick
  cooking spray

6 (4-ounce) portions halibut,
  without skin

3½ teaspoons za'atar, divided

½ teaspoon fine sea salt,
  divided

¼ teaspoon freshly ground
  black pepper

¼ teaspoon turmeric

2 tablespoons extra-virgin
  olive oil

1 tablespoon red-wine
  vinegar

Halibut does not have a naturally strong flavor, so it takes on spicing, like za'atar mix and sauces, wonderfully. Fresh halibut should have a firm, wet appearance and a whitish-creamy color. Cut away any pieces of fatty layer from the back. Check carefully for bones.

Halibut is a nutrient-dense fish. It's a rich source of the minerals selenium, magnesium, phosphorus, and potassium; a good source of the B-vitamins B_{12}, niacin, and B_6; and of course, a contributor of the heart-protective omega-3 fatty acids.

Za'atar, my favorite Middle Eastern spice blend, is so versatile. In addition to fish, it can be used on meats, vegetables, rice, eggs, and bread.

Preheat oven to 450°F.

Spray both sides of each halibut fillet with nonstick cooking spray. Place onto broiler pan.

In a small bowl, mix 2½ teaspoons za'atar, ¼ teaspoon salt, and pepper. Pat spice mixture onto the top of each fillet. Roast, uncovered, for 10 minutes.

Meanwhile, prepare the dressing: In a small bowl, whisk remaining ¼ teaspoon salt, remaining 1 teaspoon za'atar, turmeric, olive oil, and vinegar.

Remove each halibut fillet to a plate. Drizzle the dressing over each fillet and decoratively around each plate.

Spinach-Panko-Crusted Trout

PARVE ■ MAKES 6 SERVINGS

6 trout fillets, with skin, pin bones removed; trim off fatty belly portion

fine sea salt

freshly ground black pepper

3 cups packed, fresh baby spinach leaves

2 teaspoons olive oil

1 cup panko bread crumbs

3 tablespoons Dijon mustard, divided

lemon slices, for garnish

Panko are Japanese bread crumbs that are cut and dried using a technique that results in crispy, crunchy, and airy crumbs that stay crisp after being cooked.

For a more kid-friendly version, this recipe can also be made with flounder or sole.

Preheat oven to 450°F.

Cover two cookie sheets with parchment paper. Place the trout fillets on the prepared sheets. Season with salt and pepper.

Place the spinach into the bowl of a food processor fitted with a metal blade. Using on-off pulses, chop until minced. This can also be done by hand. Place the minced spinach into a medium bowl. Add the olive oil and panko. Mix well.

Brush 1½ teaspoons mustard on the top of each fillet. Pat the panko crust in an even layer over each fillet.

Bake for 8–10 minutes.

Transfer to plates or platter. Garnish with a twisted lemon slice.

Cedar-Planked Salmon

PARVE ■ MAKES 10–12 SERVINGS

1-2 untreated cedar planks, soaked in water according to manufacturer's directions

½ teaspoon garlic powder

¼ teaspoon oregano

½ teaspoon smoked paprika, such as McCormick®

½ teaspoon fine sea salt

¼ teaspoon freshly ground black pepper

6 salmon fillets, with skin; pin bones removed

Pacific Northwest Native Americans cooked salmon on long cedar planks over smoking coals. The wet plank infused flavor into the seafood as it smoldered, while the moisture steamed the food, keeping it moist and tender. Purchased cedar planks, available in better supermarkets or upscale houseware stores, are a modern-day way to get the same flavors at home.

Boards for smoking fish can be made of cedar, oak, or alder. Make sure they are 1-inch thick. Completely immerse the plank in water for as long as the manufacturer suggests, usually a few hours, or it will burn when grilled. Feel free to serve the fish on the planks, but don't reuse them. Select planks big enough so the fillets are not touching, or use two planks.

This method of cooking allows you to savor the full flavor of the fish without any added fat. The only fats within this recipe are the heart-healthy omega-3 fatty acids within the salmon itself.

Smoked paprika is a perfect spice to enhance the smoky barbecued flavor.

Preheat the barbecue or outdoor grill. Place the wet plank on the grill for 10–15 minutes, until fragrant.

Meanwhile, in a small bowl, mix the garlic powder, oregano, smoked paprika, salt, and pepper. Pat the spice rub over the top of the salmon fillets.

When the plank is ready, place the salmon on the plank. Cover the grill and allow to cook for 8–10 minutes.

Transfer salmon to a platter or carefully move the plank to the table. If you remove the fish, allow the plank to cool on the grate before removing.

Salmon Burgers

PARVE ■ MAKES 6 SERVINGS

2 pounds salmon fillets, pin bones and skin removed

¾ teaspoon garlic powder

½ teaspoon onion powder

½ teaspoon celery salt

¼ teaspoon dried dill

⅛ teaspoon cayenne pepper

nonstick cooking spray

¼ cup yellow mustard

1 tablespoon balsamic vinegar

½ cup chopped fresh dill

whole wheat buns

mesclun lettuce

Use the freshest salmon you can for this wonderful light lunch or dinner dish. Fresh salmon never smells fishy and should look moist, never dry.

The addition of mustard packs a zesty zing for a mere 5 calories per teaspoon and brings with it some mighty health benefits. As a member of the chili family, mustard increases blood circulation and clears sinuses, just as a decongestant does. It can also act as a digestive stimulant.

Slice the salmon into 2-inch strips. Place into the bowl of a food processor fitted with a metal blade. Using on-off pulses, chop the salmon; don't pulse too many times or you will grind the salmon too finely. Transfer the salmon to a medium bowl. Mix in the garlic powder, onion powder, celery salt, dill, and cayenne. Form into 6 patties.

Spray a large grill pan with nonstick cooking spray. Heat over medium-high heat. Cook the salmon burgers for 2–3 minutes per side, until just cooked through.

In a small bowl, stir the mustard with the vinegar and fresh dill.

To serve, place each burger on a bun. Top with the mustard dressing and lettuce.

Snapper With Cucumber Harissa

PARVE ■ MAKES 6 SERVINGS

6 (4-ounce) portions red snapper fillets

1 lemon, divided

1 tablespoon plus 2 teaspoons extra-virgin olive oil, divided

¼ teaspoon cayenne pepper, divided

1½ teaspoons ground cumin, divided

1½ teaspoons ground coriander, divided

1 English (hothouse) cucumber, peeled, cut into 6 pieces, seeded

1 tablespoon fresh cilantro leaves

3 cloves fresh garlic

½ teaspoon fine sea salt

1 teaspoon crushed red pepper flakes

1 teaspoon caraway seeds

This dish is really hot stuff … and it's worth the heat! Cayenne pepper and red pepper flakes aid the digestive system as well as the heart and circulatory systems. The anti-inflammatory powers of cayenne power may even soothe a sore throat!

Although not authentic, this cucumber harissa is also spicy, like its namesake.

Preheat oven to 375°F.

Place the snapper fillets onto a parchment-lined baking sheet. In a small bowl, whisk the juice from ½ lemon, 2 teaspoons olive oil, ⅛ teaspoon cayenne, ½ teaspoon cumin, and ½ teaspoon coriander. Brush the fillets with the spice mixture. Bake, uncovered, for 18–20 minutes, until fish flakes with a fork when tested.

Meanwhile, in the bowl of a food processor fitted with a metal blade, process the cucumber with the cilantro, garlic, remaining teaspoon cumin, salt, red pepper flakes, remaining tablespoon olive oil, remaining teaspoon coriander, juice of remaining lemon half, remaining ⅛ teaspoon cayenne, and caraway seeds. Pulse until a chunky salsa forms.

Serve the snapper with a dollop of the cucumber harissa.

Eggs, Pasta, and Dairy

Greek Frittata Ring

DAIRY ■ MAKES 16 SERVINGS

1 (15-ounce) can diced tomatoes

nonstick cooking spray with flour in the can

2 teaspoons olive oil

1 green pepper, seeded, cut into ¼-inch pieces

1 small red onion, very thinly sliced

¼ cup packed baby spinach leaves

6 large eggs

2 egg whites (from large eggs)

1½ cups egg substitute, such as Egg Beaters®

⅓ cup low-fat milk

1 teaspoon dried oregano

½ teaspoon fine sea salt

¼ teaspoon freshly ground black pepper

⅓ cup all purpose flour

½ cup light feta cheese, crumbled

¼ cup Kalamata olives, pitted and chopped

Eggs, containing 6 grams of high-quality protein and all 9 essential amino acids, have gotten a bad rap over the years. Today, even the American Heart Association says that one egg a day is acceptable, but you need to keep in mind the cholesterol in that egg along with the cholesterol in other foods you eat in that same day.

Studies have shown that because of their carotenoid content, specifically lutein and zeaxanthin, eggs may be important for eye health and possibly help prevent macular degeneration. With 300 mgs. of choline per yolk, eggs may also help regulate the brain, nervous system, and cardiovascular system.

Although an egg contains 5 grams of fat, only 1.5 grams are saturated fat. (And remember that egg whites contain no fat or cholesterol.)

This is nice served with a salad that is lightly dressed with a red-wine vinaigrette.

Preheat oven to 350°F.

Empty the tomatoes into a strainer and drain very well.

Heavily coat a bundt pan with nonstick cooking spray. Set aside.

Heat the oil in a medium skillet over medium heat. Sauté the pepper and onion for 5–6 minutes, until they start to wilt. Shred the spinach leaves and add to the pan. Sauté for an additional 2 minutes.

Meanwhile, in a medium bowl, whisk the eggs, egg whites, egg substitute, milk, oregano, salt, pepper, and flour until frothy. Mix in the sautéed vegetables and the tomatoes. Stir in the cheese and olives. Pour into prepared pan.

Bake for 45 minutes or until set. Using a small offset spatula or a knife, loosen the edges of the frittata and around the tube as well. Unmold. Slice and serve.

Huevos Rancheros

DAIRY ■ MAKES 6 SERVINGS

2 cups store-bought salsa

1 (15.5-ounce) can black beans, rinsed and drained

2 teaspoons lime juice

6 whole wheat tortillas

nonstick cooking spray

6 large eggs

6 tablespoons grated low-fat cheddar or Monterey Jack cheese

1½ Haas avocados, pitted, peeled, cut into ½-inch pieces

pinch paprika, for garnish

chopped cilantro, for garnish

lime slices, for garnish

I love this filling Mexican classic. Although the eggs have to be fried at the last minute, the rest can be made earlier, so I turn to this recipe when having a small group for brunch. I like using the fresh salsa that is in the refrigerator section of the supermarket, because it is chunkier and brighter tasting. Go as mild or spicy as you like.

Some people shy away from using canned beans because they fear that they're too high in sodium. Did you know that by rinsing the beans before you use them, you can slash the sodium content by one-third? Rinsing will also help you wash away some of the complex sugars that sometimes cause gas. So if you're trying to keep your sodium intake at bay, you don't have to avoid this often-unappreciated superstar vegetable. If you skip the beans, you'll miss out on their many benefits, including reducing your risk of heart disease, diabetes, and cancer.

Place the salsa, black beans, and lime juice into a medium pot. Heat over medium until warm, stirring occasionally.

Heat an empty large nonstick skillet over medium-high heat. Add a tortilla and toast until it starts to bubble; flip it over and toast on the other side. Transfer to a plate. Repeat with remaining tortillas.

Off the heat, spray the skillet with nonstick cooking spray. Break in the eggs and allow them to cook 3–4 minutes, sunny-side-up, until the white is opaque.

To serve, top each tortilla with some of the warm salsa mixture and a tablespoon of the cheese. Place a fried egg on top. Toss some avocado chunks onto each plate. Garnish with a sprinkle of paprika, cilantro, and a lime slice.

Brown Rice Lasagne

DAIRY ■ MAKES 12 SERVINGS

nonstick cooking spray

1 (10-ounce) box brown rice lasagne noodles

1 tablespoon olive oil

1 (12-ounce) bag soy crumbles, such as Meal Starters® from Morningstar Farms

1 (16-ounce) can tomato sauce

½ teaspoon dried oregano leaves

½ teaspoon garlic powder

¼ teaspoon dried basil

¼ teaspoon freshly ground black pepper

1 (16-ounce) bag frozen chopped spinach, completely defrosted; can use microwave

3 cups low-fat ricotta cheese, divided

2 (14-ounce) cans stewed tomatoes, with liquid

12 ounces light mozzarella, shredded

Brown rice pasta, specifically the Tinkyada brand, is gluten-free and great-tasting. It tastes so much like regular pasta you will be shocked; just make sure to cook until just al dente and not longer.

The soy crumbles are used in place of ground beef and enable you to make an authentic "meat style" lasagna. You can even prep the mock-meat mixture, stuff it into peppers, and bake them.

Soy is rich in protein, calcium, and many other vitamins and minerals. Soybeans also contain phytochemicals called isoflavones, believed to help strengthen bones, fight cancer, and protect your heart. Although it's not a good idea to overdo your soy intake, some researchers say we should be consuming one serving of soy everyday.

Preheat oven to 400°F.

Spray a 9- by 13-inch baking pan with nonstick cooking spray. Set aside.

Prepare the noodles according to package directions until al dente.

Meanwhile, prepare the mock-meat filling: Heat the oil in a large skillet over medium and add the soy crumbles. Sauté until fragrant, about 4–5 minutes.

Pour the tomato sauce into a small bowl and season with oregano, garlic powder, basil, and pepper. Set aside.

Squeeze all the liquid out of the spinach. Set aside.

Arrange a layer of three noodles in the bottom of the pan. Using an offset spatula, spread 1 cup of ricotta cheese over the noodles. Top with a third of the "meat" mixture and a layer of stewed tomatoes with some of the liquid from the can. Sprinkle with a layer of spinach. Top with ½-cup of the mozzarella. Repeat this two more times. End with a layer of noodles.

Pour the seasoned tomato sauce over the top of the lasagne and top with any remaining cheese.

Place the lasagne into the oven and bake for 10 minutes, or until the cheese is melted. Serve hot.

Ultimate Veggie Burger

PARVE ■ MAKES 6 BURGERS

¾ cup (1 medium) carrot, peeled, shredded on large holes of grater

¾ cup (½ medium) raw sweet potato, unpeeled, cut into ¼-inch dice

¼ cup water

1½ cups cooked brown rice, prepared on stove or in microwave

8 crimini mushrooms, stems trimmed

⅓ cup raw sunflower seeds

¼ cup all-purpose flour

1 heaping teaspoon vegetable consommé powder

zest of 1 lemon

2 very leafy basil stems

3 sprigs fresh oregano

½ cup canned white beans, rinsed and drained

3 egg whites (from large eggs), beaten

1 teaspoon fine sea salt

½ teaspoon freshly ground black pepper

3 tablespoons olive oil

6 whole wheat pitas or buns

6 tomato slices

thin slices of cucumber

thin slices of red onion

I love veggie burgers and this one tops the list! This is a great do-ahead meal. Do all the prep, shape the burgers, and store in the fridge for up to 3 days until ready to cook.

These burgers are bursting with nutrient value! This melange of colorful vegetables provides an array of vitamins and minerals, and the protein is well complemented with the combination of egg whites, beans, and brown rice.

Place the carrot and sweet potato in a small microwave-safe bowl. Add ¼-cup water. Loosely cover and heat on high until just cooked through, about 4 minutes.

Place the rice, mushrooms, sunflower seeds, flour, consommé powder, and lemon zest into the bowl of a food processor fitted with a metal blade. Remove the leaves from the basil and oregano stems and add leaves to the bowl. Pulse until everything is uniform but you can still see grains of rice.

In a medium bowl, fold together the mushroom mix, carrots, sweet potato, white beans, egg whites, salt, and pepper.

Heat the olive oil in a large skillet over medium heat. If you will need to cook the burgers in batches, heat only 1½ tablespoons of oil per batch. Using rounded ½-cups, form 6 patties, pressing lightly to form the burgers. Sear for 3–4 minutes per side.

Serve in or on pitas or buns, with slices of tomato, cucumber, and red onion.

Multigrain Pasta
With Roasted Pepper Pesto

PARVE ■ MAKES 6 SERVINGS

1 small head roasted garlic (see note on page 90)

3 red bell peppers

1 (14.5-ounce) box multigrain rotini pasta

6 sun-dried tomato halves

2 teaspoons pine nuts

⅓ cup extra-virgin olive oil

1 teaspoon balsamic vinegar

2 tablespoons water

½ teaspoon dried basil

¼ teaspoon garlic powder

¼ teaspoon fine sea salt

⅛ teaspoon cayenne pepper

Every time I tried passing off whole wheat pasta to my kids, I ended up with a mutiny and full plates of dinner left over. That was until I discovered Barilla Plus Multigrain pasta. Each serving contains 17 grams of protein and is loaded with omega-3 fatty acids and fiber. But the best news is that the toughest pasta audience, kids ranging in age from 5–13, gave it the thumbs-up. I love that they are consciously making healthy choices and that I don't have to try to slip anything by them.

This flavorsome creation also adds the powerful antioxidant, cell-protecting properties of basil. The health benefits of basil include its ability to treat nausea, motion sickness, indigestion, constipation, and respiratory problems. Basil is also a good source of Vitamin A, magnesium, potassium, iron, and calcium.

This dish is great served at room temperature, so it works well on a buffet, at a barbecue, or as part of a menu that can be made in advance.

While the garlic is roasting, prepare the peppers. You can either keep the peppers whole and char them on top of the gas burner, using tongs to turn them as they blacken so each surface is black, or cut the peppers in half, discard the seeds, and roast skin-side-up on a jelly-roll pan under the broiler. Either way, when the skins are blackened, place the peppers into a ziplock bag and allow to steam in the bag for 5 minutes. Remove from the bag and slip the skins off. It is okay if some of the blackened bits remain; they will add a nice smoky flavor to the pesto. If the pepper was whole, discard the stems and seeds.

Cook the pasta according to the package directions.

Place the prepared peppers, sun-dried tomatoes, pine nuts, olive oil, vinegar, water, basil, garlic powder, salt, and cayenne into the bowl of a food processor fitted with a metal blade. Squeeze the roasted garlic into the bowl as well. Pulse to form a thick pesto.

When the pasta is done, drain and immediately transfer to a serving bowl. Top with the pesto and toss to blend. Serve hot or at room temperature.

Tacos

1 tablespoon grapeseed oil

½ small onion, cut into ¼-inch dice

½ yellow bell pepper, seeded, cut into ¼-inch dice

½ red bell pepper, seeded, cut into ¼-inch dice

½ small jalapeño pepper, minced

1 (12-ounce) package LightLife SmartGround Original® or Taco/Burrito Ground® crumbles

2 teaspoons chili powder

2 teaspoons paprika

1 teaspoon ground cumin

½ teaspoon garlic powder

½ teaspoon onion powder

1 (8-ounce) can tomato sauce

1 cup water, more if needed

6 taco shells

SAUCE:

2 cups organic ketchup

1 teaspoon chili powder

½ teaspoon ground cumin

Tacos are a fun meal where all the family members can help themselves, stuffing their taco shells with loads of healthy choices. Start with the "meat" mixture below and set each of the "fixings" out in bowls. The sauce calls for organic ketchup, as regular ketchups usually contain high-fructose corn syrup.

One of the hottest topics in nutrition today revolves around foods that can reduce inflammation, and this "hot" dish certainly fulfills that role. Peppers of any type, whether bell or jalapeño, help battle cancer (particularly of the skin and prostate) and the pain of arthritis and headaches. In addition, some peppers contain twice the amount of Vitamin C in citrus fruits, making them powerful antioxidants, too.

Heat large sauté pan over medium-high heat. Add oil. Sauté onion, bell peppers, and jalapeño just until fragrant. Add the crumbles and cook about 3 minutes or until they start to brown. Immediately add the seasonings; toast till browned. Add the tomato sauce and 1 cup water. Simmer, uncovered, over low to medium-low heat, about 15 minutes. The filling should be thickened, but still saucy. If all the liquid has evaporated, add more water to reach desired consistency.

Prepare the sauce: In a medium bowl, whisk the ketchup, chili powder, and cumin.

Fill each taco shell with the seasoned "meat." Serve immediately with taco fixings and top each taco with sauce.

FIXINGS:

avocado, peeled, pitted, cut into ¼-inch dice

shredded lettuce

shredded low-fat cheddar cheese

store-bought salsa

chopped fresh tomatoes, seeded

canned black beans, rinsed and drained; or canned refried beans

fat-free sour cream

sliced olives

sliced scallions

Blueberry Pancakes

DAIRY ■ MAKES 8 PANCAKES

½ cup fat-free milk

1 large egg

3 tablespoons sugar

1 teaspoon pure vanilla
    extract

3 tablespoons canola oil,
    divided

2 tablespoons water

1 cup flour, see note

2 teaspoons baking powder

½ teaspoon fine sea salt

½ cup fat-free cottage cheese

heaping ½ cup fresh
    blueberries

fat-free sour cream

light pancake syrup

In developing this recipe, I tried four side-by-side batches; one with all-purpose flour, one with plain whole wheat flour, one with whole wheat pastry flour, and one with white whole wheat flour. They all worked fine. My kids preferred the ones made with all-purpose flour, but when I told them they were doing something better for their bodies with the whole wheat pastry flour or the white whole wheat, they felt that the difference was not significant enough to matter. The pure whole wheat flour had a darker color and a bit of a nutty but blander flavor that did not appeal to my kids but may to yours. Experiment on your own family and see what they prefer. Either way, this is a great way to start your day.

Also feel good in knowing that these are healthier than any pancakes you'd get anywhere else! Most pancakes do not contain as much protein (milk, egg, cottage cheese) or antioxidants from the blueberries. These fiber-filled sweet treats are extraordinarily rich in antioxidants, topping most other foods. The blue pigments, called anthocyanins, have been shown to inactivate a number of common carcinogens. Blueberries also store longer than most berries — up to five days fresh and for several months when frozen.

In a medium bowl, whisk the milk, egg, sugar, vanilla, 2 tablespoons oil, and 2 tablespoons water.

In a small bowl, combine the flour, baking powder, and salt. Stir the dry ingredients into the wet. With a spatula, mix in the cottage cheese and fold in the blueberries.

Heat remaining tablespoon of oil in a nonstick skillet over medium heat.

When the skillet is hot, drop the batter by ¼-cup measures. An ice cream scoop works well. If using straight whole wheat, you may need to stir in a little milk to thin the batter. Cook for 3 minutes until golden; flip and cook another 2 minutes.

Serve with fat-free sour cream or light pancake syrup.

Mexican Mini-Quiches

nonstick cooking spray

6 large flour tortillas,
can be plain or spinach

5 large eggs

5 egg whites (from large eggs)

1 cup low-fat milk, 1% is fine

½ teaspoon freshly ground
black pepper

½ teaspoon chili powder

¼ cup sliced scallions

¼ cup shredded low-fat
cheddar or Monterey Jack
cheese

¼ cup bottled salsa,
for garnish

¼ cup fat-free sour cream,
for garnish

chopped fresh cilantro
leaves, for garnish

Most people don't realize that garlic is not the only gem in the allium family. Medicinal benefits are also derived from onions, scallions, shallots, and chives. These foods help to enhance the immune system, curtail coronary risk factors, and perhaps reduce the incidence of certain cancers.

You can make these quiches in advance, omitting the salsa and sour cream garnishes. Once completely cooled, place in an airtight container and in the refrigerator. To reheat, place on a jelly-roll pan, uncovered, and bake in a 375°F oven until heated through, about 10 minutes. Garnish and serve.

Preheat oven to 375°F.

Heavily coat 2–3 muffin tins with nonstick cooking spray.

Using a 4½-inch round cookie cutter, cut 3 circles from each tortilla.

Press one circle into each muffin cup, pleating as necessary to fit.

In a medium bowl, whisk the eggs, egg whites, milk, pepper, and chili powder until foamy. Stir in the scallions and cheese. For ease of pouring, transfer the batter to a liquid measuring cup or other spouted bowl. Pour the egg filling into each cup, almost to the top of each tortilla cup, without overflowing.

Bake until the tops are set, about 15–20 minutes. Cool for 5 minutes; remove from tin. Garnish each warm quiche with a teaspoon of salsa and a dab of sour cream. Garnish each plate or the platter with chopped cilantro.

Pastel Omelet for Two

PARVE ■ MAKES 2 SERVINGS

- 2 large eggs
- 4 egg whites (from large eggs)
- 2 teaspoons canola oil
- ½ zucchini with skin, cut into ¼-inch pieces
- ½ red bell pepper, seeded, cut into ¼-inch pieces
- ¼ teaspoon fine sea salt
- ⅛ teaspoon freshly ground black pepper
- ¼ teaspoon dried thyme
- ¼ teaspoon dried oregano
- ⅛ teaspoon cayenne pepper
- ½ beefsteak tomato, cut into 4 wedges

Egg-white omelets top the list of healthy breakfasts for all dieters. I did try them, but all-egg-white omelets turn out flat and dry. This compromise recipe, which uses mostly egg whites, includes 2 whole eggs to give body. The yield equals two 3-egg omelets.

The beauty of the egg-white omelet is that is that it is a low-calorie, fat-free, nutrient-dense vehicle for carrying all types of vegetables. This versatile dish can be eaten for breakfast, lunch, or dinner, accompanied by multigrain toast. By combining protein and carbohydrates, you'll be fueled with energy that lasts.

In a medium bowl, whisk the eggs and egg whites. Set aside.

Heat the oil in a nonstick 10-inch skillet over medium heat. Add the zucchini and red pepper and sauté for 3 minutes, until shiny. The zucchini should be tender and have a little color. Season with salt and pepper.

Meanwhile, heat a small skillet over medium heat. In a small bowl, mix the thyme, oregano, and cayenne. Sprinkle over the tomatoes. Place the tomatoes into the hot pan and cook for 1 minute to get a nice charred flavor. Set aside.

Push the zucchini and red pepper into the center of the skillet in a single layer. Add the eggs. Once the eggs start to solidify, tilt the pan away from you. This will allow gravity to help flip half the omelet over itself as you fold it over with a thin metal spatula.

Serve the omelet with the charred tomatoes.

Side Dishes

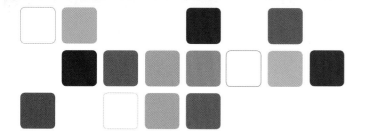

Teriyaki Butternut Squash Rounds

PARVE ■ MAKES 6 SERVINGS

2 large butternut squash,
  peeled
¼ cup apricot preserves
4 teaspoons teriyaki sauce
1 teaspoon yellow mustard

I share the same Ashkenazic palate as many of my readers, and sometimes desire something sweet and sticky on the side. These yummy squash rounds fit the bill without adding too much sugar. I always make more than I need because they don't always make it to the table — they are so delicious to snack on!

Select a squash that has a long neck so you will get a lot of even, round slices. Although the benefits of butternut squash are many, did you know that this squash, high in Vitamin C and beta-carotene, also works as an anti-inflammatory aid for children with asthma and may reduce the number of wheezing episodes?

Preheat oven to 375°F.

Cover 2 large cookie sheets with parchment paper.

Starting from the neck end, thinly slice the squash into rounds that are less than ¼-inch thick. Stop when you get to the seeds; save that part of the squash for another use.

Lay the squash slices on the prepared baking sheets. Set aside.

In a small bowl, whisk the apricot preserves, teriyaki sauce, and mustard until smooth.

Lightly brush both sides of each squash round with the sauce.

Bake 40 minutes, until roasted and sticky.

Remove to a serving plate or platter.

Oatmeal Apple-Butter Muffins

PARVE ■ MAKES 18 MUFFINS

1 cup all-purpose flour

½ cup white whole wheat or whole wheat pastry flour

½ cup quick-cooking or 1-minute oats

½ cup sugar

1 tablespoon baking powder

1½ teaspoons cinnamon, divided

½ teaspoon baking soda

½ teaspoon fine sea salt

1 cup unsweetened or plain soy milk

½ cup apple-butter

1 large egg

3 tablespoons canola oil

1 teaspoon pure vanilla extract

1 Braeburn or McIntosh apple, peeled, cored, and cut into ¼-inch dice

1 tablespoon dark brown sugar

These muffins are delicious as a side dish but just as good toasted for breakfast or as a snack. They are loaded with the rich soluble fiber of oats, which help lower cholesterol and triglyceride levels and stabilize blood sugar. And don't be fooled by the name apple "butter," since this product doesn't contain any butter at all. In fact, instead of raising cholesterol, which butter could do, apples contain pectin, a beneficial soluble fiber that can lower heart-clogging fats.

Preheat oven to 350°F.

Line muffin tins with paper liners, for a total of 18 muffins.

In a medium bowl, whisk the all-purpose flour, whole wheat flour, oats, sugar, baking powder, ½ teaspoon cinnamon, baking soda, and salt. Set aside.

In a medium bowl, whisk the soy milk, apple-butter, egg, oil, and vanilla.

Fold the wet ingredients into the dry ingredients, making sure to incorporate well and not to over-mix. A few lumps are okay. Fold in the apple.

Using a 2-ounce (2-inch) ice cream scoop, portion out the batter into the prepared tins.

In a small bowl, mix the remaining teaspoon cinnamon with the brown sugar. Sprinkle evenly over each muffin.

Bake 20 minutes, or until a toothpick inserted into the center comes out clean.

Twice-Baked Sweet Potatoes

PARVE ■ MAKES 6 SERVINGS

6 small sweet potatoes

1 teaspoon ground cumin

½ teaspoon ground coriander

¼ teaspoon ground cayenne pepper

⅔ cup sweetened dried cranberries, like Craisins®, very finely chopped

½ teaspoon fine sea salt

¼ cup real maple syrup, NOT pancake syrup

2 tablespoons chopped pecans, divided

I love sweet-potato pie and was looking for a healthier stand-in last Thanksgiving. Once I took out the eggs, crust, sugar, and flour, I wasn't left with much to work with, so I took the star of the sweet-potato pie show and put it out on its own. I think it shines.

Sweet potatoes are among the most nutritious foods in the vegetable kingdom. They possess a natural sweetness that's enhanced after cooking. This dish can, of course, accompany meat or fish and boost the nutritional value of any meal. What most people don't realize is that this dish also makes a super-charged snack, filled with vitamins, minerals, and fiber, yet not filled with calories. With its creamy texture and sweet taste, sweet potatoes don't require the addition of an abundance of butter or sugar, often seen in many traditional recipes.

Preheat oven to 450°F.

Using a fork, prick each sweet potato along the top. Double-wrap each potato in aluminum foil.

Place the potatoes into the oven and roast for 45–55 minutes.

When they are cool enough to handle, cut off a lengthwise slice, about ½-inch from the top. Place the orange flesh from these slices into a bowl, discarding the skins. Using a melon baller, scoop out the potato and add it to the bowl, leaving a small wall of sweet potato to help retain the shape of the skins.

In a small bowl, mix the cumin, coriander, and cayenne. Mix into the sweet potato flesh. Add the cranberries, salt, and maple syrup. Mix.

Refill each potato shell with the mashed sweet potatoes. Sprinkle each with 1 teaspoon pecans.

Place the potatoes onto a baking sheet and return to the oven for 10 minutes. Transfer to a serving platter.

Squash Halves
Stuffed With Black-Bean Salsa

PARVE ■ MAKES 6 SERVINGS

3 small acorn squash

2 (14.5 -ounce) cans whole stewed tomatoes, Italian flavored, drained

1 (15.5-ounce) can black beans, rinsed and drained

1 (7-ounce) can yellow corn, drained

1 (7-ounce) can white shoepeg corn, drained

¾ teaspoon dried cilantro

¼ cup seasoned rice vinegar

¼ teaspoon coarse sea salt

I serve any extra black-bean salsa to my kids after school. They scoop it out with baked tortilla or multigrain chips for a fiber-rich treat. Most people are shocked when they discover just how much protein beans contain: ½ cup of black beans provides the same amount of protein that's in 1 ounce of meat, with lots more fiber and heart-healthy features.

Preheat oven to 400°F.

Place the 3 whole squash into the oven on a jelly-roll pan and roast for 45–55 minutes, until softened.

Meanwhile, prepare the salsa: On a cutting board, coarsely chop the tomatoes. Transfer the tomatoes into a shallow container. Add the beans and both types of corn. Stir. Season with cilantro, vinegar, and salt. Mix with a spoon.

When the squash are soft, carefully remove them from the oven and cut each one in half lengthwise.

Scoop out and discard the seeds.

Using a slotted spoon, fill each squash half with the black-bean salsa.

Transfer to a platter and serve warm.

Mulled Spaghetti Squash

2 spaghetti squash

1 tablespoon ground cinnamon

1 teaspoon fine sea salt

¼ teaspoon ground allspice

¼ teaspoon ground nutmeg

8 teaspoons olive oil

½ cup apple cider, divided

4 tablespoons honey, divided

Spaghetti squash gets its name from the likeness it bears to spaghetti. If you run your fork across the flesh after it is roasted, it separates into strands. They are delicious seasoned up in a variety of ways. Spaghetti squash is low in calories and high in fiber, so it adds bulk to dishes. I serve it as a side dish and sometimes make a nest of it under a portion of chili. My girlfriend uses the cooked flesh in place of shredded potatoes in latkes. I have even floated some strands in soup.

Here you will find simple spicing that mimics sweet, mulled apple cider flavors, but don't be afraid to go savory with this vegetable as well. If you're a spaghetti lover but you're trying to eat fewer calories and more vegetables, spaghetti squash may be your answer. The flesh of this winter squash is firm and stringy and makes a great partner for tomato or pesto sauce. One cup of spaghetti supplies a whopping 40 grams of carbohydrates and 197 calories, while the same amount of spaghetti squash provides a slimming 10 grams of carbs and 42 calories, as well as a wealth of beta-carotene, Vitamins B and C, folic acid, and fiber.

Preheat oven to 450°F.

Cut each spaghetti squash in half lengthwise. Scoop out and discard the seeds.

In a small bowl, combine the cinnamon, salt, allspice, nutmeg, and oil. Drizzle the spice mixture into the 4 cavities. Pour 2 tablespoons apple cider into each cavity. Mix with the spices in the cavity and brush some of the mixture onto the flesh of the squash. Drizzle 1 tablespoon of honey over each squash half. Wrap each half individually in aluminum foil. Place onto a cookie sheet.

Roast the squash for 50–60 minutes, or until tender.

Remove from oven and, when cool enough to handle, remove and discard the foil. Cut each half in half again, making 8 portions.

Pull a fork lengthwise though the flesh to produce strands that resemble spaghetti. Mix the spices in the center cavity into the spaghetti strands. Transfer to a serving bowl.

Ratatouille Polenta Pie

MEAT OR PARVE ■ MAKES 8 SERVINGS

- 5 cups chicken or vegetable stock
- 1 teaspoon fine sea salt
- ½ teaspoon freshly ground black pepper, divided
- 1¾ cups cornmeal
- ⅛ cup honey
- nonstick cooking spray
- 1 cup tomato sauce
- ½ zucchini, with skin, sliced paper-thin
- ½ small eggplant, with skin, sliced paper-thin
- ½ yellow squash, with skin, sliced paper-thin
- 2 plum tomatoes, sliced thin
- 2 cloves fresh garlic, minced
- 1 tablespoon extra-virgin olive oil
- 1 teaspoon dried oregano
- fresh basil leaves, for garnish

Polenta is corn meal, which can be used to make the breakfast cereal grits and other comfort foods. Some recipes prepare it so it takes on the consistency of mashed potatoes. Here it forms a base for an elegant pie that holds all the makings of ratatouille. This recipe combines a medley of powerful veggies to give you a dish that not only keeps calories in check, but could also fight viruses and harmful bacteria and protect against cell damage that could set the stage for cancer.

Heat the stock, salt, and ¼ teaspoon pepper in a medium pot over high heat. Slowly whisk in the cornmeal. Reduce the heat to low. Keep whisking until the mixture is fluffy and not grainy. If the heat is too high, the polenta will get too thick before it is fully cooked. Add the honey and whisk continuously until the polenta is pulling away from the sides of the pot, about 7 minutes total. Remove from the heat.

Spray a 10-inch springform pan with nonstick cooking spray.

Press the polenta into the bottom of the pan, forming a base.

Top with tomato sauce. Scatter the slices of zucchini, eggplant, squash, and tomato over the top of the pie. Season with the minced garlic. Drizzle with olive oil. Scatter on the oregano and remaining pepper.

Set the broiler to high. Place the pie 8 inches from the heat source and broil for 10–12 minutes.

Remove from oven. Place on a plate and carefully release the sides of the pan. Garnish with basil leaves. Slice and serve.

Summer Harvest Quinoa

MEAT OR PARVE ■ MAKES 6 SERVINGS

1 cup uncooked quinoa

2 cups chicken stock or water

1 tablespoon olive oil

½ zucchini, with skin, cut into ½-inch dice

½ yellow squash, with skin, cut into ½-inch dice

1½ cups sugar snap peas, threads removed, quartered

½ cup red grape tomatoes, halved

½ cup yellow grape tomatoes, halved

½ teaspoon fine sea salt

½ teaspoon freshly ground black pepper

½ teaspoon freshly minced ginger

¾ teaspoon garlic powder

6 large fresh mint leaves, very finely chopped

6 large fresh basil leaves, very finely chopped

juice of 1 lemon

Pronounced "keen-wa," this seed can be found as a cereal and in the form of flour, grain, or pasta. Of all grains, quinoa has the highest protein content, and the protein contained is of excellent quality, which enhances other foods within the dish. Other benefits of eating quinoa include its ability to fight cancer and lower cholesterol levels. And don't forget about the iron, potassium, riboflavin, Vitamin B$_6$, niacin, and thiamin you'll be providing your body with too … all from this little grain!

Rinse the quinoa thoroughly either in a strainer or in a pot and drain. Do not skip this step or a bitter-tasting, natural, soap-like coating will remain. Once the quinoa is drained, place it into a medium pot with the water or stock. Bring to a boil. Reduce heat and simmer, uncovered, until the liquid is absorbed, about 10–15 minutes. You will know when it is done as the grains turn translucent and the outer layer pops off. Drain any excess water that may remain.

Meanwhile, prepare the vegetables. Heat the olive oil in a large skillet over medium heat. Add the zucchini and squash. Sauté for 2–3 minutes, tossing to coat with oil. Add the snap peas and sauté for 2 minutes longer. Add the red and yellow tomatoes and sauté for a final 2 minutes. Season with salt and pepper. Add the ginger and the garlic powder. Stir in the mint and basil. Add the quinoa. Mix until all the colors are distributed. Squeeze in the lemon juice. Transfer to a bowl or container to cool. Best served at room temperature.

Roasted Red Onions

PARVE ■ MAKES 6 SERVINGS

1 tablespoon water

3 medium red onions

olive oil

6 tablespoons honey

¼ cup good-quality balsamic vinegar

1 teaspoon fresh thyme leaves

¼ teaspoon fine sea salt

Simplicity at its best. Roasting the onions brings out the natural sugars. This colorful dish pairs perfectly with steak or other meat. I slice up any leftovers the next day into a spinach salad.

Don't cry over onions … they could help you battle cancer because they contain quercetin, a potent flavonoid antioxidant. Onions also provide Vitamin C, folate, and fiber, thus reducing the risks of heart disease, too.

Preheat oven to 350°F.

Pour 1 tablespoon water into a baking dish.

Peel onions and cut in half horizontally. Place cut-side-down into the baking dish. Drizzle with olive oil. Cover with aluminum foil and bake for 1 hour.

In a small bowl, whisk the honey, vinegar, thyme, and salt.

Turn the onions cut-side-up. Drizzle with the honey-mixture and bake, uncovered, 15 minutes more.

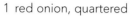

Moroccan Spiced Vegetables

PARVE ■ MAKES 10 SERVINGS

1 red onion, quartered

2 large leeks, trimmed, halved lengthwise

1 acorn squash, seeded, cut into 2-inch chunks, with skin

1 butternut squash, seeded, cut into 2-inch chunks, with skin

2 sweet potatoes, cut into 2-inch chunks, with skin

1½ cups baby carrots

2 parsnips, peeled, cut into 2-inch chunks

2 zucchini, cut into 2-inch chunks, with skin

1 (15-ounce) can chick peas, rinsed and drained

½ cup raisins

1 cup olive oil

juice of 1 lemon

5 cloves garlic, minced

1 tablespoon paprika

2 teaspoons coarse sea salt

1 teaspoon ground cumin

1 teaspoon ground ginger

2 teaspoons turmeric

leaves from 3 sprigs parsley, chopped

leaves from 3 sprigs cilantro, chopped

A potpourri of color, this filling side dish can be the centerpiece of a dinner table.

Acorn and butternut squash and sweet potatoes all share a gorgeous orange color that shouts with vitamins and minerals. The darker flesh of these winter squashes are more nutritious and richer in complex carbohydrates, fiber, and beta-carotene, compared with summer varieties of squash, like zucchini.

Preheat oven to 375°F.

Place the onion, leeks, squashes, sweet potatoes, carrots, parsnips, zucchini, chick peas, and raisins into a large oven-to-table baking dish.

In a medium bowl, whisk the olive oil, lemon juice, minced garlic, paprika, salt, cumin, ginger, turmeric, parsley, and cilantro. Pour over the vegetables and toss to coat.

Bake, uncovered, 1½ hours, or until the vegetables are tender. Serve warm.

Faux Potato Kugel

MEAT OR PARVE ■ MAKES 12 SERVINGS

¼ cup plus 2 teaspoons canola oil, divided

1 very large or 2 medium onions, chopped into ¼-inch pieces

2 large eggs

8 egg whites (from large eggs)

2 medium heads (2 ½ pounds florets) cauliflower, cut into coarse dice

1 large (10-ounce) Idaho potato, peeled, chopped into coarse dice

2 tablespoons chicken stock or water flavored with 1 teaspoon parve chicken consomme powder, divided

2½ teaspoons coarse sea salt or kosher salt

2½ teaspoons coarse ground or cracked black pepper

2 tablespoons all-purpose flour

My family was lucky enough to have a special friend, Ancie Cohenson, live with us for a few months last year. This octogenarian has more energy than people who are decades younger. Sometimes, as a pre-Shabbos treat, she would venture into my kitchen and whip us up an old-country favorite, potato kugel fried in oil on the stovetop. After she moved back home, we missed her and her kugels terribly. I developed this recipe to stand in and my family grudgingly approved. Look, nothing tastes exactly the same as potato kugel almost deep-fried in oil, but this is a great compromise. The cauliflower bulks up the kugel, while the pepper gives it great kick. If you don't like your kugel so peppery, cut down the amount. At close to 2,000 calories per cup of oil (yes, that's 2,000 calories!), this recipe can save you a day's worth of the calories you need! Although oil, particularly olive and canola oils, are rich in monounsaturated fats and are important members of the heart-healthy family, they also add up in calories a lot quicker than you realize when you turn that bottle over, so pour with caution. This recipe showcases the splendor of these nutritionally potent veggies — without the guilt.

Preheat oven to 425°F.

Pour ¼ cup canola oil into a 9- by 13-inch baking pan. Place into the oven while it heats. The oil will get very hot.

Heat the remaining 2 teaspoons canola oil in a medium nonstick skillet over medium heat. Add the onions and sauté until golden, about 10 minutes.

In a medium bowl, whisk the eggs and egg whites.

In the bowl of a food processor fitted with a metal blade, process half the cauliflower with half the potato. Add half the egg mixture and 1 tablespoon chicken stock or consomme. Process until smooth. Remove to a large bowl and process remaining cauliflower, potato, egg mixture, and stock. Add to the first half. Mix in the salt, pepper, and flour. Distribute the spices well.

Gently fold the sautéed onions into the mixture. Carefully remove the pan from the oven; the oil will be very hot. Add the batter to the hot pan. If any oil comes up in the corners, brush or spoon it over the batter in the center of the pan.

Bake, uncovered, for 1 hour 15 minutes. Serve warm.

Stir-Fried Cabbage

PARVE ■ MAKES 6 SERVINGS

½ very small purple cabbage, hard, outer leaves discarded

½ large Napa cabbage, also known as Chinese cabbage

2 tablespoons canola oil

3 carrots sliced with julienne peeler, or 1½ cups shredded carrots

⅛ teaspoon ground cumin

¼ teaspoon ground coriander

¼ cup low-sodium soy sauce

1 teaspoon roasted or toasted sesame oil

¼ teaspoon ground ginger

1 teaspoon garlic powder

The benefits of consuming blue and purple foods are many. These foods are rich in flavonoids called "anthocyanins," which help increase circulation, lower cancer risk, improve memory, and encourage urinary-tract health. On the aesthetic side, they also add a beautiful contrast to other vegetables within the dish.

Remove the core from the purple cabbage half. Slice cabbage into ½-inch thick slices. Separate into strands. Thinly slice the Napa cabbage as well.

Heat the canola oil in a very large skillet over medium heat. Add both cabbages and the carrots. Season with cumin and coriander. Cook for 10 minutes, stirring occasionally; the cabbages will soften. Turn off the heat. Add the soy sauce, sesame oil, ginger, and garlic powder. Mix well. Transfer to a serving bowl.

Kasha Pilaf

The flavor of the pilaf is greatly enhanced by the broth, so use a good-quality broth or stock. Don't overcook or it will turn mushy.

Buckwheat is the new jewel in the cholesterol-fighting crown! This grain contains a flavonoid called rutin, which lowers LDL, or bad cholesterol levels, and it keeps blood flowing more freely. Buckwheat is an excellent source of soluble fiber and contains a list of other antioxidants, including Vitamin E, selenium, and phenolic acids.

Place the broth and salt into a large soup pot. Add the sweet potatoes, broccoli, and pepper. Bring to a boil over medium-high heat.

When the mixture comes to a boil, add the kasha and stir. Cover; reduce heat and simmer for 8–10 minutes, or until most of the water is absorbed but the kasha is not mushy.

Remove the pot from the heat. Add the oil, basil, and lemon juice. Fluff the pilaf with a fork. Transfer to serving bowl. Serve warm or at room temperature.

3 cups chicken or vegetable broth

½ teaspoon fine sea salt

3 small sweet potatoes, peeled, cut into ¼-inch dice

florets from 2 stalks broccoli, chopped into small pieces

¼ teaspoon freshly ground black pepper

2 cups whole granulation kasha, also known as roasted buckwheat groats

¼ cup extra-virgin olive oil

11 large basil leaves, shredded

juice from 1 large lemon

Spicy Fries

PARVE ■ MAKES 4 SERVINGS

1 large butternut squash, peeled

nonstick cooking spray

1 teaspoon coarse sea salt or kosher salt

½ teaspoon cayenne pepper

½ teaspoon paprika

½ teaspoon garlic powder

¼ teaspoon chili powder

¼ teaspoon dried oregano

⅛ teaspoon dry mustard powder

There is a fabulous website called hungrygirl.com. It is administered by a woman who claims she is not a nutritionist, she is just always hungry. She uses her website to talk about great low-fat products that she comes across and to share recipes and tips for dieters. She has an awesome recipe on her site for faux fries made from butternut squash that is simply sliced with a crinkle-cut cutter, salted, and roasted at high heat. In my house, skinny spicy fries reign supreme, so I played with her recipe and developed a version for spicy fries, which my kids now actually prefer to real spicy fries — boy, that is an accomplishment! They can sometimes get soft after roasting, but they are still yummy. Any shape is fine, from shoestring to chunky. Reheat uncovered.

Spicing up this dish with the fiery taste and bright-red appearance of red cayenne pepper, paprika, and chili powder will make it hot in healing power as well as in taste. These spices have been effective in promoting pain relief, they aid in digestion, and they have also been linked to preventing heart disease. And if spicy food does not suit your taste, know that even small amounts of these spices have therapeutic benefits.

Preheat oven to 425°F.

Line a jelly-roll pan with parchment paper. Set aside.

Using a sharp knife, carefully cut the squash in half lengthwise. Discard the seeds. Thinly slice into French-fry shapes; I like long, skinny fries.

Place the cut squash in a single layer on prepared pan. Spray liberally with nonstick cooking spray.

In a large bowl, mix the salt, cayenne, paprika, garlic powder, chili powder, oregano, and mustard powder. Toss the fries into the spice mixture to coat all sides. Return in a single layer to the pan.

Roast, uncovered, for 35–40 minutes; cooking time may be shorter for skinny fries, longer for fatter ones. Shake the pan halfway though cooking. The fries are done when they are crisp. Serve hot.

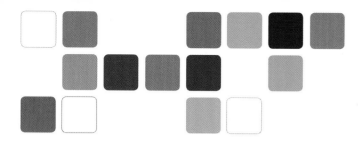

Brussels Sprouts Poppers

PARVE ■ MAKES 8 SERVINGS

20 ounces Brussels sprouts

2 tablespoons extra-virgin olive oil

1 tablespoon roasted sesame oil

3 cloves fresh garlic, minced

½ teaspoon cracked or coarse black pepper

½ teaspoon coarse sea salt or kosher salt

Talk about a bad reputation! Brussels sprouts have topped the most-hated list of childhood veggies for decades. That is all about to change with this munchable recipe. You will love the nutty toasted flavor of these roasted poppers. The high-heat cooking method crisps and caramelizes the tops while the insides become creamy.

Roasted sesame oil adds more than just a captivating aroma; this oil is high in linoleic acid, an essential fatty acid our body cannot produce. This fatty acid helps keep our skin supple and plays an important role in maintaining healthy blood vessels, regulating blood pressure, and controlling cholesterol. Deficiencies of linoleic acid result in hair loss, arthritis-like conditions, and possible mood swings. Sesame oil is also rich in oleic acid, believed to benefit the cardiovascular system.

Preheat oven to 400°F.

Line a jelly-roll pan with parchment paper. Set aside.

Trim the root end from each Brussels sprout and cut each sprout in half lengthwise. If they are really large, cut into quarters. Place into a medium mixing bowl.

Add the olive oil, sesame oil, garlic, pepper, and salt. Toss to coat evenly. Transfer to prepared pan.

Roast, uncovered, for 25–30 minutes. The outsides will be dark and crisp. Smaller Brussels spouts will cook faster, so keep an eye on them. Serve hot.

Baked Brown Rice and Edamame

MEAT OR PARVE ■ MAKES 6 SERVINGS

2 cups short-grain brown rice

4 cups chicken or vegetable stock

1 carrot, julienned, or 1 cup shredded carrots

1 cup shelled edamame; can be frozen

¼ cup low-sodium soy sauce

1 tablespoon roasted or toasted sesame oil

Short-grain rice will give this dish a great texture, almost like barley, but it is harder to find. You may need a more upscale supermarket like Whole Foods. If using parboiled rice, like Uncle Ben's, cut the cooking time to 1 hour.

Edamame (pronounced ed-a-mah-may) really packs a punch! Just ½ cup of this fabulous bean provides 9 grams of fiber (the same amount you'd find in 4 cups of zucchini) and 11 grams of protein, as well as containing the same amount of iron found in 4 ounces of chicken breast — all in only 120 calories.

Preheat oven to 350°F.

Place the rice and stock into an 11- by 13-inch baking pan. Stir to combine. Cover tightly with foil. Bake for 1 hour 30 minutes.

Remove the foil, add the carrot, edamame, soy sauce, and sesame oil. Stir to combine. Return the pan, uncovered, to the oven and cook for 5 minutes to heat the edamame though.

Can be served warm or at room temperature.

Greens and Garlic

PARVE ■ MAKES 6 SERVINGS

3 tablespoons extra-virgin olive oil

5 large cloves fresh garlic, sliced

1 pound fresh baby spinach leaves

¼ teaspoon coarse sea salt or kosher salt

Garlic is here to stay. Garlic is one of the oldest known medicinal plants and its bold flavor has been strongly linked to fighting heart disease, lowering blood pressure, and helping to stave off the common cold. Whether the cloves are crushed, cut, or chewed, garlic's sulfur-containing compound, allicin, is responsible for its therapeutic qualities, including lowering cholesterol and blood pressure.

Here is a great trick to evenly slice the garlic to the perfect thickness for this recipe. Lay a garlic clove horizontally on your cutting board. Place a fork across the length of the garlic clove, also horizontally. Slip your knife between the tines of the fork to cut perfectly even slices of garlic.

Heat the oil in a large skillet over medium heat. Add the garlic and cook until fragrant; do not allow it to brown. If it starts to brown, lower the heat.

Wash the spinach well; shake off excess water but don't dry the leaves. The water that clings to the leaves will help steam them. Add the spinach to the skillet. Use tongs to turn the spinach in the pan. Sauté until wilted but still bright green. If there is a lot of liquid, carefully drain excess water. Return the skillet to the heat to warm through. Season with salt.

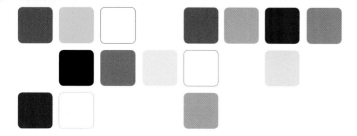

Saffroned Barley

MEAT OR PARVE ■ MAKES 6 SERVINGS

½ cup raisins

½ cup golden raisins

½ cup orange juice or tea

2 cups uncooked pearl barley

1 tablespoon olive oil

large pinch saffron threads

6½ cups chicken or vegetable stock

½ cup sliced almonds

2 tablespoons fresh minced parsley

¼ teaspoon fine sea salt

Gorgeous color and great texture make this barley a great accompaniment to roast chicken as well as to lamb, turkey, or beef. Serve the barley loose, or, for a more formal presentation, you can make timbales by packing the barley into plastic-wrap-lined ramekins and unmolding them onto serving plates.

Saffron is considered to be the most precious spice in the world. It takes thousands of royal purple flowers of the crocus plant to produce a single ounce of saffron. This golden spice comes from the plant's stigma, of which there are only three per flower. Luckily, due to its intense flavor and coloring power, only a tiny amount of saffron is needed to make its presence known in whatever dish you create. This herb has been linked to alleviating asthma, coughs, and the common cold, as well as to treating acne and skin conditions. Saffron also has antibacterial and antiviral properties, thereby protecting the body from disease.

Mix the raisins together in a small bowl. Add the orange juice or tea and allow the raisins to soak in a warm place, such as near the stove, while you prepare the recipe. Or, place the raisins and liquid in a small pot and simmer over medium for 2 minutes. This will help to plump and flavor them.

Place the barley and olive oil into a large pot. Toast over medium heat for 5 minutes; the barley will become fragrant as it toasts. Add the saffron threads and stir. Add the stock. Cook, uncovered, over medium-low heat for 40 minutes, until the liquid is absorbed and the barley is tender.

Drain the raisins, reserving 2 tablespoons of the liquid. Add the raisins and the reserved liquid to the barley, along with the almonds. Toss to combine. Add the parsley and salt, and toss. Transfer to a serving bowl.

Harvest Bread

PARVE ■ MAKES 16 MUFFINS OR 10 MINI LOAVES

nonstick cooking spray

2 cups all-purpose flour

1 cup whole wheat flour

1 teaspoon baking powder

½ teaspoon baking soda

¼ teaspoon cinnamon

⅛ teaspoon nutmeg

½ teaspoon fine sea salt

½ cup olive oil

½ cup unsweetened applesauce

3 large eggs

1⅓ cups sugar

1 cup packed baby spinach leaves

¾ cup corn kernels (can be frozen) or kernels from 1 small cob

2 medium zucchini, unpeeled, grated

Baked breads like zucchini breads are usually so heavy due to white flour and sugar. I think this remake will capture your attention. It can also be made in a 9- by 13-inch pan, baked for 45 minutes, and cut into small squares. Serve it as a side dish or toasted for breakfast, with a cup of coffee.

Zucchini is available year round and can add texture and nutritional value to a wide variety of dishes without adding fat and barely adding any calories. One average zucchini has just 25 calories and is composed of 95% water. Rich in lutein, zucchini also promotes eye health.

Preheat oven to 350°F.

Place paper liners into a 12-cup muffin tin or spray mini (2- by 4-inch) loaf pans with nonstick cooking spray. Set aside.

In a medium-large bowl, whisk the flour, whole wheat flour, baking powder, baking soda, cinnamon, nutmeg, and salt.

In the bowl of a stand mixer set at medium speed, mix the oil, applesauce, eggs, and sugar. Add the dry ingredients in two batches.

Using a silicone spatula, stir in the whole baby spinach leaves, corn, and zucchini. Pour into prepared pans.

Bake, uncovered, until a toothpick inserted into the center comes out clean. The muffins should take 30–35 minutes, the mini loaves 35–40 minutes.

Tangy Mediterranean Vegetables

PARVE ■ MAKES 10 SERVINGS

VEGETABLES:

- 1 head cauliflower, cored, cut into florets (can use 2 pounds fresh florets)
- 2 small Italian eggplants, stems discarded, cut into 1-inch chunks
- 1 red bell pepper, seeded, cut into 1-inch chunks
- 1 small Meyer lemon, with peel, cut into ¼-inch chunks; discard loose seeds (can use regular lemon)
- 1 red onion, cut into 1-inch chunks
- 12 cloves fresh garlic, whole
- 2 cups cherry tomatoes
- 16 pimento-stuffed olives
- 16 dried plums (prunes)

DRESSING:

- ¼ cup red-wine vinegar
- ¼ cup olive oil
- 2 teaspoons stone-ground Dijon mustard
- 4 cloves fresh garlic, minced
- 1 tablespoon dried oregano
- 4 fresh mint leaves, minced
- ½ teaspoon dried rosemary, crumbled

The tang from this dish will be apparent when you get one of the pieces of lemon. The roasting turns it soft and edible, like preserved lemons. Preserved lemons are a Moroccan condiment; lemons are soaked in oil and salt, and after a month-long soak they lose their sourness. Meyer lemons work best in this recipe because they are not as tart as regular lemons and the thinner peel is slightly sweet.

Cauliflower, a member of the cruciferous family, contains disease-battling nutrients, including sulforaphane. This photonutrient helps the liver produce enzymes that block cancer-causing chemicals from causing damage and may play a role in reducing tumor growth in breast and prostate cancer. Cauliflower is also rich in vitamin C and folic acid.

Preheat oven to 400°F.

Place the cauliflower, eggplant, bell pepper, lemon, onion, garlic, tomatoes, olives, and prunes into a large roasting pan. Set aside.

Prepare the dressing: In a medium bowl, whisk the vinegar, oil, mustard, garlic, oregano, mint, and rosemary.

Pour dressing over the vegetables and toss to distribute.

Bake, uncovered, for 60 minutes. Toss once or twice during cooking.

Allow the vegetables to cool for 10 minutes to allow the flavors to mellow.

Quinoa Oreganata

PARVE ■ MAKES 10 SERVINGS

5 whole plum tomatoes, halved lengthwise, seeds scooped out

1½ cups dry quinoa

3 cups water

⅓ cup minced red onion (about ½ small red onion)

4 sun-dried tomato halves, re-hydrated in warm water, finely minced

⅓ cup (about 15) Kalamata olives, pitted, chopped

4 sprigs fresh oregano, leaves removed, stems discarded, chopped

2 tablespoons extra-virgin olive oil

¼ teaspoon garlic powder

2 teaspoons lemon juice

Kalamata is both an olive variety and an olive-oil-producing region. This olive is rich in nutrients such as Vitamin E, copper, and fiber. Although olives are high in fat, the type of fat contained within is monounsaturated, believed to be of great benefit when it comes to fighting cholesterol levels. Although olives are high in sodium, good things come in small packages … if you watch your portion sizes, a small quantity can add a lot of flavor.

Preheat oven to 375°F. Cover a cookie sheet with parchment paper. Place the tomato halves on the sheet, cut-side-up. Cut a thin sliver from the bottom of any tomato half that is not stable. Set aside.

Rinse the quinoa thoroughly either in a strainer or in a pot and drain. Do not skip this step or a bitter-tasting, natural, soap-like coating will remain. Once the quinoa is drained, place it into a medium pot with the water. Bring to a boil. Reduce the heat and simmer, uncovered, until the water is absorbed, about 10–15 minutes. You will know it is done when the grains turn translucent and the outer layer pops off. Drain any remaining water.

Meanwhile, in a medium bowl, combine the red onion, sun-dried tomatoes, olives, oregano, oil, garlic powder, and lemon juice. Toss to combine.

Add the drained quinoa and toss to combine. Place a heaping scoop of quinoa into each plum tomato half. Return the filled tomato halves to the prepared cookie sheet. Bake for 20 minutes.

Transfer to a serving dish.

Pumpkin-Barley Risotto

5 cups chicken or vegetable stock

1 tablespoon unsalted margarine

3 medium shallots, cut into ⅛-inch dice

16 ounces pearled barley

10 ounces (2 cups) fresh pumpkin or butternut squash, peeled, seeded, cut into ½-inch dice, or 10 ounces frozen cubed butternut squash

1¼ cups good white wine, such as Sauvignon Blanc

1 tablespoon nondairy sour cream, such as Tofutti brand Sour Supreme®

¼ teaspoon fine sea salt

¼ teaspoon freshly ground black pepper

1 tablespoon fresh minced chives

1 tablespoon fresh minced parsley leaves

If making this dish in advance, reserve the final cup of chicken stock and stir it in as you are reheating the dish to bring back some of the creaminess. As with all risotto, this is best served fresh, but is still a delicious side dish on the reheat.

Pumpkin and winter squash contain high levels of antioxidants and carotenes, particularly vitamins C and E, and therefore may lower the risk of cancer, heart disease, cataracts, and strokes. And if you're using fresh pumpkin, don't throw away those seeds! Pumpkin seeds have been coupled with prostate protection, better bladder function, and improved levels of LDL cholesterol. Because of their rich zinc content, pumpkin seeds may be a natural protector against osteoporosis. Some say these seeds have been linked to treating mild depression as well.

Heat the broth in a small pot over medium heat; do not allow it to simmer.

Melt the margarine in a large skillet that has a lid. Add the shallots and sauté over medium heat for 2 minutes, until translucent. Add the barley and toast, shaking the pan, until fragrant and lightly golden, about 5–6 minutes. Add the fresh pumpkin or squash. If using frozen pumpkin or squash, add it after half the stock has been added.

Add the white wine and cook, stirring constantly, until the wine evaporates, 1–2 minutes.

Over a 15–20 minute period, add the stock one ladleful at a time, reserving one cup. As you add each ladleful, stir almost constantly with a wooden spoon until all the stock is absorbed. The barley will still be slightly al dente but not dry. Add remaining stock, stir, and cover the pot. Allow to cook for 10–15 minutes, until all liquid is absorbed.

Remove lid. Stir in sour cream, salt, and pepper. Stir in chives and parsley. Serve immediately.

Desserts

Coconut-Lime Tart

DAIRY OR PARVE ■ MAKES 12 SERVINGS

CRUST:

nonstick cooking spray

1 cup low-fat graham cracker crumbs (about 8 whole graham crackers pulsed in the food processor)

½ cup ground walnuts or pecans

2 tablespoons sugar

3 tablespoons melted butter or margarine

1 tablespoon extra-virgin olive oil

FILLING:

zest of 1 lime

½ cup sugar

2 tablespoons all-purpose flour

2 large eggs

1 egg white (from large egg)

½ cup lime juice, from about 5 limes

¼ cup skim milk or original-flavor soy milk

5 tablespoons shredded sweetened coconut, divided

The benefits of coconut and coconut oil can be attributed to its combination of lauric, capric, and caprylic acids, and the important role they play in fighting infection and disease, especially for those who have compromised immune systems. Coconut oil has been used regularly in skin- and hair-care products and has been known for its stress-relieving properties.

Preheat oven to 350°F.

Spray a 9-inch springform pan with nonstick cooking spray. Set aside.

Prepare the crust: Mix the graham cracker crumbs, ground nuts, sugar, butter or margarine, and olive oil in a medium bowl. Using your palm, press into the bottom and slightly up the sides of the prepared pan. Wipe out the bowl.

Prepare the filling: Place the lime zest and ½ cup sugar into the bowl. Rub the sugar and zest together between the palms of your hands. Whisk in the flour. Add the eggs, egg white, lime juice, and milk or soy milk. Whisk to combine.

Pour this mixture into the crust. Sprinkle with 3 tablespoons coconut.

Bake for 25–30 minutes, until the lime curd is just set in the middle.

Allow to cool for at least an hour. Release the sides of the springform pan. Chill until ready to serve. Sprinkle remaining 2 tablespoons coconut over the top. Thinly slice.

Raspberry Mousse Triflettes

PARVE ■ MAKES 8-10 SERVINGS

6 ounces frozen raspberries, not in syrup, rinsed with hot water, drained

½ cup sugar

1 teaspoon fresh lemon juice

⅛ teaspoon coarse sea salt

4 egg whites (from large eggs)

4 ounces nondairy whipping cream

1 pint fresh raspberries

1 (3-ounce) box soft ladyfingers (24 ladyfingers)

Whether frozen or fresh, these garnet-colored beauties are healthy as well as delicious. Raspberries are full of vitamins, minerals, antioxidants, and fiber and are a welcome addition to your meal or great for a snack. Abounding in quercetin, an antioxidant, and ellagic acid, a phenolic compound, raspberries can help fight cancer, and their fiber content can benefit digestion.

Place the raspberries, sugar, lemon juice, and salt into the bowl of a food processor fitted with a metal blade. Do not turn on the machine. Allow the raspberries to stand and defrost for 15 minutes. Run the machine for a full 2 minutes to purée and form a smooth mixture.

Place a fine mesh strainer over a large bowl. Pour the raspberry mixture into the strainer and, using the back of a wooden spoon, press the mixture through so it all strains through. Discard the seeds. Set aside.

In the bowl of a stand mixer fitted with the whisk attachment, beat the egg whites at medium speed until soft peaks form. Whip at high speed until stiff peaks form.

Gently fold the egg whites into the raspberries, a large scoop at a time.

Place the whipping cream into the bowl of a stand mixer and whip on medium-high speed until stiff peaks form. Gently fold the cream into the raspberry mixture, a large scoop at a time.

Drop a few fresh raspberries into the bottom of a wine glass. Stand 3–4 ladyfingers in the wine glass, with their rounded sides facing out. Add a dollop of raspberry mousse in the center, pressing lightly so it gets down into the glass and between the ladyfingers. Top with a fresh raspberry. Depending on the size of your wine glasses, you may have extra mousse.

Place into refrigerator. Chill 3–4 hours or overnight to set.

Fudge Brownie Torte

DAIRY OR PARVE ■ MAKES 12 SERVINGS

nonstick cooking spray

2 ounces semisweet chocolate, chopped

1 cup sugar

3 tablespoons butter or margarine

2 tablespoons chocolate syrup, like Bosco®

2 tablespoons canola oil

½ cup Dutch process cocoa powder (I like Droste®)

¾ cup all-purpose flour

½ teaspoon fine sea salt

¼ teaspoon baking powder

2 large eggs

1 egg white (from large egg)

2 tablespoons low-fat or nondairy sour cream

1 teaspoon pure vanilla extract

1 teaspoon instant coffee dissolved in 2 tablespoons warm water

low-fat whipped cream

strawberries, quartered

To me, this recipe symbolized what I was trying to accomplish by writing this book. If I was going to get my family, which includes 4 children, to live a healthier lifestyle for the long run, it had to be about more than steamed spinach and chicken without the skin. Practically, I needed a repertoire of healthier versions of things they would naturally crave and expect. What could be more apt than a brownie dessert?

I spent days working on brownies. I tried versions substituting applesauce, prunes, dates, mayonnaise, and canola oil for the stick and a half of margarine in the brownies I usually make. I played with chocolate extract, sugar-free chocolate chips, and cocoa in place of 12 ounces of semi-sweet chocolate. Whole wheat flour, self-rising flour, water, brown sugar, you name the variable and I tackled it. I had more charts and post-it notes than an air traffic controller but disappointment reigned. Instead of fudgy dense brownies I was getting cake-like, low flavor results. There were batches that I could not get a kid to take a second bite of. I came close to conceding that it could not be done and that the low-fat brownie was a pipe dream. I took one last crack. I added back some of the fat which brownies just seem to need, the syrup for moisture and depth of flavor, and added the coffee to enhance the chocolate flavor and I struck brownie gold.

This brownie torte is moist and dense with a nice chocolate taste. The chewiness is there and the amount of sugar is strong enough without being cloying. While not a health food, it is a realistic recipe that my kids and their friends will happily eat. By shaving off a lot of fat and sugar from my old standards, I've taken another step in the right direction.

Preheat oven to 350°F.

Spray a 9-inch springform pan with nonstick cooking spray. Set aside.

In a double boiler, or a metal bowl set over a pot of simmering water, melt the chocolate, sugar, margarine or butter, chocolate syrup, and oil. Stir until melted and smooth.

Meanwhile, in a medium bowl whisk the cocoa, flour, salt, and baking powder. Set aside.

In the bowl of a stand mixer, beat the eggs, egg white, sour cream, vanilla extract, and coffee. Mix until smooth. Add in the melted chocolate mixture. Combine.

With the machine running, add in the cocoa mixture in two parts. Mix until smooth and creamy. Scrape down the sides as necessary. Spread the batter into the prepared pan.

Bake for 25 minutes. Do not overbake and don't test with toothpick. Release the sides of the pan. Allow to cool. Top with whipped cream and strawberries.

Frozen Pumpkin Pie

DAIRY OR PARVE ■ MAKES 12 SERVINGS

- 2 low-fat honey graham crackers
- 2 tablespoons finely chopped pecans
- ½ cup plus 1 tablespoon dark brown sugar, divided
- 1 teaspoon pure maple syrup
- 1 teaspoon ground cinnamon, divided
- 2 pints vanilla low-fat yogurt (I like Häagen Dazs®) or parve ice cream
- 1 cup canned pure pumpkin, NOT pumpkin-pie filling
- ⅛ teaspoon ground nutmeg

Pumpkins are full of fiber and other nutrients and are an excellent source of the all-important antioxidant, beta-carotene. They are high in lutein and beta-crypoxanthin, which scavange free radicals in the lens of the eye. This may help prevent the formation of cataracts and reduce the risk of macular degeneration.

When shopping for canned pumpkin, be sure to check the label and see that you're not getting sweetened pumpkin. Although it will still have pumpkin's potent carotenoid and beta-cryptoxanthin, which help to maintain healthy eyes, skin, bones, and immune system, it will also contain 4 times the sugar.

Just a note: When making the parve version, the fat content, at least in the parve ice creams that I have found, goes way up, compared to low-fat vanilla ice cream.

Place the graham crackers into a heavy ziplock bag. Break into small pieces, trying not to crush too finely; you want some texture. Pour into small bowl. Add the pecans, 1 tablespoon brown sugar, maple syrup, and ½ teaspoon cinnamon. Mix to combine. Set aside.

Remove the ice cream from the freezer to soften slightly.

Cut two sheets of parchment paper or aluminum foil. Fold each in half lengthwise. Set inside the rim of a 9- or 10-inch springform pan. Tape as necessary to the outside of the pan to form a collar 3–4 inches above the rim of the pan. Set aside.

Place the ice cream into the bowl of a stand mixer fitted with a paddle attachment. Beat on medium-high speed until smooth. Add the pumpkin, ½ cup brown sugar, remaining ½ teaspoon cinnamon, and nutmeg. Beat until fully combined and creamy. Transfer to prepared pan. Sprinkle on the graham cracker topping. Place, uncovered, in the freezer for at least an hour or overnight.

Remove from the freezer. Release the sides of the springform pan. Discard the parchment. Slice and serve immediately.

Peanut Butter Pizza

PARVE ■ MAKES 8 SERVINGS

1 thin-crust pre-baked pizza crust, 12-inch diameter
½ cup natural peanut butter
1 tablespoon honey
½ cup chocolate chips
½ cup mini marshmallows
1 banana, thinly sliced

Regular brands of peanut butter contain sugar, preservatives, and shortening. Natural peanut butter typically contains peanuts, salt, and sometimes additional oil. While regular peanut butter has nutritional value (fiber, protein, vitamins), natural is healthier because of what is does NOT have — all the additives. For ease of use, try to find the no-stir kind; I like the MaraNatha brand.

The peanut is a legume, the same as a bean or a pea. Peanuts are high in good-quality protein (25 grams per 100-gram serving). Peanut butter is also a good source of niacin, which may help raise HDL (good) cholesterol levels. Peanuts also have more resveratrol than grapes, an antioxidant also found in red wine that helps fight heart disease. And don't forget the fiber ... one ounce provides 2 grams, or 9% of the fiber you need each day.

Preheat oven to 350°F.

Cover a jelly-roll pan with parchment paper. Place a cookie cooling rack into the pan. Set aside.

Spread a thin layer of peanut butter over the crust. Drizzle with honey. Scatter the chocolate chips and marshmallows over the top. Place the pizza onto the cooling rack. Elevating it will allow air to circulate, ensuring a crisp crust.

Place into the oven for 20 minutes. Remove and scatter banana slices over the top.

Cool for 2 minutes. Using a pizza cutter, cut into 8 slices. Serve warm.

Peach-Berry Tart

DAIRY OR PARVE ■ MAKES 8 SERVINGS

CRUST:

nonstick cooking spray

¾ cup blanched slivered almonds

1 cup whole wheat pastry flour or white whole wheat flour

¼ cup old-fashioned rolled oats

3 tablespoons dark brown sugar

¼ teaspoon kosher salt

⅛ teaspoon ground cinnamon

4 tablespoons cold butter or margarine, cut into 8 pieces

1 tablespoon unsweetened applesauce

3 tablespoons ice water

FILLING & TOPPING:

16 ounces frozen peaches or nectarines, defrosted and sliced

8 ounces fresh raspberries, divided

8 ounces fresh blueberries, divided

12 ounces fresh strawberries, sliced or diced, divided

3 tablespoons all-purpose flour

3 tablespoons sugar

½ teaspoon ground cinnamon

3 tablespoons good-quality, seedless raspberry preserves

The taste of a juicy, succulent peach is hard to resist, and here are some other reasons why you should regularly include this fuzzy fruit in your diet: peaches provide almost 75% of the Vitamin C you need each day in only 100 calories. They are a great source of the phytochemicals lycopene and lutein, sweetly protecting you from heart disease, cancer, and macular degeneration. Peaches also contain iron and potassium.

Preheat oven to 350°F.

Spray a round 9-inch tart pan with removable bottom with nonstick cooking spray. Place on cookie sheet or jelly-roll pan, and set aside.

Place the almonds into the bowl of a food processor fitted with a metal blade. Pulse for 20 seconds or until the almonds resemble coarse bread crumbs. Add flour, oats, brown sugar, salt, and cinnamon. Pulse another 8 seconds. Add the butter or margarine and applesauce. Pulse for another 10 seconds, or until the mixture is evenly crumbly. Add the ice water; pulse for 5 seconds.

Gently pat the dough into the bottom and slightly up the sides of the pan. Arrange the peaches or nectarines in overlapping slices on the dough.

Combine 4 ounces raspberries, 4 ounces blueberries, and 6 ounces strawberries in a medium bowl. Toss with the flour, sugar, and cinnamon. Pour the coated berries over the peaches and bake, uncovered, for 45 minutes. Remove from oven and immediately top the tart with the remaining 4 ounces raspberries, remaining 4 ounces blueberries, and remaining 6 ounces strawberries.

In a small microwave-safe bowl or ramekin, heat the preserves until liquefied, about 30 seconds. Using a small spoon, a silicone pastry brush, or heat-resistant squirt bottle, drizzle the fruit with the melted preserves. Chill for 3 hours, or until ready to serve.

Chocolate, Fruit, and Nut Bark

PARVE ■ MAKES 18 SERVINGS

16 ounces semisweet chocolate, at least 62% cocoa, finely and evenly chopped

½ cup whole almonds

⅓ cup dried blueberries

5 dried apricots, snipped into small bits

2 tablespoons sweetened dried cranberries

My mom is not a big nosher, but I remember that when I was a kid, her favorite indulgence was a Chunky bar. This is an upscale, healthier version of that treat that I created for her.

Researchers have shown that dried fruits may have up to four times the antioxidant content of their fresh counterparts. Dried fruits are also higher in fiber and may help naturally relieve constipation and lower cholesterol levels. Depending on the fruit, most are also rich in iron, potassium, and selenium. These sweet treats certainly have a place in a healthy diet.

And don't forget to make room for some dark chocolate! It contains a chemical that triggers the release of feel-good endorfins in the brain. Dark chocolate contains powerful antioxidants that protect from cell degeneration. Rich in cocoa phenols, dark chocolate may help lower your blood pressure and protect your heart. The higher the cocoa content, the more healthful the chocolate. Commercial candy bars do not fit this bill, as they contain refined sugar and trans fats. But before you dig in, remember that 3 ounces of dark chocolate contain around 500 calories. This may be a tasty treat that's better than other snacks that have no health value, but proceed with caution. Don't replace healthier foods with chocolate!

Cover a jelly-roll pan with parchment paper. Set aside.

Place the chocolate into a microwave-safe bowl. At 50% power, microwave the chocolate for 45-second intervals, stirring between rounds, until mostly melted. Stir until completely smooth. This can also be done in a double boiler.

Pour the chocolate onto the prepared sheet. Use an offset metal spatula to spread it into a ¼-inch-thick chocolate layer. Immediately sprinkle the almonds, blueberries, apricots, and cranberries over the chocolate.

Place the pan into the refrigerator for at least 30 minutes. Cut or break into irregular pieces, serving 2 shards per person. Serve slightly chilled. Can be stored in the refrigerator for up to one week.

Ginger-Molasses Biscotti

PARVE ■ MAKES 30 BISCOTTI

1¼ cups all-purpose flour
1¼ cups whole wheat flour
1½ teaspoons baking powder
½ teaspoon baking soda
¼ teaspoon fine sea salt
1½ teaspoons ground cinnamon
1½ teaspoons ground ginger
½ cup sugar
2 large eggs
1 egg white (from large egg)
2 tablespoons mild molasses
¼ cup canola oil

Molasses is the thick syrup that's left after sugar beets or cane are processed for table sugar. Blackstrap molasses is a very good source of iron: just 2 teaspoons will sweetly supply you with 13.3% of the daily recommended value for this mineral. Unlike sugar, blackstrap molasses also contains calcium, copper, manganese, potassium, and magnesium.

Preheat oven to 350°F.

Cover a cookie sheet with parchment paper and tear a second piece of parchment paper to fit the sheet. Set aside.

In a medium bowl, whisk the all-purpose flour, whole wheat flour, baking powder, baking soda, salt, cinnamon, and ginger. Set aside.

In the bowl of a stand mixer, at medium speed, beat the sugar, eggs, egg white, molasses, and oil until well combined. In batches, add the dry ingredients until the mixture forms a loose dough.

Halve the dough and turn each portion onto one of the pieces of parchment paper. With wet hands, and using the parchment paper to help, spread each dough into an even 10- by 3-inch loaf. Place the loaves, tucking the parchment as necessary, side-by-side on the cookie sheet. Bake until the loaves are just beginning to crack, about 25 minutes, turning the cookie sheet halfway through the baking time. Remove from oven and cool for 5 minutes. Using a serrated knife, cut each loaf diagonally into ⅜-inch-thick slices. Lay the slices about ½-inch apart on the baking sheet, cut-side-up, and return them to the oven. Bake for 10 minutes. Remove from oven and flip each of the biscotti. Return them to the oven for 5 minutes. Transfer the biscotti to a wire rack and cool completely.

Biscotti can be stored in an airtight container for up to 3 weeks.

Apple-Blueberry Cake

PARVE ■ MAKES 16 SERVINGS

nonstick cooking spray
with flour in the can

1 cup fresh blueberries

1 medium MacIntosh apple,
peeled, seeded, cut into
¼-inch dice

1 tablespoon cinnamon/
sugar

2 cups all-purpose flour

1 cup white whole wheat
flour or whole wheat pastry
flour

2 teaspoons baking powder

¼ teaspoon baking soda

½ teaspoon fine sea salt

zest ½ orange

juice of a whole orange

½ cup canola oil

½ cup olive oil

3 large eggs

2 egg whites (from large
eggs)

1 tablespoon pure vanilla
extract

1½ cups sugar

2 teaspoons confectioner's
sugar

Every once in a while you just want a good piece of cake to end the meal. In general, that is going to cost you some calories and, due to the oil in this recipe, this one is no different in that respect. However, if you are going to have cake, this is a good one to have. The changes here are that we are using heart-healthy oils in place of shortenings, whole wheat flour in place of all white flour, and some fruit for added vitamins. Keep recipes like this for that "once in a while" craving and keep the portions small.

Sifting dry ingredients results in fluffier cake. When working with oil as your fat, it is especially important to sift the dry ingredients, or else they will form clumps in the oil.

An integral ingredient that has not been focused on in so many recipes is nonstick cooking spray. It can now be found in a number of varieties and it has become quite popular in recent years, for good reason: each tablespoon of oil provides a whopping 120 calories. This may not sound like a lot, but if you regularly use oil to grease your pans, the calories can add up. Nonstick cooking spray, on the other hand, fulfills the same purpose, allowing your favorite dishes to separate from your pans without a fuss and without any calories!

Preheat oven to 350°F.

Heavily spray a 9- by 13-inch cake pan with nonstick cooking spray.

Place the blueberries and apple into a small bowl. Toss with cinnamon/sugar. Set aside.

In a medium bowl, sift the flour, whole wheat flour, baking powder, baking soda, and salt. Set aside.

In the bowl of a stand mixer set at medium speed, beat the orange zest, orange juice, canola oil, olive oil, eggs, egg whites, and vanilla. Gradually beat in the sugar.

Slowly add the dry ingredients and mix until a smooth batter forms.

Pour half the batter into the prepared pan. Top with blueberries and apples. Gently spoon remaining batter on top, spreading to cover fruit as best you can.

Bake for 40 minutes, or until a toothpick inserted into the center comes out clean. Allow to cool in pan for 10 minutes. Turn the cake out and allow it to cool completely on a rack. Dust with confectioner's sugar passed through a fine mesh strainer.

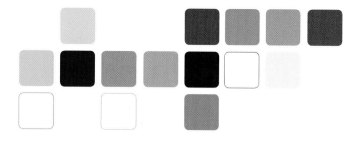

Apple-Rum Croustade

DAIRY OR PARVE ■ MAKES 10 SERVINGS

nonstick cooking spray

1 tablespoon butter or margarine

2 large Granny Smith apples, peeled, cored, cut into ¼-inch pieces

2 Macintosh or Braeburn apples, peeled, cored, cut into ¼-inch pieces

1 tablespoon orange juice

3 tablespoons dark brown sugar

1 teaspoon ground cinnamon

2 tablespoons cornstarch

2 tablespoons dark rum

12-14 sheets (½ of 16-ounce box) phyllo dough, defrosted overnight in the refrigerator

1½ ounces (usually ½ bar) good-quality semisweet chocolate, such as Schmerling Noblesse®, broken on the score marks into 1-inch squares

Although it is purchased from the freezer section, keep phyllo in the refrigerator until ready to use. It can last there, unopened, for up to a month, and is easier to work with than if defrosted right from the freezer.

"An apple a day" may be sage advice, and here's why: in addition to an apple's boron content, the flavonoid phloridzin, found only in apples, may increase the strength of bones in post-menopausal women, thereby protecting them from crippling osteoporosis. Apples have also been connected with relieving wheezing symptoms of asthma in children, as well as protecting brain cells in adults with Alzheimer's disease. Due to an apple's rich pectin content, this fruit can play a role in lowering cholesterol and in reducing colon cancer by promoting a healthier digestive tract. A Brazilian study has even linked apples to weight loss!

Preheat oven to 350°F.

Heavily spray a 9-inch springform pan with nonstick cooking spray.

Melt the butter or margarine in a large nonstick skillet over medium heat. Add the apples and orange juice and sauté for 3 minutes. Add the brown sugar and cinnamon, stirring to distribute. Cook for 4 minutes, until apples are soft but not mushy.

In a small bowl, dissolve the cornstarch in the rum. Carefully add the rum to the pan; if the rum ignites flames, they will quickly die down. Cook until the mixture thickens and the apples are caramelized. Remove from heat.

Unwrap the phyllo dough. Working quickly, fold a sheet of phyllo in half lengthwise. Spray with nonstick cooking spray. Lay the sheet into the prepared pan so one end touches the middle and the other end comes up the side and hangs over the pan. Fold a second phyllo sheet lengthwise and spray with nonstick cooking spray. Lay it into the pan so that one end touches the center of the pan and the rest hangs over and overlaps the first sheet by 1-inch. Repeat with remaining phyllo, arranging the strips in a spoke-like fashion around the pan, until the pan is completely covered.

Pour the apples into the center of the pan. Starting with the last sheet of dough placed in the pan, lift the end and twist it towards the center of the filling. Coil and tuck the end under to form a rosette. The center filling should be visible. Repeat with remaining phyllo strips in the reverse order in which they were placed. When you are done, there should be a complete crown of rosettes and a 4-inch circle of filling visible. Tuck the chocolate pieces into the apple filling.

Bake for 30 minutes until pastry is golden. Remove the sides of the springform pan. Slice and serve warm.

Grapefruit Brûlée

3 white or red grapefruits, or a mix of the two

6 teaspoons apricot preserves, divided

12 teaspoons sugar, divided

This pretty dish can be either an appetizer or a dessert. A mini butane torch works even better than a broiler to caramelize the sugar to an even, hard caramel top.

Grapefruit, screaming with immune-boosting Vitamin C, may help reduce cold symptoms and reduce the effects of inflammation by protecting your heart. This superb citrus fruit has also been connected to relieving the symptoms of asthma, osteoarthritis, and rheumatoid arthritis. Be sure to choose the pink and red types, high in lycopene, known for anti-cancer status.

Preheat the broiler to high, with a rack positioned 4–6 inches from the heat source.

Halve each grapefruit, then loosen segments by cutting along their membranes with a grapefruit spoon or paring knife. Discard seeds. If a grapefruit half is not stable or is rolling to one side, cut a thin strip off the bottom to form a flat base. Pat the tops of each half with paper towels to absorb some of the juice.

With a small offset spatula or back of a spoon, spread 1 teaspoon apricot preserves over the top of each grapefruit half.

Sprinkle 2 teaspoons sugar evenly over the tops of each half-grapefruit. Place grapefruit halves on a jelly-roll pan. Broil until the sugar browns, watching carefully and rotating the pan as necessary, about 3 minutes. Serve warm.

Ancie's Carrot Cake

PARVE ■ MAKES 12 SERVINGS

nonstick cooking spray with flour in the can

2⅔ cups (6-8 medium) carrots, peeled, cut into large chunks

1 cup all-purpose flour

1 cup whole wheat pastry flour or white whole wheat flour

1½ teaspoons baking powder

1 teaspoon baking soda

1 teaspoon fine sea salt

1 teaspoon ground cinnamon

¾ cup canola oil

1¾ cups sugar

1 (4-ounce) jar baby food carrots

¼ cup unsweetened applesauce

1½ teaspoons pure vanilla extract

3 large eggs

1 egg white (from large egg)

¾ cup finely chopped walnuts

½ cup raisins

¾ cup (4-ounces) semisweet chocolate chips

This is a trimmed-down favorite of mine from one of my favorite women. I hope you will agree it is the perfect ending to a meal.

This cake stands up beautifully on its own but if you must add a cream cheese frosting and it's for a dairy meal, beat ½ cup reduced-fat cream cheese with 1 tablespoon honey. Spread over the top and sides of the cake.

This cake freezes beautifully; just defrost and slice.

As the richest vegetable source of the pro-vitamin A carotenes, carrots' powerful antioxidant compounds not only promote good vision (particularly night vision), but they also help protect against cardiovascular disease. Carrots have been associated with decreasing the incidence of certain cancers, including breast, bladder, cervical, prostate, colon, and esophageal cancers. Research suggests that foods rich in carotenoids may be related to lowering blood-glucose levels and reducing insulin resistance, therefore playing an important role in controlling diabetes.

And here's an interesting tip: cooking carrots slightly can release their beta-carotene more freely, allowing your body to absorb it more readily. (But if your kids will only eat carrots raw, don't discourage them!)

Preheat oven to 350°F.

Heavily coat a nonstick 10-inch bundt pan with the nonstick cooking spray. Set aside.

Place the carrot chunks into the bowl of a food processor fitted with a metal blade. Using on-off pulses, do 7 (10-second) pulses. Scrape down the bowl and run the machine for another 10 seconds. Measure out 2⅔ cups grated carrot. Set aside.

Sift the all-purpose flour, whole wheat pastry flour, baking powder, baking soda, salt, and cinnamon into a medium bowl. Set aside.

In the bowl of a stand mixer set at medium speed, beat the oil and sugar until smooth. Add the baby food carrots, applesauce, and vanilla. Beat. With the machine running, add the eggs and egg white, one at a time.

With the machine still running, using two large or wooden spoons, add large alternating dollops of the dry mixture and the 2⅔ cups grated carrots, until both are completely added. Beat in the walnuts, raisins, and chocolate chips. Mix until blended. Pour the batter into the prepared pan.

Bake for 55–60 minutes, or until a toothpick inserted into the center comes out clean. Cool in the pan for 10 minutes; then turn the cake out onto a rack or plate to cool completely.

Vanilla Bean Angel Food Cake

PARVE ■ MAKES 12 SERVINGS

1½ cups superfine sugar

1 vanilla bean

12 egg whites (from large eggs), at room temperature

1¼ teaspoons cream of tartar

½ teaspoon fine sea salt

1 teaspoon pure vanilla extract

½ teaspoon almond extract

1 cup cake flour, sifted

fresh strawberries, for garnish

This is certainly one dessert that you can assuredly say "contains no cholesterol." Although the whole egg is one of the richest sources of cholesterol in the diet, egg whites contain none. Two egg whites provide the same amount of protein as one whole egg, with less than half the calories. In most recipes, you can try substituting 2 egg whites for one whole egg.

Preheat oven to 350°F.

Line a 10-inch tube pan with a parchment circle. If you can't find the rounds with a pre-cut hole for tube pans, cut your own out of parchment paper. Set aside.

Place sugar into a medium bowl. Using the tip of a knife, slice the vanilla bean down the center. Scrape the seeds from the bean pod into the sugar. Rub the sugar and vanilla between your fingers to combine.

In the bowl of an electric mixer fitted with the whisk attachment, beat the egg whites on medium until foamy. Beat in cream of tartar, salt, vanilla, and almond extract. Increase speed to medium-high and beat to soft peaks. Reduce speed to low and beat in the vanilla sugar, 1 large spoonful at a time. Beat until stiff peaks form.

Using a spatula, carefully fold the flour, ¼ cup at a time, into the egg whites, being careful not to deflate the egg whites.

Spoon the mixture into the ungreased, lined tube pan. Cut through the batter with a knife to break any air pockets. Bake for 35–40 minutes, until top is spongy to the touch, and a toothpick inserted into the center comes out clean.

Cool the cake in the pan by hanging it upside-down on a wine bottle or, if your pan has legs, upside-down on a cooling rack, for at least 1 hour before removing from the pan. Slide a narrow spatula around the sides of the pan to separate the cake from the sides. Slice with a serrated knife. Serve with strawberries.